THE OCCUPATION THESAURUS:

A Writer's Guide to Jobs, Vocations, and Careers

ANGELA ACKERMAN
& BECCA PUGLISI

THE OCCUPATION THESAURUS:
A WRITER'S GUIDE TO JOBS, VOCATIONS, AND CAREERS.

Copyright 2020 © by Angela Ackerman & Becca Puglisi

ISBN: 978-0-9992963-7-0

Edited by Michael Dunne (www.michael-dunne.com/) and
C.S. Lakin (https://www.livewritethrive.com)
Book cover design by JD Smith Design (http://www.jdsmith-design.com)
Book formatting by JD Smith Design (http://www.jdsmith-design.com)

MORE WRITERS HELPING WRITERS® BOOKS

TABLE OF CONTENTS

IT'S ALL IN THE DETAILS …

Wherever you are on the creative path, sooner or later one question pokes its way to the center of your thoughts: What does it take to become a masterful storyteller?

The answer? So many possibilities. Is it tenacity—a butt-in-chair mentality that keeps authors chipping away at their stories, no matter how many drafts it takes to get it right? Is it hard-won knowledge acquired from thousands of hours of focused reading, studying, and applying one's craft? Is it a passion for uncovering a character's deepest layers to give readers realistic players who have desires, fears, and vulnerabilities just as they do?

Honestly, it would be hard to list all the contributing factors for becoming a great storyteller, but one thing is certain: skilled writers display a willingness to see the job through. Whether they are researching, planning, drafting, or revising, they seek to unearth what's meaningful, which requires paying careful attention to the details.

And details? Well, they matter—in careers, life, and storytelling.

Let's consider the focal point of any work of fiction: the protagonist. We know that readers respond to the ones who are relatable and interesting and whose behaviors make sense within the story. To create characters like these, we authors must know a lot about them: their personality traits, emotional wounds, passions, hobbies, quirks, and so much more. These details are important because they'll reinforce our protagonists' desires, goals, fears, and needs, which, in turn, define their arcs and determine their actions throughout the story.

One detail often overlooked by writers is the character's occupation. Perhaps it seems insignificant—an aspect of characterization that simply rounds the character out rather than lending strength to the story. And if this were the case, a writer could just assign their character a profession they've personally done or that they find fascinating, and move on. But here's the thing: used to their full potential, occupations can be powerful drivers in the story, helping to characterize, steer the plot, generate conflict, reveal dysfunction, and provide a route for character arc growth—and that's just to start.

So, insignificant? Not in the slightest. Because a job can influence so many story factors, careful thought should go into selecting one.

Think about this from your own perspective. When it comes to your current occupation (or past jobs), were they chosen randomly, without much thought? Probably not. You may have been drawn to them because of your interests and areas of giftedness or because the job met a need, such as supporting your family or making a difference in the world. Maybe it was a simple matter of convenience and what was available. Regardless, there were reasons behind every employment decision you've made.

The same should be true for our characters. If we choose their jobs thoughtfully, readers will have a better understanding of who they are, what skills they possess, and their motivations and priorities. Not only do jobs provide valuable characterization indicators, they tie in to the plot itself, providing characters with the abilities and knowledge they'll need to succeed or by creating obstacles to hinder them along the way.

A well-chosen occupation can strengthen your story on many levels, but there are so many options. Let's start by delving into the reasons behind career choices so you can home in on your own character's motivations.

THE MOTIVATIONS BEHIND CAREER CHOICE

Because so much of a person's time is spent at work, occupations are usually chosen with thought and care. Personality and hobbies can influence this decision, but by themselves, they're just not weighty enough to prompt a choice that might span many years or even a lifetime. No, big-time decisions like a career need a lot of consideration, and the primary factor that often tips the scales in favor of one over another is motivation.

Simply defined, **motivation** is the reason behind a choice or behavior. For any given decision there are multiple possible motivations. As parents, for instance, we often explore the reasons behind our children's troublesome actions. If we can figure out why they engage in certain behaviors, we can guide them into changing those habits for the better. *Why does my kid lie?* is a question many parents have asked. The answer will be determined by the circumstances and any number of reasons from the child's perspective:

> He doesn't want to get in trouble.
> He doesn't want to disappoint his parent.
> He's protecting someone else.
> He's looking for a reaction.
> He's trying to boost his esteem by claiming things that aren't true.
> He doesn't understand that lying is wrong.
> He truly forgot and has remembered the details wrong, making his story sound like a lie when it's really not.

Like us, our characters have many possible reasons for the choices they make—including the jobs they pursue. Their motivation typically boils down to one of two drivers: basic needs or unresolved wounds.

BASIC NEEDS

According to famed psychologist Abraham Maslow, every person has five basic needs that, when met, make them feel fulfilled. Destabilization of one or more of these needs will cause discomfort—a ripple that disturbs a relatively calm surface. Should this discomfort grow too big or last too long, a person will feel compelled to set things right again by addressing the need that is most vital.

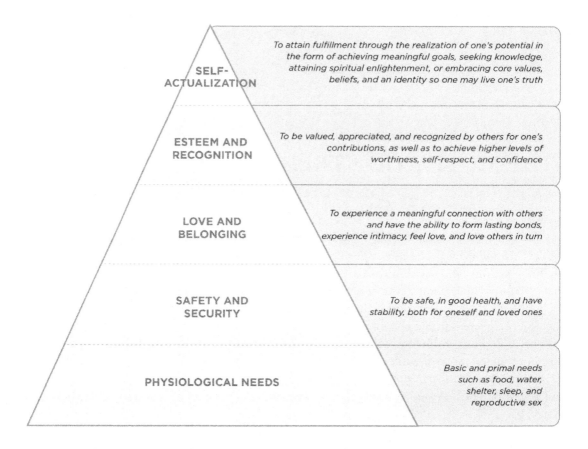

As the diagram shows, the foundation of the pyramid represents our physiological needs because those are the most important; without food, water, air, and the like, we would cease to exist. Should our physiological needs become threatened, we will be driven to reinforce them. Safety is the next most critical need, followed by love and belonging, esteem and recognition, and self-actualization.

Here's how this works. If an armed intruder breaks into your house, your sense of security will be threatened. Even if everyone escapes unharmed, you may still feel unsafe at home. To feel protected, you might take certain actions, such as installing a security system, taking a self-defense class, or buying a gun. You might tighten the rules for your children, requiring them to be home earlier at night or call more often when they're out. All these choices are driven by your need for safety and security.

Basic human needs are important motivators for our behavior. Because fiction reflects real life, they also galvanize our characters and will push them toward certain actions and choices, including the all-important decision of which career to pursue. Let's take a deeper look at this need-occupation connection.

Physiological Needs
Food, water, shelter, and sleep are some of the most basic needs. A character worried about survival will look for work that pays enough to guarantee it. This probably won't be his dream job, one he's most qualified for, or even something that brings him great satisfaction. Depending on

his level of desperation, it might even be unhealthy or toxic, putting other needs at risk. We've all heard of real-life scenarios in which someone turns to prostitution or dealing drugs out of a critical need to make money to survive. The job may endanger them physically, strain their personal relationships, and kill their self-esteem, but none of that will matter because the first order of business is to stay alive.

While most jobs don't create this level of distress, many people do choose them to solve an immediate problem. The job may be temporary—one that is abandoned when the physiological needs are taken care of—or the character might stick with it out of habit. Either way, if physiological needs are in peril, the character will be compelled to fix the situation immediately, and they won't have the luxury of being choosy about the work they do.

Safety and Security

Once survival is no longer at stake, the next most critical need is safety, health, and security for the character and her loved ones. For instance, someone living in a dangerous area where gang members are trying to recruit her children might decide to take on a second job so she can afford to move to a safer area. She might not love janitorial work or driving a taxi, but that doesn't matter when her family is being threatened. Tough decisions have to be made in this situation, and job choice is one of them.

Love and Belonging

Next on the hierarchy is our need for meaningful connections. This includes loving others, being loved by them, and experiencing true intimacy. *Okay*, you think, *I can see how this is important to people, but what does it have to do with occupations?* The truth is, deliberately or subconsciously, jobs are sometimes chosen more out of regard for other people than for ourselves.

A character from a tight-knit family may accept a position that's closer to home, even if it's less desirable than other offers. Someone else might pursue a career because she comes from a family of first responders or nurses or teachers, and following in her loved ones' footsteps provides a sense of belonging. In another scenario, a character who loses her father to cancer may take over his real estate practice as a way to honor him and keep his legacy alive. In situations like these, the character's need for love or belonging drives her decision-making.

Esteem and Recognition

Every person, and therefore every character, needs to feel valued, appreciated, and respected by others while also having a healthy regard for themselves. If a character longs for esteem and recognition, it can push her toward a certain career. As examples, consider these scenarios:

> Someone seeking the esteem of others may choose to become a doctor or hedge fund manager simply because, to her, these fields are prestigious and impressive.

> A character might pursue a career in a competitive field because she knows that succeeding will bring her recognition and accolades.

If the culture teaches that certain employment opportunities are more respectable than others (white collar vs. trade skills, owning your company vs. working for someone else, etc.), the character may chart a career course that will bring her the most recognition.

A character might choose a challenging occupation because she wants to prove to herself that she's capable. She gets a charge from doing something that few people can do.

Self-esteem is also part of this need, so a character may choose a job because she's good at it and it gives her confidence.

The esteem and recognition section of the pyramid may appear small, but don't underestimate its importance. Characters looking to blaze a path for themselves, escape feelings of low self-worth, or prove to others what they can do are likely to choose careers that will raise their esteem and bring about internal satisfaction.

Self-Actualization

It may seem as if this need is the least important, but, in reality, it's what most people strive for. Humans want to be fulfilled and satisfied, achieving their full potential. Many times, this means living according to their beliefs, values, and true identity. A character seeking to meet this need may very well choose a job to achieve one of the following:

Freedom and Independence. She may stay with an occupation that isn't perfect because it provides her the money and freedom to pursue personal activities that make her happy, such as traveling, learning new skills, or spending more time with family.

Validation of Values and Moral Beliefs. Characters who are focused on something bigger than themselves may gravitate toward careers that reinforce their ideals. Choosing work that is rewarding (rehabilitating animals, providing humanitarian medical care in a third-world country), allows her to serve others (social work, nursing), or solves a global problem (being an inventor, pursuing a career in the sciences) would potentially generate a great deal of satisfaction.

Purpose. Some characters may feel called to a certain profession—even from an early age. Working in that field will provide a sense of purpose for them, resulting in gratification because they know they're doing what they were meant to do.

Fulfillment through Philanthropy. If it's true that the ends sometimes justify the means, a character could choose a career because it enables her to help others. The work may be stressful and the hours long, or it might be downright boring. But to her it's worthwhile if it provides the time or funds needed to help people or advance causes she believes in.

Happiness. This is an important part of our self-actualization need. It's key to people doing what they do; whenever possible, they choose a profession that brings them joy.

UNRESOLVED WOUNDS

While a missing need can be a big motivator, there's another factor that might push your character toward (or away from) a career: an emotional wound. These painful past traumas leave them feeling so vulnerable and exposed, they become willing to do almost anything to avoid experiencing that kind of pain again. In the aftermath, fears take root, along with lies a character may believe about himself or the world (*I'm worthless, you can't really know or trust anyone*). This not only damages his sense of self-worth; it also leads to dysfunctional behaviors and attitudes that are meant to keep potentially hurtful people and situations at bay.

The choices characters make after a wounding event will differ from ones made had nothing bad ever happened to them. To avoid risk, they may underachieve, turn away from passions, resist change, or refuse to take chances—all of which will sow unhappiness and cause unmet needs.

A good example of this is the protagonist from the movie *Good Will Hunting*. Will is a genius, able to memorize everything he sees and solve math problems that stump most of the world. As a result, we'd expect him to be working as a code-breaker for the government or teaching advanced mathematics at a prestigious university. But the first scene of the movie shows him pushing a mop down a hallway. Why is one of the most brilliant young men in the country working as a janitor? The answer lies in his traumatic past.

Abandoned by his parents and abused in the foster care system, he has serious trust issues. This means that when he finds someone he can count on, he's incredibly loyal. This results in him choosing a job that enables him to stay close to his friends. And, despite his brilliance, he's plagued by self-doubt, which causes him to avoid any career that would require him to live up to expectations or be responsible for others.

This fictional situation is realistic because it shows how things work in real life. Wounds influence behavior and choices, so tying your character's past trauma to his career adds layers and authenticity that will resonate with readers.

Wounds run the gamut from mild to deeply traumatizing, and each character will respond uniquely to them. When it comes to choosing an occupation, this can go one of two ways: wounds can push characters toward certain jobs or repel them from the ones they really want.

Choosing a Job because of a Wounding Event

Imagine a protagonist named Casey, who was raised by a career criminal. Her father's knack for keeping his nose clean and thwarting the authorities kept him mostly out of prison, which meant he was constantly around to belittle and humiliate her. He was proud of his professional accomplishments, which were abhorrent to Casey, birthing shame despite her having done nothing wrong. His professional network involved a lot of family members and close friends, so she could easily have followed in his footsteps. But she decides to go a different route and becomes a cop.

And she's good at her job. No wrongdoer can give her the slip. Tough as nails, she does what needs to be done in the most unforgiving environments. But she has no compassion to soften her sharp edges. This keeps her from being a great cop. And it causes problems at home, because when her kids break the rules, she sees them headed down the same path as her father, and she absolutely can't have that …

It's easy to see why Casey chose the field of law enforcement: she can't stand her father and wants to be nothing like him. He flouted the law, so she becomes the law, ensuring that the people she pursues face justice. This is her duty and her penance, her way of dealing with the shame inflicted upon her by her outlaw father. Her behavior also shows how unresolved wounds are impacting her in the present. The resulting attitudes and habits will need to be dealt with for her to successfully traverse her character arc.

Avoiding a Job because of a Wounding Event
Just as wounds can lead characters toward specific careers, they can also cause them to avoid the ones they most desire.

Imagine a character who has suffered his whole life from a debilitating speech impediment. Mike is highly intelligent and gifted in science, but the social aspect made school a nightmare—the bullying, the behind-the-back snickers, the well-meant pity from his teachers. As a result, he spent his free time alone, studying his passion: forensics. He dreamed of becoming a coroner, but that would've required additional schooling, and after graduation he swore he'd never set foot in a classroom—real or virtual—again.

So as a young twenty-something, he works as a crime scene cleaner. It's a quiet background job where he only has to talk to a few co-workers. It also allows proximity to the kind of cases he might have worked had he pursued his dream. Each day, as he cleans up crime scenes and natural death environments, his brain can't help but notice the clues and try to piece them together to see the whole picture. But the picture is always incomplete. His work scratches the itch but never quite alleviates it. And it gets worse as time goes on.

In a situation like this, the character's wounding event (a speech impediment) is keeping him from his dream job. He's chosen the next best thing, but it's unsatisfying because he's living below his full potential. Throughout the course of Mike's story, this lack of fulfillment is going to grow until it becomes something that he must address. He'll eventually have to recognize that his un-dealt-with wound is festering, causing a malignancy that is slowly infecting his whole being. And he'll be faced with a decision: continue in a safe but miserable existence or face his fears and risk being hurt again so he can ultimately live his best life.

Remove the backstory from either of these scenarios, and we have no idea why the characters chose their careers. But once we learn their history, we understand. The characters become real and vulnerable and so much more interesting. We know not only what happened in their past, we can also see their path forward—the realizations and changes they'll have to make to be fulfilled both professionally and personally.

CAREERS THAT CHARACTERIZE

Let's say you're at a party, and you strike up a conversation with someone new. What's one of the first things you're going to ask?

"So, what do you do?"

The reason this question comes up in this context is jobs characterize. Like it or not, we tend to size people up and put them in boxes. And a person's chosen field of work can reveal a lot about who they are.

Granted, not every stereotype is accurate, and we obviously want to avoid clichéd characters; individualization is an important part of the character-building process, so we'll discuss this in-depth in just a bit. But, at first blush, a character's job can provide a baseline for readers about things that are probably true, shortening the learning curve in the getting-to-know-you process. Here are a few things your reader may infer about a character simply by knowing his occupation.

PERSONALITY TRAITS

Certain traits will make it easier for a person to succeed at a given job. And usually people want to be successful; that's one reason we gravitate toward careers that play to our personality. So when a reader sees a character working in a specific field, they're going to draw some conclusions. This gives authors a leg up when it comes to characterization, enabling them to show personality simply by revealing that cast member's job.

To test this theory, what positive qualities come to mind when you think of a kindergarten teacher? Traits like compassion, gentleness, and patience probably top the list. It looks different, though, for an ER physician, who might be pegged as intelligent, decisive, and calm under pressure. There are exceptions, but certain traits do help make someone a good teacher or doctor or farmer. (For more information on the jobs associated with specific dominant traits, see Appendix A.)

Conveying your character's personality to readers without resorting to info dumps and long passages of narrative can be challenging. This is where occupations can come in handy, enabling you to kick-start characterization with a minimum of words.

TALENTS AND SKILLS

Every career requires a skill set that goes beyond personality. Talents and abilities are special aptitudes and areas of exceptionality that can make a person good at her job. A chef is going to be skilled at cooking or baking. A bouncer is likely adept at self-defense. When readers are introduced to a professional poker player, they can surmise that the character will know how to read people.

Unless an unmet need or other higher motivation is steering them, characters will pursue jobs they're good at and enjoy (just as we do in the real world). Talents and skills are found in that intersection and often will lead someone toward a particular job. Because readers make associations about what it takes to succeed in various occupations, your character's choice in this area will naturally showcase his aptitudes, no infodumps needed.

HOBBIES AND PASSIONS

Many careers are born from a favorite pastime. This may be the case for a museum docent who knows every possible thing about ancient South American civilizations and wants to share his knowledge with others. A geologist may pursue that career because he's spending his free time studying geology anyway, so why not get paid for doing what he loves? This is the reason many people choose a creative or artistic field of work. In cases like these, a career can loudly proclaim the character's interests and preferred diversions, offering insight into what sets them apart from others.

PHYSICAL DETAILS

Some jobs can give readers a hint about the character's appearance. Models tend to be attractive by society's established standards. Laboratory technicians wear lab coats. Professional athletes are physically fit. Whether it's the uniform or expectations that go with the job, an occupation can provide many unspoken clues about how a character looks and behaves at work.

PREFERENCES

Sometimes a character will work in a field because he's forced to or it's the only thing available. But when he's free to choose, a job will usually indicate certain preferences. An outdoor guide will be a nature enthusiast who would rather work outside than in a cubicle. A personal shopper should enjoy shopping. A nanny hopefully likes working with kids. While characters in a given career will have their own personal passions, that employment choice will often reveal something about their basic preferences.

IDEALS AND BELIEFS

Another reason a character may choose a profession is that it aligns with his deepest beliefs. A clergy member may follow this path because, to him, helping people find God is the highest possible calling. A career in the military is often preceded by a strong sense of patriotism and respect for one's country. Careers like these can immediately say something to readers about the character's ideals and values.

ECONOMIC STATUS

As indelicate as the subject may be, many jobs are associated with economic status. A character who is a successful lawyer, doctor, or business tycoon is going to read *rich* while someone in an entry level or blue-collar position (cashiers, car drivers, babysitters, or bouncers) may be perceived by readers as being less privileged.

Even without any fine-tuning or individualizing—which is always a good idea, to avoid clichés or stereotypes—an occupation can suggest many things about a character. Unless you have a strong story-worthy reason for doing so (and we'll get into those later), picking a career for your character that doesn't gel with his personality, beliefs, and skills is going to weaken him. Like pieces from separate puzzles, they won't quite fit together. Make sure his job is perfect for *him* in this story, and you're on your way to creating a character that rings true with readers.

JOBS AS SOURCES OF
TENSION AND CONFLICT

Conflict provides a steady stream of challenges on the path to the character's goal, so it's a necessary ingredient in any story. The formula is quite simple: a character wants something, and obstacles get in her way. Conflict comes in many forms—barriers, problems, crises, opposition—and if we bring our A-game to the keyboard, these complications will hit our character from different directions.

Some conflicts are small—micro challenges that increase the tension within a scene, making the figurative wall blocking the way to the character's goal that much higher and harder to scale. Other conflicts are more significant, providing serious obstacles for her to fight past, which threatens her ability to win and raises the stakes. These macro conflicts often have wider, story-encompassing effects, because when stakes are raised due to something personal being at risk, the character and everyone involved will have something to lose. The power of conflict is that it forces your character again and again to recommit to her goals, prove her dedication, and (if she is on a change arc) stick to the journey of growth that is necessary for her to succeed.

Whether you need macro or micro conflict for a scene, occupations can provide a vast field of potential land mines. We know that people work for many reasons: to provide for themselves and those they love, to feel valued, and to find meaning—to name just a few. Because a job integrates so thoroughly with your character's life, it naturally creates soft spots and sensitivities that can be poked. As the author, you can decide which foundations you want to shake and how hard. Even the threat of conflict can awaken insecurities. Let's look at some of the ways your character's job can cause problems in different areas of her life.

RELATIONSHIP CONFLICT

The people closest to a character have insider access to her thoughts, ideas, beliefs, and emotions, which, when you think about it, is no small thing. In most cases, these are people your character invited into her life—meaning, the relationships are personal and therefore are important to her. But, at work, she's not able to choose, and circumstances may force her to share space with people she normally wouldn't seek out, such as a racist co-worker or a demanding boss. It may be a constant struggle for your character to decide whom she will let in and who must be kept at arm's length.

High expectations, tight deadlines, small margins, and too much responsibility (perhaps for too little pay) can supercharge emotions, generate friction, and create the perfect storm for conflict around the office. Among co-workers, a range of problems can crop up and derail a character's plans. For example, being saddled with the boss's entitled, incompetent kid when productivity is paramount could put your protagonist's bonus in peril. In itself, this is bad enough, but throw in a five-digit gambling debt, and you've got a nightmare scenario. Or what if your protagonist is competing for a promotion against a conniving co-worker who doesn't think twice about interoffice sabotage and throwing people under the bus? How will your hero come out on top?

At work, people have differing viewpoints, opinions, manners, and personalities that are not always compatible. And, in most occupations, everyone is expected to put differences aside and work as a team. Only … is that what happens, especially these days? You don't need a physical watercooler to spread gossip when everyone in the office has text-messaging. And why risk being overheard bad-mouthing a co-worker when you could use IMs and memes instead? Face it, around the office, smiles can hide knives.

Here are some of the ways work and relationships often make bad dance partners.

Power Imbalances

In any organization, some people will have power over others, maybe because of their prestigious position, seniority, or friends in high places. Wherever your character lands in the food chain, he will have to answer to those in charge, and as we all know, not all bosses are created equal.

It's unfair, but sometimes the best-suited people don't always get the coveted positions, especially in management. An internal shuffle might drop a supervisor into a role he's not capable of handling, or it could award him a position due to bias or nepotism. It doesn't matter if the boss is unethical, lazy, egotistical, or plain bad at his job; your character must find a way to work with him. This might mean having to kid-glove his temper, follow insensible processes, ignore his hypocrisy, or cater to his narcissism. Power in the workplace can be a carrot or a stick, promising advancement if the character falls in line or a layoff if he doesn't.

And it's not just the boss who can make life easy or hard for your character. Other people will control the budget for new purchases, decide who is eligible for company training, and dictate who gets the graveyard shift. All sorts of factors might go into the decision-making, including pettiness. At a grocery store, the head cashier is usually tasked with assigning where the service clerks will work. If your character gets on that person's bad side, she might find herself consistently running the slowest register and bagging groceries unassisted all day long.

Industry or personal bias (gender discrimination, ageism, racial or religious prejudice) by higher-ups could also block your character from advancing professionally. If she's being harassed or marginalized in the workplace, this could cause big problems and reawaken psychological wounds, threatening everything she is trying to achieve.

Power imbalances can also come from unusual places. Consider a new hire who, to your protagonist's horror, is someone from his past, and there is an ocean of bad blood between them. Imagine the leverage this new guy would have because he knows all about your hero's shady past, or he's privy to a secret that, if revealed, could mean jail time. Conflict resulting in a loss of control for your character can be electrifying, resulting in readers who are glued to the page and agonizing over what will come next.

The Land of Bad Decisions: Workplace Romances

A common trope in fiction is the office romance, when the lines between personal and professional relationships blur. Long, late nights trying to meet a deadline or a desire to cut loose at the conclusion of a successful project can lead to bad decisions, such as an impromptu tryst with a co-worker or inviting the boss's hunky assistant into the boardroom for something other than dictation. Office romances are usually forbidden for good reason—they produce unwanted drama. And when the sparks inevitably fizzle, everyone else may need chainsaws to cut the tension, which could undermine the unity and teamwork needed for your character to achieve her goals.

Another problem with these relationships is that both parties don't always end up on the same page. For one, the break room booty is all fun and games, but for the other it may become serious. If a careless "I love you" or "When are you going to leave your husband?" spills out, a cold breeze might blow in. The lovestruck whispers change to "We should really stop" and "This was fun, but let's keep it professional from here on out." Heartbreak is never easy, but when you're forced to see and work with the person who discarded you, it can lead to resentment, anger, and the desire for revenge.

With bad breakups at work, the possibilities are endless for delicious conflict. Some staples, such as career sabotage, blackmail, and threats to tell the wife, are often used because they work. But instead of replaying the same old recording, add a twist that readers haven't seen. What if the jilted love interest threatens to tell the boss's angst-ridden teenage kid instead of his wife? Ouch. And it would take a special kind of vengefulness to bypass family members and hand evidence of the affair to the chin-waggers at his church. Sharpen your imagination to come up with creative ways to get even, and remember that sometimes small cuts cause the most damage.

Problems at Home

Work-related conflict can cause relationship fallout when the two biggest parts of the character's life collide: their work persona and their at-home identity. Just because the uniform is hung up, it doesn't mean that the character's brain has turned off. Bouncy kids eager to see their parents after a long day, a hungry spouse asking about dinner, or a cat with digestive problems can send your character over the edge, leading to overreactions and an evening of regret and apologies.

Demanding careers can impact the character's personal relationships in a myriad of ways. Relocations for work disrupt friendships, schedules, and a sense of belonging. Shiftwork means having to lean on a spouse or grandparents to help with child care. Too much travel, late nights, and missed violin recitals or little league games can pile on the stress for a character who's just doing what he has to do to keep his job. He might suffer guilt for not prioritizing family time while the partner taking on the most at-home responsibility feels underappreciated or abandoned. Frustration can build as both people make demands that the other can't meet. And if the couple becomes so exhausted by work and domestic responsibilities that they're unable to nurture their marriage, they may forget why they joined forces in the first place.

Money has always been a common friction point in relationships, and this can play in your favor. What about a husband who doesn't support his wife's career because it doesn't pay enough? That judgment might cause her to doubt herself and question her own worth, and eventually she'll resent him for making her feel this way. Or perhaps jealousy is the issue and he's unsupportive because her job brings in more money and accolades than his, which bruises his ego.

Another real-world scenario is when one partner's career is assigned a higher priority than the other's. Consider Steve, a personal trainer who's working toward opening his own studio, and Alicia, a street performer who works nights so she can be home with their physically disabled son. Everything is going smoothly until a recording of Alicia's act goes viral online. Suddenly the phone is ringing nonstop with booking requests and agents clamoring to sign her as a client.

But making that jump will require her to work more hours, and someone has to be at home with their boy. So Alicia sits Steve down for some straight talk: this is a once-in-a-lifetime opportunity, a chance for her to see how far she can go. So Steve needs to quit his job to care for their son.

Maybe Steve doesn't want to quit work, especially when he's so close to finally achieving his own goals. If he recognizes this as his wife's big moment, he may reluctantly agree, but how will this impact his fulfillment? And how will the relationship be changed by the implication that his wife's dreams are more important than his own?

Conflicts that pit work against family responsibilities cause some of the most difficult situations to navigate. They're also a great way to explore deeper emotions as your character is forced to make hard choices about her needs, identity, and duty to others. Choices are always key for our characters, providing opportunities for them to decide what happens next. If they're able to redirect energy from work to something else because it's the right thing to do, they're choosing to reshape their goals, which can lead to fulfillment. But a character who feels that a loved one is forcing him to sacrifice something he loves may grow resentful, unhappy, and jaded at how unfair life can be.

Readers understand the difficulties of balancing work, family, and relationships. Including this kind of common-ground conflict scenario can add a sense of realism to scenes and put readers more firmly on the character's side.

MORAL CONFLICT

Characters are formed in the mixing bowl of past experiences: how they were raised, who influenced them, and what they were taught. All this produces a specific worldview—an attitude about society, the people in it, and how everything works. Embedded within this perspective is something powerful enough to influence a character's everyday behavior and actions: moral beliefs that form how he discerns right from wrong. These beliefs can be so charged with emotion that they become part of the character's identity, driving him to risk everything to uphold them. But, as happens in the real world, not every situation is straightforward—meaning, right and wrong aren't always easy to define.

Different Lines in the Sand

Work brings together people from all backgrounds, cultures, and experiences, each with their own worldview, moral code, and goals. As a result, not everyone shows up with the same values and right-or-wrong boundaries. This can result in behavior that interferes with the job or causes a moral crisis.

Let's say our character, Gary, works for an antiques dealer. One day, he overhears his boss lying to a customer about the history or condition of an item. Gary brings this up later, but his employer brushes it off, saying the customer isn't savvy enough to know the difference, anyway.

This bothers Gary because it goes against his ethics to work for someone who scams people. But the moral conflict might not be easy to resolve if he really needs his job—maybe because his wife just had heart surgery, and he's got a mountain of bills to pay. Loyalty can also confuse the matter if his employer hired Gary after he was released from prison and couldn't find work elsewhere.

Moral conflicts involving others are often messy, so it can be tempting to try to sidestep them by doing nothing. But we've all heard the old maxim about not choosing still being a choice. Morals are tied to a person's identity, so doing nothing is often synonymous with condoning. No, a choice must be made, and either way, consequences will follow. If a character acts unethically, going against his deepest beliefs, it may result in loss of self-worth or reputation. If he stands his ground and holds true to what he believes is right, he might still lose something important: his freedom, influence, power, or job.

In Gary's case, he might choose to ignore his employer's dishonesty. But, as time goes on, it will become harder for him to look himself in the mirror. Deep down, he'll know that while he isn't the one lying to customers, he's allowing it to happen, and that makes him complicit.

No matter what the moral conflict is, your character's actions and choices will say a lot about him and convey his deeper (or shallower) side to readers. Additionally, this internal tug-of-war can be effective for demonstrating your character's growth. In the same way that an alcoholic must say *no* to the next drink in order to bring about a larger change, your character must also reject the temptations that may further him professionally but wreck him personally. Once a conflict grows strong enough to trigger his deepest morals and values, he'll no longer be able to avoid his problems and will be forced to do the hard, internal work that will bring about meaningful change.

The Slippery Slope of "Just This Once"

Like other types of conflict, moral challenges cause problems of varying degrees. But even small dilemmas in this area are dangerous, since they can slowly erode someone's moral fiber. A character may decide that using petty cash one day to pay for his lunch is justified, considering all the off-hour work he does. Then he does it again. And again. Over time, it becomes a habit. Where does this pattern of line-crossing end? Will he recognize himself down the road, when he's finally caught dipping into those funds to pay his electric bill?

This bending of the rules in small conflict scenarios can quickly escalate to something more substantial. A character may agree to cover for a co-worker who wants to cut out early, believing that an hour is no big deal. But what if the co-worker's ex-boyfriend goes missing shortly after she left work, and his mutilated body is discovered a few days later? Now your character's life is upended as he becomes a key player in a murder investigation. And he must come to grips with the knowledge that he may have aided a killer.

When Duty Meets Morality

Sometimes a character's loyalty is tested when duty clashes with moral beliefs. A soldier might be ordered by a dictator to kill innocent villagers as a lesson to others. Does he do so or refuse? If threatened, will he yield?

Issues can also arise when a character experiences conflicting needs, desires, beliefs, or goals. In the movie *Sleepers*, four life-long friends from Hell's Kitchen embark on a vendetta to destroy their childhood abusers. When two of the friends are arrested (legitimately) for murdering a former tormenter, they petition their priest to provide their alibi. His former altar boys—once young and innocent, victims themselves of a horrible crime—are essentially asking him to lie under oath to save them, leading to a heart-wrenching decision that, either way, will result in tremendous loss.

PERSONAL CONFLICT

When personal choices begin impacting job performance, it can threaten career stability and throw other parts of the character's life into chaos. Take a character who drinks to cope with life stress. One day she's able to control her intake, and the next she's not, and it's affecting her productivity and quality of work. If she continues, she may eventually be let go without a reference that would help her find a new job. Well-connected friends in the industry may not vouch for her because they're unwilling to risk their reputations for someone who has become unreliable. In this situation, the friction between her and her peers combined with her inability to find employment becomes a one-two punch of conflict that will cause even more problems.

Personal Sacrifice

Some jobs are demanding, and to do them well, a sacrifice is required—time and energy that normally would be dedicated to other things. This tradeoff might seem fine at first, but it can lead to a crisis down the road. Take Lydia, a dancer who dedicated herself to her art, sacrificing personal goals and relationships in order to be the best. She's achieved acclaim and success, but now that younger dancers are entering the field of competition, getting roles is not as easy as it once was.

Then it happens—the contract with her dance company is not renewed. Lydia is gutted when her career ends without warning.

The aftershocks of being cast aside spread through her whole life, threatening important areas of need that used to be secure. For example, she hasn't invested in building meaningful relationships outside her company, so she struggles to feel connected to anyone (love and belonging). She refuses to be around other dancers and endure their pity because she feels used up and worthless (esteem and recognition). Worst of all, Lydia feels like her identity has been stolen. She was a dancer; it was her dream. Without it, she doesn't know who she is (self-actualization).

The future seems bleak. How will she support herself? All her education revolved around dancing, so unless she can transition to a secondary career as an instructor, studio owner, or choreographer, she'll be in big trouble. She can go back to school to gain skills in another area, but that means not getting paid for a while. Once her savings is gone, she will have no way to pay for her apartment, food, or other necessities (physiological needs).

When a career that demanded dedication and personal sacrifice ends, it's common for a person to feel victimized. Like Lydia, a character may harbor ill will toward the industry that used her up, resent the society that ignores her mistreatment, and even be angry with family and friends who are not as supportive as they could be. Regardless of the job, when it is taken away, navigating that new reality is a challenge. Lots of difficult emotions need to be processed.

The good news about this scenario is that we're all familiar with the heartache and disillusionment of something precious ending prematurely. We can use the character's painful circumstances to remind readers of a time when things went sour for them, encouraging empathetic bonds to form.

Feeling Evil? Use Maslow's Hierarchy to Compound Conflict

We shared earlier how Maslow's hierarchy can be used to identify missing needs that could contribute to a character's choice of career. But, as we all know, life happens, and what was once satisfying can become ho-hum, frustrating, or downright dangerous, given the right circumstances. On-the-job conflict can be the corrosive element that eats away at a character's needs or puts them at odds, leading to a workplace showdown.

Dara is an assistant to a hip-hop singer, managing her transportation, hotel, and travel details when they go on tour. She also organizes her interview and appearance schedules, ensures everything in the singer's rider is supplied, and runs other errands as needed. Dara loves having access to celebrities and the glamourous lifestyle that goes with the job, and while it's tasking and she doesn't always get enough sleep, it's fulfilling, it pays well, and she wouldn't trade it for anything in the world.

One night after a show, Dara accompanies the singer to their hotel and picks up mail at the front desk—mostly cards and letters from fans. The year before, her boss was targeted by a stalker (who was eventually caught and thrown in jail, thankfully), so Dara monitors mail closely to avoid passing along anything upsetting.

While the singer changes for an after-party, Dara stays in her adjoining room and plucks a red envelope out of the mail pile. When she opens it, white powder spills out, coating her hands. She gasps and drops the card before realizing she's just inhaled the substance into her lungs.

The doorknob connecting her suite to the celebrity's rattles. Dara throws herself against the door and yells to the singer to call the police and get out of the hotel. While Dara waits for emergency services, she uses a pen to open the card and slide out a photo. It was taken over the shoulder of the singer as she signed an autograph—the stalker's familiar calling card. Shaking and numb, she collapses into a chair, wondering how he got out of jail, how security didn't spot him. He's probably even more unstable after all that time in prison, and if he blames the singer for his incarceration, how far might he go to get back at her?

She stares at white-dusted hands. Is it anthrax? Ebola? She rushes to the bathroom and scrubs her skin raw. Her breath grows short, her chest tightens, and she's sweating profusely by the time first responders arrive.

After a few days being quarantined and surrounded by doctors in special suits, Dara is given the all-clear. The tests have proven the powder to be simple cornstarch and her initial symptoms no more than a panic attack induced by the event.

When she returns to the hotel to pack up her things, it's filled with flowers and cards from well-wishers in the industry who had heard what happened. The singer is in tears, apologizing, mortified that one of her fans had done this. She goes on about how tough Dara is and asks if three days will be enough time off. Dara smiles and says all the right things, but deep down she knows that she's done. The cameras flashing in her face in front of the hotel, the paparazzi yelling out questions about it all being a PR stunt, the closeness of strangers and their access to her—mentally, she's already writing her resignation letter.

Basic human needs are powerful. A person can have everything in place, feel completely fulfilled and in love with what they do, but if something comes along to significantly threaten that stability, everything tilts. Dara's safety and security were shaken, reminding her how fragile life is. The danger that comes with proximity to those in the spotlight is no longer a risk she's willing to take to feel self-actualized.

Warring human needs create big problems in storytelling. Your character who found love and belonging in the community of law enforcement may retire to pursue safety and security after being shot. Your mechanical engineer can enjoy what she does but have her self-esteem damaged by a demanding and belittling supervisor, causing her to leave her dream job to work for someone else. There are infinite ways basic human needs can intersect with your character's job, forcing her to make choices she wouldn't otherwise have to make.

What about the Dream Job?

Sometimes a character sets his sights on a position that he believes will completely fulfill him. But the reality rarely lives up to the hype, and he may end up disappointed mid-career, wondering if he made a mistake.

If he's invested a lot to get to this point, letting it go can seem terrifying—and possibly stupid, if he's good at what he does, makes decent money, and has earned the esteem of the people around him. This creates inner turmoil, because leaving a job is a scary prospect, yet deep down he knows that staying might make him overworked and unfulfilled.

A character can get stuck in this place between settling and risking because both options lead to uncertainty. Staying in the position might result in regret because he lacked the courage to reboot and move on. Switching also carries costs, such as debt for new education, losing time as he builds new skills, and other factors. And what if he fails, or years down the road yearns to return to his previous career because, in hindsight, he realizes it was better?

Choosing a job, whether for the first time or during a life pivot, requires a leap of faith. Faith is not always in large supply for a character who has been beaten down by people and circumstances. With each negative experience, the risk of decision-making holds more weight. Showing characters wrestle with the age-old life question of "Is this what I really want to do?" is a great way to humanize them to readers through real-world commonalities.

SCENARIOS OUTSIDE THE CHARACTER'S CONTROL

If you're looking for general conflict ideas that could happen across many professions, try these on for size:

Technology Shifts

Unfortunately, innovation and advancements sometimes result in jobs being phased out. As technology streamlines processes and robots replace heartbeats, becoming obsolete is a worry for many.

Company Mergers

Companies in competitive markets must grow stronger or risk being put out of business by larger, more aggressive rivals. A merger can help with this, but one of the first tasks on the docket will be identifying any redundancies so departments, products, and people can be whittled down to a profitable core.

Economic Downturns

When the markets struggle, so do many industries, and companies within those industries don't always have sufficient buffer to keep them afloat in the lean times. Recessions, pandemics, wars, natural disasters, and political volatility can all destabilize global and local economies, forcing business owners to cut costs. They might chop underperforming services or products, scale back on new developments, and consider what their biggest costs and areas of risk are, all of which can result in mass layoffs. If a lot of workers are let go at once, finding another job will be harder for your character because a flood of people will be doing the same thing, and fewer companies may be hiring.

When a single industry is experiencing problems, it may seem that it will only impact people within that field, but this isn't always the case. Whenever people are laid off, have had their hours reduced, or are forced into paid leave, they tend to spend less. The trickle-down effect causes other business owners to feel the pinch as fewer customers walk through their doors. They, in turn, may be forced to tighten their own wallets to weather the storm. This can cause a wider economic crisis across multiple industries.

New Owners
Whenever a business changes hands, the employees hold their breath. Why? Because no one knows what will stay the same and what will change. The new owners might be fine with maintaining the status quo in the short term, but bigger changes are likely coming down the road. They may ditch certain services or products, shift the company's direction, go niche or wide with their offerings, or change the company's culture. At the end of the day, employees who are no longer a good fit will be shown the door.

PR (Public Relations) Problems
Sometimes, a company goofs. They fail to test a product enough and it results in a recall, or a poorly planned marketing campaign receives backlash from the community. Maybe they didn't conduct enough research, or they partnered with a service provider that gets caught doing something unethical, and the business becomes guilty by association. Whatever the reason, when a company's reputation is damaged, it often results in financial losses.

To regain the trust of the public, the business must make the situation right. This usually involves holding people accountable. If your character was involved, he may be fired or demoted. Even if he wasn't responsible, companies need someone to blame, and your character could become their convenient scapegoat.

Societal Shifts
If your story takes place in the real world (or is similar to it), society's opinions will influence the economy. With information so readily available, public opinion can upset industries quickly, forcing businesses to adapt or die. Look no further than the growing awareness of climate change and how consumers are turning to reusables. Stock in a company that makes plastic straws might tank overnight when people are encouraged by influencers and politicians to stop using them. If this business is unable to change their product line quickly, they'll go under.

HOME OFFICE CONFLICT
Working from home is an increasingly common situation, which, as you might imagine, can lead to spectacular clashes between the character's two worlds. A buffet of conflict scenarios can derail productivity, distract from critical work, and make him appear unprofessional to those who hold power over his career.

Here are a few ideas to plunder when you need work-at-home conflict for your storyline.

Interruptions

Is there anything worse than being interrupted at a crucial time? Packages requiring signatures, kids tattling on their siblings, the internet crashing, a spouse wanting to discuss the color of paint for the bathroom, a repairman updating the homeowner on the broken dryer—the options are endless.

If your character is anything like a real person, he's probably also prone to self-interruptions. We're all tempted to procrastinate when it comes to unappealing tasks. Text notifications, social media, hunger pangs—even the obnoxious siren call of a messy apartment can interrupt the flow of work. If your character falls behind, stress and emotional volatility escalate, and it might cause him to rush through a job, leading to errors and mistakes.

Scheduling Conflicts

Unless your character lives alone, he's sharing his space with others. If he has kids at home, house guests, or a steady stream of his spouse's clients coming and going, it might be hard to concentrate. And what about if child care falls through or resources must be shared (like a teen needing the computer for research or a spouse taking over the office to attend an online meeting)?

Another interesting possibility is if your character works with team members in other parts of the world. It may be necessary to have conference calls or video meetings at unusual hours when quiet surroundings aren't available. Having to run a call during a playdate or family gathering may make your character seem unprofessional and earn the disapproval of higher-ups.

Exposed Secrets

Some people are very careful to keep their home and work life separate. But if your character is suddenly forced to work from home because of an illness, condition, injury, or company policy, it could expose things they'd rather keep hidden. For instance, a hoarder will find it difficult to hide that tendency during a video conference. Also, if your protagonist lives with others in a small space, privacy can be a problem. What if his drunken partner can be heard swearing in the background, or an elderly parent with dementia wanders into view half-dressed?

The Little Things

With the rise of home-based businesses (hair salons, massage therapy, Reiki treatments, dog grooming, and the like), your character may need to keep a tidy house for when clients visit. A dog who steals and relocates undergarments from the laundry bin, a dishwasher that decides to messily self-terminate, or even an innocent nosebleed that turns the entryway into a murder scene can create imaginative and embarrassing complications when a client arrives.

To get the most mileage out of your micro or macro conflict, know its purpose in a scene. It should have a function other than simply to throw rocks at your character. Obstacles and opposition can be a catalyst for epiphanies; there's nothing like conflict to bring a blind spot or misguided priority into sharp focus. It can force a stubborn character to realize when he's in over his head or reveal that his work situation needs to be reimagined.

JOBS CAN SUPPORT STORY STRUCTURE AND CHARACTER ARC

Between word count guidelines and discerning readers whose lives are full of distractions, the details that go onto the page have to pull their storytelling weight. And like the gift that keeps on giving, your character's occupation once again comes through. Not only will a source of employment reveal important aspects about personality, beliefs, and interests, it can also reinforce certain structure points in a novel and reveal the layers of character arc.

A story's opening is a great example of this, because, let's face it—there's a mountain of pressure on writers to nail the beginning. We have to introduce the protagonist and what matters most to him, show his ordinary world in a way that reflects his current situation and needs, and hint at what could go wrong. Oh, and make it all interesting to read, of course! A tall order, as any writer will attest, but it must be done.

Here are some pivotal ways a career choice can be used to set foundational pieces for the story.

USING A CAREER TO SET THE STAGE

Imagine a story opening that introduces a lawyer protagonist. But he's not at a big firm with fancy leather furniture and a secretary manning a sleek desk in the land of *by appointment only*. No, our lawyer's office is crammed inside a storage room in the back of a nail salon. Rather than expensive artwork and rugs, his space contains a dusty water heater and dented filing cabinet. A phone sits within reach on a scabby old desk, and the character taps his fingers, willing it to ring.

As we watch this scene unfold, what can we assume? Well, if he's a lawyer, he must be intelligent, hardworking, and walk-the-line crafty—someone who is very good at reading a chessboard and playing to win. The fact that he's not with a firm suggests he's either new, a maverick, or not very good at his job.

But this is where questions creep in. Of all the places to practice law, why here? People needing legal services tend to trust professionals who look successful, so that's the persona lawyers emulate. Even someone fresh out of law school who's determined to strike out on his own would rent the best office he could afford in a good location, because appearances are everything. Yet this lawyer doesn't seem to care about that, which raises more questions. Why not? How would clients find him hidden back there, anyway? And while we're on that topic, what sort of clientele would hire a lawyer working out of a dingy storage room?

Fans of *Better Call Saul* will recognize Saul Goodman, a lawyer in Albuquerque, New Mexico, who has interesting layers, questionable ethics, and complex motivations for practicing law. But even if you didn't recognize him, look at what this setup gives readers: an introduction to the protagonist, details that characterize, a view of his ordinary world, suggestions that something is off, and a boatload of questions that act as hooks, pulling readers in. These are all ingredients of a strong opening, delivered through the lens of Saul's profession.

Because a career is often a big part of a character's life, it makes a great window into their everyday world and what isn't quite right about it. The character's behavior at work will allude to the story to come and raise questions:

Is he passionate about the job while chafing at its rules and constraints?

Does he feel overworked and underappreciated and wish others would recognize his contributions?

Is there a bias keeping him stuck in a position, suggesting the presence of a glass ceiling to bust through?

Does he meekly do as he's told, believing he's only capable of supporting rather than leading?

Showing a character's unhappiness through work—how he's trapped in a role he doesn't like or one that doesn't fit who he is—is a terrific way to provide a snapshot of his life before everything changes (hopefully for the better). To maximize this technique, though, we need to follow through by providing clues about why he chose it in the first place:

Was he pushed down this path by a domineering parent?

Does he have responsibilities that keep him in this job even though it gives him no satisfaction?

Was this a "safe" choice, causing him to settle rather than risk trying for something better?

Was this the only job he could get because he isn't suited for anything else?

A profession, whether we like it or not, becomes part of our identity. We usually choose the work we do, even if narrow options make it feel as if the choice is being made for us. In the rare case in which someone falls into a job randomly, the person still *chooses* to stay there, and the reasons always matter, both in life and in story. Your readers are hardwired to follow the *whys*, especially when they hint at a character's secrets, his painful past, or the deeper layers of who he is, so make sure to provide answers to their questions as the story progresses.

Now, not all characters are black holes of misery on page one. Sometimes it's the opposite, and life is all rainbows. Even then, an occupation can prime the audience for what will happen next. A story opening about a successful, in-love-with-his job character will prime readers to pop mental popcorn and turn pages. Why? Because this isn't their first rodeo—they've read enough stories to realize that happy characters don't stay that way. They know the protagonist is about to get smoked in the head by life, and his perfect situation will crumble.

HOW JOBS CAN AWAKEN CHARACTERS TO CHANGE

Due to its importance in a character's life, a career can also be used as a vehicle for change. A protagonist at the start of a story should be different than who he is at the end. With change arcs specifically, the lead character (and possibly others) will undergo an inner transformation during which he learns to harness his inner strengths, regain lost self-belief, and let go of the fears and wounds of the past. To get to this point, though, the character must awaken to the fact that something is off about his life, causing him to feel unhappy, hollow, and unfulfilled.

This feeling of a need going unmet can be a bit nebulous. The character may know he's yearning for something without knowing what it is, and he'll have to dig for the cause. Because work is a big portion of his life, it's packed with opportunities to bring about this revelation. A character who is unhappy in his job might connect the dots a bit quicker, but it really depends on the underlying reasons.

As an example, take Adam, who works on the family's ranch, training to take it over from his aging father. The world of cattle is all he knows—the routine of caring for animals and mending fences and the quiet hours of reflection as he leads the herd to grazing pastures and home again. Adam loves the sunsets and sunrises and roaming the wide-open spaces on horseback, but he also knows that something isn't quite right. Let's consider how his job might help him pinpoint what is causing this dissatisfaction.

What if ranching is a duty, not a dream? Maybe he herds cattle yet imagines a different life, one with streets and shops, with high-rises and yellow cabs, a world busy with lights and sounds. He might think about university and the different possibilities available to him. Perhaps Adam is fascinated with buildings—their shape and flow, the beauty of glass and steel. To him, buildings are art, and he's realizing he has a passion for how they are made.

As time goes on, ranching becomes drudgery; he becomes fixated on the less enjoyable tasks rather than the ones he likes. Most of his school friends have left to pursue education and build their own lives. Feeling trapped and lonely, he wants to experience new things too.

In this case, two things are awakening Adam to a need for change: a growing dissatisfaction with the work he does and the feeling that a window is closing. As his friends move forward, Adam believes he must do the same, and soon. This sense of urgency might help Adam evaluate his priorities about what's important—studying to be an architect and having a different future—which will push him to have a difficult conversation with his dad.

Now let's consider a different scenario in which Adam doesn't dream of the city and being an architect. In fact, he loves everything about ranching. But he's constantly butting heads with his father, who likes things to function a certain way. Always micromanaging, he points out what Adam misses rather than mention what he's doing right. It doesn't seem to matter how proactive his son is or how hard he works; his dad always complains about something Adam could have done better.

Adam is becoming increasingly unhappy, so when friends from college return home with enthusiastic stories about life at school, he can't help but question whether ranching is for him. He longs for independence and a break from the constant criticism. As he and his friends meet in a pub, they talk about their lives. Some are excited about what they're learning, but others seem overwhelmed and perhaps envious of Adam. On the drive home, he is uncertain what to feel. Life on the other side of the fence maybe isn't as great as he first thought.

Giving your character conflicting information will create mixed feelings, which in turn sends their gaze inward to reflect on their situation and what's bothering them. In this case,

Adam begins to realize that it's not the ranching life he's struggling with but his dad. An honest discussion about the problems might help Adam see his father's criticism as well-meaning—a way to prepare him for the challenges of managing a ranch. Understanding that viewpoint can help him grow. Or maybe the conversation doesn't go well and reinforces his dad's need for control. If this can't be worked through, another difficult conversation will have to happen, this time about Adam starting a ranch of his own.

A decision like this could be hard on both characters. Adam's dad will be disappointed and possibly angry, and it will take time for him to understand his son's decision to leave. Adam will also be taking a risk, walking away from a profitable ranch where all the kinks have been worked out. But if he is ready to fight for his independence, it means he's realized something important: chasing what you want isn't easy and involves risk. And while this situation with his dad will be difficult to navigate, doing so will lead to greater self-confidence and empowerment—the self-growth he needs to steer his own future.

OTHER WAYS A JOB CAN OFFER INSIGHT

Whether your character's stuck in a job that's wrong for her or she's trying something new, both her responsibilities and people she interacts with can generate epiphanies.

A Co-Worker on a Bad Path

The things your character witnesses can serve as an echo of her own problems. Imagine a protagonist whose peer is always embroiled in power struggles with the boss. Standing on the sidelines, she watches as that work relationship erodes. Finally, the boss reaches his limit and fires the co-worker. This consequence can serve as a wake-up call for your protagonist, who happens to be experiencing her own power struggle at home: if she and her spouse can't figure out how to tackle the problem of their burgeoning debt, their relationship might be in danger.

A Co-Worker on a Good Path

Positive examples can be just as illuminating as negative ones, such as a co-worker who helps your character see that the status quo isn't always enough. Let's say your protagonist is a reporter with a desk mate who is tired of having no control over which stories are being printed. He decides to start his own publication, and he hands in his resignation.

Your character may also feel unfulfilled in her role, but the steady paycheck keeps her in her seat. Predictability is safe, after all. But as she stares at the empty desk across from her own, her mind turns to the novel she really wants to write and wonders whether she, too, should trade predictability for passion.

Positive Experiences at Work

Sometimes a powerful work experience can transform how the character sees the world. Imagine Sandra, a social worker carrying the heavy emotional wound of growing up in a broken, dysfunctional home. She decided long ago that she didn't want a family, and her experience with abused children has only strengthened her resolve. But when roles are shuffled at the office, her caseload changes, and she finds herself servicing families who have been separated after a crisis. Seeing genuine, loving bonds and being part of beautiful reunions might awaken her to what she is missing. If she changes her mind about having a child, it might also repair a point of friction with her husband, who has always wanted a family.

Characters should have blind spots when it comes to their own struggles, faults, and failings, but, like real people, they are natural observers and learners. Help them reach that *aha* moment about what's missing in their life by exposing them to an event or situation that will resonate with them on a deep level.

PROFESSIONS THAT HELP OR HINDER GOAL ACHIEVEMENT

Because a character's career usually relates to their talents or areas of interest, it can be instrumental to him achieving his overall story goal. Look at Indiana Jones. Would he have found the Ark if he'd been a tattoo artist or orchestra conductor? Possibly, and those choices might have made an interesting movie, but we all can agree that the traditional story worked well because of how Jones's archaeology gig played directly into his main objective. If you know your character's overall story goal, consider choosing a vocation that will provide the knowledge and experience necessary for him to succeed.

Alternatively, a job that gets in the way of that goal can provide beautiful opportunities for conflict: an inventor who must destroy his best creation; a 1940s librarian being forced to burn books; a paparazzi-hounded celebrity who needs privacy to kill someone and dispose of the body.

Sometimes the choice of work indicates that the character is limiting himself as punishment for a past mistake, or he's settling for an ill-fitting job because he believes trying for something more will only lead to disappointment. Walter White from *Breaking Bad* comes to mind—the talented chemist who left the company he co-founded before it went big. Success was within his grasp and he stepped away from it, leading to the biggest regret of his life. Is it any wonder that, rather than try to hit the jackpot again, he settled for the safe job of an overqualified high school chemistry teacher?

This is why it's satisfying for fans when Walter comes into his own as Heisenberg, the powerful methamphetamine kingpin—because he finally chose a career that gave him the recognition and power he'd always craved. None of it could have happened, though, without Jesse Pinkman, the drug-dealing student who helped Walter access the drug trade. So, ironically Walter's teaching job made his dark ascension possible.

Conflict is really about choices and consequences. Your character is forced into a corner by undesirable circumstances and he must react, facing the problem head on, working around it, or hiding from it. Each decision leads to a cost, reward, or both.

If you're writing a positive change arc and must choose work-related obstacles for your character, think about how those roadblocks might nudge him toward embracing growth and change, leading to positive outcomes. This will move him one step closer to the transformation required for him to complete his arc and achieve the story goal. If you're writing a failed arc, use conflict primarily to show your character relying on old, dysfunctional habits and defense mechanisms. This will supply the subtext of anti-growth that grounds him in the denial and fear that eventually will be his undoing.

VOCATIONS AS THEMATIC DEVICES

One thing that will make your story unique is the imprint you as the author leave upon it: a worldview that belongs solely to you. This imprint will be delivered through a central idea known as **theme** and a **thematic statement**, which is your opinion on an aspect of that theme. For example, if the central idea of your story is *family*, a possible thematic statement could be *True family is chosen, not predetermined* or *Blood is thicker than water* (depending on the message you want to share with readers). The thematic statement is something that will be woven into the fabric of the story and supported by your character's actions throughout.

Let's say you've chosen the first thematic statement: *True family is chosen, not predetermined.* Your story will likely contain scenarios in which family members fail when given the opportunity to do right by your protagonist. Maybe your character will be betrayed by a loved one or find himself isolated, ostracized, and cast out for not conforming to the family's wishes. Then, in contrast, other people—friends, neighbors, co-workers, or strangers—step up, caring about and advocating for your protagonist. They respect the character, endure hardship for him, and generally choose to help when they don't have to. This loyalty and kinship will help your protagonist regain the self-worth stolen by his blood relatives and lead to the realization that true family is made of people you choose because they do right by you and vice versa.

Some writers plan their theme and thematic statement so they can apply symbolism as they write, reinforcing their viewpoint throughout the story. Others only fully realize the scope of a theme after the draft is complete. Then, in revision, they seed recognizable symbols and motifs meant to crystalize this underlying idea for readers.

A symbol can be anything—a person, place, or thing—and draws its power through the associations a reader makes: hearts are a universal symbol for love, the color white is a symbol for purity, and so on.

It might surprise you to know that one of the most versatile symbols is the character's vocation. A carefully chosen career can not only fit into the theme but the character's behavior in response to job-related conflict, responsibilities, and trials can embody the thematic statement.

Let's consider *sacrifice*—the act of giving up something meaningful for a higher purpose—and how an occupation could reflect this theme. A character could learn that his wife is pregnant and realize they'll need financial stability when the baby comes. So he gives up his pursuit of becoming a professional photographer and returns to teaching and a steady income. Another character may trade his youth to study and become a highly specialized transplant surgeon so he can save others the way his twin sister was saved as a child. A Marine will sacrifice safety for duty, and a nurse will often give up work-life balance in favor of patient care. In each case, the character's choice of career is intentional, making the theme of sacrifice clear.

Careers can be surrogates for other central ideas as well, like *fear*. Imagine a deep-sea commercial diver who, after a near-drowning, switches to a low-risk job as a mail carrier. His change of career becomes a representation of his fear. That fear can also be reinforced through your character's behavior at work rather than via the job itself. A professional poker player might only join less-lucrative games because he believes he'll mess up when the stakes are high. A politician could stick to the middle on all issues to avoid alienating voters and, as a result, never bring about any significant change. Underachievement, or the character clinging to his comfort zone at work, will underscore his fear of failure to readers.

OCCUPATION, THEME, AND EMOTIONAL WOUNDS

Chances are, if a fear is prominent in the story, it's likely part of an unresolved emotional wound, and the character's dysfunctional behavior becomes a representation of it. Just as avoidance and fear of failure can indicate a past wound, so can self-sabotage. If your poker player purposely joins the high-stake games regardless of how it decimates his finances, and your politician pushes the envelope to bring about changes that are polarizing and erratic, your readers will know something isn't quite right. This recklessness might be self-punishment for a past mistake, which, in turn, supports a thematic statement: *You can't run from the past,* or *Betrayal also hurts the one holding the knife.* When actions like these are used, readers will feel compelled to find out why your character is nuking his career.

Another way an occupation can point to a past wound is when it reveals an obsession. Imagine someone who grew up next to a farm without knowing his neighbors hoarded and tortured animals. When they were finally caught, your character was unable to forgive himself for not noticing what terrible things were happening next door. Driven to make up for the past, he became an animal rescue worker who specializes in rehabilitating abused farm animals, taking cases that others view as lost causes. His obsessive behavior will clarify that this isn't just a passion and that something is pushing him to try to save the unsavable. The work he does and the fervor with which he does it is a sign to readers that he's never been able to let go of what happened or move past his own perceived failure.

JOBS AND CLASHING THEMATIC ELEMENTS

Occupations can also show **thematic contradictions**. For example, in the film *Mr. Brooks*, Earl Brooks is a prominent businessman and philanthropist who also happens to be a serial killer. Controlled and careful, Earl has a system that allows him to satisfy his dark urges so even his family won't know what he is.

Then his daughter returns home from college with a shocking secret: despite not knowing the truth about him, she has unwittingly followed in his footsteps and become a killer herself. However, lacking her father's finesse and control, she left a messy crime scene that points right to her. Earl knows she'll be caught unless he does something, so he risks exposure and travels to her college town to give detectives a copycat murder to investigate while providing a rock-solid alibi for his daughter.

Let's look at the contradictions at work here: Earl is a pillar of the community, yet he takes lives. He is a dedicated family man who, if caught, will ruin the lives of his loved ones. Self-preservation motivates him to keep his second life hidden, yet love for his daughter causes him to risk capture to help her. He is a case study in opposites and identity contradictions.

Another technique that can be fun to play with is **purposeful contrast**. If *Power corrupts* is your thematic statement, you might be tempted to choose a profession for your character that comes with influence and moral flexibility (such as a power-hungry politician or businessman) so the corruption seems believable. But how much more shocking would this thematic statement be if your protagonist was a librarian, teacher, or nanny?

Careers like these provide a contrast that will put the character under the microscope in interesting ways, peeling back the layers of their needs and morality to explain why they might trade a piece of their identity for power. It also encourages creativity when it comes to the story, allowing you to explore new plot niches and stakes to show how the corruptive lure of power might pull a librarian, teacher, or nanny under.

Another contrast might arise when a character has outgrown a career he once loved, and their search for something new ties into a theme the author wishes to explore. Let's consider *equality* in the story of a famous chocolatier whose designer treats are popular with society's elite all over the globe. Bringing joy to people through chocolate was once fulfilling, but he's slowly becoming disenchanted creating confections for the rich. This shift came about in small increments but now feels tectonic when he begins visiting certain cacao plantations to procure the highest-quality ingredients. With every trip, the disparity between the poverty-stricken, oppressed cacao farmers and his clients becomes harder to ignore. Now his thoughts constantly return to those workers, and he wonders if there's a way for him to utilize his knowledge of chocolate to become an advocate for those in the industry who so desperately need one.

CHOOSING A CAREER FOR YOUR CHARACTER

At this point, we hope you can see the value a carefully chosen career can add to your story. Now it's a matter of figuring out which ones will work for your characters. A lot of components can factor into their choice or encourage you, as the author, to select one over another.

STORY APPLICATIONS

The more you know about your character, the easier it will be to figure out which job best suits her. But what if you don't really know her yet? For writers who like to hammer out the plot before choosing the story's cast, it's often easier to decide which careers might be necessary to the story, then tailor the character to fit.

For example, sometimes a story requires a certain kind of job. *Jurassic Park* needed a paleontologist as one of the protagonists. Likewise, Ian Fleming's series is about a spy; there really is no other option for the James Bond character. So if you know straight out of the gate that certain professions are necessary to further your plot line, plan your characters around them.

If theme plays a large part in your premise, you may want to start there rather than with characterization. In *Parasite*, a movie that explores social status and inequity, the Kim family seeks to pull themselves out of poverty primarily by securing jobs that give them access to wealth. Those positions play a crucial part in the writers being able to convey their message to viewers. If you know the theme your story will explore, ask yourself which careers might tie into it or provide opportunities for scene-level symbolism.

MOTIVATION

We've discussed how motivation plays into career choice. When it's time to figure out your character's job, put that information into practice. What's motivating her? Is there a void in her life in one of the five critical areas? Did this unmet need come about as a result of an emotional wound? How can that lack spur her to pursue (or avoid) a certain job? If there is no void in any area, could she be chasing a vocation in an attempt to shore up a need that's important to her or a little shaky?

Jobs don't only demand a commitment of time and energy, they also require a piece of the self, so part of a character's *why* will be tied to identity—who she is at her core and possibly who she wishes to become.

Consider the deepest parts of your character and how personal fulfillment might have led to her career. The work she does may be a means to an end, giving her income so she can self-actualize in other ways, provide for a family, or make her feel as if she has a place in the world. It could also help more directly with fulfillment by fostering her love of knowledge, allowing her to improve the lives of others, or providing an avenue for her to be true to her beliefs and values.

PERSONALITY TRAITS, SKILLS, AND INTERESTS

Personality figures largely into career decisions, so you'll want to know some of the basics for your character before choosing an occupation for her. What positive attributes does she possess? Which flaws will create roadblocks and much-needed conflict? Does she have specific talents, skills, or interests? All these personality aspects will figure into her choice of work, so be sure to take them into account.

OPPORTUNITIES

While personal motivation plays a huge part in determining someone's career, many jobs are taken simply because of their convenience. It's important to know if this is the case for your character because situations like these often lead to dissatisfaction, apathy, or resentment. Consider the following factors to determine if they might influence your character's choice:

Proximity: It's close to home, the kids' school, or another important location, such as the bus stop (if the character lacks reliable transportation of his own).

Family Pressure: The job will please the character's loved ones or allow her to carry on a family business or legacy.

Exposure: Her parents were involved in a certain industry (as actors, models, business tycoons, etc.), and the character is comfortable with and knowledgeable about that field.

Nepotism: The character is related to an influential player at the firm who can get her a job. Maybe it's not really what she wants to do, but if it's an enviable position that no one in their right mind would pass up, how could she say no?

Obstacles: What roadblocks stand in your character's way that steer her toward (or away from) a certain job? Cultural bias, lack of education, a criminal record, physical or mental challenges, homelessness, personal duties or responsibilities that interfere with work, being in the witness protection program—there are so many possibilities that could limit your character's career options.

Any combination of these factors might help you figure out which careers will work best for your story and your characters. So, in the planning stage, explore these areas. When you've gathered enough information, consult our table of contents to see which jobs might meet your needs. The good news is that when it comes to occupations, there is no right or wrong choice. Any number of jobs might accomplish your purposes. Start with one and see how it goes. If it doesn't pan out, it's much easier for a character to change jobs than it is for you or me.

CREATE AN OCCUPATION SHOWDOWN

If you are struggling to pick a job, try thinking in terms of opposites by building two lists. The first one should contain perfect potential careers for the character because they are fulfilling and play to her strengths, interests, and personality. Choose options that allow for a good work-life balance (if that's important to her) or are reward-driven, if that is a motivator for achievement.

The second list should comprise jobs that are the opposite—ones the character would not want to do or feels she is not suited for. What occupations are a miss in terms of personality, ethics, interests, or skills? What type of work would be a nightmare as far as her personal life goes—placing demands on family, blocking other meaningful goals, and ultimately leading to unhappiness?

Now, look carefully at these lists. Think about the character's arc, the complications you want her to face, thematic elements you'll be exploring, and the overall goal. Which occupations align best with your story, either helping your character reach her goal or standing in the way of it? If your character starts out in a career that is a terrible fit due to an unmet need or an emotional wound, her growing dissatisfaction will eventually push her to pursue the job she really wants. What will that be?

Any of these components might point you toward possible occupations for a character, but if you can find a job associated with multiple factors, it will make even more sense. Appendix B contains a Career Assessment that can help you put all the pieces together.

ADDITIONAL TIPS FOR WRITING ABOUT OCCUPATIONS

Once you've decided on the best career for your character, it's time to incorporate that information into your story. In the past, you may have skimmed over the details of her work. If so, it's time to make a change. Building a layered, credible, and interesting character is important, so we don't want to undo it all by glossing over this big piece of her life.

As with any aspect of characterization, there are a few gaffes to avoid as well as enhancements to consider to get the most mileage out of a character's career.

SKIPPING THE BORING STUFF

We would be remiss if we didn't include a section on the importance of showing—not telling—as much as possible about a character's occupation. (And would a Writers Helping Writers thesaurus be complete without it?) As a technique, *showing* should be a staple for every writer because it invites the reader to participate in the character's story rather than sitting back and being told about it. It also encourages us, as authors, to zero in on the details that matter, keeping the writing meaningful and concise.

Consider the following example.

> Jeanette hates her summer student job as a concierge, but it's a means to an end, giving her access to the hotel owner, who she believes to be her father. Matching guests with great restaurants, shows, and experiences might be fun if it weren't for her micromanaging supervisor's constant criticism. Once Jeanette gets the information she needs, she plans to leave.

This example tells readers what Jeanette's job is and how she feels about it, but that's about it. They're getting an incomplete picture of Jeanette, and the bland details don't do justice to an interesting hook: a girl trying to locate her biological father. But if we *show* her at work instead of simply explaining the situation, we can do more:

> Remy Lorado's voice boomed across the deserted lobby as he and the general manager returned from lunch. As it always did when her maybe-father was nearby, Jeanette's heart made like a greyhound released from the starting gate. She adjusted the stack of perfectly placed flyers and wiped nonexistent dust from the concierge desk, using the cover of movement to study him. His hair was the

same midnight black as her own…or was that just the oil he used? His lashes were short and thick, but she supposed that was a common enough feature. Scrubbing at a stubborn speck of nothing, she mentally urged the manager to say something funny; she thought she'd spotted a dimple when Remy had grinned earlier, but it had happened so fast—

"How's it going over here?"

Jeanette jerked upright and flashed a smile. Wonderful, another check-in from the Little Dictator. Why couldn't she take longer lunch breaks?

"Great, Mrs. Fisher. Just great."

Her supervisor's head barely cleared the counter, but her narrowed gaze swept over the whole station. Jeanette touched her scarf, making sure it was centered. She'd already been lectured once about the dress code, and if it happened in front of Remy, she would die.

"Ready for the dinner rush?" Mrs. Fisher went on. "Even in downtime, there are things you can be doing. With the weekend coming, guests will be looking for entertainment venues. Have you familiarized yourself with opening and closing times? Pricing? Family discounts?"

"Yes, ma'am. All taken care of." *Please, God, don't let there be a quiz.*

Madame Dictator rattled off more items. Jeanette half-listened, tracking Remy as he headed for the elevator. It had to be him. She'd seen him rolling his neck just like she did when she was sick of studying for mid-terms, and his laugh was a lower-pitched echo of her own. But before she announced herself, she had to know for sure. The DNA kit had been weighing down her purse for weeks, but how, exactly, did one go about getting a swab from a prospective parent? And what if she was wrong? Her poor mother had been near-delirious at the end. What if she'd said the wrong name—

"Did you hear me?" Mrs. Fisher's voice jumped an octave.

"Yes, of course." Jeanette scrambled for the details. "Felipe's. They've, uh, expanded their vegetarian options."

Mrs. Fisher gave a crisp nod. "The stir fry was acceptable. Add it to your mid-range list of restaurants."

Jeanette pulled out her notebook to make a notation, then fumbled it. Remy was helping himself to some citrus water from the complimentary lobby cooler. He drained it and dropped the plastic cup into the trash.

"Thanks, Mrs. Fisher." Jeanette paused as if just remembering something. "By the way, your phone's been ringing. The office door was locked, so I couldn't answer, but I know you've been waiting to hear from Cirque du Soleil. Maybe they left a message?"

As soon as her supervisor was gone, Jeanette made for the trash bin. She needed that cup.

This sample gives readers much more information about Jeanette and her job. Without stating anything outright, we've revealed to readers the following details:

What Jeanette does for a living

Some of her work responsibilities and duties

What she thinks about her job

Aspects of characterization (she's college-aged, has lost her mother, and she's both driven and an out-of-the-box thinker)

The reason she took the job—not out of passion or a way to use her gifts, but to gain access to the man who might be her father

Conflict and workplace dynamics (external strife with her boss and internal tensions as she yearns to answer the question that haunts her)

Her emotions, made clear through physical indicators and thoughts

A recent wounding event (the premature loss of her mother) that makes the unresolved wound of not having a father in her life that much more painful

Her story goal: to find her biological father

That's a lot of mileage to cover with just a few paragraphs, and the content is revealed to readers while the story is happening without the yawn-worthy feel of a lecture. Everything is shared as the character goes about her day, and without knowing it, the reader is taking the journey with her.

It should be noted that a vital part of showing involves choosing the right details. There are many parts of Jeanette's job that we could have shared, including her schedule, a deeper description of her environment, and other work-related duties. But that information wasn't necessary. By identifying what we want to accomplish in a scene, then choosing the details that will convey that information, we eliminate filler. Every word has purpose as we use the character's job to tell readers just what we want them to know, and no more.

DISMANTLE STEREOTYPES
Now, it should be noted that there's not always a lot of distance between truth and cliché. If a job caters to people with certain traits, it's easy for those pairings to become overdone in fiction. As authors, we need to know what works for a given occupation, but it's also up to us to save our characters from being clichéd, stereotypical, or downright offensive.

Whether the character is a headliner or a supporting cast member, we want to deliver fresh details rather than circle the basics. Therapists are compassionate and discerning; a yoga instructor is spiritual and physically fit. Without thoughtful layering, a character can easily look like everyone else in their field. And in fiction, being unremarkable is the kiss of death.

Make sure your character breaks the mold in some way. Try giving her an unusual trait that may not normally be associated with people in that career (but still makes sense for her).

Maybe your therapist is a control freak who thrives on diagnosing people and dictating their course of treatment. Or your yoga instructor is spiritually-minded but tends toward pessimism instead of optimism, making him the Eeyore of Chakra. If this surprising trait also happens to be the one holding your character back (at work, in life, or both), it can feed right into her character arc journey and provide conflict and friction along the way.

Another option is to incorporate a hobby, talent, or quirk that is unexpected for someone in this profession. Remember, though, that characterization isn't like vegetable soup; you can't just throw a bunch of stuff together and end up with a great result. Every element should contribute to the ideal characterization whole, so make sure each detail makes sense for the character and the story.

When you're thinking of careers for your character and how to set her apart from the pack, it's a good idea to also challenge any existing gender assumptions. Certain jobs may have been traditionally dominated by a specific gender, but you don't have to play into that stereotype. Your female character might be a receptionist or flight attendant, but she also could be a skydiving instructor, corrections officer, or bounty hunter.

If your character has more of a walk-on role, you won't need to plan her career as thoroughly. In this case, a job that challenges gender stereotypes might make her stand out. You could also choose an unorthodox profession that offers more interesting conflict opportunities than one tied to common occupations.

BE SPECIFIC
The difference between intriguing and *blah* characters is almost always in the details. If their career choices feel a little generic, be more specific. Instead of making one a teacher, zoom in on an exact type of instruction—working with special needs students or teaching computers to middle schoolers, for instance. You could also place her in an unusual location, such as teaching a second language in a foreign country or working in a juvenile detention center or private boarding school. Whatever your character's job, there are plenty of small details that will help you characterize her and give her work a fresh angle or twist.

HOW DOES YOUR CHARACTER SEE HIM OR HERSELF?
If you pare jobs down, you really end up with two kinds: **fixed** and **open-ended**. Fixed careers follow a set route, like a nurse who enters school, gets her degree, and moves into a nursing career. This involves patient care, certain responsibilities, and advancement gained through seniority and specialization. Other examples of fixed careers might include a construction worker, a bus driver, a lawyer, or an electrician. These jobs are relatively steady and stable, ones where knowledge, skill, and work ethic allow the person to eke out a sustainable living (provided the outside world continues to tick along as it always has). These job paths are mapped out, and all a person has to do is follow the route.

Open-ended careers are unpredictable and riskier, because what they look like and the character's level of success will depend on many factors, the most important being the character herself. Think about a freelance copywriter, a small business owner, a painter, a winemaker, or a promoter. Success or failure will depend on how hard the character works, how talented she is, if there's a market for her product or service, how much competition there is, and other considerations.

Some people feel comfortable in predictable jobs where they start at the trailhead and follow the path to its conclusion. Others prefer to choose (or create) an occupation that will allow them to innovate and are free to focus on a niche area of interest.

When it comes to choosing a type of work, ask yourself if your character is more of a traditional rule-follower who appreciates predictability and stability. If so, choose a profession with a fixed path. If, instead, your character has a pioneer's spirit, abhors being placed in a box, struggles with repetition, and chafes at the status quo, an open-ended career might suit her best.

FINAL WORDS FROM THE AUTHORS

One of the most difficult parts of writing this book was knowing that we couldn't create a comprehensive list of occupations; there are just too many. So we had to decide which ones would make the cut. We aimed for a mixture of popular jobs and unusual careers in hopes of providing a wide range of brainstorming opportunities.

To help you find what you're looking for, we've included a few different search engines: our Table of Contents, which contains a simple alphabetized list, and Appendix A, where the same jobs are sorted by foundational personality traits. If your desired job isn't included, look for careers in that field or explore ones with similar responsibilities, risk, or theme to get you started. And keep in mind that the Occupation Thesaurus at One Stop for Writers (www.onestopforwriters.com) isn't limited by page count, so you will find more of our entries there.

We've also included a blank template at the end of the thesaurus section of this book in case you'd like to explore a specific career yourself. For your convenience, this can be downloaded from the Tools for Writers page at www.writershelpingwriters.net.

Should you like to check out a set of truncated occupation entries, peruse this unofficial collection of jobs (https://writershelpingwriters.net/contributed-occupations/) compiled from fans of the Writers Helping Writers site. (Note: we haven't verified these contributions, but they contain insight into a plethora of jobs that may inspire your choices.)

When using the thesaurus, keep in mind that the training, duties, and terminology for a given job will vary widely between countries or even within a state or municipality. For this reason, we've often stuck to general information about training and education. If your story takes place in a specific area and these elements will be a factor, we encourage you to do the necessary additional research.

You'll also see that we've included many conflict scenarios for each occupation. Because friction is such a powerful generator of conflict both at the scene and story level, we've included an array of realistic and creative options for each entry.

The information in this thesaurus was gathered from different sources, and many of the entries were vetted by people with experience in that field. If you need further information on a career choice (either one in this collection or a job you'd like to explore), reach out to friends, family members, and acquaintances who have worked in that field. By and large, people enjoy talking about what they know, so it's likely they'll be willing to answer your questions.

Our hope is that this book will help you become the ultimate casting director for your story. Add interest by exploring a previously unconsidered field of work that fits your character perfectly. Think carefully about which careers will propel your characters forward or spin them into much-needed turmoil as they try to achieve their goals. Reflect on which occupations can reinforce the overall theme. Most of all, don't let your character's job be just a conversation starter. Use it to tie multiple elements together, taking your story to the next level.

THE
OCCUPATION
THESAURUS:

ACTOR

OVERVIEW
This is one of the few professions that is so familiar it needs little defining. Actors play the roles of various characters and strive to entertain, inform, challenge, or emotionally move audiences. They can work in television, movies, or the theater.

NECESSARY TRAINING
While there is no formal education required for this career, the business is cutthroat and over-saturated, meaning it's a good idea to gain any advantage. To this end, budding actors may take classes or attend drama schools to attain necessary skills.

While talent is needed, who you know is also extraordinarily important, so networking (and trying to catch the eye of an agent) are part of the job. Actors usually need to cut their teeth on entry-level jobs like acting in commercials, doing voiceovers, or working as extras.

In addition to on-screen time, actors must rehearse lines, research characters, practice their skills, and even exercise to maintain the physique often necessary for success in this field. Multiple talents can help an actor stand above the rest, so they may also work to become skilled in singing, dancing, and writing scripts.

USEFUL SKILLS, TALENTS, OR ABILITIES
Charm, creativity, good listening skills, making people laugh, multitasking, performing, photographic memory, promotion, public speaking, research, writing

HELPFUL CHARACTER TRAITS
Adaptable, adventurous, ambitious, bold, charming, confident, cooperative, creative, curious, enthusiastic, extroverted, flamboyant, focused, friendly, funny, materialistic, melodramatic, obsessive, passionate, patient, perfectionist, persistent, persuasive, quirky, responsible, sensual, spontaneous, spunky, studious, supportive, talented, uninhibited, witty

SOURCES OF FRICTION
Working with pretentious or self-involved co-workers
Too many actors competing for too few roles or losing a role to a rival
Blowing an important casting call
Creative differences among co-workers
Working with a difficult or unrealistic director
Being typecast
Sexual (and other kinds of) harassment
Not winning an award the character thought they deserved
Poor contracts or getting fleeced by an agent
Pressures of the limelight leading to dysfunction (addiction, infidelity, etc.)
Getting romantically involved with another cast member
Being blackballed by influencers
Being asked to do something in a role that goes against the character's moral code
Having no privacy, clashing with paparazzi, or being stalked

Being slandered in the media due to personal beliefs
Skeletons in the closet coming to light and threatening the character's career
Challenging work schedules causing problems at home
Having to choose between pursuing a career or having a family
Fame driving a wedge between the character and long-term friends

PEOPLE THEY MIGHT INTERACT WITH

Other actors, directors, producers, agents, makeup artists, stylists, a personal assistant, a personal trainer, members of the crew (camera operators, writers, set designers, etc.)

HOW THIS OCCUPATION MIGHT IMPACT THE CHARACTER'S NEEDS

Self-Actualization: Actors who get pigeonholed into certain roles or kinds of projects may begin to feel stifled, believing that they're unable to reach their full potential.

Esteem and Recognition: If an actor's career doesn't gain traction, he can begin to doubt himself or his abilities.

Love and Belonging: Actors work difficult hours and spend a lot of time traveling, which can cause doubt and jealousy to fester. Successful actors may have reason to doubt the sincerity or intentions of anyone who expresses romantic interest.

Safety and Security: Many factors of this career can contribute to addiction and substance abuse, putting the actor's physical and mental well-being at risk.

Physiological Needs: Actors may attract stalkers who are unhinged and violent.

TWISTING THE FICTIONAL STEREOTYPE

With so many stories featuring actors, it's not surprising that numerous stereotypes have emerged: the vapid bombshell who's only good for sex appeal, the absent-minded method actor, the washed-up character so desperate to stay in the business that they'll take any role.

To avoid clichés like these, make sure your character is well-rounded and unique. What are their positive attributes and negative flaws? Where do they draw their moral lines? What motivation is driving them in this profession? Make sure there's something different about them that will set your actor apart from overdone portrayals.

CHARACTERS MIGHT CHOOSE THIS PROFESSION BECAUSE THEY...

Grew up in a star-studded, famous family
Long to become someone else and escape feelings of low self-worth brought on by an abusive upbringing
Have a dramatic or flamboyant personality
Hope that fame will lead to parental approval
Are enamored with Hollywood glamour and celebrities and want to emulate them

AIR TRAFFIC CONTROLLER

OVERVIEW

Air traffic controllers oversee and maintain the safety of those traveling in the air and on runways. They provide instructions to pilots for taking off and landing their planes, as well as monitoring and changing the flight patterns for aircraft. Once a plane is out of range, controllers relinquish responsibility to other air traffic centers. They also may be responsible for training, managing, and providing stress defusing for team members. Constant focus and quick decision-making are necessary during shifts, making this job a stressful one.

NECESSARY TRAINING

Many branches of the military offer training programs for this career. For civilians, at minimum, an associate degree in air traffic control is needed, as is certification by the Federal Aviation Administration. To obtain the latter, one must pass a written and practical exam and accumulate the appropriate amount of experience. Reference letters and recommendations can help characters enter additional training programs, most of which are specific to the unit or sector of application.

Acceptance into an air traffic control position is rare for anyone over the age of thirty, especially if the applicant is new to the field. Anyone with a criminal history will likely be turned down.

USEFUL SKILLS, TALENTS, OR ABILITIES

Detail-oriented, equanimity, good with numbers, multilingualism, multitasking, predicting the weather, research, strategic thinking

HELPFUL CHARACTER TRAITS

Alert, analytical, calm, cautious, disciplined, focused, intelligent, meticulous, obedient, observant, organized, patriotic, proactive, professional, responsible

SOURCES OF FRICTION

Bad weather that hinders visibility and communication
Pilots who don't heed instructions or advisories
Co-workers with clashing personalities, opinions, or approaches to giving commands
Pilots and other air traffic control personnel with accents that are difficult to understand
Lack of communication between units
Large amounts of air traffic to monitor
Inconsistent shifts and long hours requiring high alertness that leads to fatigue
Spotty radar coverage that could compromise communication
Staffing shortages
Unexpected events that require split-second decisions
Juggling multiple tasks at the same time
High stakes attached to every decision (mistakes come with grave consequences)
Stressed personal relationships due to demanding hours
Close relationships with co-workers that may cause jealousy with family members

Unexpected shift changes that interfere with family plans
Medical issues that could hinder job performance
Sudden illness that impacts focus (coming down with a cold, an upset stomach, etc.)
Stressful personal situations that seep into a character's mindset, making compartmentalization at work hard

PEOPLE THEY MIGHT INTERACT WITH
Pilots, other air traffic controllers, airport personnel on the ground, military personnel and federal employees, onsite security officers

HOW THIS OCCUPATION MIGHT IMPACT THE CHARACTER'S NEEDS
Esteem and Recognition: Confidence is crucial for a character who holds the lives of others in their hands. Making even a minor mistake that could have led to tragedy can allow doubt to fester, leading to more errors or a crisis of faith.

Love and Belonging: Due to the extensive hours required and the close connections formed outside of their immediate family, characters in this field could find their personal relationships strained.

Safety and Security: Especially when staffing shortages occur and extra shifts are required, basic needs such as sleep might not be met. Chronic fatigue and extreme exhaustion are common and can affect decision-making and response time, putting others in danger.

TWISTING THE FICTIONAL STEREOTYPE
Especially when it comes to action plots, a common portrayal of air traffic controllers is that they are somewhat robotic and militant due to their high-stress job. Make sure to show other sides of your character to help personalize them to the reader. Providing moments of levity through humor, sharing snippets of personal information during a workplace conversation, or showing the character struggling with job-related stress can provide interesting and realistic layers.

CHARACTERS MIGHT CHOOSE THIS PROFESSION BECAUSE THEY...
Were pressured by a family member, friend, or mentor to pursue it
Were unable to become a pilot and air traffic control was their fallback plan
Lost a loved one in a plane crash
Love aircraft and want to pursue a career in aviation
Are good at multitasking and want to seek a challenging career
Are able to avoid a problematic relationship by working long hours
Thrive under pressure
Have a desire to keep others safe and prevent fatalities
Require access to planes and other aviation equipment
Desire power or authority
Get off on being in control of the lives of others

ANIMAL RESCUE WORKER

OVERVIEW

Many different jobs fall under the umbrella of animal rescue work: owners and managers of shelters, veterinarians and technicians, trainers, deployment workers, animal control officers, and even wildlife rehabilitation workers, just to name a few. This entry will focus on rescue deployment workers, who are called out to assess, and if needed, rescue domestic animals in distress. The animals may be at risk due to hoarding situations, abandonment, dog-fighting rings, puppy mills, factory farms, or displacement of animals in the aftermath of a disaster.

Rescue workers may also help with fundraising and public awareness, shooting video to document rescue work, engaging with the public on social media, and interacting with locals to share information.

NECESSARY TRAINING

To join a rescue group, often a person only requires a high school diploma. The organization will then provide any necessary assessment training, such as determining the condition and age of an animal, possible risk factors, if abuse has occurred, and identifying injuries or diseases. They'll also be taught about the safe handling of animals, different risk scenarios, basic care, and rehabilitation. If a person wishes to move up the chain, either in animal-focused work or management, they likely will need to obtain a related associate's degree. Some rescue workers may have a psychology background or schooling in the art of handling people to help them de-escalate situations with owners.

To rescue and re-home pets in disaster situations, workers would receive additional training to set up a base of operations, adhere to safety protocols, gather and manage volunteers, work in tandem with other aid-based groups, collect supplies, provide animals with medical care, and reunite pets with owners in the aftermath.

USEFUL SKILLS, TALENTS, OR ABILITIES

A knack for making money, a way with animals, basic first aid, exceptional memory, gaining the trust of others, multilingualism, multitasking, photographic memory, promotion, swift-footedness, wilderness navigation

HELPFUL CHARACTER TRAITS

Adaptable, adventurous, affectionate, alert, calm, cautious, cooperative, courageous, disciplined, fanatical, kind, merciful, nature-focused, nurturing, organized, passionate, persistent, persuasive, protective, pushy, socially aware

SOURCES OF FRICTION

Owners who do not want to give up their animals
Knowing abuse is occurring but not being able to prove it
Having to put a rescued animal down due to severe injury or illness
Discovering acts of cruelty but being unable to find the person responsible
Dealing with repeat offenders in hoarding or cruelty cases
Always struggling with funding issues

Having too many animals to rescue and not enough shelter space
Suffering from compassion fatigue
Struggling with depression or thoughts of suicide
Being bitten by an abused or ill animal
Hoarders who hide or temporarily move their animals so they can't be taken
Being tempted to personally take in more animals than the worker can afford
Working so many criminal cases that the character becomes suspicious, seeing abuse where there is none
Working long days where the character is mostly on their feet
Being peed on by a frightened animal
Volunteers who want to play with the animals instead of completing necessary duties

PEOPLE THEY MIGHT INTERACT WITH

Animal rescue workers, pet owners, ranchers and farmers, police officers, people from other aid organizations, veterinarians, animal health technicians, vet clinic staff members, shelter workers, dog groomers, rehabilitation specialists, animal foster families, animal rights advocacy groups

HOW THIS OCCUPATION MIGHT IMPACT THE CHARACTER'S NEEDS

Self-Actualization: A character in this occupation could suffer a crisis of faith in humanity at seeing the cruelty people are capable of.

Esteem and Recognition: A rescue worker who is unable to save animals in time may internalize their pain and feel like a failure, questioning their own self-worth and abilities.

Love and Belonging: Frequent travel and long hours may not leave much time for other people, especially if the rescue worker is also caring personally for animals.

Safety and Security: Certain calls may pose a danger to rescue workers, both from people—violent owners or criminals using animals for profit—and the animals themselves, which may have rabies or be violent due to mistreatment.

CHARACTERS MIGHT CHOOSE THIS PROFESSION BECAUSE THEY...

Were raised in a neglectful or abusive home and are choosing a nurturing path for the future
Want to advocate for those who cannot fight for themselves
Love animals
Are compensating for a past wrong—say, growing up in a family that hoarded pets
Believe animals are safer than people (a belief stemming from exposure to violence that created mistrust and fear of others)
Want to make up for a perceived past failure, such as being unable to help someone and feeling responsible for what happened to them
Have a deep-seated moral belief that all life is sacred and must be protected

ANIMAL TRAINER

OVERVIEW
Animal trainers teach animals for a variety of purposes—to make them better pets, prepare them for work in the entertainment field, or develop them into service or work animals. They may choose to specialize in dogs, horses, marine species, or exotic animals, to name just a few.

Work settings will vary depending on what kind of animal is involved. Marine trainers will likely be employed by a zoo or aquarium, horse trainers are most often found at a farm, stable, or personal residence, and dog trainers can work out of a vet's office, doggy day care, animal shelter, or come to a client's home. Trainers may also be employed long-term by a search and rescue organization, police force, or other business. People pursuing this profession can be freelance or employed by an animal organization, such as a zoo or shelter.

NECESSARY TRAINING
While marine animal trainers often need a degree in an animal-related field (such as marine biology, veterinary studies, or animal studies), other animal training jobs typically only require a high school diploma—though further certifications and a certain amount of on-the-job experience will be necessary.

USEFUL SKILLS, TALENTS, OR ABILITIES
A way with animals, basic first aid, empathy, gaining the trust of others, leadership, mentalism, out-of-the-box thinking

HELPFUL CHARACTER TRAITS
Affectionate, alert, calm, centered, disciplined, empathetic, enthusiastic, gentle, kind, loyal, nurturing, observant, passionate, patient, persistent, persuasive, playful, resourceful, socially aware, trusting

SOURCES OF FRICTION
Being injured by an animal
Working with an animal that is difficult to train (due to low intelligence, stubbornness, a neurotic disposition, etc.)
The heartbreak of dealing with neglected or abused animals
Suspecting an owner of abuse
Owners with unrealistic expectations for their animals
The owner's inconsistency or poor practices undoing all of the trainer's hard work
Working with an aggressive or dominant animal
Realizing that an animal is untrainable and having to break the news to the owner
Vouching for an animal and having it attack or injure someone
The untimely death of an animal
Moral struggles regarding animals trained for entertainment
The character suffering from an injury or chronic illness that makes the job difficult
Social difficulties that make it hard to communicate with clients
A trained animal being injured or killed from a behavior it shouldn't have exhibited, such as

running into traffic despite being taught not to leave the yard without permission

Being asked by friends to train their pets for free

Being asked to train an animal that is not suitable to a specific venue and cannot be cared for properly (an elephant housed in tiny living space at a zoo or circus, for example)

Developing an allergy to the animals one trains

Forming a strong bond with an animal and having to relinquish it to the owner after training

PEOPLE THEY MIGHT INTERACT WITH

Animal owners, veterinarians, shelter workers, other employees (if the trainer works at a facility), other trainers, those working with the animals (police officers, rescue workers, patients in a hospital, etc.)

HOW THIS OCCUPATION MIGHT IMPACT THE CHARACTER'S NEEDS

Self-Actualization: A character may discover poor living conditions and unethical treatment when onsite to train certain animals for entertainment purposes. This could challenge their morals and change their view of the work they do.

Esteem and Recognition: This occupation doesn't pay a whole lot, so the character may feel inadequate if other people look down on them for their humble financial status.

Love and Belonging: Animal trainers are animal lovers. If they pair up with someone who hates animals, this could spell trouble for the relationship.

Safety and Security: There are ample ways a trainer could be injured or infected on the job, putting their safety at risk.

Physiological Needs: It's rare that trainers are killed, but it does happen, so this is a possibility.

TWISTING THE FICTIONAL STEREOTYPE

Animal trainers are usually nurturing-but-disciplined types—gentle, but firm. Consider throwing some unusual character traits into the mix to set yours apart: quirky, whimsical, disorganized, antisocial, etc.

There's also a common representation of animal trainers as socially awkward people who relate better to animals than humans. If this is the case for your character, make sure you have a reason for this, and consider an option that may be unusual or surprising for readers.

CHARACTERS MIGHT CHOOSE THIS PROFESSION BECAUSE THEY...

Grew up around animals and want to work with them

Are unable to have children, and animals provide a substitute

Believe that people can't always be trusted, but animals can

Suffer from a physical, mental, or social deficit that makes working with people hard

Have a natural love for animals

Want to fill a love and belonging deficit caused by their inability to make meaningful connections with people

Love someone with a disability and want to serve that person and their community by training animals to help them

Have a special ability to connect and communicate with animals

ANTIQUES DEALER

OVERVIEW

In a nutshell, antiques dealers purchase old items and re-sell them. This requires extensive knowledge in the field, including the ability to tell true antiques from fakes, knowing how much certain items are worth, and being able to sell them. People in this profession may own a shop or work with other dealers. They may work with general antiques or be specialized with particular items (art, furniture, coins, jewelry), a specific time period or setting (Egyptian antiques, Victorian-era items, Hollywood nostalgia), or certain hobbies and interests (car racing, stamp collecting, oddities, etc.).

NECESSARY TRAINING

Most up-and-comers in this field start out in an apprentice-like position, such as being an assistant to a successful dealer or an intern in an auction house. Higher education isn't required, though some courses (such as art appreciation, history, and business basics) can supplement their knowledge and skills.

USEFUL SKILLS, TALENTS, OR ABILITIES

A knack for making money, charm, exceptional memory, gaining the trust of others, haggling, multilingualism, promotion, reading people, research, sales, strategic thinking

HELPFUL CHARACTER TRAITS

Ambitious, charming, confident, cooperative, courageous, courteous, curious, decisive, devious, diplomatic, disciplined, enthusiastic, extroverted, friendly, greedy, industrious, intelligent, passionate, patient, persistent, persuasive, professional, responsible, studious

SOURCES OF FRICTION

Dishonest sellers who try to pass off fakes as authentic antiques
Ambitious competitors stealing customers and horning in on the dealer's business
The dealer doubting their knowledge in certain areas
Having to trust an "expert" associate to evaluate an item but being unsure of their abilities
Lack of funds to buy the items needed to build up inventory
Purchasing an expensive item but being unable to find a buyer for it
A catastrophe in the shop (a fire, a burst pipe, vermin, or mold, etc.) that ruins inventory
Inept or untrained associates overpaying for items
Selling an item that turns out to be a fake
Being unable to properly restore a purchased item
Becoming attached to a piece or collection and being unable to part with it
Wanting to sell an item but not agreeing with how it will be used (if it will be altered, ruined, etc.)

PEOPLE THEY MIGHT INTERACT WITH

Other dealers, customers, auctioneers, experts in various fields (historians, archaeologists, etc.), museum docents and owners, sales associates, people associated with the character's store (a landlord, janitors, delivery people, the owner, etc.)

HOW THIS OCCUPATION MIGHT IMPACT THE CHARACTER'S NEEDS

Self-Actualization: Those dealing with antiques are likely enthusiastic about what they do; their job is also their passion. Self-actualization can be undermined when that passion is threatened—say, when an unethical shop owner encourages the dealer to undervalue merchandise or knowingly sell fakes.

Esteem and Recognition: In this career, a person's knowledge of their subject area can mean the difference between success or failure. When a dealer knows they lack expertise in an area, or when respected members in the field distrust the character's abilities, this need can become impacted.

Safety and Security: Antiques are expensive, and, therefore, valuable. A dealer may be vulnerable to theft or attack as a result.

TWISTING THE FICTIONAL STEREOTYPE

Because antiques are expensive, dealers are usually portrayed as sophisticated, fashionable, and suave. What about one who is on the scruffy side but has a keen eye and so does well in the business?

Items such as rugs, furniture, and Civil War memorabilia are common specialties for antique aficionados. But what about a dealer who collects something unusual, like ancient torture devices, artifacts associated with serial killers, or old items known to be haunted?

It might also be interesting to have a dealer who acquires his knowledge of antiques through an unusual method. Think Connor MacLeod from *Highlander*, whose collection consists of the items he's gathered from his many years living as an immortal.

CHARACTERS MIGHT CHOOSE THIS PROFESSION BECAUSE THEY...

Were raised by a relative who frequented garage sales, flea markets, and antiques stores and taught the character how to identify valuable artifacts

Have a love of history

Want to be a protector of beauty in all forms

Are an avid collector of something and want to turn that passion into a career

Are seeking access to something taboo or difficult to acquire (Nazi-era propaganda posters, contraband items, stolen collections, etc.)

Need to subdue a hoarding tendency; being a dealer allows them to collect items but then sell them to others

Have a fascination with the past and want to live in a simpler time

Enjoy the treasure-hunting aspect of finding rare items

Have a keen eye for antiques and are adept at spotting forgeries

ARCHITECT

OVERVIEW
An architect is responsible for designing physical structures, such as homes, office buildings, shopping centers, religious buildings, factories, and bridges. They create plans not only for function and safety but with an eye for design, as well.

NECESSARY TRAINING
A college degree in architecture is required to pursue this career. You must also acquire a license to practice from the local state or municipality, which is granted upon completion of an internship and an examination. This is the training necessary in the US, but requirements differ from place to place, so research this aspect of the job carefully.

USEFUL SKILLS, TALENTS, OR ABILITIES
Creativity, good with numbers, multitasking, out-of-the-box thinking, strategic thinking, vision

HELPFUL CHARACTER TRAITS
Ambitious, analytical, confident, cooperative, creative, diplomatic, disciplined, focused, honorable, meticulous, obsessive, organized, passionate, patient, perfectionist, persuasive, professional, responsible, studious, talented

SOURCES OF FRICTION
Indecisive clients who keep changing their minds
Having to jump through bureaucratic hoops to obtain licenses and permits
Nitpicky inspectors
A worker being hurt or killed on the job
A finished structure being faulty and injuring the inhabitants
Being given an assignment that conflicts with the character's moral beliefs (building a strip club, drawing plans for a dog racing track, etc.)
Workers taking shortcuts that compromise the safety of the project
Being passed over for a promotion
Fighting for a specific project and losing to an inferior co-worker
A client whose design aesthetic or preferences are very different from the character's
Being unable to collect money from the client to cover expenses
Becoming romantically involved with an inspector, government official, or someone else who makes the job difficult when the relationship sours
A project going over budget or past its deadline
Incomplete information from a client resulting in a design that doesn't meet their needs
Working in a location where bribes are necessary to push a project through
A degenerative disease or disorder that becomes a challenge on the job (failing mental faculties, a knee or hip issue that makes climbing stairs or scaffolding difficult, etc.)
Having to keep up with technological advances in drafting
Losing a loyal client

A creativity drought (especially if they are known for designing highly creative structures)
An angel investor pulling out of the project at a critical time
Climate change, erosion, or other environmental factors that make a design complex

PEOPLE THEY MIGHT INTERACT WITH
Other architects, construction workers and contractors, clients, inspectors, licensing and permitting officials, interior designers, landscape designers

HOW THIS OCCUPATION MIGHT IMPACT THE CHARACTER'S NEEDS
Self-Actualization: Many architects enter the profession hoping to work in a certain field, but that doesn't always pan out, and they end up doing more generic work. In this case, the job supplies a paycheck instead of providing the satisfaction they once dreamed of.

Esteem and Recognition: An architect who is unable to distinguish himself (due to being given uninspiring projects, being surrounded by architects who are more talented or creative, or through personal doubt and insecurity) may yearn for the esteem of his colleagues and his community.

Safety and Security: Construction sites are high-risk places and rife for accidents if workers aren't paying close attention. An architect who experienced an injury on the job might find it difficult to return to the site and do his best work there.

TWISTING THE FICTIONAL STEREOTYPE
Historically, architects have been male; this stereotype is changing, so it's good to keep in mind and get the women involved in this career.

It's also common for architects to become associated with a certain kind of form or building. Why not get your character involved in an unusual project or aesthetic, like amusement parks, artistic structures, or medieval design?

CHARACTERS MIGHT CHOOSE THIS PROFESSION BECAUSE THEY...
Want to be remembered through buildings which will be around for generations
Love building and designing structures
Are strategic thinkers
Have artistic roots and wish to use buildings, bridges, or other structures as their canvas
Want to create permanent things to make up for a nomadic or homeless childhood
Are compensating for something important that has been torn down (the bonds of family, a marriage, a family business run into the ground, etc.)
Are gifted mathematically and have an eye for design
Love their city and want to enhance it through architecture

AUTO MECHANIC

OVERVIEW
Mechanics inspect, repair, and maintain vehicles. Some have a general knowledge of engines and parts while others specialize in an area, choosing to focus on a certain type of vehicle (cars and trucks, big rigs, boat engines, imports) or specific parts of the engine (air conditioners or transmissions). Mechanics can own their own garage, work at a dealership's service center, or be part of someone else's shop.

NECESSARY TRAINING
While some shops require their mechanics to receive post-secondary education and become certified through various programs, not all of them do. Completing these programs does, however, improve their chances of being hired and making better money. Educational opportunities can be found at trade schools and community colleges, specialized mechanic schools, and through the military. The apprenticeship or on-the-job training model is also very common in this career field.

It should also be noted that some shops require their mechanics to supply their own hand tools; because of the expense, this could be a barrier to employment for some.

USEFUL SKILLS, TALENTS, OR ABILITIES
Dexterity, hot-wiring a car, mechanically inclined, photographic memory, strategic thinking

HELPFUL CHARACTER TRAITS
Alert, analytical, curious, focused, honorable, independent, industrious, meticulous, observant, resourceful, responsible, studious

SOURCES OF FRICTION
Being unable to correctly identify the problem with a vehicle
Missing a problem that results in a breakdown
Inattentiveness or fatigue that leads to an injury
Breaking an important tool or piece of machinery
Having to use old or sub-standard machinery
Weather conditions, such as extreme heat or cold, that make the job difficult
Impatient or irate customers
Difficulty keeping up with changes in the industry
Falling behind in training or certification
Not making enough money to support a family or achieve desired goals
Being pigeon-holed into a certain area of work when the character really wants to be doing something else
Customers parking in front of garage bay doors, preventing vehicles from entering or leaving the service area
Constantly being asked by friends to diagnose their cars' problems for free
Being accused of dishonesty by customers who buy into the stereotype that mechanics are swindlers

Wanting to start a business but being unable to do so
Employing a mechanic who cuts corners and hurts the shop's reputation
Working with mechanics who don't take proper care of the shop's tools
Onsite theft (of tools, supplies, equipment)
Employees who don't follow safety regulations

PEOPLE THEY MIGHT INTERACT WITH

Car owners, other mechanics, the shop owner, vendors, inspectors

HOW THIS OCCUPATION MIGHT IMPACT THE CHARACTER'S NEEDS

Self-Actualization: A character might become dissatisfied with this career if it began as a temporary endeavor, say as a steppingstone to being able to work on race cars. If that end goal never materialized, they may feel stuck doing something they don't fully enjoy.

Esteem and Recognition: While everyone would agree that a mechanic's job is important, there are those who view blue-collar jobs in a negative light. A character experiencing this kind of prejudice could feel looked down on by others.

Love and Belonging: If the character is struggling financially, it could put a strain on his or her personal relationships.

Safety and Security: While industry standards require a minimum of safety requirements, working with people who are stingy or cut corners could create an unsafe environment where injuries are more likely to happen.

TWISTING THE FICTIONAL STEREOTYPE

As with so many other professions, this one is predominantly male. Throw in a female mechanic (think Mona Lisa Vito from *My Cousin Vinny*), and you've got an interesting twist.

The field is also a blue-collar one, so what about a mechanic from a white-collar family pursuing this career?

CHARACTERS MIGHT CHOOSE THIS PROFESSION BECAUSE THEY...

Grew up working on cars and have a passion for them
Love vehicles, engines, and making things work as they should
Are good with their hands and have a mind for mechanics
Like working independently and avoiding people
Enjoy the challenge of puzzles and finding solutions for them
Struggle socially (due to a disfigurement, speech impediment, cognitive challenge, etc.)
Believe themselves to be incapable of love (due to a past trauma) and use vehicle maintenance as a way to show caring and affection
Want to honor or feel connected to a deceased loved one who was passionate about cars and taught the character about maintenance

BABYSITTER

OVERVIEW
A babysitter will watch over children while their parents are away from home. Typically, they will entertain the kids during the day (playing games, watching movies, taking them to a local park), and prepare easy meals, read stories, and get the children ready for bed. Occasionally they may be asked to perform a few menial chores, such as washing the dinner dishes or straightening up a playroom once the kids are asleep. Babysitting is typically done by responsible teens or college-aged individuals wanting to supplement an allowance or make money while attending school.

NECESSARY TRAINING
This type of work can be done without any training or certification, although there are specific programs that can enhance a sitter's skill set. Many parents prefer babysitters that have completed certain courses (such as one in CPR or basic first aid) and are a specific age. Typically, parents will interview a potential sitter to get a feel for who they are, their experience, their attitude toward kids, and whether they have completed any courses or have first aid training. Once responsibilities and payment have been negotiated, the sitter can begin work.

USEFUL SKILLS, TALENTS, OR ABILITIES
Basic first aid, charm, creativity, empathy, enhanced hearing, enhanced sense of smell, equanimity, gaining the trust of others, haggling, intuition, making friends, making people laugh, peacekeeping, reading people, stamina, swift-footedness, throwing one's voice

HELPFUL CHARACTER TRAITS
Adaptable, adventurous, affectionate, alert, calm, charming, confident, controlling, creative, diplomatic, easygoing, flamboyant, friendly, imaginative, independent, know-it-all, mature, nurturing, obedient, observant, paranoid, persuasive, playful, responsible, spontaneous, spunky, tolerant, whimsical, wise

SOURCES OF FRICTION
Kids who don't respect the babysitter's rules or authority
Kids whose parents are lax with discipline and act spoiled, demanding, and entitled
Discovering something disturbing, such as signs of illegal activity or drug use in the home
Learning a family secret through something a child says
House guests who show up unannounced
Trying to reach a parent in an emergency but being unable to
One of the children growing violent
Kids sneaking out or trying to run away
Kids trying to do something dangerous such as playing with matches or a kitchen knife
Parents who don't come home when they say they will, disrupting the babysitter's schedule
Parents who underpay
Friends showing up without permission and expecting to hang out while the character is working

Parents who expect a list of chores to be completed before they return

Parents who have grounded the kids from certain activities (no TV, computer time, or outside play, etc.) that make the sitter's job more difficult

An emergency (an injury, a power outage, a lost child, a break-in, etc.)

Living in a neighborhood with few children (increased competition for jobs)

Losing a loyal and steady customer (due to them relocating, the kids growing up, etc.)

Poor time management that leads to overbooking or gigs that conflict with school projects, family obligations, etc.

Being accused of something the character didn't do (theft, child abuse, neglect, etc.)

PEOPLE THEY MIGHT INTERACT WITH

Parents, friends and older siblings of the kids, neighbors

HOW THIS OCCUPATION MIGHT IMPACT THE CHARACTER'S NEEDS

Esteem and Recognition: A low-income sitter working for a wealthy family may have unwanted feelings of inferiority or shame, especially if they're close in age to one of the children in the house.

Love and Belonging: Being around a tight, loving family may make it difficult for a sitter who lacks a nurturing home life, since it reminds them of what they do not have.

Safety and Security: A sitter may be in danger if the family they work for is targeted by criminals (due to being in a high crime neighborhood, the family being wealthy, etc.)

TWISTING THE FICTIONAL STEREOTYPE

While babysitters in fiction and film are often female, this job can provide income for anyone. Consider it for a male character who wants a little extra cash.

Babysitters in fiction and film are often two-faced, acting responsible with adults and then neglectful and rude to the children. Try to avoid this well-worn stereotype, if only because kids are likely to rat out a narcissistic teen they don't want as a sitter anyway.

CHARACTERS MIGHT CHOOSE THIS PROFESSION BECAUSE THEY...

Want to escape a difficult family situation, if only briefly

Want to be paid under the table and fly under the radar (if they're in the country illegally, are wanted by the law, etc.)

Like working with kids, possibly because they have no siblings themselves

Are saving for college, a car, or another big-ticket item

Need to stockpile money to escape their current situation

Want access to other people's homes (because they're a voyeur, to assess it for a future break-in, to steal small items that won't be noticed, etc.)

Need a flexible job that works around school or another part-time position

BAKER

OVERVIEW
Bakers typically work in a shop or factory setting and are responsible for preparing and decorating baked goods. They also oversee quality control of the products, help gather ingredients, and fulfill orders. In the course of a shift they mix batters and doughs to produce breads, buns, cookies, cakes, pies, and other goods the bakery specializes in. They also oversee the cooking and packaging of products, following health and safety protocols. Bakers also test new recipes and adjust existing ones to improve them. Depending on the setting, bakers could be creating items for individual customers or large orders for a wholesaler.

NECESSARY TRAINING
Though bakers often receive training through culinary school or an apprenticeship, in most cases, no formal education is required. Bakeries, restaurants, and factories usually have specialized training through that facility to teach the necessary skills for the position. However, any prior experience is beneficial, and basic knowledge of food safety is a must. It's common to start at an entry-level position before moving up into a specialty field. If the baker is also the owner, having experience in running a business, hiring and overseeing employees, managing inventory, and understanding marketing and sales are also necessary.

USEFUL SKILLS, TALENTS, OR ABILITIES
A knack for making money, baking, creativity, dexterity, enhanced sense of smell, enhanced taste buds, multitasking, sales

HELPFUL CHARACTER TRAITS
Adventurous, creative, curious, efficient, imaginative, independent, industrious, passionate, talented, uninhibited, whimsical, workaholic

SOURCES OF FRICTION
Having too many or too few customers
Running low on inventory
Equipment that is always breaking
Working with employees who do not take direction well
Staff members struggling to work as a team or who have personal conflicts with one another
Impatient customers
Struggling to build a company from the ground up
Being in a location that doesn't offer opportunities for growth
Having competitors in the area
Working in a hot and messy environment
Lacking the tools needed to complete production
Staffing shortages
Carpal tunnel syndrome, arthritis, or other health issues that could hinder job performance
Irregular work hours that often require night and early morning shifts
Working under strict deadlines

Standing for long hours with little rest
Being accused of stealing someone's recipes or designs
Being great at baking but no good at business
Food contamination that makes someone sick and brings health inspectors onsite

PEOPLE THEY MIGHT INTERACT WITH

Other bakers, senior chefs or pastry chefs, customers, apprentices, grocers and other suppliers, equipment manufacturers, members of the public health administration

HOW THIS OCCUPATION MIGHT IMPACT THE CHARACTER'S NEEDS

Self-Actualization: If a character wants to move up but doesn't have the dexterity, creativity, or other skills required to be an exceptional baker, they may need to say goodbye to a dream and adjust their career goals.

Esteem and Recognition: As in any creative arena, it's easy to compare oneself to others. Bakers who always find themselves lacking or who fail to bring their own ideas to fruition may suffer from feelings of inferiority and low esteem.

Safety and Security: Hot ovens, sharp knives, deep fryers, and other equipment can impact safety when they're not handled properly.

TWISTING THE FICTIONAL STEREOTYPE

A common misconception about bakers is that they're overweight. A character who maintains a healthy lifestyle or is physically fit could combat the stereotype.

Another way to give this occupation a fresh twist is to think carefully about the type of goods your baker produces. Instead of providing generic offerings, maybe they specialize in nontraditional treats, such as vegan desserts or baked goods in unusual flavors.

CHARACTERS MIGHT CHOOSE THIS PROFESSION BECAUSE THEY...

Had family members in the food industry
Needed a local job they could easily get to
Grew up watching famous chefs and want to live the same lifestyle
Had a parent, now deceased, who taught them to bake, and being in the kitchen makes the character feel connected to him or her
Enjoy the creativity and challenges that being a baker offers
Are artistic and good with their hands
Relieve anxiety and stress through baking
Have many fond childhood memories in the kitchen
Believe food brings people joy and sweets do most of all
Like the nontraditional hours
Want to own their own business and be part of the local community

BARISTA

OVERVIEW
A barista is someone who makes coffee and espresso drinks—and, in some countries, other beverages. In many commercial and chain shops, the job entails being able to work the necessary machinery and caring for customers. A barista in a specialty or independent shop may be more knowledgeable about the products, including knowing where the beans come from, how the plants are cultivated, and the tastes and strengths of the different roasts. They also may take more ownership of the processes, such as grinding the beans and making an extra effort with presentation.

Wherever a barista works, they'll need to interact with customers, keep items stocked, work the cash register, and maintain a clean environment for guests. Because this job is often seen as a stepping stone to other opportunities (rather than a permanent career), it can be a good choice for teenagers and people in transition.

NECESSARY TRAINING
No formal education is required; most training will be received on the job.

USEFUL SKILLS, TALENTS, OR ABILITIES
Charm, creativity, enhanced sense of smell, enhanced taste buds, good listening skills, hospitality, multitasking, promotion, sales

HELPFUL CHARACTER TRAITS
Adaptable, calm, charming, cooperative, courteous, efficient, enthusiastic, equanimity, funny, honest, hospitable, kind, observant, passionate, responsible, sensible

SOURCES OF FRICTION
Working with malfunctioning equipment
Running out of supplies
Employees calling in sick with little warning or not showing up at all
Working alongside dishonest, lazy, or uncooperative co-workers
Dealing with a micro-managing or absentee boss
Customers who are demanding, fussy, or difficult
Failing a health inspection
Serving a drink containing an allergen to a customer with food sensitivities
A customer slipping and falling
Being called out for sampling the wares, driving up food costs and depleting inventory
Having to work in a cramped space
Bad PR for the shop
Having a passion for coffee that the establishment doesn't share or care about
Developing an allergy or sensitivity that makes the coffeeshop a difficult place to work—e.g., becoming pregnant and not being able to stand the smell of coffee
Discovering that something underhanded is going on, such as beans being purchased from unethical sources, etc.

Being pressured by peers to give them free drinks

Vouching for a friend's employment, and them turning out to be a poor choice (being lazy, quitting with no notice, not cooperating with co-workers, stealing from the company, etc.)

PEOPLE THEY MIGHT INTERACT WITH

Other baristas and employees, a manager, a store owner, delivery people, customers, health inspectors

HOW THIS OCCUPATION MIGHT IMPACT THE CHARACTER'S NEEDS

Self-Actualization: Someone with a passion for coffee may find their enthusiasm squashed if the management is only interested in doing the same old thing. This could lead to a lack of fulfillment for the barista.

Esteem and Recognition: It's likely that most would view this job as a short-term opportunity. If your barista is happy and wants to make a career out of it, they may be judged by family and friends who vocalize they are settling and should want something more.

Safety and Security: While most retail jobs are fairly safe, a barista's security may be at stake in the event of a robbery or if the store is located in a dangerous area.

TWISTING THE FICTIONAL STEREOTYPE

This job is often a temporary one, but what might drive a character to pursue it as a long-term career?

To create some pizzazz for your barista, consider what you can change about the coffee shop itself. Where would an interesting location be? What other businesses might be run out of or in conjunction with the shop (a bakery or stationary store)? What charity might the owner be excited about, like a cat adoption program, that could be supported by the shop?

CHARACTERS MIGHT CHOOSE THIS PROFESSION BECAUSE THEY...

Lack the education needed for higher paying jobs

Are highly social

Have a passion for coffee

Want to gain access to someone who works at or frequents the shop

Like the flexible hours

Have no reliable transportation and the job is close to home

Are young and jobs available for their age group are scant

Need extra income for a short period of time (at Christmastime, to pay for a desired sports camp or summer program, etc.)

BARTENDER

OVERVIEW

Bartenders are responsible for providing alcoholic drinks to customers in a social environment. They can find employment in clubs, sports bars, pubs, restaurants, and at special events like weddings, private parties, or entertainment venues. As well as being legal age to distribute alcohol, they must adhere to any requirements specific to the venue.

NECESSARY TRAINING

Some people in this profession may attend bartending school, but others are self-taught. Having a wide knowledge of popular drinks and how to mix them, understanding the many varieties of beer (lagers, ales, IPA, etc.), and being able to make recommendations to customers is key. Some locations, such as a wine bar, may also require their bartenders to have special knowledge of a particular beverage.

Depending on the location of your story and the type of venue, a bartender may have to obtain different certificates (such as a license to serve alcohol) or take alcohol awareness classes. A food handling permit might be required in a pub or restaurant where meals will be served. And when working a location with high-profile clientele, the bartender will likely have to pass a security check.

USEFUL SKILLS, TALENTS, OR ABILITIES

Charm, enhanced taste buds, equanimity, exceptional memory, gaining the trust of others, good listening skills, hospitality, making people laugh, peacekeeping, reading people, self-defense

HELPFUL CHARACTER TRAITS

Adaptable, alert, calm, charming, creative, diplomatic, discreet, efficient, flirtatious, friendly, funny, hospitable, industrious, organized, perceptive, persuasive, spontaneous, talented, witty

SOURCES OF FRICTION

Dealing with drunk patrons
Domestic abuse situations that play out in the bar
Patrons determined to play out the fantasy of bringing a hot bartender home
Patrons who are unable to pay their bills
Customers who have taken drugs or prescriptions that lead to accelerated intoxication
Drunk patrons who refuse to get a cab and want to drive home
Disputes over bills
Tip theft among staff members
Tempers flaring among partygoers, resulting in arguments and fights
Impaired patrons who become belligerent or hostile when their drinking is cut off
Witnessing someone putting a substance in another patron's drink
Underage patrons using fake IDs to try and score drinks
Being robbed
Front-of-house vs. back-of-house friction (pettiness and fighting between bartenders, serving

staff, and kitchen staff)
Co-workers who drink on shift
Late shipments or being unable to obtain a popular drink
Chaotic, crowded events that make tracking orders and payments difficult
Sexual harassment (patrons getting handsy or making crude, unwanted remarks)

PEOPLE THEY MIGHT INTERACT WITH

Servers, management, patrons (drunk, sober, high, amorous, etc.), delivery people, cooks, police officers, bouncers, alcohol reps, inspectors (liquor, health and safety, food, etc.)

HOW THIS OCCUPATION MIGHT IMPACT THE CHARACTER'S NEEDS

Self-Actualization: Some venues prefer to hire attractive female bartenders, believing they will sell more product. This kind of gender and appearance bias can limit opportunities for those who don't meet the requirements, leading to a jaded outlook that sours the dream.

Esteem and Recognition: Appearance bias can produce feelings of inferiority in both male and female characters who find themselves being shortchanged based on their looks.

Love and Belonging: Bartenders are often flirtatious on the job, seeking an increase in tips to supplement their paychecks. Romantic partners may become jealous, believing there is more behind the behavior than there actually is.

Safety and Security: Bar fights, rowdy patrons, and possible illegal activities happening during a shift can create safety issues for employees.

TWISTING THE FICTIONAL STEREOTYPE

Rather than a bartender relying on their good looks, give them something else that makes them successful, such as a specific personality trait, a flare for the dramatic, or a creative spirit for inventing new beverages. Maybe they know exactly how to handle difficult patrons, can read the minds of their customers, or are known for performing sleight-of-hand tricks while slinging drinks. Think outside the box with this occupation so you can deliver something unique and fun to readers.

CHARACTERS MIGHT CHOOSE THIS PROFESSION BECAUSE THEY...

Want to supplement their income with good tip money
Enjoy the club lifestyle
Love meeting new people
Need a second job with flexible hours
Want to one day own a bar, club, pub, or restaurant
Are seeking access to potential romantic partners without worrying about commitment
Need to remain semi-anonymous or hide from the world
Are an addict and want easy access to alcohol
Have a condition where sleeping is dangerous and the energized environment keeps them awake

BOOK CONSERVATOR

OVERVIEW
Book conservators assess books and other documents through careful handling to determine how best to preserve them, preventing further deterioration. They then restore the item to the best of their ability given its current condition. Knowledge about the restoration process, materials to be used, and history of the object is essential.

NECESSARY TRAINING
Because multiple skill sets and expertise in a variety of subjects are required for this occupation, most employers prefer that their conservators obtain a master's degree in conservation. Prior experience through an internship or apprenticeship is usually recommended and the conservator must be proficient in many restoration techniques. Often a person in this profession will also be able to read and speak various languages.

USEFUL SKILLS, TALENTS, OR ABILITIES
Detail-oriented, dexterity, exceptional memory, multilingualism, out-of-the-box thinking, research, teaching, writing

HELPFUL CHARACTER TRAITS
Analytical, centered, curious, efficient, focused, fussy, gentle, independent, industrious, intelligent, introverted, meticulous, observant, patient, persistent, protective, resourceful, responsible

SOURCES OF FRICTION
Health risks from the chemicals used in the process
Aches and pains from sitting in one position for long periods of time
A workspace that is messy or otherwise unconducive to the restoration process
Stress at working on original copies of items that cannot be replaced
Having to go where the work is due to limited opportunities
Having to travel for jobs
Working with surly, uncommunicative, or condescending co-workers
Unhappy customers or ones with unrealistic expectations
Lacking the funds or tools needed for projects
Tedious work that requires intense focus and high dexterity
Accidentally damaging an item during the restoration process
Taking over a project that another conservator has bungled
Having to work on multiple projects at once
Lacking the necessary skills for a particular project
Being interrupted at a sensitive point in the process
Clients who change their expectations
A job taking longer than usual, resulting in blown deadlines
Micromanaging or incompetent bosses who don't appreciate the character's process
Discovering a fake document

PEOPLE THEY MIGHT INTERACT WITH
Other conservators, library or museum staff, private individuals, members of historical societies, suppliers of cleaning products and tools

HOW THIS OCCUPATION MIGHT IMPACT THE CHARACTER'S NEEDS
Esteem and Recognition: Restoration, when properly done, goes relatively unnoticed by anyone untrained in it. A character who thrives on recognition and praise may be have a hard time in this position.

Love and Belonging: Working in this occupation can be solitary, so characters who are extroverts or who like frequent social interactions might feel isolated.

Safety and Security: The mold and mildew present in old books and documents can affect a conservator's health. This can be an even bigger problem for a character working in an area that lacks proper ventilation or someone with a preexisting condition such as asthma or allergies.

TWISTING THE FICTIONAL STEREOTYPE
It's a common belief that people in this field can fix anything; however, there may be times when an item cannot be repaired. A talented book conservator who still fails periodically at restoring objects can not only switch up this stereotype, it may also provide you with realistic conflict scenarios for your story.

Another misperception is that book conservators only work on important historical artifacts. While they may occasionally get this opportunity, their job more often involves restoring everyday documents. A character who is mostly commissioned by private individuals or small institutions may offer a fresh (and realistic) alternative.

CHARACTERS MIGHT CHOOSE THIS PROFESSION BECAUSE THEY...
Grew up in a home where history, knowledge, and books were valued

Have a sense of purpose when they're restoring historically significant documents

Find the restoration process to be relaxing

Are seeking access to certain documents or information

Have a love of history, knowledge, and literature

Are patriotic and feel it's their duty to keep their country's history alive

Want access to certain kinds of information without drawing the attention of others

Love traveling to new locations and gaining a deeper understanding of other cultures

Struggle socially and want a career where they can work on their own

Need the knowledge and tools to forge documents

Love books and research

Belong to an organization that protects significant historical artifacts from those who would destroy them

Feel emotionally connected to the past and prefer it to the present

BOUNCER

OVERVIEW

A bouncer serves as hired security for an establishment where alcohol is served. They have many duties, including vetting patrons on entry to ensure they are of age and aren't dangerously intoxicated. In addition, they watch for scenarios that could escalate as alcohol or drugs is added to the social environment. They also look for situations that could put the club at legal risk.

A bouncer is typically very fit and imposing. If necessary, they will employ the intimidation factor to de-escalate situations, but using physical interaction to expel a customer is usually a last resort. Instead, quick thinking, humor, and staying calm under pressure are tools better used to avoid trouble. If a situation does become physical or someone is at risk, then police will be called to take over.

What a bouncer can and cannot do to remove someone from the premises varies depending on the laws of the state or province, so if you are writing a real-world bouncer, be sure to research local regulations. In most cases, the bouncer has no more rights than an average citizen; this means they will try to avoid actions that put them or the establishment at legal risk. They will engage physically to defend themselves, but only with reasonable force. Most will not carry a weapon, even if it is legal to do so. Their work attire may be casual (jeans and a shirt bearing the bar's logo) or upscale (a business suit) depending on the event and location.

NECESSARY TRAINING

Most bouncers enter a training program to better understand the scope of their work, or are trained by the establishment. They may need to pass a drug test, have a background check, or obtain a high school diploma to be hired.

Bouncers can work a variety of venues, including clubs, concerts, beer gardens, celebrity functions, special celebrations, strip clubs, invite-only private functions, casinos, restaurants, and bars. Their roles will be tailored to suit the location and event.

USEFUL SKILLS, TALENTS, OR ABILITIES

Basic first aid, blending in, charm, clairvoyance, empathy, enhanced hearing, enhanced sense of smell, exceptional memory, gaining the trust of others, haggling, high pain tolerance, hospitality, lip-reading, making people laugh, multilingualism, peacekeeping, reading people, self-defense, strength, throwing one's voice

HELPFUL CHARACTER TRAITS

Adaptable, alert, analytical, calm, cautious, centered, charming, confident, courageous, courteous, diplomatic, disciplined, discreet, easygoing, efficient, empathetic, evasive, humorless, impatient, inflexible, macho, observant, persistent, persuasive, proactive, professional, protective, responsible, sensible, suspicious, temperamental, tolerant, witty

SOURCES OF FRICTION

Underage patrons with fake IDs
Drug dealers on the premises

A patron who smuggles in alcohol, drugs, or a weapon

Male bouncers having to break up a fight between women

Bartenders or servers being threatened or hit on

Pick-pocketing at the event

Working a big event where there isn't enough security

A patron throwing a punch and the bouncer defending himself with excessive force

Sexual predators looking for potential marks

Monitoring bathrooms, hallways, and other enclosed areas

People who are unsafely intoxicated being abandoned by their group of friends

Rivals or ex-lovers running into each another

Special venue inclusions that make the area difficult to monitor (celebrations with distracting decor that restrict visibility, costumes, celebrity guests and media in attendance, etc.).

PEOPLE THEY MIGHT INTERACT WITH

Patrons, bartenders, management, liquor reps, celebrities, private security for celebrities and other important personalities, wait staff, cab drivers, police officers, media covering the event

HOW THIS OCCUPATION MIGHT IMPACT THE CHARACTER'S NEEDS

Esteem and Recognition: A character in a position of power can easily get an inflated ego, which can lead to mistakes on the job.

Safety and Security: Any character who goes up against people who have been drinking and possibly using drugs is stepping into a risky situation where physical injury is a real likelihood.

TWISTING THE FICTIONAL STEREOTYPE

Not all bouncers are beefy, intimidating men. Women can also be bouncers and often can be better at talking down situations with both men and women because they are not as physically imposing. Some clubs will always have a female bouncer on staff to handle situations specifically to do with women, enter areas where women frequent (such as the bathroom), and to help calm down situations where egos and testosterone are at play.

CHARACTERS MIGHT CHOOSE THIS PROFESSION BECAUSE THEY...

Were injured and are unable to pursue their dream job that made use of their physique (as a professional athlete, military officer, etc.)

Are physically intimidating and want to use that to their advantage

Need a steady paycheck while pursuing a professional body building career

Fear failure and are afraid to go after the career they really want

Have friends who value and accept only "tough" jobs

Want to help others and keep the peace

BOUNTY HUNTER

OVERVIEW

Bounty Hunters apprehend fugitives who are running from the law. While a suspect awaits a court date, they're often released on bail. If they can't pay the money themselves, they get it from a bail bondsman, and if the suspect doesn't appear for his court date, he becomes a fugitive. In this situation, the bail bondsman may hire a bounty hunter to find the suspect in exchange for a portion of the bail amount. Bounty hunters may work directly for a bondsman or do freelance work on their own.

In some ways, bounty hunters have more freedom than police officers because they can enter the fugitive's home without a warrant and cross state lines to apprehend them. Their work might include such activities as interviewing family and friends, canvassing the fugitive's neighborhood, staking out certain locations, tracing phone records and license plates, and confronting the suspect when he's found. Because of the inherent danger in this job, most bounty hunters work in teams or pairs.

NECESSARY TRAINING

In the U.S., you must be twenty-one years old and hold a high school diploma or GED to pursue this career. While many bounty hunters have a background in law enforcement or the military, no official training is necessary. Because they must be licensed in most states, they'll have to pass an exam that covers the laws and limitations for their trade area. Someone new to this profession would likely apprentice with an experienced hunter to learn the trade.

USEFUL SKILLS, TALENTS, OR ABILITIES

Basic first aid, blending in, charm, clairvoyance, computer hacking, equanimity, exceptional memory, gaining the trust of others, good listening skills, haggling, high pain tolerance, knife throwing, mentalism, networking, out-of-the-box thinking, parkour, reading people, self-defense, sharpshooting, stamina, strategic thinking, strength, survival skills, swift-footedness, wrestling

HELPFUL CHARACTER TRAITS

Adventurous, alert, bold, callous, cautious, confrontational, decisive, discreet, focused, humorless, industrious, just, manipulative, nosy, observant, obsessive, patient, persistent, persuasive, protective, pushy, rebellious, resourceful, responsible, rowdy, sensible, suspicious, uninhibited, vindictive, wise

SOURCES OF FRICTION

Trying to get information from uncooperative sources
Being confined by the law
Being tempted to circumvent the law to catch a fugitive
Not being able to find the fugitive
Receiving incorrect information from a source
A job going over budget or schedule
An important contact—e.g., a primary investigator or bondsman—going out of business

Conflicts of interest (the fugitive being a person the bounty hunter knows, having a family member who was victimized by the fugitive, etc.)
Suffering a physical injury that makes it difficult to do the job
Being wounded or taken captive by the fugitive
Working with an impatient bail bondsman
Taking a case that multiple bounty hunters are also working
Do-gooders questioning the character's methods
Having to enter dangerous neighborhoods and talk to volatile people to get information
A moral conflict with a job (for example, being tasked with going after a felon charged with assault after attacking a predator who has targeted his child)

PEOPLE THEY MIGHT INTERACT WITH
Bondsmen, law enforcement officers, people associated with the fugitive (family members, friends, neighbors, former bosses, etc.), contacts within an area the bounty hunter frequently works (shop owners, wait staff, prostitutes, etc.), administrative personnel

HOW THIS OCCUPATION MIGHT IMPACT THE CHARACTER'S NEEDS
Self-Actualization: A bounty hunter who chose the profession because he was unable to pursue the career he really wanted (such as one in the military or law enforcement) might soon become restless and feel unfulfilled.

Safety and Security: The danger associated with this job, the fugitives involved, and the neighborhoods they frequent mean their safety is often at risk.

Physiological Needs: A bounty hunter could lose their life tracking down a dangerous fugitive who will do anything to remain uncaught.

TWISTING THE FICTIONAL STEREOTYPE
Bounty hunters are often portrayed as rough and grubby, which helps them blend into the environments where their subjects are hiding. To switch things up, consider a bounty hunter who takes on only high-profile cases and must share the upscale appearance of the fugitives he hunts.

CHARACTERS MIGHT CHOOSE THIS PROFESSION BECAUSE THEY...
Needed a job when their career in the military came to an end
Are seeking control (due to having no control in other areas of life)
Have extensive knowledge of a certain city and its inhabitants
Thrive on risk and danger
Have a natural desire to protect others
Have an inherent respect for justice
Have a passion for hunting and solving mysteries and want to turn those hobbies into a career
Have an emotional wound where they were victimized and the perpetrator escaped justice

BUSINESS TYCOON

OVERVIEW
A business tycoon is someone who is extremely successful in their industry, be it banking, social media, finance, automobiles, media, real estate, or other area. They tend to be entrepreneurial, coming up with innovative ideas or solutions that help them rise to the top. Some (Henry Ford, J.P. Morgan, Mark Zuckerberg, Warren Buffet) are so famous as to become household names, while others are simply well-known by people in their fields. Because of their success, these leaders tend to be very wealthy and influential.

NECESSARY TRAINING
This will depend on the industry. Many successful business people have degrees—sometimes, multiple degrees—from institutions of higher education. Others are entirely self-taught. But most of these individuals share a drive to learn, grow, and improve through whatever means will enable them to move toward success.

USEFUL SKILLS, TALENTS, OR ABILITIES
A knack for making money, equanimity, exceptional memory, haggling, leadership, multitasking, networking, out-of-the-box thinking, promotion, public speaking, research, sales, strategic thinking, vision

HELPFUL CHARACTER TRAITS
Adaptable, adventurous, ambitious, analytical, bold, confident, decisive, devious, diplomatic, disciplined, disloyal, efficient, greedy, industrious, intelligent, materialistic, meticulous, passionate, patient, perfectionist, persistent, persuasive, talented, wise

SOURCES OF FRICTION
Competitors that threaten the character's position at the top of the food chain
Bad PR for the business
Rushing to market a product or service that isn't ready
Losing a great deal of money in a bad investment
Being sued or blackmailed
Discovering disloyalty among their inner circle (sharing sensitive research with a competitor, leaking financials and reports, engaging in internal sabotage, etc.)
Being targeted by powerful competitors who seek to damage the character's business dealings
Long work hours creating conflict with family members
Being unable to solve a particular problem
Gold diggers and opportunists making the character doubt the motives of others
Being hounded by paparazzi
Their personal life becoming the topic of tabloids and national headlines
Changing regulations that create problems for the character's production methods
A whistleblower exposing the company's dark side
Unethical practices from the past coming to light and threatening the character's reputation

PEOPLE THEY MIGHT INTERACT WITH

Other business people, investors, board members, employees, news reporters, personal secretaries or assistants, mentors in the field, celebrities

HOW THIS OCCUPATION MIGHT IMPACT THE CHARACTER'S NEEDS

Self-Actualization: A business person finding themselves doing things they never intended (acting unethically, becoming a workaholic, engaging in unhealthy relationships due to their wealth or prestige) may suddenly realize they no longer know who they are.

Esteem and Recognition: A tycoon who started their business out of a need to prove their mettle (to themselves or others) may find that, despite success, they still lack esteem. This revelation may drive them to find the true root of their problems.

Love and Belonging: A character used to opportunistic people and manipulations in business may have trust issues and be unable to fully surrender their heart to anyone.

Safety and Security: A business mogul's safety could be at risk should they become a target for a stalker, rival, disgruntled employee, or some other unhinged individual.

TWISTING THE FICTIONAL STEREOTYPE

Business tycoons are typically portrayed as greedy, unethical, heartless, and willing to do whatever it takes to further their bottom line. Twist this stereotype by creating a different kind of mogul—maybe one who is humble and principled, perhaps seeing wealth and power as a way to become influential and bring good into the world.

This occupation can also be freshened up by thinking outside the typical billionaire box. Instead of your tycoon being successful in banking or real estate, how else might they achieve greatness? Growing exotic trees and plant hybrids? Revitalizing the public education system? Inventing a food source that burns calories?

Lastly, consider your business person's appearance. People with a lot of money tend to be more attractive than most, due to the money they're able to spend enhancing their looks. Consider giving your rich business mogul something that others would consider to be a physical shortcoming—one they choose not to "correct" once they have the wherewithal to do so.

CHARACTERS MIGHT CHOOSE THIS PROFESSION BECAUSE THEY...

Grew up with a successful parent or sibling and want to achieve their own success
Grew up poor and want to amass wealth and be financially solvent
Have an entrepreneurial spirit
Are a visionary with an idea that can help society or better the world
Have a knack for building companies and selling them for profit
Desire power and want to rule in certain arenas (politics, education, business reform, etc.)
Have a philanthropic nature and want to make money to help others
Are outrunning feelings of inadequacy that blossomed from an emotional wound (an abusive upbringing, a toxic relationship, neglectful parents, conditional love, etc.)

CARPENTER

OVERVIEW
Carpenters build and repair fixtures made primarily of wood. They might be involved in large-scale projects, such as the construction of houses, commercial buildings, and bridges. Others may find smaller, more specific jobs to their liking; in this case, they may take pride in creating custom cabinetry, crown molding, doors, bookshelves, or furniture. Another common carpentry job is creating forms for concrete and masonry projects. Carpenters may obtain skills in multiple areas of woodworking, or they may specialize in just a few.

NECESSARY TRAINING
While a high school diploma is the minimum requirement to go into carpentry, an associate degree is often preferred, as is formal training through a vocational or technical program. Any prior experience, such as an apprenticeship, is also beneficial.

USEFUL SKILLS, TALENTS, OR ABILITIES
Good listening skills, mechanically inclined, multitasking, organization, repurposing, strength, whittling, woodworking

HELPFUL CHARACTER TRAITS
Ambitious, analytical, cooperative, creative, diplomatic, disciplined, efficient, enthusiastic, honest, honorable, humble, industrious, intelligent, meticulous, organized, passionate, perfectionist, resourceful

SOURCES OF FRICTION
Losing a project to a competitor
Inexperienced helpers, or those lacking knowledge of the proper tools
Elevated prices of materials
Unrealistic deadlines
Receiving incorrect materials or broken parts
Clients who are indecisive or have unrealistic expectations
Gender-based discrimination
Overly strict inspectors
Difficult co-workers or overbearing supervisors
The carpenter's work being damaged by other tradespeople (e.g., a plumber or electrician)
Having to wait on other tradespeople to complete their work
Being picketed by protestors
Working in harsh weather conditions
Insufficient funds for materials, or material prices that fluctuate
Fears that could impact job performance (heights, small spaces, etc.)
Struggling to handle multiple roles (if the character is self-employed)
Sustaining a back injury from carrying too-heavy loads
Working in an enclosed space or one with improper ventilation
A medical condition, such as carpal tunnel syndrome, that impacts fine-motor skills

Eye strain from poor lighting
A shortage of supplies

PEOPLE THEY MIGHT INTERACT WITH

Engineers, architects, other tradespeople (stonemasons, iron workers, roofers, etc.), clients, receptionists, business owners, job site managers, inspectors, distributors, delivery personnel

HOW THIS OCCUPATION MIGHT IMPACT THE CHARACTER'S NEEDS

Self-Actualization: Characters who are not given the freedom or the opportunity to carry out their visions for a project could begin to feel stifled. The same is true for those who are talented carpenters but lack the necessary skills to manage their own business.

Esteem and Recognition: In a field where word-of-mouth is key to gaining visibility and rising above the pack, bad reviews can make or break a career. They also can make a creative carpenter doubt their abilities.

Safety and Security: Working with dangerous tools puts carpenters at risk for injuries. In addition, some job sites, such as bridges and highways, could increase the danger due to traffic, heights, and tight spaces.

TWISTING THE FICTIONAL STEREOTYPE

A common misconception about carpenters is that they chose trade work because they couldn't get into college. To combat this stereotype, consider having a college-educated character who chooses to go into this field to pursue their passion for woodwork and artistic designs. Or, have your tradesperson do as well in their career as someone who went the higher education route. Plenty of people in the trades make an excellent living because they are talented, have a strong client base, and a head for business.

CHARACTERS MIGHT CHOOSE THIS PROFESSION BECAUSE THEY...

Had a parent who was a skilled carpenter
Grew up in a series of foster homes or had a nomadic family and so having a career where things are made to last is both satisfying and therapeutic
Were encouraged by a mentor to go into the field
Found carpentry to be an escape from their problems as a youth
Grew up in a run-down house and wanted to provide something better for their family
Enjoy working with their hands
Enjoy the variety that each work project offers
Get a sense of accomplishment from creating something from nothing
Feel compelled to create high-quality pieces for others
Enjoy the medium of wood and what can be done with it

CASHIER

OVERVIEW

A cashier is someone who handles transactions with customers, accepting payments for goods. During slow times they may have other duties such as straightening the checkout area, wiping down counters, or other small tasks. If the bagging of items is required, the cashier may do this, removing tags if requested. Cashiers are also the "front line" when it comes to dealing with customers, so they must be personable and able to problem solve or de-escalate situations that involve unhappy customers.

Cashiers with seniority in larger stores may be put in charge of the front end (customer support), working more with management and less on cash, performing duties such as scheduling hours for cashiers and clerks, creating break assignments for front-end employees, restocking the checkout area, attending to price checks, and recoding prices within the store's computer system. They will also handle customer inquiries and some paperwork.

A cashier may work at a grocery store, gas station, convenience store, retail shop, restaurant, cafeteria, movie theater, hardware store, coffee house, fast food or takeout place, recreation spaces, or any service industry business that sees regular foot traffic.

NECESSARY TRAINING

Most of these jobs require no formal education, but on-the-job training is provided. Cashiers either attend special training sessions to learn how to run the register and perform related duties, or they are shadowed for the first few shifts by more experienced co-workers. Because they handle money, trust is paramount. For this reason, it is unlikely that someone with a known criminal record would be hired in this position.

USEFUL SKILLS, TALENTS, OR ABILITIES

Charm, empathy, enhanced hearing, exceptional memory, gaining the trust of others, good listening skills, hospitality, making people laugh, mechanically inclined, multilingualism, multitasking, photographic memory, promotion, reading people

HELPFUL CHARACTER TRAITS

Calm, charming, cooperative, courteous, diplomatic, disciplined, discreet, easygoing, efficient, friendly, honest, hospitable, independent, loyal, obedient, observant, organized, proactive, professional, witty

SOURCES OF FRICTION

Angry customers who feel they are being overcharged or can't find the product they want
People soliciting customers outside the store without permission
Underage customers trying to buy alcohol or cigarettes
Employees not showing up for their shift, causing staff shortages at peak times
Co-workers who use seniority to get out of menial duties
Money that goes missing from the till
Customers who are inebriated or belligerent
Customers who act violent

Shoplifters

Robberies

The character's hours being reduced when they can't afford to lose any income

Being blamed for something so the management can save face

Being unable to move up in the company

Having a personal conflict with someone in seniority who makes life difficult (being given undesirable shifts, cut hours, frequently stationed on a problematic cash register, etc.)

Frequent turnover in the workplace, requiring the cashier to constantly be training new hires

Having ideas about how to improve the business but not being taken seriously by management

A prolonged power outage that forces the cashier to ring people up manually

The establishment being shut down by the health inspector

Customer complaints about the cashier because an unreasonable demand went unsolved

PEOPLE THEY MIGHT INTERACT WITH

Customers, other store employees, management, delivery people

HOW THIS OCCUPATION MIGHT IMPACT THE CHARACTER'S NEEDS

Self-Actualization: A cashier who is unable to find employment elsewhere due to job shortages may feel under-employed and unfulfilled.

Esteem and Recognition: If a cashier is looked down on because their work doesn't require much education, the character's self-esteem may suffer.

Safety and Security: Because they handle the money, cashiers may be endangered in the event of a robbery.

Physiological Needs: Because this job pays very little, a character with no other means may find themselves unable to secure basic needs, such as food and shelter.

TWISTING THE FICTIONAL STEREOTYPE

Cashiers are often portrayed as run-down women who have fallen on hard times and hate their job. Why not give us a character who genuinely loves the work and interacting with people?

CHARACTERS MIGHT CHOOSE THIS PROFESSION BECAUSE THEY...

Needed a second source of income

Required a job close to home

Are unable to get higher paying work (due to low education, family obligations, etc.)

Need the flexible schedule for specific parenting or caregiving needs

Want a low-stress job that doesn't spill over into their home life

Erroneously believe they're not suited for anything more complicated or skilled

Have social difficulties and are seeking a way to connect with others

Have a condition that creates limitations, yet cashiering is a good fit

Wish to work their way up into store management

CHEF

OVERVIEW

Chefs are generally responsible for food preparation. They may plan menus, oversee and direct others in its preparation, select ingredients, order supplies, and manage the kitchen staff. Individual duties will vary depending on the chef's position within the business.

Chef-Owners are responsible for the restaurant's success, and so oversee the kitchen (and restaurant) from a business standpoint. They may hire, fire, set prices, and have the final say over the menu. An **Executive Chef** oversees the daily operation of the kitchen, which includes food preparations, ordering, and menu planning. A **Sous Chef** oversees the kitchen in the Executive Chef's absence, is responsible for training new chefs, and ensures the food leaving the kitchen is of the highest quality and presentation. A **Senior Chef** is part of the team and is typically assigned to a station within the kitchen where they are responsible for a specific dish or aspect of food preparation (such as plating).

It should be noted that chefs and cooks hold different positions. Cooks don't have as much training and generally fill the entry-level positions in a restaurant or work as part of a small staff in smaller establishments.

NECESSARY TRAINING

Most chefs require an associate's degree in culinary arts and certifications in specific areas. Their courses will include things like nutrition, butchery, grilling, pastry creation, kitchen safety and basic first aid, garnishing and plating, hospitality training, menu planning, and possibly business courses that cover kitchen operations and management. Training is both classroom-based and hands-on.

Candidates will often start in entry level jobs and apply for apprenticeships to gain the work experience needed to become a chef. Specialized positions (pastry chefs, grill chefs, pantry chefs, sauce chefs) will require specific training.

USEFUL SKILLS, TALENTS, OR ABILITIES

A knack for making money, baking, basic first aid, creativity, enhanced sense of smell, enhanced taste buds, equanimity, exceptional memory, hospitality, leadership, multilingualism, multitasking, photographic memory, promotion, sculpting, strength, swift-footedness

HELPFUL CHARACTER TRAITS

Adaptable, ambitious, analytical, centered, cocky, cooperative, creative, disciplined, focused, hospitable, imaginative, judgmental, know-it-all, independent, industrious, meticulous, observant, obsessive, organized, passionate, perfectionist, professional, talented, thrifty, workaholic

SOURCES OF FRICTION

Long work hours
Demanding employers and customers
Customers who insist on certain substitutions or exclusions that will ruin a dish
Kitchen hazards (burns, cuts, back issues from standing for too long, dehydration from hot conditions, etc.)

Having to work holidays and so missing out on family events
Working for meddling owners who have little knowledge of how a kitchen should be run
Poorly designed kitchens with too little storage and counter space
Working with poorly maintained equipment
Hiring lazy staff
Team members who are out of sync and mess up the food delivery timing
Dealing with customer complaints
Last-minute diners who arrive right before closing
Kitchens that are not stocked and prepped properly for the next day
The kitchen staff being blamed for mistakes made by a server
Performance-related stress; competition among chefs
Employers who want to direct the menu when they do not have a sophisticated palate
Food spoilage from improper storage, handling, or incompetence

PEOPLE THEY MIGHT INTERACT WITH
Customers, kitchen staff, wait staff, management, owners, other chefs, cooks, delivery people, health inspectors, grocers

HOW THIS OCCUPATION MIGHT IMPACT THE CHARACTER'S NEEDS
   Self-Actualization: Dealing with demanding or rude customers, working long hours, and being in an environment where the chef's skills are not appreciated can cause a character to wonder if they're following the right dream.
   Esteem and Recognition: A chef on the lower end of the kitchen hierarchy may find it difficult if their contributions are not being recognized or they're being mistreated by haughty senior chefs.
   Love and Belonging: The long hours, weekend shifts, and after-work exhaustion can make personal relationships hard to maintain. Family may come to resent the character's profession as it will often come before them.
   Safety and Security: A kitchen contains many hazards that could lead to a life-changing injury, such as losing a finger while chopping, being scalded and disfigured, or sampling too much and gaining an unhealthy amount of weight.

CHARACTERS MIGHT CHOOSE THIS PROFESSION BECAUSE THEY...
Grew up in a home where the kitchen was a place of diverse tastes and experimentation
Grew up in a family that ran a restaurant or other food-based business
Had a large family where everyone pitched in to prepare meals
Have an enhanced palate and love food
Are highly hospitable, deriving satisfaction from bringing people together in fellowship
Want to make people happy by providing them with a powerful, enjoyable experience
Have an intense desire to create art through food

CHILDREN'S ENTERTAINER

OVERVIEW
A children's entertainer performs at group events where kids are present. An act may include music, magic, puppets, face painting, crafts, juggling, or any other activity a young audience might find enjoyable. Entertainers are most commonly hired for parties, weddings, community events, special school events, and other such occasions.

NECESSARY TRAINING
No formal education or training is necessary to become a children's entertainer. However, any prior experience, either through volunteer work or via a mentor, could be helpful. Depending on the performer's area of expertise, courses in acting or public speaking may help to make them better at their job.

USEFUL SKILLS, TALENTS, OR ABILITIES
A knack for making money, creativity, dexterity, empathy, enhanced hearing, equanimity, gaining the trust of others, hospitality, making friends, making people laugh, mimicking, multilingualism, parkour, performing, public speaking, reading people, sleight of hand

HELPFUL CHARACTER TRAITS
Adventurous, confident, creative, enthusiastic, extroverted, flamboyant, friendly, funny, gentle, happy, imaginative, kind, mischievous, playful, quirky, spontaneous, spunky, uninhibited, whimsical

SOURCES OF FRICTION
Working a gig with poorly behaved children
Bad weather (if the performance takes place outside)
Lack of funds for props and supplies
Parents who disengage and treat the performer like a glorified babysitter
Scheduling snafus (cancellations, an unexpected change of location, etc.)
Accidently double-booking appointments
Losing out to a competitor for a promising gig
A show that takes longer than anticipated
Dealing with demanding parents
Kids that are too old for the character's form of entertainment
Working with cheaply made supplies or malfunctioning equipment
Inconsistent hours and employment that means constantly having to hustle for jobs
Low wages that force the character to get a second job
Clients that don't pay on time
Family and friends who belittle or scorn the character's job
Having to cancel family plans when a work gig comes up
Trying a new routine that doesn't go over well
Picking up an illness from being around children

Unexpected situations that interfere with work (a son being home sick from school, having to take a sick pet to the vet, etc.)

Being falsely accused of something terrible and potentially career-ending (inappropriate touching, stealing something from a home, sexual advances toward a parent, etc.)

PEOPLE THEY MIGHT INTERACT WITH

Children of all ages, parents, staff members at party venues, vendors, circus staff, other entertainers, equipment and product suppliers

HOW THIS OCCUPATION MIGHT IMPACT THE CHARACTER'S NEEDS

Self-Actualization: If the entertainer has a passion for a specific style of performance (magic, song and dance, juggling) and the interest level wanes among the audience, it may leave the character feeling jaded and unfulfilled.

Esteem and Recognition: Making a living as an entertainer is difficult. If your character is the type to let money get under their skin, being surrounded by family and friends with high-earning jobs, or having a successful, well-compensated spouse might give them an inferiority complex.

Love and Belonging: Family members who don't understand the character's passion for entertaining children may result in veiled disappointment and lackluster support of their career. This could drive a wedge into those relationships.

TWISTING THE FICTIONAL STEREOTYPE

One portrayal we sometimes see in fiction is the child entertainer as someone who isn't going places or who isn't motivated enough to seek more prestigious work. Why not give your character a successful long-term career in this field or make it clear that they are doing this because it's something they're passionate about?

The specific paths within this occupation can also become somewhat cliché, such as a magician who's always pulling a rabbit out of their hat or the creepy, off-putting mime. For a fresh perspective, consider a nontraditional act for your character.

CHARACTERS MIGHT CHOOSE THIS PROFESSION BECAUSE THEY...

Were unemployed and jobs in this field were available

Had strict, domineering parents who robbed them of a childhood

Enjoy working with children

Have a natural knack for entertaining kids and are good at performing

Enjoy being able to reconnect with their inner child

Can adopt a fun persona that allows them to leave their struggles behind for a time

Love to bring joy to others

Want easy access to children (if they are criminally inclined)

Feel more at ease around children than adults

Love to perform a variety of acts and seeing the positive reactions to their work

CHOCOLATIER

OVERVIEW
Chocolatiers conceptualize and prepare confections and displays made from chocolate. They are intricately involved in the process of production, overseeing others and preparing the recipes to be used. Chocolatiers are responsible for choosing what chocolate to use, tempering, and revising the methods used in making these sweets before testing the finished product. They often have knowledge about the history of the craft as well as the preparation processes that help them determine if the final quality is acceptable.

NECESSARY TRAINING
An associate's degree from a bakery and pastry arts program is not required but is highly encouraged, as is additional training at a chocolate school. Apprenticeships are also helpful. It's not uncommon for someone in this field to begin as a pastry chef or baker before becoming a chocolatier.

USEFUL SKILLS, TALENTS, OR ABILITIES
A knack for making money, baking, creativity, detail-oriented, dexterity, enhanced sense of smell, enhanced taste buds, multitasking, photographic memory, sculpting, stamina, vision

HELPFUL CHARACTER TRAITS
Adventurous, creative, curious, efficient, imaginative, independent, industrious, meticulous, observant, obsessive, passionate, persistent, resourceful, responsible, talented, whimsical

SOURCES OF FRICTION
Working with people who have little education in chocolate
Staff who do not adhere to strict processes and conditions, affecting quality
Equipment malfunctions or an environmental change that has a negative impact on the product (a power outage, humidity issues making temperature hard to regulate, etc.)
Poor time management from co-workers
Long hours of standing all day and lifting heavy trays
Expensive ingredients leading to narrow profit margins
Supply issues causing quality inconsistency
Tempering failures that cause blooms, rendering batches unfit for sale
Products that don't meet quality standards or aren't uniform
Challenging shipping conditions, such as hot weather
Employees who aren't passionate about the job
Falling short of the health inspector's standards
Being passionate about chocolate but not about running a business
Impatient or demanding customers
Internal sabotage at the hands of a disgruntled employee
An economic downturn that causes consumers to cut down on discretionary spending
Customers who default on an order after it has been made
High-risk investments for supplies, equipment, or property

PEOPLE THEY MIGHT INTERACT WITH
Other chocolatiers, bakers and chefs, workers at food companies and private bakeries, customers, suppliers, cocoa farmers, equipment manufacturers, inspectors

HOW THIS OCCUPATION MIGHT IMPACT THE CHARACTER'S NEEDS
Self-Actualization: Characters who have passion but lack skill despite extensive education may become disillusioned if they try to make a name for themselves (either by entering competitions or opening a business in a tight market) and fail.

Esteem and Recognition: Chocolatiers who are talented but do not get the same recognition as their peers (in the form of awards, cookbook deals, or media attention) might feel like they are always coming up short.

Safety and Security: A chocolatier must sample as they go, meaning they may ingest high amounts of sugar. This can impact their health by increasing their risk for diabetes, causing weight issues, or creating other issues.

TWISTING THE FICTIONAL STEREOTYPE
A common stereotype in this field is that chocolatiers might have a certain body type because they consume so many treats. Having a character who breaks that mold and maintains a healthy lifestyle regardless of their body type could make for an interesting perspective.

Chocolate is a fan favorite, meaning many people are interested in all aspects of chocolate-making, not just eating the final product. Consider a chocolatier who uses other talents (such as sculpting, design, teaching, or videography) to showcase chocolate in different ways. Perhaps your character is known for entering reality TV sculpting competitions, teaching online classes to teens, or creating videos on chocolate experimentation, letting chocolate lovers peek behind the curtain.

CHARACTERS MIGHT CHOOSE THIS PROFESSION BECAUSE THEY...
Wanted a work schedule that would allow them to avoid holidays and gatherings with their volatile family

Were pressured into running the family chocolate business

Grew up in poverty, and chocolate was a luxury they couldn't afford

Enjoy chocolate and working with their hands

Are artistic and enjoy creating things, particularly edible confections

Enjoy making something that brings universal joy

Are passionate about chocolate and wish to invent new ways to consume it

Have fond childhood memories of working with chocolate alongside a grandmother or uncle

CLERGY MEMBER

OVERVIEW
Clergy is a general term referring to the people in charge of an organized religious group. Pastor, bishop, priestess, rabbi, and imam are some of the titles used to indicate this leadership role in various religions.

The main duties of a clergy member may include interpreting sacred texts, educating followers, ministering to their parishioners and others within the community, and seeing to certain religious duties. This might cover a wide variety depending on the religion: offering sacrifices, intervening with the deity on behalf of the people, taking confessions, and overseeing sacraments specific to the religion, such as baptism, communion, prayer, and ordinances associated with holy days. If your character is a clergy member with a real-world religious group, you will want to research that group for specifics.

NECESSARY TRAINING
Some religions require their leaders to attend an affiliated religious institution for a certain period of time and receive a degree before starting work. Others might require their clergy to go through an apprentice-like situation where they work with an existing leader and learn as they go. Clergy members in remote locations may have no formal training beyond a passion for their religion and a basic knowledge of its tenets.

USEFUL SKILLS, TALENTS, OR ABILITIES
Charm, empathy, gaining the trust of others, good listening skills, hospitality, leadership, multitasking, networking, public speaking, reading people, research, teaching, vision, writing

HELPFUL CHARACTER TRAITS
Bold, centered, charming, confident, courteous, creative, diplomatic, disciplined, discreet, empathetic, enthusiastic, extroverted, fanatical, honest, honorable, hospitable, humble, idealistic, inspirational, intelligent, just, kind, loyal, manipulative, merciful, nurturing, obedient, passionate, perfectionist, persuasive, philosophical, spiritual, studious, subservient, superstitious, supportive, unselfish, wholesome, wise

SOURCES OF FRICTION
The clergy member not being paid enough to support him or herself
Bureaucratic red tape that keeps the character from doing the important aspects their job
Disagreements with parishioners or higher-ups about doctrine
Politics within the religious organization
Conflict with the public when the religion's beliefs go against cultural norms
Clashes with traditional parishioners over modern ideas
Knowing a follower needs a certain kind of help but they're unwilling to listen
Dealing with misperceptions and unfair stereotypes about the religion
Being persecuted for religious beliefs
A clergy member risking their life to lead people in a society where the religion is outlawed
Struggling with temptations and addictions (alcohol abuse, sexual transgressions, etc.)

Being a leader for others but having no one to confide in or go to for advice
Personal doubts about religious ideology

PEOPLE THEY MIGHT INTERACT WITH

Parishioners or followers, officials within the religious hierarchy, those that they serve outside of the "church" (the homeless, social pariahs, the poor, etc.), members of the media, other staff members, local clergy members, strangers seeking something the religion may be able to provide (peace, absolution, knowledge, community, physical care, etc.), politicians

HOW THIS OCCUPATION MIGHT IMPACT THE CHARACTER'S NEEDS

Self-Actualization: Spirituality and being true to oneself are big parts of being fully actualized. A clergy member who's required to sacrifice their personal beliefs, needs, and priorities to serve may suffer a crisis of faith.

Esteem and Recognition: If your clergy member is seeking to move up in the organization to have more influence yet internal politics prevent it from happening, it could impact their need for respect and esteem.

Love and Belonging: A clergy member who too-strictly interprets religious laws may lose a chance to find a life partner and the benefits of a loving, unconditional relationship.

Physiological Needs: In many cultures, both past and present, the practice of certain religions has been outlawed. In these cases, breaking the law may lead to jail time, physical abuse, banishment, or execution.

TWISTING THE FICTIONAL STEREOTYPE

Some stereotypes have been used so much they've become tropes for clergy members in literature. For instance, the clergy members who adhere to their religious beliefs to the point of hateful and abusive behavior, or the hypocritical, two-faced sexual deviant. Take these stereotypes into account and create multi-dimensional characters instead.

CHARACTERS MIGHT CHOOSE THIS PROFESSION BECAUSE THEY...

Feel called by a higher power to serve in this way
Steadfastly believe in the compassion of God and want to lead others to the same idea
Want to make up for a past transgression, failure, or mistake
Feel a duty or obligation (to the church, to family, etc.)
Want to give back to their church
Desire to shape a religious order (by making it more appealing to modern parishioners, encouraging collaboration with other organizations to meet larger needs, etc.)

CONCIERGE

OVERVIEW
A concierge typically works at a hotel, assisting guests and making their stay as enjoyable as possible. Their tasks often include scheduling transportation, making reservations, answering questions, and offering advice on local events to attend. The best concierges will go above and beyond their expected duties to provide guests with extraordinary service.

NECESSARY TRAINING
Both a high school diploma and previous hotel experience are preferred but aren't required. Knowing the immediate area well and being familiar with its current events and goings-on is a must for providing excellent service. A concierge should also be able to relay succinct and clear directions. In some locales, knowing multiple languages may be a requirement.

USEFUL SKILLS, TALENTS, OR ABILITIES
Charm, good listening skills, hospitality, multilingualism, multitasking, networking, research

HELPFUL CHARACTER TRAITS
Adaptable, confident, courteous, curious, diplomatic, discreet, enthusiastic, hospitable, know-it-all, nosy, observant, passionate, patient, perceptive, persuasive, pessimistic, professional

SOURCES OF FRICTION
Handling needy guests or ones who are difficult to please
Being looked down on by co-workers who view the character's position as inferior
Miscommunication with a guest or other facility
A facility issue that is beyond the character's control (the Wi-Fi going down, overbookings due to a popular event in the area, a problem with filters that forces the pool to close, etc.)
Working in a dirty or otherwise unpleasant environment
Being expected to have immediate answers
Sustaining an injury or having a physical disability that limits mobility
Working long days for little pay
Working in an unorganized facility
Being new to the area and having to learn on the job
Having to work weekends or holidays
Being asked by staff to do things that aren't in the character's job description, such as making coffee, placing a personal reservation with a local restaurant, etc.
Verbose guests who don't respect the concierge's time
Low tips from guests
Dealing with guests who are jet-lagged, inebriated, or traveling with fractious children
Working an overnight shift where little is going on
Bad public relations for the hotel that results in local establishments not wanting to associate with them
People not returning phone calls

PEOPLE THEY MIGHT INTERACT WITH

Guests, family members and friends of guests, receptionists, housekeeping staff, hotel managers, speakers for hotel events, celebrities, travel agents, staff at local entertainment facilities and restaurants, airline personnel

HOW THIS OCCUPATION MIGHT IMPACT THE CHARACTER'S NEEDS

Self-Actualization: A concierge with a certain level of sophistication may find themselves frustrated working in a hotel where the clientele's interests flow in a different direction; if they're passionate about opera and wine-tasting, they may soon tire of researching tractor pulls or providing directions to the world's biggest ball of string.

Esteem and Recognition: Workers in the hotel industry are known for their hospitality, professionalism, and ability to meet the needs of clients. A concierge who is not as well-connected as a peer working for a competitor may doubt themselves and their abilities if they can't provide the same level of insider access, discounts, and perks as their counterpart can.

TWISTING THE FICTIONAL STEREOTYPE

Concierges are often depicted as old men who are lackluster and no longer have a passion for their job. Creating a young character in this profession who has great communication skills and thrives on helping others could reduce this stereotype.

Another common misconception is that concierges sleep all day, and when they're working, they're not much help. Having a character who goes above and beyond the duties of their position and enjoys the challenges it offers could put a fresh twist on things.

CHARACTERS MIGHT CHOOSE THIS PROFESSION BECAUSE THEY...

Were offered a promotion to this position by the hotel manager
Grew up in a low-income tourist town and were seeking an opportunity to escape
Needed to combat an overwhelming sense of loneliness due to a lack of personal interactions
Enjoy giving the ultimate experience to guests at hotels
Are personable and excel at problem solving
Enjoy the challenge of having to juggle many things at once
Want to escape a needy spouse or unsatisfactory home situation
Are seeking access to others' personal belongings
Have lived in the area forever and long to share their knowledge with others
Like to be the "I know a guy" person and procure and provide things others can't
Like the idea of wearing a fancy uniform and working in a high-end hotel
Want access to the elite and powerful (if they work in a high-end hotel)

CONDUCTOR

OVERVIEW
Conductors direct orchestras, symphonies, choirs, and other musical ensembles, interpreting the music and setting the tempo for the musicians. Their responsibilities include studying the musical scores, planning and overseeing rehearsals, and leading performances. They may also network with potential donors and help with fundraising. In addition, conductors taking on a secondary role of music director will select the music and schedule guest performances for their program.

Conductors are most often associated with top-end symphonies and choirs. But they're needed for all levels of musicianship, providing career opportunities in schools and universities, community groups, musical theater companies, and military organizations, as well.

NECESSARY TRAINING
A four-year degree is required and a master's degree is often preferred. Conductors should also have significant mastery of one or more instruments. Practical experience is imperative; many aspiring conductors achieve this by attending conducting workshops to gain the advice of a master, enrolling in a grad school program to study with a teacher, and conducting small groups and ensembles.

USEFUL SKILLS, TALENTS, OR ABILITIES
Enhanced hearing, exceptional memory, good listening skills, multilingualism, multitasking, musicality, photographic memory, promotion

HELPFUL CHARACTER TRAITS
Alert, ambitious, analytical, appreciative, bold, confident, cooperative, decisive, disciplined, enthusiastic, focused, imaginative, inspirational, meticulous, passionate, perfectionist, persuasive, studious, talented, uninhibited, whimsical

SOURCES OF FRICTION
Musicians with a diva mentality
Oversensitive musicians who can't take criticism
The conductor's authority being challenged
Creative differences with the musicians or composer
Facilities issues (the building having terrible acoustics, a broken heating or A/C system, etc.)
Language barriers
A show or tour being cancelled
Flagging ticket sales
A show or performance getting poor reviews
Losing a major donor or benefactor
A conductor becoming romantically involved with one of their musicians
A physical ailment that threatens their career (hearing or vision loss, a degenerative bone disease that makes it difficult to stand, etc.)
Being uninspired by the piece the conductor must conduct

Being unable to advance to a more desirable program
Working with poor musicians who are in the orchestra because of something other than musical proficiency (nepotism, tenure, they're blackmailing someone, etc.)
Being accused of favoritism, harassment, or other inappropriateness by an orchestra member

PEOPLE THEY MIGHT INTERACT WITH

Musicians, a music director, composers, donors and benefactors, other conductors, facilities staff, journalists

HOW THIS OCCUPATION MIGHT IMPACT THE CHARACTER'S BASIC NEEDS

Self-Actualization: A conductor in a lower-level organization with a dream of working with a top-tier ensemble may become disgruntled at his or her inability to move up.

Esteem and Recognition: A conductor who isn't respected by his peers might begin to feel resentful or insecure.

Love and Belonging: People who are highly passionate about their work often find it difficult to share their time, attention, and passion with others, which could lead to an inability to foster meaningful connections.

TWISTING THE FICTIONAL STEREOTYPE

Conductors, by and large, are male, so consider a female for this leading role.

When we think of people in this role, they're usually wealthy, pretentious, and snobby. Twist the stereotype by giving your conductor some unorthodox traits, making them quirky, timid, sloppy, or uncouth.

Instead of putting your conductor in charge of a highbrow ensemble, consider the less-represented options. Maybe she conducts the army band, an orchestra for an off-Broadway show, or an inner-city children's choir.

CHARACTERS MIGHT CHOOSE THIS PROFESSION BECAUSE THEY...

Experienced music as a means of escape and want to provide that sense of safety for others
Excelled in music at school while underperforming in other areas
Deeply love music
Have an obsession with music that drove them to immersing themselves in it
Are proficient with many instruments and have a knack for musical interpretation
Have an adored role model who was a music aficionado
Are compensating for a lack of control in other areas of life
Are highly creative and want to express themselves through music
Want to achieve an esteemed and prestigious position in the musical field
Are a natural leader with a passion for orchestral or classical music

CORONER

OVERVIEW
Coroners are elected or appointed officials responsible for investigating deaths to determine what caused them. In addition to performing autopsies, a coroner's duties include collecting evidence at a crime scene, conducting investigations, speaking to eye witnesses, testifying in court, studying medical records, establishing identities, filling out death certificates, and arranging for the notification of next of kin. Each coroner's duties will be determined by their jurisdiction and their training.

NECESSARY TRAINING
While many coroners hold a college degree (usually in a medical or science field), it may not always a requirement in every jurisdiction in the US. Many will be required to pass a test proving basic necessary knowledge, and it helps if their resumé includes medical or investigative work. Their education, experience, and other factors will determine their official job title, such as that of a medical examiner (physician). Many people in this field start out as deputy coroners and complete an apprenticeship, of sorts, before moving up to the official coroner position. If you are using a real world location and education is a factor for your coroner, check into the requirements of wherever your story takes place.

USEFUL SKILLS, TALENTS, OR ABILITIES
Dexterity, empathy, exceptional memory, gaining the trust of others, good listening skills, reading people, research, strategic thinking, talking with the dead

HELPFUL CHARACTER TRAITS
Adventurous, analytical, calm, cautious, confident, cooperative, courteous, curious, decisive, diplomatic, discreet, efficient, focused, honest, honorable, intelligent, just, meticulous, morbid, nosy, objective, observant, obsessive, organized, passionate, patient, persistent, professional, pushy, responsible, sensible, studious, suspicious, workaholic

SOURCES OF FRICTION
Tension with family members due to being on call 24/7
Evidence that has been tainted due to inept collection techniques
Evidence purposely being tampered with
Pressure from influential people to come to a certain decision in a case
Suspecting foul play but being unable to prove it
Arriving at a crime scene and recognizing the corpse
Being unable to determine a definitive cause of death
Working in a small jurisdiction and being faced with a case beyond the character's ability to solve
A contentious election for the job
Being smeared by a rival
Losing an election to a less-qualified candidate
Being tempted to tamper with evidence or make an unethical call so justice will be done

Having to testify in an emotional or disturbing case

Suffering from a mental or physical ailment that makes the job difficult (memory loss, nerve damage in the fingers, etc.)

Finding a cause of death that suggests the start of an epidemic

Dealing with people who think that coroner work is repugnant and creepy

Being asked by nosy or morbid people for details about confidential cases

Seeing a pattern of deaths that suggest police involvement in a coverup

PEOPLE THEY MIGHT INTERACT WITH

Police offers and detectives, other coroners or medical examiners, a deputy coroner, lawyers and judges, public health officials

HOW THIS OCCUPATION MIGHT IMPACT THE CHARACTER'S NEEDS

Self-Actualization: A person in this position who, due to lack of education or opportunity, is unable to perform all the necessary duties may feel that they're unable to live up to their full potential or help people as they'd like to.

Esteem and Recognition: A coroner with fewer credentials and job responsibilities may feel inferior to medical examiners or forensic pathologists who are able to do more.

Love and Belonging: Many people might look down upon someone who works with dead bodies, believing the job to gross or off-putting. If this puts off potential love interests, your coroner may yearn for connections yet be unable to make them materialize.

Safety and Security: While precautions should always be in place, contagion could become an issue in certain cases for a coroner who is distracted or doesn't follow procedures.

TWISTING THE FICTIONAL STEREOTYPE

Coroners tend to be drawn as either humorless and no-nonsense or over-the-top quirky. To understand their personality, be sure to know why they chose the career. This can give you some insight into the kind of person they really are.

CHARACTERS MIGHT CHOOSE THIS PROFESSION BECAUSE THEY...

Suffered a death-related trauma that fed their desire to seek justice for victims who couldn't speak for themselves

Wanted to serve in law enforcement but had a condition or impairment that made certain roles impossible

Are naturally investigative and interested in unraveling the mysteries of the human body

Are curious about death and want to steer that interest in a healthy direction

Are obsessed with ghosts, the afterlife, or other supernatural phenomenon associated with death

Enjoy puzzles, mysteries, and other problem-solving scenarios that involve gathering data and putting the pieces together to form a conclusion

Are seeking access to dead bodies for a darker purpose

CORRECTIONS OFFICER

OVERVIEW

A corrections officer (also known as a prison guard) oversees inmates who are serving out their sentences, ensuring they are afforded their legal rights while obeying facility rules and local laws. They rotate through assignments in different areas, including the gatehouse, observation towers, and unit deployments (accommodation wings, infirmary, recreation area, etc.). Some positions are very hands-on while other assignments are less so, such as monitoring controls, running headcounts, checking rooms for contraband, and overseeing paperwork. They also may assist with vocational training for prisoners and help inmates address behavioral issues that are tied to their offenses.

Corrections officers are responsible for the safety and rights of the inmates as well as their fellow officers. They may have to respond to fights, medical emergencies, and other incidents and should know what to do in each situation, displaying complete authority. Inmates constantly test officers to determine any weak points, especially if the guard is new. It's important for a corrections officer to maintain discipline by remaining professional, adhering to protocol, following through on their word, and treating everyone equally. Responsibilities will vary at the municipal and federal levels, so research will be required to ensure the duties of your corrections officer match their situation.

NECESSARY TRAINING

Non-federal prisons require a high school diploma or a completed equivalency diploma, while federal prisons require a bachelor's degree or three years of counseling and supervising others. Officers must also pass background checks and both a mental and physical health assessment.

New hires are usually placed in an academy and then continue with on-the-job training. In addition to comprehensive education in facility procedures, institutional policies, and legal restrictions, officers receive training in firearm use, learn self-defense, and are taught how to restrain and disarm prisoners and neutralize threats. If an officer is part of a tactical response unit, they will be trained in how to respond to riots, hostage-taking, and any other dangerous situation that may occur. Training is usually ongoing, both to continually hone their skills and to keep them updated as new procedures and policies take effect.

USEFUL SKILLS, TALENTS, OR ABILITIES

Basic first aid, blending in, clairvoyance, enhanced hearing, enhanced sense of smell, equanimity, exceptional memory, gaining the trust of others, good listening skills, haggling, high pain tolerance, lip-reading, making people laugh, multilingualism, peacekeeping, photographic memory, reading people, self-defense, sharpshooting, strategic thinking, strength, survival skills, swift-footedness, wrestling

HELPFUL CHARACTER TRAITS

Alert, analytical, bold, centered, confident, confrontational, controlling, cooperative, courageous, courteous, diplomatic, disciplined, focused, honorable, just, observant, organized, persistent, persuasive, proactive, professional, responsible, stubborn, tolerant

SOURCES OF FRICTION
Trying to manage friction between gangs
Overcrowding issues
Poor quality of life that contributes to volatility in prisoners
Prison rapes and attacks
Discovering inappropriate conduct between a guard and a prisoner
A corrections officer who is unreliable
Family problems due to shift work and work being brought home from the job
Disagreeing with a fellow officer's way of managing prisoners
Witnessing a bribe
Having to break up altercations between prisoners
A riot
A murder
Being accused of misconduct
Seeing injustice, such as mentally ill prisoners going untreated in the general population

PEOPLE THEY MIGHT INTERACT WITH
Prisoners, prison staff, administration, the warden, psychologists, doctors and nurses, police officers, investigators, FBI agents, visitors, lawyers, delivery people

HOW THIS OCCUPATION MIGHT IMPACT THE CHARACTER'S NEEDS
Self-Actualization: Because this work is mentally taxing and can drain the spirit, it is easy to adopt a jaded, negative worldview. This could prevent the character from fulfilling a life pursuit that has personal meaning or even seeing society at large as being worth saving.

Love and Belonging: Shift work and overtime can impact the character's ability to keep family relationships strong or make time for loving relationships.

Safety and Security: Prisoners can be deceptive and violent and have nothing to lose. This puts correction officers constantly at risk—especially in pod situations where one guard may be responsible for watching a large number of prisoners.

Physiological Needs: Being overtaken during a riot or being taken in an attempted hostage situation would put the guard's life in imminent danger.

TWISTING THE FICTIONAL STEREOTYPE
These characters are commonly portrayed as cruel or even sadistic people who enjoy abusing their charges. We see a nice twist on this in Stephen King's *The Green Mile*, with Paul Edgecombe being compassionate and open-minded, believing that everyone deserves respect. Look past the easy stereotypes for this occupation by examining your character's morals. How do their deepest beliefs dictate who they are at work?

CHARACTERS MIGHT CHOOSE THIS PROFESSION BECAUSE THEY...
Were morally opposed to the criminal activity that was common in their family
Lived in a town where the prison was the best-paying option for work
Want to feel power by dominating others
Have a fiercely protective instinct

CRIME SCENE CLEANER

OVERVIEW

A crime scene cleaner blocks off, washes, and sanitizes areas where a crime has occurred. Sometimes this includes discarding bedding, furniture, carpet, and other items contaminated by biological substances. It may also require arranging for minor home repairs, such as replacing flooring or patching and painting over drywall holes. Cleaners are often called in by family members or businesses hoping to spare individuals the emotional heartache and pain of having to deal with the task themselves.

NECESSARY TRAINING

Extensive on-the-job training will prepare new hires for this line of work, so a high school diploma or GED is usually all that's necessary to begin. As part of that training, many agencies will require their cleaners to obtain certifications having to do with related subjects, such as blood-borne pathogens, the proper care of hazardous materials, how to operate larger equipment and tools, and other safety techniques and protocols. Additional licenses and permits may be required, depending on the location. Former experience isn't necessary, but a resumé that includes work in related fields (such as public health or forensics) can be beneficial.

Cleaning jobs can be exhausting, especially when shifts run long or arise unexpectantly. Physical and mental fortitude are a must to succeed long-term in this career.

USEFUL SKILLS, TALENTS, OR ABILITIES

Blending in, empathy, equanimity, multitasking, organization, stamina

HELPFUL CHARACTER TRAITS

Adventurous, cautious, confident, cooperative, courageous, courteous, disciplined, discreet, easygoing, efficient, enthusiastic, focused, fussy, humorless, industrious, merciful, meticulous, morbid, organized, perfectionist, professional, responsible, supportive, tolerant

SOURCES OF FRICTION

Long hours away from family and friends
Dealing with a gory scene that leaves an emotional impact
Working in high-crime areas
Risk of health issues from close contact with bodily fluids
Law enforcement members who view cleaners or their work as inferior
Working in unpleasant environments
Clients who have unrealistic expectations
Working with improper protective gear or other equipment
Running out of cleaning supplies
Accidentally destroying or damaging evidence
Dealing with a difficult item to clean, such as a car, ventilation system, or machinery
Working in an environment with unpleasant odors
Exposure to sharps and other dangerous items
Family and friends of the victim trying to interfere

Defective clean-up containers that tear or spill during use
The cleaner being underappreciated for their efforts
Being pressured to complete a job quickly

PEOPLE THEY MIGHT INTERACT WITH
Law enforcement officers, investigators, firefighters, medical personnel, representatives of associated agencies (OSHA, NIOSH, DOT, EPA, etc.), family members or co-workers of the deceased, secretaries, managers of industrial facilities or other businesses

HOW THIS OCCUPATION MIGHT IMPACT THE CHARACTER'S NEEDS
Self-Actualization: Because of the need for precision and precisely-followed protocol, characters in this career who are highly creative or prefer a variety of work might struggle.

Esteem and Recognition: This profession is largely a background one, with crime scene cleaners working quietly behind the scenes and bringing as little attention as possible to themselves or the environment. As a result, those who thrive on recognition and praise may become frustrated in this regard.

Love and Belonging: Some characters may have trouble handling the emotional terrain inherent with this vocation; those who become numb or find the need to tamp down their feelings may encounter problems in their personal relationships.

Safety and Security: Cleaners deal consistently with hazardous substances and chemicals that put them physically at risk. In addition, long-term exposure to the aftermath of violent crimes could lead to psychological trauma.

TWISTING THE FICTIONAL STEREOTYPE
One misconception is that people in this field only deal with crime scenes; however, they are more frequently called to clean homes or businesses where a natural death has occurred. An interesting twist might be an empathic character or one with psychic abilities who senses the presences of the recently departed and can provide comfort to those left behind.

Because the job requires dealing with intensely gross situations, it's often assumed that workers in this field are apathetic. Creating a character who is compassionate and sympathetic toward those affected by trauma can help combat this stereotype.

CHARACTERS MIGHT CHOOSE THIS PROFESSION BECAUSE THEY...
Want to bring comfort to families who have lost a loved one
Enjoy cleaning and aren't squeamish
Want firsthand knowledge about crimes
Want to have an "in" with law enforcement
Are seeking information on how to cover up a murder
Want to come to terms with their own personal loss of a loved one
Desire to serve others in their darkest moments
Have a passion for taking what is dirty or "ruined" and making it as good as new

DANCER

OVERVIEW
Dancers are professional performers who tell stories with their bodies, using choreographed routines to entertain audiences. They usually participate in productions for theatres, television, and movies. When they're not performing, dancers spend much of their time rehearsing and attending classes to improve their skills.

NECESSARY TRAINING
No degree is necessary, but many dance companies require formal training through accredited schools and/or a minimum amount of experience. In addition, dancers will need to audition, either with a video submission or in person.

USEFUL SKILLS, TALENTS, OR ABILITIES
Creativity, dexterity, enhanced hearing, exceptional memory, high pain tolerance, mimicking, musicality, networking, parkour, performing, stamina, strength, strong breath control

HELPFUL CHARACTER TRAITS
Ambitious, creative, disciplined, focused, industrious, inspirational, mature, obedient, obsessive, passionate, persistent, sensual, talented, thrifty, uninhibited, workaholic

SOURCES OF FRICTION
Competition over a role in a production
Family members who don't support their career choice
A lack of funds to pay for classes or outfits
The company cancelling or not renewing the dancer's contract
Failing to move up within the company
Body image or self-worth issues due to constant comparisons to others
Intense pressure to do well paired with unrealistic expectations
Secondary jobs that conflict with class or performance times
Weight gain that can lead to a difference in appearance and balance
Long hours that put a strain on relationships and leave little time for other hobbies
Performance anxiety
Taxing moves that strain the body and can cause damage, especially to the feet
Forgetting the moves during a performance
Having to miss important family events because of recitals
Being treated like an expendable member of the group
Dealing with unfair treatment or favoritism
The character being criticized for their performance, weight, appearance, or dedication

PEOPLE THEY MIGHT INTERACT WITH
Other dancers, instructors, additional staff members at a dance company, movie or televisions producers, actors and actresses, audience members, critics

HOW THIS OCCUPATION MIGHT IMPACT THE CHARACTER'S NEEDS

Self-Actualization: To succeed, dancers give everything they have because anything less can end a career. But no matter how skilled they are, as dancers age, they will hit a ceiling where they can move up no further. This can be a huge blow, especially as up-and-coming dancers are seeking to further their own aspirations.

Esteem and Recognition: The constant pushing and criticism from trainers and producers often comes at a cost: negative views about the dancer's bodies and abilities, which can impact self-esteem.

Love and Belonging: A sense of love and belonging will be tested in this occupation, as dancers are constantly compared to others and graded on how well they perform. If a character is let go from their company, this could leave them feeling cast out and abandoned.

Safety and Security: Stress fractures and other physical injuries occur frequently for dancers. Eating disorders are also common as they try to manage their weight. These concerns, along with the high costs needed to pursue this career, can cause health struggles and make financial security problematic.

TWISTING THE FICTIONAL STEREOTYPE

Sometimes in fiction and film, male dancers are portrayed as not being as masculine as other same-sex athletes. Don't shortchange your character with such stereotypes; masculine and feminine traits run on a spectrum and vary from one person to another, so understand how personality and behavior work together to write any character with authenticity. Because female dancers tend to dominate the field, telling the story from a male perspective can offer readers the added benefit of a fresh perspective.

Another stereotype is that the only way to make money as a dancer is to be an exotic performer. Giving your character a successful career as a ballet, ballroom, contemporary, or other traditional type of dancer can help break that stigma.

CHARACTERS MIGHT CHOOSE THIS PROFESSION BECAUSE THEY...

Dreamed of being a dancer from a young age
Experienced trauma as a youth and learned to cope with the pain through dance
Have great body awareness and a natural ability to move to music
Live in an area that offers many performing arts opportunities
Come from a family of athletes or dancers
Feel a sense of freedom from dancing—a safe place to let go and be vulnerable
Are highly talented, competitive, and disciplined

DEEP SEA DIVER (COMMERCIAL)

OVERVIEW
Deep sea diving is the act of descending into water and remaining there for an extended time using a breathing apparatus. This type of diving is done for a variety of reasons: recreation, salvage, industrial work, and research, to name a few. This entry will focus on commercial diving—specifically offshore. Offshore work is primarily done in the oil and gas sector, where a specially trained diver installs and repairs underwater equipment and piping in deep water. Some of this work may require saturation diving, which involves extended stays in a pressurized environment (usually a hyperbaric chamber on the surface or an ambient pressure underwater habitat). This allows a diver to remain at lower depths for a greater amount of time to avoid the bends.

Deep sea divers have a variety of tasks that may require special skills. Welding, underwater detonations, construction, installations and pipe-fitting, checking connections and inspections, troubleshooting malfunctioning equipment, overseeing operations such as trenching and pipeline stabilization, search and recovery, and running other industry-specific equipment all demand specialized knowledge by the diving team.

A diver in this field must be physically and mentally fit, as the work is very demanding. The environment and the physicality of the job make it a dangerous one, resulting in most divers being on the younger end of the spectrum.

NECESSARY TRAINING
Some countries don't require divers to have a commercial diving certification, but in North America and many other developed countries, this is necessary. A basic, entry-level program is about two months in length, but more extensive programming will take anywhere from four to twelve months. To earn more advanced certifications, a person will have to log hours in the field and on working dives.

Divers must understand physics, adhere to safety protocols, have training in first aid and CPR, and know how to identify and treat diving injuries and diseases. Offshore divers will also learn technical skills, such as welding, that factor into their work.

USEFUL SKILLS, TALENTS, OR ABILITIES
Basic first aid, enhanced hearing, equanimity, exceptional memory, gaining the trust of others, good listening skills, high pain tolerance, knowledge of explosives, lip-reading, mechanically inclined, multitasking, photographic memory, regeneration, repurposing, stamina, strategic thinking, strength, strong breath control, survival skills, wilderness navigation, woodworking

HELPFUL CHARACTER TRAITS
Adaptable, adventurous, alert, ambitious, analytical, bold, calm, cautious, centered, cooperative, courageous, disciplined, efficient, focused, independent, industrious, intelligent, observant, persistent, proactive, professional, resourceful, responsible

SOURCES OF FRICTION
Poorly maintained equipment, malfunctions with air tanks or diving gear
Budget cutbacks
Sharks and other dangers
Getting the bends
A malfunction in a decompression chamber
Being stuck in a hyperbaric chamber or habitat with confrontational or unlikable divers
Exhaustion due to long hours of hyper-focus
Working with people who don't follow safety protocols
Demanding companies that require prolonged diving times that are unsafe
Industrial accidents
Being pressured to adhere to a tight or nearly impossible timeline
Personality conflicts playing out within small living quarters
An illness that makes it difficult to dive
Claustrophobia and other fears

PEOPLE THEY MIGHT INTERACT WITH
Boat operators, other divers, project managers, ship employees, oil and gas employees, doctors, scientists, engineers

HOW THIS OCCUPATION MIGHT IMPACT THE CHARACTER'S NEEDS
Esteem and Recognition: Women are not as common in this industry and so may run into prejudice which could limit their ability to climb the ladder.
Love and Belonging: Divers are often away for extended time periods, which can make building and keeping personal relationships a challenge.
Safety and Security: Many hazards and dangers could threaten your character's security: a run-in with a shark that births a fear of death, a malfunction while diving that brings about phobias of drowning or claustrophobia, and crippling industrial accidents could all put a diver's safety at risk and make it difficult for them to continue in their career.

TWISTING THE FICTIONAL STEREOTYPE
You could give your diver a crippling weakness or secret they must hide, like a fear of sharks, darkness, or even drowning.

CHARACTERS MIGHT CHOOSE THIS PROFESSION BECAUSE THEY...
Wanted to conquer a phobia (of drowning, suffocation, etc.)
Prefer to be solitary rather than social
Are fascinated by the unexplored corners of the world
Have a powerful "mind over matter" mindset and enjoy pushing their body to its limits
Want to do something very few people in the world are able to do

DENTIST

OVERVIEW
Dentists are responsible for overseeing the oral health of their patients. This includes examining, analyzing, and caring for multiple areas of the mouth while primarily focusing on the teeth and gums. Some treatments involve removing tooth decay or disease, filling cavities, or mending fractured teeth. Dentists can also give referrals to other specialists, such as orthodontists, when warranted.

While the majority of dentists work in private practices, this isn't their only option. They can also treat patients in a hospital, work in a community setting to promote dental health, conduct research, or teach.

NECESSARY TRAINING
A bachelor's degree in science will usually be necessary, as is training through a four-year program at a dental school. To obtain a license to practice, expertise in a clinical setting must be demonstrated. This is done through a practical and written exam; however, specifics of that exam and the skills required for certification will vary by location. Additional education is needed for those wanting to become a dental specialist or to teach others in the field.

USEFUL SKILLS, TALENTS, OR ABILITIES
A knack for making money, basic first aid, charm, dexterity, empathy, gaining the trust of others, good listening skills, leadership, promotion, research, teaching

HELPFUL CHARACTER TRAITS
Ambitious, analytical, charming, confident, decisive, diplomatic, disciplined, discreet, efficient, empathetic, focused, friendly, honest, honorable, hospitable, intelligent, kind, meticulous, nurturing, observant, organized, passionate, perceptive, perfectionist, persuasive, professional, studious, thrifty, workaholic

SOURCES OF FRICTION
Examining patients who have anxiety about dental work
Dealing with difficult pediatric patients
Late patients or ones who cancel frequently
Poor scheduling that results in an unproductive or stressful day
Debt from education and training
Tedious and precise work that can lead to physical and mental exhaustion
Exposure to contagious diseases
Working alone in a practice and feeling isolated
The stress of managing a business
Dental hygienists who overstep their boundaries
Long hours of often tedious work
Spending most of the day in close contact with others
Working on a patient with bad breath or problematic oral conditions
Office drama

Being on call over weekends and nights
Having a certification that doesn't transfer from one state to another
Patients who are behind on payments
Conflicts with insurance companies
Spending most of the day in a small, windowless office

PEOPLE THEY MIGHT INTERACT WITH
Patients, secretaries, other dentists, dental assistants and hygienists, dental specialists (orthodontists, periodontists, oral surgeons, etc.), dental suppliers, accountants, insurance companies, auditors

HOW THIS OCCUPATION MIGHT IMPACT THE CHARACTER'S NEEDS
Self-Actualization: A dentist who desires to open his own practice might feel stifled if he is unable to do so due to unpaid school loans, being tied to a small-town location where the field is dominated by a tenured dentist, or another limitation.

Esteem and Recognition: Most people don't like going to the dentist, a fact that can weigh on these healthcare practitioners—especially when their patients aren't shy about sharing their feelings. Always having to treat patients who are fearful, anxious, or even angry about visiting the dentist can negatively impact self-esteem.

Love and Belonging: Fears of being perceived as preferential to some because of a closer relationship may cause your dentist character to keep all staff at an arm's length, hampering any sense of belonging in the workplace.

TWISTING THE FICTIONAL STEREOTYPE
While many dentists do work in private practice, volunteerism can put them in unusual locations, such as a refugee camp, community clinic, or even a third-world country. A simple change in locale can provide a fresh twist—and interesting conflict scenarios—for an established occupation, so keep this in mind.

CHARACTERS MIGHT CHOOSE THIS PROFESSION BECAUSE THEY...
Are compensating for being neglected or not cared for as a child
Want to care for others
Desire a steady source of income
Are detail-oriented and have an interest in the medical field
Are taking over a family business
Are obsessed with clean mouths and dental hygiene
Find it easier to connect with patients temporarily than to build meaningful long-term relationships with others
Want access to medication or supplies

DIETICIAN

OVERVIEW
Dieticians manage a client's diet and provide recommended adjustments based on the individual's medical information and lifestyle practices. As licensed professionals and experts in human nutrition, they are equipped to diagnose and address diet-related issues. They can work in a variety of locations, including hospitals, nursing homes, schools, and other medical facilities.

NECESSARY TRAINING
To pursue this career, a bachelor's degree in a health-related field is required, and state registrations are essential in order to practice on patients. Licenses can be obtained by completing necessary coursework approved by the appropriate accreditation facility. Passing a national exam is also required. To work in a specific field alongside other specialists, further training may be necessary.

USEFUL SKILLS, TALENTS, OR ABILITIES
Basic first aid, charm, detail-oriented, empathy, gaining the trust of others, good listening skills, hospitality, multitasking, networking, organization, promotion, reading people, research, sales, strategic thinking

HELPFUL CHARACTER TRAITS
Cooperative, courteous, diplomatic, discreet, empathetic, enthusiastic, hospitable, kind, nurturing, objective, observant, optimistic, organized, perceptive, persuasive, professional, resourceful, responsible, studious, supportive

SOURCES OF FRICTION
Patients who are resistant to changing their habits
Unclean facilities, or ones where exposure to illness is prominent
A lack of necessary diagnostic tools
Working with critical care patients
Family or friends who don't support the dietician's career path
Co-workers who look down on them because they don't have the same training as doctors
Being constantly asked professional questions after hours
People who expect the dietician to be an expert in every area of nutrition
The diet industry pushing for things that aren't healthy
Dealing with clients who have been given a lot of misinformation
Dishonest clients who blame the dietician for their lack of progress
Issues with insurance companies
Facing criticism for being overweight themselves
Being judged if they eat something unhealthy
Family and friends feeling criticized or judged by the dietician for their food choices
Struggling to keep up with new or changing information in the field
Providing incorrect information to a patient
"Armchair expert" clients who disagree with the dietician's recommendations and cite bad

science articles found on social media to back up their opinions

Resistant parents who do not want to adopt new habits to help their children be healthier

PEOPLE THEY MIGHT INTERACT WITH

Patients (both adults and children), food service individuals, doctors, insurance providers, nurses, secretaries, accountants, facilities personnel (hospital, school, nursing home, etc.)

HOW THIS OCCUPATION MIGHT IMPACT THE CHARACTER'S NEEDS

Self-Actualization: Characters often enter this field to make a difference in people's lives. A dietician with this motivation whose clients fail to change poor eating habits may grow jaded and question their choice of career.

Esteem and Recognition: Someone could be very good at this job yet experience bias because of other health-related issues, such as having a skin disorder or being overweight. Criticism and shame for physical issues that are outside of their control can not only hurt their career but also their sense of esteem.

Love and Belonging: A dietician pushing unsolicited advice on friends and family may find it isn't well-received. This could create rifts in those relationships.

TWISTING THE FICTIONAL STEREOTYPE

A major stereotype for dieticians is that they are never overweight or don't make poor food choices themselves. For a fresh perspective, consider a character who has a weight issue. Maybe it's much easier for them to help others than to help themselves.

Because of their interest in health and nutrition, they're often portrayed as being fanatical or obsessive about food and exercise. What about a dietician who is fastidious about food but unapologetic about other unhealthy habits, like smoking, drug use, or poor hygiene?

CHARACTERS MIGHT CHOOSE THIS PROFESSION BECAUSE THEY...

Overcame poor dietary habits or an eating disorder and want to help others do the same

Were teased for being overweight as a child

Lost a loved one to health issues that could have been prevented with a better diet

Had a loved one with a debilitating condition that they corrected through diet

Have an interest in food and health

Enjoy caring for others

Come from a medical family and are expected to go into a medical field

Want to help others work through a negative relationship with food

Desire to educate the public and stop the spread of misinformation

Is a vegan and wants to help others successfully manage this diet choice also

DIPLOMAT

OVERVIEW

Diplomats are public servants appointed to represent their home nation to other countries. They have many responsibilities, including negotiating treaties, gathering and reporting information, issuing visas, protecting their citizens overseas, and influencing other nations in regard to various issues, such as war and peace, economics, the environment, and human rights. Whatever the job, the diplomat should always represent the interests and policies of their home country.

While diplomats may remain in their home nation, they most often are posted to an embassy in another region. Many assignments are short-term, lasting two to four years, after which time the diplomat will be reassigned to a new country. Newbies are required to do consular work and can move up to other more desirable postings and assignments once they've gained some experience.

There are different kinds of diplomats. The names and responsibilities vary between countries and can include any of the following, ranked by seniority: ambassador, chargé d'affairs, envoy, counsel, and attaché.

NECESSARY TRAINING

Each country's requirements are different, but as an example, someone wanting to become a diplomat in the US must be an American citizen between the ages of 20 and 59. They must take a written aptitude test and go through a rigorous interview process to determine their suitability for the job. Following a successful background check, the applicant will enter the Foreign Service Institute for training that can last up to nine months.

Candidates must understand up front that they will be posted where they're needed rather than where they might want to go. In some of the more dangerous postings, the diplomat's family may not be allowed to accompany them.

USEFUL SKILLS, TALENTS, OR ABILITIES

Charm, empathy, equanimity, exceptional memory, gaining the trust of others, good listening skills, haggling, hospitality, leadership, making friends, mentalism, multilingualism, networking, out-of-the-box thinking, peacekeeping, promotion, public speaking, reading people, strategic thinking, writing

HELPFUL CHARACTER TRAITS

Adaptable, adventurous, ambitious, analytical, appreciative, bold, calm, charming, confident, cooperative, courteous, decisive, diplomatic, discreet, empathetic, enthusiastic, evasive, extroverted, honorable, hospitable, intelligent, manipulative, meticulous, nosy, organized, passionate, patient, patriotic, perfectionist, persistent, persuasive, proactive, protective, socially aware, sophisticated, suspicious, tolerant, wise

SOURCES OF FRICTION

Making a mistake in a meeting due to not being properly informed of current events or cultural norms

An attack on the diplomat's embassy

Language barriers that make communication difficult

Officials from the hosting country who are inflexible and uncooperative

A diplomat being assigned to a posting where their family can't accompany them

Complicated political friction which must be handled carefully

Being reassigned and having to leave a beloved place and close friends behind

The diplomat's children having difficulty adjusting to frequent moves

Family members struggling with culture shock after a move

Failing in a negotiation

Being threatened with or targeted for assassination

Getting caught in a civil uprising or war

Homesickness

PEOPLE THEY MIGHT INTERACT WITH

Ambassadors, envoys, attachés, foreign diplomats, reporters, translators, government officials and heads of state

HOW THIS OCCUPATION MIGHT IMPACT THE CHARACTER'S NEEDS

Self-Actualization: Anyone working in politics is subject to the whims of those in charge. A diplomat may work very hard to achieve their given objectives on an assignment only to learn they've been used as part of a political scheme. Getting burned too many times in this way could leave them jaded and disillusioned.

Esteem and Recognition: There's a clear diplomatic ranking in most countries. Someone at the bottom of the ladder who has trouble working their way up may become discouraged by the lack of respect for their position.

Love and Belonging: A diplomat must be flexible, going where he's sent and changing countries frequently. This can cause friction within the family unit.

Safety and Security: Diplomats are often needed in places defined by unrest and instability. These circumstances can make such assignments dangerous.

Physiological Needs: Should a country's situation devolve into violence, the residing diplomat's life could easily be threatened.

CHARACTERS MIGHT CHOOSE THIS PROFESSION BECAUSE THEY...

Grew up in a political family

Wanted to escape an undesirable home life

Love to travel and explore other cultures

Have a knack for hospitality, persuasive speaking, and gaining the trust of others

Want to promote peace and improve living conditions around the world

Are seeking to avoid intimate relationships via a job that requires frequent relocation

Need information about a certain country, situation, or government official

DOCENT

OVERVIEW
A docent educates visitors at museums and similar institutions by providing tours, giving demonstrations, and hosting other activities. They are trained to share information about the exhibits, collections, and individual items specific to that establishment and may also participate in research projects for the facility. Though docents are often volunteers, there are many paid positions in this field.

NECESSARY TRAINING
Though no formal education is required, many institutions prefer their docents to have a high school diploma or equivalent. Teaching experience is beneficial but not mandatory. Docents are usually expected to complete training provided by the establishment before starting the position.

USEFUL SKILLS, TALENTS, OR ABILITIES
Detail-oriented, hospitality, making people laugh, performing, photographic memory, public speaking, reading people, research, stamina, teaching

HELPFUL CHARACTER TRAITS
Confident, courteous, curious, efficient, enthusiastic, flamboyant, focused, friendly, funny, honest, inspirational, melodramatic, objective, organized, passionate, persuasive, socially aware, studious, tolerant, uninhibited, witty

SOURCES OF FRICTION
Visitors who don't want to comply with the rules
Curators and co-workers who look down on the docent's position
Working for a disorganized institution
Working in an establishment that presents biased information
Scheduling conflicts that result in too-large groups
Not being trained properly for the position
Broken or out-of-order exhibits
Construction to the museum or surrounding areas
Accidentally breaking an artifact
Leading a rowdy group of visitors
Not knowing the answers to a guest's questions
Giving a tour to bored or distracted guests
The character losing their voice or having a sore throat
Visitors with language or cultural barriers
Disruptions or noises that impede presentations
Lacking an adequate wardrobe for the position
Visitors who litter or don't treat the exhibits with respect
Having to answer the same questions over and over
Dealing with people who ask soapbox questions that have nothing to do with the exhibit: *Do*

you agree the men of this era were completely misogynistic?
Being assigned to undesirable groups or parts of the museum
Being physically handicapped and working in a facility that isn't up to code
Leading a tour for a school field trip where the parents are inattentive or chatting loudly
A guest in the docent's group deliberately or inadvertently wandering off
Being ill-prepared and running out of things to share with a group
Having to work a long shift and walk all day while sick

PEOPLE THEY MIGHT INTERACT WITH

Visitors, curators, archivists, conservators, teachers and lecturers, students, exhibit designers, historians, museum educators, security officers, preparators, public relations officers, registrars

HOW THIS OCCUPATION MIGHT IMPACT THE CHARACTER'S NEEDS

Self-Actualization: Characters who like variety in their day and dislike following guidelines and routines might begin to feel stifled in this career.

Esteem and Recognition: Recognition and praise in this industry is sparse, so a docent who depends on either may find this need going unfulfilled.

TWISTING THE FICTIONAL STEREOTYPE

People in this position are often depicted as elderly retirees. Instead, brainstorm unusual choices for a part-time docent, such as a college student who is passionate about history or a stay-at-home dad who gives tours while the kids are at school.

Another misconception is that docents spend their time immersed in history and are out-of-touch with current events. Consider someone who is as passionate about the modern world as they are with the past. Maybe they find ways to weave today's headlines into their presentations as cautionary tales or to reinforce historical events.

CHARACTERS MIGHT CHOOSE THIS PROFESSION BECAUSE THEY...

Saw a posting for the position at a local museum and decided to apply
Have great communication skills and like leading activities
Are studying in a related field and the job provides experience
Want to create a welcoming atmosphere for visitors
Have fond memories as a child of museums and want others to have good experiences, too
Feel accomplished and successful when they can tell others what they know
Feel obligated to correct misinformation about historical events
Want to contribute to and connect with their community
Are passionate about a certain culture or historical period and want to share their knowledge with others

DOG GROOMER

OVERVIEW

Dog groomers maintain a canine's physical appearance using various shears, trimmers, scissors, brushes, shampoos, and other products. They will wash, dry, cut, and shape a dog's coat to the specifications of the owner. Other grooming duties include trimming nails, brushing their teeth, cleaning their ears, and looking for illnesses or problems such as swellings, sores, thrush, ticks, or other parasites. Some groomers may offer additional services such as fur dying and designer cuts.

Groomers typically work at shelters, kennels, pet stores, in a mobile unit, or out of their own homes. Some may also practice out of a larger veterinary clinic that serves many pet owners.

NECESSARY TRAINING

Most groomers will need a high school diploma to work in this field. In addition to on-the-job training and mentoring, employers may also require a certification from a recognized grooming school or post-secondary school apprenticeship program.

USEFUL SKILLS, TALENTS, OR ABILITIES

A knack for making money, a way with animals, basic first aid, charm, empathy, enhanced hearing, enhanced sense of smell, exceptional memory, gaining the trust of others, multitasking

HELPFUL CHARACTER TRAITS

Adaptable, affectionate, calm, centered, charming, easygoing, efficient, empathetic, focused, friendly, fussy, gentle, industrious, nurturing, observant, professional, responsible, stubborn, talented, thrifty, tolerant, workaholic

SOURCES OF FRICTION

Developing an allergy to dogs or grooming products
A fellow groomer suddenly quitting, leaving the character with too many clients to handle
Demanding pet owners (who expect perfection, request difficult cuts, etc.)
Dogs that are unsocial and difficult to work with
Animals with a history of abuse that bite and scratch
Dog owners who refuse to provide paperwork to prove up-to-date vaccinations
A dog getting loose and taking off when a gate is left open
Dog owners who are cheap and complain at the price or don't tip
Accidentally causing an injury
Discovering animal abuse and having to report it
Trying to pay the bills with a dog groomer's salary
A dog having an allergic reaction to a product
A pet owner not disclosing a condition or allergy
Pet owners requesting a full shave when it is not needed, or it is dangerous to give one
Pet owners who show up too early or too late
Wanting to be creative with cuts but having to follow strict guidelines

Having to complete other duties on the job that are boring or unpleasant (stocking shelves, cleaning bathrooms, etc.)

PEOPLE THEY MIGHT INTERACT WITH
Dog owners, pet sitters, pet store employees or veterinarian staff (if located within a pet store or vet clinic), other groomers, delivery people

HOW THIS OCCUPATION MIGHT IMPACT THE CHARACTER'S NEEDS
Esteem and Recognition: Characters in this job may feel they are not being valued by others, since some customers only see the price tag and don't appreciate the time and energy that goes into caring for their pet.

Love and Belonging: In some cases, groomers can be overloaded with appointments, and the long hours and tiring work can leave little energy for loved ones, causing resentment.

Safety and Security: This job doesn't pay particularly well, making financial security hard to obtain unless other members of the household are also contributing.

TWISTING THE FICTIONAL STEREOTYPE
Anyone involved with animals tends to be portrayed as nurturing, kind-hearted, and maybe a little quirky. But what about a surly or anti-social dog-groomer who chose the job because of a social or mental difficulty? An overwhelmed one who is so focused on their own problems that they have no extra time or effort to share with even a dog? Or a cruel character who might have chosen the profession for nefarious reasons? Occupations can be useful for characterizing, hinting at backstory, and defining motivation, so utilize this information to avoid stereotypes.

CHARACTERS MIGHT CHOOSE THIS PROFESSION BECAUSE THEY...
Love animals, especially dogs
Find animals easier to read and be around than people (due to negative past experiences)
Mistrust people and find it easier to bond with dogs (who are inherently trusting)
Want to move past a trauma involving animals—e.g., a fear of dogs induced by being bitten
Want to be able to notice abuse and do something about it
Are suffering or grieving and find comfort from animals
Can no longer practice as a vet or trainer, and this job provides the access to animals that the character craves

DREAM INTERPRETER

OVERVIEW

A dream interpreter analyzes and interprets their clients' dreams to extract possible meanings. The information they glean might be used to help their clients with self-growth and development. Other times, it can offer a window to the past, with the interpreter focusing on symbolism and contextual clues to unveil the client's buried feelings, emotional trauma, and resulting mental health concerns.

Dream interpreters may work in a private practice, out of a commercial office, or their personal residence. They might also work online, interpreting dreams via chat or video.

NECESSARY TRAINING

No formal training is required for this career, though courses on dream interpretation can be taken. Psychologists who use dream therapy in their practices will have pursued coursework in this specialized area.

USEFUL SKILLS, TALENTS, OR ABILITIES

Clairvoyance, empathy, gaining the trust of others, good listening skills, hospitality, intuition, out-of-the-box thinking, promotion, reading people, research

HELPFUL CHARACTER TRAITS

Analytical, confident, courteous, curious, discreet, easygoing, empathetic, friendly, gentle, hospitable, inspirational, observant, perceptive, persuasive, philosophical, professional, supportive, tolerant, uninhibited, wise

SOURCES OF FRICTION

Clients who are skeptical about dream interpretation
Being frequently pestered by a needy client
Friends or family members who don't support the character's career path
Getting conflicting or confusing information from a client's dreams
Failing to get enough clients
Clients who don't pay on time
Not being able to provide answers for a client
Overthinking dreams to the point of obsession or exhaustion
Giving an interpretation that turns out to be false or causes a client to make a poor decision
Negative reviews leading to bad PR
Not having a consistent source of income
Being viewed as shady or as someone who is only out to make money
Working from home and having clients who know where the character lives
Inconsistent work hours
Clients with unrealistic expectations
Lack of support from the scientific community
Living in a traditional or small town where the character's career isn't accepted or respected
The interpreter finding something disturbing in their own dreams

PEOPLE THEY MIGHT INTERACT WITH

Clients, friends or family members of clients, psychologists, other counselors or therapists working with a client

HOW THIS OCCUPATION MIGHT IMPACT THE CHARACTER'S NEEDS

Self-Actualization: As with many careers in the health field, a character with this job very likely has a desire to help others. But if their clients are resistant or won't take advice to make positive change, an interpreter may begin to feel that they're wasting their time.

Esteem and Recognition: Many people view this field with skepticism and even scorn. A character seeking esteem or recognition in their career will soon find themselves lacking in this department.

Love and Belonging: A dream interpreter in a small town with largely traditional perspectives may find it difficult to connect with others.

TWISTING THE FICTIONAL STEREOTYPE

Dream interpreters are often seen as eccentrics who believe in the supernatural and other controversial subjects. To combat this, create a character who is very down-to-earth and rooted in facts. If they're part of the scientific community, that could make for an even more interesting twist.

Another stereotype is that dream interpreters are swindlers and are only in it to make a quick buck. Skeptics with this viewpoint might also believe that dream interpreters don't really care about their clients and are only putting on a show or telling them what they want to hear. Consider a character who is passionate about interpreting dreams and has a very caring nature towards others, perhaps even following up on their clients on a regular basis out of concern for their well-being.

CHARACTERS MIGHT CHOOSE THIS PROFESSION BECAUSE THEY...

Had a supernatural or otherworldly experience growing up
Were gifted with a special ability to interpret dreams
Are interested in how people's minds work
Are fascinated by dreams and felt called to this career
Enjoy helping others get in touch with their emotions and needs
Want to open others' minds to alternate possibilities
Are extroverted and want to work with people
Want to control others and manipulate their choices
Have heeded warnings in their own dreams and it saved their life or helped them avoid hardship, and now they wish to do the same for others

DRIVER (CAR)

OVERVIEW
Drivers get people from one place to another, receiving payment that's based on the length of the trip. Typically, they're employed by a service and are assigned jobs either by a dispatcher or via an app. They may use their own vehicles or those owned by the company or employer. Personal drivers are often hired by corporations or wealthy individuals and are kept on retainer to drive people where they need to go.

NECESSARY TRAINING
Drivers must have a current license and many services require a certain amount of experience before hiring. Drivers with companies must have a background check, be fingerprinted, and purchase additional insurance. Drivers using their own cars may have to pass an inspection to ensure the vehicle is acceptable.

Hiring a freelance driver or ride sharing via an app have become common ways to get around but requirements and licenses are shifting with the times. If your character is a driver for these services, do your research to stay up to date.

USEFUL SKILLS, TALENTS, OR ABILITIES
A good sense of direction, defensive driving, enhanced hearing, exceptional memory, good listening skills, good sense of direction, hot-wiring a car, making people laugh, multilingualism, reading people, self-defense

HELPFUL CHARACTER TRAITS
Adaptable, alert, calm, confident, courteous, discreet, extroverted, focused, friendly, observant, patient, proactive, sensible, tolerant

SOURCES OF FRICTION
Getting traffic tickets that could threaten the character's employment as a driver
Getting into an accident
Picking up a dangerous customer
Getting stiffed on a fare
Having to drive someone the character finds morally reprehensible
Driving a passenger who wants to talk about touchy subjects, such as politics or religion
Being accused of inappropriateness by a passenger
Being accused of over-charging a customer for a fare
Getting lost
Getting caught overcharging a customer
Being late for a scheduled pick-up
Driving a passenger who is clearly ill or inebriated
A drunk passenger puking in the driver's car
Calling in sick or taking the day off and missing scheduled pick-ups
Being car-jacked
The car breaking down or becoming unreliable

Suspecting passengers of being involved in something illegal, such as drug smuggling

Recognizing a passenger as someone who is wanted by police

Believing that a passenger may be a victim (of abuse, trafficking, etc.)

A deteriorating ailment that makes the job difficult (failing eyesight, a back injury, etc.)

A slow shift that results in boredom

Passengers who are rude, abusive, and hurl racial slurs

A security camera malfunction that fails to capture important events (evidence of a passenger's violence, robbing the driver, a hostage situation, etc.)

PEOPLE THEY MIGHT INTERACT WITH

Customers, a dispatcher, other drivers employed by the same service, a manager, police officers, mechanics, car-detailing employees

HOW THIS OCCUPATION MIGHT IMPACT THE CHARACTER'S NEEDS

Self-Actualization: A commercial drive with higher aspirations may eventually grow dissatisfied with their current occupation.

Esteem and Recognition: If a driver is looked down upon or treated as inferior by his passengers, he may begin to feel badly about himself and his chosen profession.

Safety and Security: A driver may be highly skilled, but there are always idiots on the road who could endanger their safety.

Physiological Needs: Risk is inherent when picking up strangers, and drivers have been known to fall victim to unstable or violent customers.

TWISTING THE FICTIONAL STEREOTYPE

Being a professional driver gives one access to people and places denied to others. For what nefarious reasons might your character have chosen this career?

Keep in mind that with the growth of driving services like Lyft and Uber, the model has changed. Drivers may be employed full-time or only when it's convenient for them. They may even only drive to places they're going themselves, such as when they're going to or from work in an urban area. Many options are available now in this field, making this a versatile career choice.

CHARACTERS MIGHT CHOOSE THIS PROFESSION BECAUSE THEY...

Like people and enjoy the interactions with others

Have certain limitations (such as illiteracy) that make other jobs impossible

Need a way to transport secret cargo (guns, drugs, damaging correspondence, etc.)

Require a flexible schedule that works around the kids' school activities, another job, etc.

Want to serve others in a practical way

Have a physical disability that makes it difficult to stand for long periods of time

Have lived all their life in the area and are intimately familiar with it

Love the sense of freedom and independence that comes with driving

EMERGENCY DISPATCHER

OVERVIEW
When someone calls 911 during an emergency, the first point of contact is the dispatcher. This person takes calls, gathers vital information, offers medical advice when necessary (such as how to perform CPR), passes the information along to the correct agencies (police, ambulances, fire department, etc.), and records the information into a database so it's available to all parties. While the job requirements are fairly technical, this position requires a lot of finesse, since the dispatcher will need to remain calm and think clearly in high pressure, life-or-death circumstances. Turnover is high in this field due to its stressful nature.

NECESSARY TRAINING
A high school diploma or GED is needed for this position. On-the-job training and extensive classroom instruction will also be necessary for new dispatchers.

USEFUL SKILLS, TALENTS, OR ABILITIES
Basic first aid, enhanced hearing, equanimity, exceptional memory, gaining the trust of others, good listening skills, knowledge of explosives, multilingualism, multitasking, peacekeeping, predicting the weather, reading people

HELPFUL CHARACTER TRAITS
Analytical, calm, centered, cooperative, courteous, decisive, discreet, efficient, empathetic, focused, kind, objective, organized, patient, perceptive, perfectionist, persuasive, proactive, professional, pushy, sensible, supportive, wise

SOURCES OF FRICTION
The dispatcher becoming emotional about a case while they're working it
Taking out workplace stress on people at home
Technical difficulties or machinery malfunctions
Hysterical callers who can't be reasoned with
Making a mistake that results in someone's death or injury
Freezing up at a critical moment
A new dispatcher taking a call that they aren't qualified or trained to handle
Receiving a call from someone the dispatcher knows
Taking a call about a large-scale emergency that has many moving pieces
Someone needing help immediately but emergency services are delayed
Something traumatic happening during the call (a death, kidnapping, abuse, etc.)
Turning off feelings at work and having difficulty turning them on again after hours
Budget cuts that result in old or faulty equipment, lack of training, etc.
Being criticized or blamed when a call goes bad
Conflicts of interest (if a loved one is a first responder with a certain team, etc.)
Physical discomfort from sitting and looking at a computer screen for long hours
Increased worry or anxiety for loved ones due to being exposed to daily traumas
Being short-staffed

An equipment malfunction that makes it difficult to hear a caller or be heard by them

Fielding a lot of difficult calls in a short period of time

Having to stay on a call longer than normal in a difficult situation (because first responders are delayed by traffic, police are having trouble entering the building, etc.)

PEOPLE THEY MIGHT INTERACT WITH

People in crisis, other dispatchers, supervisors, first responders

HOW THIS OCCUPATION MIGHT IMPACT THE CHARACTER'S NEEDS

Esteem and Recognition: The stakes don't get higher than they do in this occupation. One mistake, memory lapse, or moment of paralysis can cost someone their life. If something does go south, it can make a dispatcher question their decisions and abilities, which may further impact their ability to function well at work.

Love and Belonging: An emergency dispatcher has a front row seat to the worst moments of someone's life, which can make them fearful of loved ones and what *might* happen. If the character becomes overly controlling, those closest to them may revolt.

Safety and Security: The situations a dispatcher encounters can become traumatizing over time. After prolonged exposure to crime, victimization, and violence, dispatchers may become paralyzed, struggling to feel safe under any circumstance.

TWISTING THE FICTIONAL STEREOTYPE

There tend to be more female dispatchers, so consider this occupation for your male characters.

This job will expose the character to a range of traumas, and odds are at some point, your character will be triggered and make an association to something from their own past. How this might play out could add interesting layers to the story, especially if the dispatcher has something significant in common with the caller.

CHARACTERS MIGHT CHOOSE THIS PROFESSION BECAUSE THEY...

Had a loved one whose life was saved by emergency personnel

Once called 911 in a time of great need and want to pay it forward

Have a powerful desire to help others in times of need

Believe they have a moral obligation to help others

Want to serve others but have a handicap or condition that requires a desk job

Have excellent communication skills and an ability to calm people down in difficult moments

Are haunted by a past failure that drives them to save others to try and make up for it

Come from a family of first responders

Are persuasive and unflappable under pressure

EMERGENCY MEDICAL RESPONDER

OVERVIEW
Emergency Medical Responders (also called EMTs, medics, and paramedics in various parts of the world) are some of the first people on-site in an emergency situation. Alongside other first responders, they provide aid in the aftermath of vehicle and worksite accidents, personal assaults, neglect cases, health-related emergencies (like a heart attack, stroke, or seizure), and other scenarios where people require medical attention. After assessing and treating patients with urgent and often life-threatening needs, they transport them to an appropriate medical facility. Upon arrival, EMRs advise emergency room personnel about the patient's condition.

NECESSARY TRAINING
In most places, EMRs must be at least 18 years old with a high school degree and no criminal record. There are three levels of certification that a person in this field can receive: basic, intermediate, and paramedic.

The basic course teaches general life support treatments along with many non-invasive procedures (such as CPR and splinting a broken bone). An intermediate certification is more complex, allowing EMRs to intubate and insert IVs. The highest level EMRs are paramedics. Their certification allows them to administer medication (in some states), clean wounds, and read X-rays or lab results. EMRs must complete this two-year course and an internship in a hospital or ambulance to become certified at this level.

USEFUL SKILLS, TALENTS, OR ABILITIES
Basic first aid, defensive driving, detail-oriented, dexterity, empathy, equanimity, gaining the trust of others, leadership, lip-reading, multilingualism, multitasking, organization, peacekeeping, research, self-defense, strategic thinking, strength, teaching

HELPFUL CHARACTER TRAITS
Analytical, calm, cautious, confrontational, cooperative, decisive, efficient, meticulous, nurturing, objective, observant, protective, resourceful, responsible, studious, unselfish

SOURCES OF FRICTION
Large patients who are difficult to lift
Combative or uncooperative family members of the patient
An important piece of equipment breaking when it's needed most
Language barriers
Being sued
A traffic jam or accident that causes delays
Bad weather that could impede driving or arrival time
Responding to a call in a high-crime area
Remaining stationary in an awkward position for a long period of time
Having limited opportunities to sit and rest
Continuously dealing with emotionally taxing situations
Medical staff who do not appreciate the EMR's skills

Working long shifts
Dealing with mass trauma or life-threatening situations
Working on a patient with a contagious disease
Having to work holidays and weekends
Remaining calm in chaotic or high-pressure situations
Caring for someone that isn't going to make it
Difficult cases involving children

PEOPLE THEY MIGHT INTERACT WITH
Patients, doctors, paramedics, other EMTs and first responders, 911 operators, family members or friends of those being treated, nurses, other medical staff

HOW THIS OCCUPATION MIGHT IMPACT THE CHARACTER'S NEEDS
Self-Actualization: An empathetic EMR who wants to improve the lives of others may become frustrated from repeatedly encountering the same situations—sometimes with the same patients. They may grow jaded and wonder if they're making a difference at all.

Esteem and Recognition: EMRs work in high-risk, fast-paced emergency situations where quick thinking and decision-making are a must. Mistakes are a part of any job, but the expectations are higher for people in this field. Criticism, along with internal blame that the character puts on him or herself, can lower self-esteem.

Love and Belonging: Long hours and shiftwork over nights, holidays, and weekends can put a strain on an EMR's personal relationships.

Safety and Security: EMRs go wherever they're needed, including violent and hazardous environments, and so are frequently at risk.

Physiological Needs: This is a dangerous field with multiple risk factors that can take the life of a first responder.

TWISTING THE FICTIONAL STEREOTYPE
As this is a male-dominant field, a female EMR can offer a fresh perspective. But take it a step further and make sure your character is unique and unexpected. Instead of the tough-as-nails female first responder, what about one who is highly empathetic and in touch with her emotions? Maybe she's petite or slight of build while still being able to meet the physical criteria for the job. Think carefully about all the aspects of your character and you can help combat misconceptions in any career field.

CHARACTERS MIGHT CHOOSE THIS PROFESSION BECAUSE THEY...
Lost a loved one who could have been saved if help had arrived sooner
Are great with people and handle emergencies well
Have family members who are first responders
Have a God complex and get off on having a role in the life and death of others

EMERGENCY ROOM PHYSICIAN

OVERVIEW
An emergency room physician is a doctor trained in trauma who assesses and stabilizes patients admitted to the ER. Different from a trauma surgeon, an ER physician will order lab tests and x-rays (and interpret the results), administer medication, and deal with a large variety of injuries and illnesses. They may do basic emergency surgery in crisis situations, but with a focus on stabilization so other specialists can then take over. They carry out or oversee life-saving procedures, set broken bones, attend to lacerations, and refer patients to appropriate medical departments for further treatment (or discharge them as needed). ER Physicians must also keep accurate records of all treatment, tests, and medicines to ensure correct insurance reimbursement (if applicable).

NECESSARY TRAINING
Medical programming for this profession covers theory, labs, and clinical rotations at the undergraduate and graduate level that results in an MD degree. These doctors then enter into a program for emergency medicine to become board certified. It can run thirty-six months in length and includes clinical rotations, training in trauma care, radiology, orthopedics, patient care, emergency room procedures, resuscitation, and pediatric critical care. ER Physicians must be state licensed. If you are writing about an ER physician in a real-world location, research the qualifications and duties for that area, since this can fluctuate.

USEFUL SKILLS, TALENTS, OR ABILITIES
Basic first aid, charm, equanimity, exceptional memory, gaining the trust of others, good listening skills, leadership, multilingualism, multitasking, photographic memory, physical stamina, reading people, research, sewing, strategic thinking

HELPFUL CHARACTER TRAITS
Adaptable, analytical, confident, decisive, disciplined, focused, intelligent, manipulative, meticulous, nosy, observant, patient, persistent, proactive, professional, studious, wise

SOURCES OF FRICTION
A large-scale crisis with not enough resources and staff to handle it
Patients who are violent or unpredictable
Patients who are untruthful about their medical history
Long hours and exhaustion causing burnout
Hospital politics getting in the way of patient care
Uninsured patients and moral dilemmas
A staff shortage due to illness
Office romances and bad judgment
Misdiagnoses, mislabeled medicines, or errors on charts that lead to medical crises
A staff member who is an angel of death
Reporters or fans trying to gain access to a celebrity or high-profile criminal patient
Family drama, arguments in the waiting room

Grieving family members suing for a wrongful death
Developing PTSD and trying to hide it, self-medicating to cope
Having to treat a friend or family member in crisis
Sending someone home who later dies
Disagreements with co-workers regarding how an incident or procedure was handled
Medicines, equipment, or supplies being stolen
Diseases or viruses unknowingly being passed from patient to doctor or between patients

PEOPLE THEY MIGHT INTERACT WITH

Other doctors, surgeons, nurses, support staff, police and detectives, paramedics, family members, insurance representatives, security personnel, pharmacy and medical company reps, delivery people, hospital board members and employees

HOW THIS OCCUPATION MIGHT IMPACT THE CHARACTER'S NEEDS

Self-Actualization: A character choosing this career for the wrong reason (such as to make family members proud or be highly esteemed in the community) may experience regret later in life for pursuing an unworthy motivation.

Esteem and Recognition: A lawsuit or accusation could damage the character's reputation with their peers and the community. Age, the onset of an illness, or another factor could also weaken their skills, leading to self-esteem issues as the character wonders if they're still able to do their job well.

Love and Belonging: Relationships almost always take a backseat in this career.

Safety and Security: There are many possible threats to an ER doctor's personal safety and job security: violent patients, grieving family members seeking revenge, a questionable diagnosis, and lawsuits, to name just a few.

Physiological Needs: Exposure to contagions, along with stress, lack of sleep, and other factors, can cause serious repercussions to an ER physician's health.

TWISTING THE FICTIONAL STEREOTYPE

ER physicians are often the perfect ideal on steroids—intelligent, fit, the best of the best. Why not choose an ER doctor that has a disability or disfigurement that makes them exceptional instead of holding them back?

CHARACTERS MIGHT CHOOSE THIS PROFESSION BECAUSE THEY...

Lost a loved one when a sub-par or incompetent doctor failed to save them
Believe that their calling is to save lives
Feel energized by the idea of playing God
Have a strong interest in the human body and how it works
Are following in the footsteps of others (e.g., having generations of doctors in the family)
Feel a sense of duty or obligation—e.g., they promised a parent to pursue this path in exchange for something they greatly desired
Want to be loved and accepted by a parent who only offers conditional love

ETHICAL HACKER

OVERVIEW

Ethical hackers are professionals employed to deliberately break into a customer's network or system to determine security vulnerabilities and offer solutions. Also called "white hat hackers," they apply the same techniques and methods that malicious hackers use, but with good intent, seeking to shore up potential issues to keep the bad guys out. They may work as independent contractors or be part of a security firm.

NECESSARY TRAINING

Training requirements vary from job to job. Because of the security risks, many employers require that their hackers have a bachelor's degree in computer science or another related field. They also may need to be certified in one of the main IT security certifications.

While it's possible to become an ethical hacker without any formal training, getting hired can be difficult. This occupation is legit and in demand, but many people are suspicious, believing that people in this field are simply bad hackers turned good. For an employer to put their company's security into the hands of a stranger, they must be able to trust that person. Many times, a degree or certification (as well as legitimate references) can be enough to convince them.

USEFUL SKILLS, TALENTS, OR ABILITIES

Computer hacking, creativity, detail-oriented, gaining the trust of others, multitasking, out-of-the-box thinking, photographic memory, research

HELPFUL CHARACTER TRAITS

Addictive, adventurous, analytical, centered, confrontational, curious, devious, discreet, egotistical, independent, intelligent, manipulative, meticulous, mischievous, observant, paranoid, perfectionist, persistent, proactive, professional, rebellious, resourceful, responsible, studious, suspicious, unethical, uninhibited

SOURCES OF FRICTION

Missing a vulnerability within a client's system that is then exploited
Being blamed for a breach in a recent client's system
The character's system being hacked, threatening their credibility
Getting caught using unethical procedures on a job
Unknowingly letting a certification lapse
Nefarious people from the past making it hard for the hacker to "stay clean and fly straight"
Word getting out about the character's illegitimate hacking activities from the past
Being blackmailed
Complications arising from the character's illegitimate hacking activities on the side
Lack of respect from loved ones who don't understand the hacker's job
Not being trusted by others (because of the inherent prejudice about the industry)
Conflict with the client's IT security team over proposed solutions

Excelling at the job but struggling with the social part (having to communicate with clients, lead meetings, engage with security teams, etc.)

PEOPLE THEY MIGHT INTERACT WITH

Clients, online certification instructors and administrators, people working for or with the client (employees, contractors, past employees, etc.)

HOW THIS OCCUPATION MIGHT IMPACT THE CHARACTER'S NEEDS

Esteem and Recognition: Ethical hackers can receive criticism from many quarters. Black hat hackers could see them as sell-outs and cowards while legitimate professionals may have a hard time trusting them. If unethical hacking is a part of their past, family members and loved ones may continue to be suspicious. If any of these dysfunctional dynamics come into play, it can impact the character's esteem.

Safety and Security: A hacker's safety may be threatened if they discover vulnerabilities in a system that a nefarious creator wants to stay hidden. This need could also be impacted if the hacker fails to protect a public system, resulting in the general population or an important grid (traffic, electricity, food distribution, etc.) being exposed.

TWISTING THE FICTIONAL STEREOTYPE

When people think of the typical hacker (even an ethical one), they picture a twenty-something male working out of his basement. Give readers a pleasant surprise by considering alternative genders, ages, and locations. How about a semi-retired grandfather working out of his assisted living facility? A stay-at-home mom who works in her she-shed during school hours? A part-time pastor or priest doing ethical hacking as a way to supplement his income?

There's also a common perception that ethical hackers weren't always ethical. Keep in mind that your character can have a squeaky-clean past and be good at this job.

CHARACTERS MIGHT CHOOSE THIS PROFESSION BECAUSE THEY...

Were scarred by a past run-in with a cyber-criminal (their identity was stolen, credit cards were scraped, etc.)
Have an affinity for computers and coding
Have control issues caused by a wound where their power or autonomy were stripped away
Get a rush from controlling others
Are highly ethical and want to protect people from theft and abuse
Want something good to come from their checkered past (turning lemons into lemonade)

FARMER

OVERVIEW
A farmer plants, grows, and harvests crops or breeds and raises animals, most often for food consumption.

NECESSARY TRAINING
Farmers don't require a formal education, but experience will help them succeed. Those who grow crops must become subject matter experts in exact types, be it grains, vegetables, berries, fruit, nuts, or seeds. They should know what each crop needs and where it will grow best and be able to fight off pests and disease. Crops will also need to be harvested and stored or sold and transported. With so many links in the food production chain, a lot can go wrong if the details aren't handled correctly.

A farmer who raises livestock must understand animal husbandry, maintain a healthy environment, provide proper nutrition and care, follow industry safety and health standards, and be able to pass livestock inspections. Once the animals are ready to be sold, the farmer must make the necessary arrangements, including transportation.

Farming is a business, meaning farmers also have to manage accounts, pay bills, oversee workers, address rotating debts (if applicable), balance books, purchase and repair equipment and other supplies, maintain buildings and property, and arrange for the product to reach markets. Margins are tight, the market fluctuates, and weather, policy, and pricing will always influence a farmer's bottom line.

USEFUL SKILLS, TALENTS, OR ABILITIES
A knack for making money, a way with animals, basic first aid, enhanced hearing, enhanced sense of smell, enhanced taste buds, exceptional memory, farming, gardening, good with numbers, haggling, mechanically inclined, multitasking, predicting the weather, repurposing, stamina, vision, woodworking

HELPFUL CHARACTER TRAITS
Adaptable, ambitious, analytical, calm, compulsive, disciplined, efficient, independent, industrious, know-it-all, meticulous, nature-focused, nurturing, observant, patient, proactive, resourceful, responsible, socially aware, thrifty, wholesome, workaholic, worrywart, wise

SOURCES OF FRICTION
An illness that decimates a crop or livestock
Climate change or extreme weather (early frosts, a long-lasting drought, flooding, etc.)
Mounting debt
Political policies and market shifts that make it difficult to get products to consumers
Pricing shifts
Market saturation
Wild animals attacking the farmer's livestock
An illness or injury that prevents the farmer from performing their duties
Too much work and not enough time

Pressure to change crops to better fit the market's needs

A blight that decimates a crop or herd

A lack of support from the government

Being over-taxed and over-regulated

Friction within the family if a member wants to trade a country life for a city one

Equipment breakdowns happening at the worst time

Family members disagreeing about the trajectory of the business

Moral conflicts regarding farming methods (knowing factory farming increases profit but also feeling that giving them less space to live or restricting their movement isn't right)

Teenage children who are unhappy with the rural lifestyle

Difficulty finding reliable and trustworthy farmhands

Being tied to the property and their responsibilities, limiting freedom

PEOPLE THEY MIGHT INTERACT WITH

Other farmers, neighbors, mechanics, suppliers, customers, inspectors, veterinarians, family members, locals

HOW THIS OCCUPATION MIGHT IMPACT THE CHARACTER'S NEEDS

Self-Actualization: A character who loves living and working in the country may question their path amid a constant, wearying fight to stay afloat.

Love and Belonging: Conflict between family members on how to work the farm, how much debt to take on, what crops to invest in, etc. may strain relationships. Pressuring adult children to stay and choose the farming life when they wish for something else may also cause rifts that will be difficult to heal.

Physiological Needs: Debt is a huge struggle for farmers that often is caused by variables outside of their control. Should they lose that battle, it can leave them and their loved ones without the necessities needed to survive.

TWISTING THE FICTIONAL STEREOTYPE

By and large, these characters are portrayed as male, with females in this role occurring as part of a farming family. Maybe your character is the head of her operation—running it on her own or with the help of women in crisis. Perhaps she grows an unusual crop, such as lavender, Christmas trees, or marijuana. Consider a popular occupation from different perspectives to give it depth and interest.

CHARACTERS MIGHT CHOOSE THIS PROFESSION BECAUSE THEY...

Grew up in a family that farmed

Were expected to carry on the family business

Want to live in the country and be self-sufficient

Love nature and open spaces

Feel more connected to God when they're working the land

Love animals and livestock husbandry

Are worried about the condition of the food production industry and want to do something about it

Want to return to a more traditional and simple way of life

Are survivalists or doomsday preppers seeking to create a sustainable environment

FASHION DESIGNER

OVERVIEW

A fashion designer envisions and produces apparel. They are involved in every step of the process from imagining a concept to procuring the materials and assembling them into a cohesive design. The garments may then be sold to individuals or companies, including retailers and design firms.

While people often associate fashion design with clothing, there are many other possibilities. A designer may also create eyewear, footwear, or accessories. They might only design for a certain audience (such as men or children) or focus on a type of clothing, like swimsuits, business attire, or leisure wear. Often, they're known for creating pieces that have a certain aesthetic or because they utilize a specific type of fabric. Designers might work independently to build their own brand of apparel or work for another designer's label.

NECESSARY TRAINING

Though no formal training is required, having a bachelor's degree in fashion design or a related area is common. For someone establishing their own brand or line of clothing, training or experience in business or fashion merchandising is helpful. An independent designer will also need to have a basic understanding of running a business, promotion, and building a successful brand.

USEFUL SKILLS, TALENTS, OR ABILITIES

A knack for making money, creativity, detail-oriented, dexterity, good with numbers, multitasking, networking, organization, out-of-the-box thinking, promotion, reading people, repurposing, sales, sewing, vision

HELPFUL CHARACTER TRAITS

Adaptable, ambitious, creative, curious, disciplined, enthusiastic, flamboyant, focused, imaginative, independent, industrious, materialistic, melodramatic, meticulous, observant, organized, passionate, persistent, persuasive, pushy, quirky, resourceful, sensible, socially aware, spontaneous, spunky, studious, talented, uninhibited, whimsical

SOURCES OF FRICTION

Being away from family due to frequent traveling
Working long hours as deadlines approach
Having multiple deadlines close together
A lack of clientele
The character's design ideas being stolen or copied
A lack of funds for materials
Income that varies, making it hard to budget and plan
Harsh criticism about the character's designs
Struggling to build a good reputation and gain visibility
Nitpicky customers who are never satisfied
Family or friends who don't support the character's career choice

A lack of knowledge about the industry or the latest trends
Frequent disruptions to the character's schedule
An injury that limits mobility of the hands or fingers
High demands from a supervisor
Eyestrain from working in poor lighting
Not having the necessary tools for a job
Having to work in a cramped or cluttered space
Social anxiety when having to network or be introduced at a show

PEOPLE THEY MIGHT INTERACT WITH
Individual clients, lead project managers, assistants, other designers, pattern makers, seamstresses, fabric suppliers, manufacturers, retail employees, celebrities, fashion influencers, photographers, makeup artists, brand representatives, hair stylists, critics

HOW THIS OCCUPATION MIGHT IMPACT THE CHARACTER'S NEEDS
Self-Actualization: When faced with too many projects or long hours the character may burn out. If their creativity diminishes, it will steal joy from a career they felt called to.

Esteem and Recognition: In an industry where the character's work is always compared to others, it's easy to experience self-doubt and insecurity about their designs.

TWISTING THE FICTIONAL STEREOTYPE
One expectation of fashion designers is for them to be dressed pristinely or spectacularly all the time. To combat this stereotype, consider having a character who doesn't care what others think of their appearance or who prefers to wear plain clothing so as not to stand out.

In fictional settings, designers usually create clothes for women or high-fashion lines. To make things interesting, consider narrowing your designer's focus to something that isn't commonly portrayed, such as menswear, shoes, plus-sized clothing, or apparel made from a certain textile or process.

CHARACTERS MIGHT CHOOSE THIS PROFESSION BECAUSE THEY...
Were teased as a child for having secondhand or outdated clothing
Had a favorite aunt who worked in the industry as a model or fashion critic
Love fashion and following current trends
Are highly creative and work well under pressure
Enjoy working on a variety of projects that make every day different
Are on a mission to save people from horribly designed clothing
Like the solitary nature of the job
Want to be famous and get a rush at seeing others wears their designs
View clothing as an art medium

FIREFIGHTER

OVERVIEW
A firefighter is a rescuer who extinguishes and prevents fires that threaten life, property, and the environment. They also respond to car accidents, chemical spills, natural disasters, and engage in water rescues. Many firefighters are certified EMTs, administering first aid until paramedics arrive. They complete inspections, educate the public on preventing fires, and conduct investigations, particularly if arson is suspected. When they're not responding to an emergency, they work on call at a fire station, maintaining vehicles and tools, staying physically fit, conducting drills, and keeping up to date with industry changes. Because shifts can last 24-48 hours, they often eat and sleep at the station.

NECESSARY TRAINING
Firefighters need a high school diploma or equivalent. Some choose to complete a two-year degree in fire science, but it is not always a requirement. They receive training at a fire academy, where they must be interviewed and pass written, physical, and psychological tests.

USEFUL SKILLS, TALENTS, OR ABILITIES
Basic first aid, empathy, enhanced hearing, enhanced sense of smell, equanimity, high pain tolerance, knowledge of explosives, stamina, strength, strong breath control, swift-footedness

HELPFUL CHARACTER TRAITS
Adventurous, alert, analytical, bold, calm, cautious, compulsive, confident, confrontational, cooperative, courageous, decisive, disciplined, efficient, fanatical, focused, fussy, humorless, intelligent, objective, observant, persistent, protective, pushy, resourceful, responsible, sensible, unselfish

SOURCES OF FRICTION
Sustaining an injury due to someone's incompetence (a firefighter, volunteer, reckless member of the public, etc.)
A fellow firefighter dying in a fire
Strained personal relationships due to the inherent danger of the work
A challenging fire investigation
An accusation of misconduct or poor decision-making by higher ups who were not on scene
Long and unusual working hours, including 24-hour shifts, holidays, and weekends
Living in the firehouse with people who have clashing personalities
Private firefighting companies competing with traditional firefighters for jobs
Showing fear in front of other firefighters
Managing post-traumatic stress
Repeated exposure to trauma
The physical demands of carrying heavy gear or working in extreme temperatures
The weight of responsibility as a rescuer
Having to fight for government funding year after year
Losing someone in a fire and feeling responsible

PEOPLE THEY MIGHT INTERACT WITH
The fire chief, other firefighters (paid and volunteer), members of the public, police officers, paramedics, fire inspectors, fire investigators, public servants, reporters, psychologists, search and rescue training specialists

HOW THIS OCCUPATION MIGHT IMPACT THE CHARACTER'S NEEDS
Self-Actualization: In high-intensity situations, firefighters might struggle to problem solve. They may be faced with difficult moral decisions, such as saving one person over another. The lack of control in some situations may be hard to square with, especially if a firefighter is highly empathetic, and leave them wondering if this is the career for them.

Esteem and Recognition: Lives may be lost while a firefighter is on the job, resulting in guilt, shame, and possibly post-traumatic stress, all of which may lower self-worth.

Safety and Security: Firefighters work near traffic accidents, buildings with compromised structures, swift-moving water, and active fires, making this is an extremely dangerous profession.

Physiological Needs: Firefighters place their lives on the line in many of the situations they face, so this is a need that is definitely threatened on the job.

TWISTING THE FICTIONAL STEREOTYPE
Firefighters do more than serve the federal or local municipalities; they also work at ports, airports, for the armed services, and for chemical, nuclear, and gas and oil industries. Why not switch up your character's workplace to bring a fresh twist to the page?

Firefighting is an overwhelmingly male occupation. Consider crafting a female character who can meet the demanding physical, emotional, and mental requirements of the job.

The public inherently trusts firefighters. Keep this in mind and craft a character that defies stereotypes and surprises the reader.

CHARACTERS MIGHT CHOOSE THIS PROFESSION BECAUSE THEY...
Grew up with a family member in the same profession
Want to make up for a perceived past mistake where they failed to rescue someone
Desire to serve the public in a meaningful way
View camaraderie with other firefighters as a substitute for family
Are drawn to exciting activities and want a job that keeps them active
Want to channel their adrenaline-junkie tendencies into a healthy outlet
Are fascinated with fire

FLIGHT ATTENDANT

OVERVIEW
Flight attendants are employed by an airline as part of the cabin crew and ensure the safety and comfort of passengers. Before the flight, they attend a briefing given by the captain to go over safety issues, equipment usage, expected turbulence, and weather conditions. They review the passenger list, focusing on those with specific needs, such as children and VIPs. They also inspect the plane's safety equipment before take-off and must replace anything faulty.

Flight attendants assist passengers in boarding the plane and are trained to observe behavior that raises suspicion and suggests ill-intent. Before takeoff, they educate passengers on safety equipment and procedures and other protocol. During flight, attendants meet passengers' comfort needs by serving food and beverages and providing items such as pillows, blankets, and headphones. They remain alert for unusual noises or activity, including medical emergencies, and prepare the cabin for landing by collecting trash and reinforcing proper safety precautions. Once the plane lands, they assist passengers in deplaning.

NECESSARY TRAINING
Flight attendant training requirements vary by airline. Some require a high-school diploma or equivalent, while others require college coursework. Individual airlines typically train flight attendants for several weeks after they are hired, but there are schools for individuals who wish to pay for their own training before finding a job.

USEFUL SKILLS, TALENTS, OR ABILITIES
Basic first aid, charm, equanimity, exceptional memory, good balance, hospitality, lip reading, making people laugh, multilingualism, peacekeeping, reading people

HELPFUL CHARACTER TRAITS
Calm, courteous, diplomatic, disciplined, discreet, efficient, friendly, hospitable, observant, organized, patient, persuasive, professional, responsible, tolerant, wise

SOURCES OF FRICTION
Passengers who ignore safety guidelines
Passengers who are behaving suspiciously
Travel delays due to weather or plane maintenance
Strict employer guidelines for personal appearance
Passengers with oversized or awkward carry-ons
An irregular work schedule, including nights, weekends, and holidays
Being on call due to having less seniority than others
Difficult or disruptive passengers, such as inebriated individuals or children
Passengers who are fearful of flying or who have social anxiety
Turbulence
An in-flight medical emergency
Low pay
Exhaustion due to an erratic schedule

Friction between passengers (personal conflicts, bickering couples, racism or biases, etc.)

The onboard entertainment system malfunctioning

A delayed takeoff where passengers are not allowed to deplane

Sexual harassment on the job

People who have too much carryon and use up too much space in the overhead bins

An issue with a lavatory that puts it out of commission for the remainder of the flight

People congregating (in galleys, near the bathroom, in an aisle) when they were told not to

Unhygienic behavior: passengers clipping toenails, putting bare feet on a table tray, etc.

PEOPLE THEY MIGHT INTERACT WITH

Passengers, captains and co-captains, other flight attendants, airport staff (such as maintenance crew members and cleaners), law enforcement officials

HOW THIS OCCUPATION MIGHT IMPACT THE CHARACTER'S NEEDS

Esteem and Recognition: Flight attendants may be viewed by passengers as waitresses or waiters in the sky," since serving food and beverages are among their more visible duties. This minimizing viewpoint may steal the esteem of your character.

Love and Belonging: Irregular hours, frequent travel, and being on call make it hard for flight attendants to maintain relationships with friends, family, and romantic interests.

Safety and Security: If violence erupts in the cabin, your flight attendant must face it, and so may be at risk.

Physiological Needs: Due to irregular schedules and time-zone changes, flight attendants can experience sleep deprivation and exhaustion, impacting their health.

TWISTING THE FICTIONAL STEREOTYPE

Flight attendants are often portrayed as being calm and in control. Consider mixing things up by creating a character with an addiction, claustrophobia, or insomnia that challenges their ability to maintain a composed persona on the job.

We think of attendants as sociable and patient. Try giving your character a lack of interpersonal skills that poses a problem with difficult passengers and crew members.

CHARACTERS MIGHT CHOOSE THIS PROFESSION BECAUSE THEY...

Wanted to beat a fear of flying or work through a traumatic experience involving air travel

Enjoy travel and spontaneity

Dislike their homelife and want a way to keep family drama at a distance

Wishing to avoid personal commitments, "settling down" and confining relationships

Feel safer in the air than they do on the ground (due to certain phobias, a past trauma, a despair of society and people in general, etc.)

FOOD CRITIC

OVERVIEW
A food critic tests and reviews food for newspapers, magazines, or blogs. They offer their educated opinion about the taste, smell, composition, and presentation of food, as well as restaurant service and atmosphere. They generally prefer to remain anonymous to avoid being given special treatment that might compromise an authentic review.

NECESSARY TRAINING
Professional critics often have a bachelor's degree in journalism, English, or communication in order to effectively write about their experiences with food. Classes in food media, food reviewing, and culinary arts are available to further sharpen their skills. Work in this field is highly competitive. Internships and writing experience through newspapers, magazines, and blogs are desirable in order to build a resumé. Food critics might also choose to travel to gain a wide range of tasting experiences and better develop their culinary palate.

USEFUL SKILLS, TALENTS, OR ABILITIES
Enhanced sense of smell, enhanced taste buds, hospitality, teaching, writing

HELPFUL CHARACTER TRAITS
Analytical, courteous, curious, enthusiastic, extravagant, focused, fussy, imaginative, objective, observant, passionate, patient, professional, spontaneous, uninhibited, whimsical

SOURCES OF FRICTION
Being accused of nepotism (if the character has ties to a certain chef or restaurant)
The critic's boss pressuring him or her to give a favorable review of a restaurant
Struggling with job stability as a freelance critic
Being "outed" or recognized during the dining experience
Struggling to self-promote while remaining anonymous
Working within publishing deadlines
Being threatened for giving a bad review
Feeling guilt when a restaurant goes under after an unfavorable review
Offering unwanted culinary suggestions to friends or family
Loved ones requesting feedback on their own cooking (when they only want to hear how good it is)
Weight gain due to rich meals and wine
Taking along a distracting diner who somehow interferes with the meal
Receiving hate mail
Difficulty having an open mind about foods they don't like
Having to give a popular restaurant or chef a negative review
The critic's reviews being scrutinized and scorned by other critics
Personal issues (a recent break-up, physical pain, etc.) preventing a critic from fully engaging with the meal experience
Backing a restaurant that ends up being shut down by the health department

Suffering from writer's block

Being interrupted while dining (by an important call, people who recognize the critic, etc.)

Having impossibly high expectations, setting the bar out of range for everyone

Health issues that impact the job (a cold that blocks smell and taste, a toothache that makes chewing painful, etc.)

PEOPLE THEY MIGHT INTERACT WITH

Editors, chefs, restaurant wait staff, restaurant management, restaurant patrons, other critics

HOW THIS OCCUPATION MIGHT IMPACT THE CHARACTER'S NEEDS

Self-Actualization: It takes time to become popular and well-renowned in this field. In the beginning, a critic must climb the ladder, taking whatever jobs they can get. If they spend too much in this phase and are unable to break through to a higher tier of clientele, they may become frustrated with their accomplishments.

Esteem and Recognition: Food critics may feel pressure to dramatize reviews to satisfy their following. Becoming too negative or callous could damage a critic's reputation and cause their peers to look down on them.

Safety and Security: Food critics may have to pay for costly meals and transportation, particularly if they freelance, making finances tight at times.

TWISTING THE FICTIONAL STEREOTYPE

Food critics are thought of as having refined tastes and opinions the public inherently trusts. But perhaps your character is not all that they seem and fears being discovered as a fraud.

Critics in fiction and film are often portrayed as being snooty, judgmental, and impossible to please. Why not create an easygoing critic—a true food enthusiast who struggles with delivering criticism?

Food critics tend to eat widely, reviewing a wide variety of restaurants. But what about a critic who only critiques certain kinds of food, like exotic fare, Mediterranean dishes, or food truck cuisine?

CHARACTERS MIGHT CHOOSE THIS PROFESSION BECAUSE THEY...

Failed as a chef or restaurant owner and became a critic to remain part of the culinary world

Grew up with parents who were critical and had high expectations

Have a passion for food and writing

Love travel and new experiences, especially culinary ones

Desire to serve the public by drawing attention to good restaurants

Love cooking but lack the talent or drive to make it a primary career

Have a refined palate

Are an adventurous eater who enjoys trying new things

FOOD STYLIST

OVERVIEW
A food stylist prepares and arranges food for cookbooks, magazines, advertisements, movies, TV shows, and more. They strive to make food look as appealing and appetizing as possible by considering the color, texture, and shape of food, as well as how different cooking methods affect the final visual product. Some professional stylists will work with art directors and photographers to create an aesthetic vision while others (such as food bloggers) may do most or all of the work themselves, including designing the scene where the food will be set. Food stylists will typically cook the food they are working with and may use inedible products (such as plastic ice cubes, "incense" steam, or spray-on deodorant for extra shine) to get the desired visual effect.

NECESSARY TRAINING
Formal education is common among successful food stylists but is not required. Many attend culinary arts programs, though food styling itself is not often a degree. A strong portfolio and resumé are more important than training when finding work. They generally work as chefs and shadow working food stylists before finding their own success.

USEFUL SKILLS, TALENTS, OR ABILITIES
Baking, creativity, detail-oriented, dexterity, hospitality, networking, out-of-the-box thinking, promotion, sculpting, writing, vision

HELPFUL CHARACTER TRAITS
Adaptable, cooperative, creative, curious, focused, fussy, imaginative, industrious, introverted, meticulous, observant, passionate, perfectionistic, persistent, quirky, sophisticated, talented, whimsical

SOURCES OF FRICTION
Trying to build a visually diverse portfolio
The cost of food and equipment (if the stylist works from home)
The stylist's vision conflicting with that of a photographer and/or art director
Having to work quickly with freshly made food
Overcooking a component of the dish and needing to start all over
Balancing perfection and messiness so the food appears beautiful but approachable
A photographer who takes unflattering photos
Moral dilemmas—being vegan but having to handle meat, for example
Allergies that make working with some ingredients difficult
Not having the necessary ingredients or materials on hand
Preparing a client's dish that wasn't well-tested, making attractive plating harder to do
Styling multiple meals to obtain many photos in a day
Managing client expectations
Clients who request difficult or unflattering ingredients
Suffering from a creative block that makes it difficult to fulfill the vision for a shoot

Craving the recognition that isn't often granted in a background kind of career
Styling in high humidity or another condition making food fragile and hard to assemble
Having to cook food that makes one ill (e.g., sensitivity to smells due to pregnancy)
Using an unfamiliar ingredient that is fussy to work with

PEOPLE THEY MIGHT INTERACT WITH
Photographers, art directors, editors, chefs, restaurant owners and other clients

HOW THIS OCCUPATION MIGHT IMPACT THE CHARACTER'S NEEDS
Self-Actualization: Because food stylists must work with art directors, photographers, and clients, they may feel limited in their ability to reach their own full creative potential.

Esteem and Recognition: A food stylist may not feel appreciated or recognized for their creative work, particularly since they're largely separated from consumers. Styling requires many skills and steps, so they may feel underappreciated even by those working closest to them.

Safety and Security: Some ingredients can present a danger to the stylist, particularly when gloved handling isn't possible or inhaled particles trigger an allergic reaction.

TWISTING THE FICTIONAL STEREOTYPE
Since food stylists must often cook the food they make and plate it quickly, they must be organized and able to anticipate problems. Why not create a character who's a perfectionist, which slows them down to the point others on the team become frustrated?

Food stylists must be good at collaboration when creating a vision for a styling. Consider crafting a character who must be in control…which leads to amazing plating because of their talent and vision but causes problems with others part of the team.

CHARACTERS MIGHT CHOOSE THIS PROFESSION BECAUSE THEY...
Failed as a chef but want to continue working with food
Had an emotional wound that led to an eating disorder and styling is helping them face their food obsessions and move past them in a healthy way
Have a passion for cooking or baking
Appreciate the aesthetic beauty of a well-balanced plate
Come from a family tied to the magazine industry (photographers, designers, etc.)
View food as a medium for art
Are highly tactile and need a creative outlet
Have lost a valuable sense (smell or taste) and making food beautiful helps make this lack seem more bearable

FUNDRAISER

OVERVIEW

Fundraisers are hired by businesses, organizations, and nonprofits to raise money on their behalf. Their job duties can include organizing fundraising campaigns and events, training volunteers, using social media to raise money, contacting potential donors or sponsors, writing grants, creating promotional materials, and keeping records of donor information.

Because they have to decide which approach and events will work best for each client, fundraisers must be familiar with the various options and be able to evaluate what has worked in the past. Their success depends largely on their dealings with others, so fundraisers must have excellent people skills and be able to network effectively. They may be freelance or work for a consulting firm.

NECESSARY TRAINING

Some clients and firms prefer that their fundraisers have a bachelor's degree—preferably in business, public relations, public administration, or a similar area—while others are more interested in a candidate's experience. Internships and volunteer work can give characters the practice they need to develop skills in this field.

USEFUL SKILLS, TALENTS, OR ABILITIES

A knack for making money, charm, creativity, empathy, exceptional memory, gaining the trust of others, good listening skills, hospitality, multitasking, networking, promotion, reading people, sales, writing

HELPFUL CHARACTER TRAITS

Adaptable, analytical, calm, charming, cooperative, courteous, creative, diplomatic, efficient, empathetic, enthusiastic, extroverted, generous, hospitable, idealistic, imaginative, industrious, meticulous, optimistic, organized, passionate, patient, persistent, persuasive, professional, resourceful, responsible

SOURCES OF FRICTION

A big event flopping
Donors promising money and not following through
Failing to meet a campaign goal
Clients with unrealistic expectations
Micro-managing clients
Taking on a client whose cause is socially unacceptable and will make fundraising difficult
Secrets from a business's past becoming public during the campaign
A venue or vendor for a scheduled event falling through at the last minute
A computer or hard drive crashing and taking the character's records with it
A personal fall from grace that makes networking difficult
A hardship for a big sponsor that causes them to cut their charitable giving
An injury or illness that makes it difficult for the fundraiser to do their job
Difficult or incompetent volunteers

Delegating an important job to a volunteer who doesn't follow through

Learning that much of the funds are going to the business owner rather than to those who need it

Missing evening and weekend time with family due to work obligations

Frequent travel causing trouble at home

An emergency that happens just before a big event

A client who has a terrible reputation or brand that doesn't resonate with most people

Wanting a backseat position (manning phones, managing paperwork) and being thrust into the limelight instead (being the Master of Ceremonies at an event, entertaining donors, etc.)

PEOPLE THEY MIGHT INTERACT WITH

Nonprofit and business owners, administrative staff, volunteers, other fundraisers and bosses at a consulting firm, vendors, venue staff, potential donors, high-profile donors (celebrities, millionaires, etc.), philanthropists, journalists and members of the media

HOW THIS OCCUPATION MIGHT IMPACT THE CHARACTER'S NEEDS

Self-Actualization: Fundraisers are often passionate about their work and the good they're able to do. Those unable to work with their preferred organizations or who are assigned to clients they don't respect may feel they're not living up to their true potential.

Esteem and Recognition: If a fundraiser's failure or shortcomings keep a worthwhile organization from receiving much-needed money, she may begin to doubt her abilities.

Safety and Security: If the client has high-profile or radical enemies who don't want them to succeed, these people may seek to sabotage fundraising efforts, catching the character in the crossfire.

TWISTING THE FICTIONAL STEREOTYPE

Fictional fundraisers are typically associated with glitzy events for wealthy clients. But even small businesses and nonprofits require money, and fundraisers need to start somewhere. What if your character started out raising funds for a local charity or cause—maybe a no-kill shelter, a health clinic, or an after-school program for kids?

CHARACTERS MIGHT CHOOSE THIS PROFESSION BECAUSE THEY...

Grew up in a home where they played a supporting role (by raising younger siblings, helping to cheer on a successful sibling, etc.)

Have an outgoing personality and enjoy a challenge

Want to raise money and attention for worthy causes, helping to bring about change

Enjoy organizing and championing a cause or event

Are a people person who enjoys the art of persuasion

Want to use their charm and gift of persuasion to do good in the world

FUNERAL DIRECTOR

OVERVIEW

Funeral directors assist with end-of-life preparations (either prior to or after a death) and have a variety of responsibilities including picking up bodies, preparing legal documentation, and working with surviving family members to arrange for funeral services. The decisions that must be made for a service are many, such as burial and cremation arrangements, choice of casket, music and slideshow selections, putting together pamphlets for the service, choosing flower arrangements, and setting up transportation. The director will coordinate with all the necessary providers and oversee the funeral, ensuring everything is run according to the wishes of the deceased and their family.

Often, the funeral director will prepare the body itself, attending to storage, embalming, body preparation (dressing and appearance), and possibly cremation. In this case, the director may be called an embalmer or mortician.

NECESSARY TRAINING

Required education may vary depending on the state or location, so if your story is set in a real-world locale, do some research for that area. In general, though, most directors will have an associate's or bachelor's degree in mortuary science. A funeral director also needs a license to practice in the state where they work. Directors must be educated in the legal aspects of body preparation and follow strict guidelines and procedures, not only for paperwork (e.g., death certificates) but also in the case of chain of evidence situations so that any legal proceedings can move forward seamlessly.

USEFUL SKILLS, TALENTS, OR ABILITIES

Basic first aid, blending in, clear communication, empathy, equanimity, exceptional memory, gaining the trust of others, good listening skills, hospitality, leadership, multitasking, peace-keeping, sales, sculpting, sewing, talking with the dead

HELPFUL CHARACTER TRAITS

Calm, centered, courteous, diplomatic, disciplined, discreet, efficient, empathetic, focused, honorable, hospitable, industrious, kind, mature, meticulous, morbid, nurturing, obedient, organized, patient, persuasive, professional, proper, responsible, spiritual, supportive

SOURCES OF FRICTION

A difficult body collection (a child, someone who died in a horrible manner, etc.)
Conflict between relatives over funeral arrangements
A break in the chain of custody
Making preparations for those who have no one to make their arrangements
Struggling to have a manageable work-life balance
Social prejudices against this career
Receiving a body that doesn't have all the necessary paperwork or instructions
Balancing the mental and emotional toll from the work
Theft of a body or associated items, such as jewelry

Families who plan for more than they can afford to pay
Problems during the funeral
Misprints in an obituary or on a death certificate
Being short-staffed
Equipment malfunctions
A body being cremated by mistake
A grieving family that is unable to make even the simplest decisions
Infighting over arrangements by siblings who don't get along
Having to pick up a body in the middle of the night or during a special event

PEOPLE THEY MIGHT INTERACT WITH
Grieving family members, church administrators, volunteers, pastors and ministers, florists, caterers, community hall organizers and church staff, representatives from the military (if the deceased was in service) who play a role in the service, police investigators, coroners, repairmen, delivery people, employees

HOW THIS OCCUPATION MIGHT IMPACT THE CHARACTER'S NEEDS
Self-Actualization: If a character is in this profession because they believe they don't fit in with the living, believing this lie will hold them back from finding their own way and steal the fulfillment that comes with discovering what they are meant to do.

Love and Belonging: A character in this industry may feel isolated if the career makes other people uncomfortable.

Safety and Security: A character may be caught in a dangerous situation if they're working on a high-profile client, such as a criminal, mobster, or person of interest in a federal investigation.

TWISTING THE FICTIONAL STEREOTYPE
People in this profession are usually comfortable with death. But what if your character isn't? What emotional wound, fear, or reason could they have for working in this industry?

CHARACTERS MIGHT CHOOSE THIS PROFESSION BECAUSE THEY...
Learned early on to respect death (due to a father who was a graveyard caretaker or a mother who officiated at funerals, etc.)
Had a near-death experience that led to a lifelong interest in the life and death cycle
Were able to adapt to loss in a healthy way and want the same for others
Are deeply spiritual in nature
Want to help people through the grief process
Have a knack for manipulation and find that grieving people are easy marks

GENERAL CONTRACTOR

OVERVIEW

A general contractor is the person in charge of a construction project. Whether the job is residential, commercial, or highway-related, the GC oversees it from start to finish. This means that their duties begin well before the first hammer falls.

A GC is responsible for putting together bids, including getting pricing on labor and materials and creating a budget and timeline for the project. Once they've landed a job, they are in charge of hiring plumbers, electricians, and other contractors, as well as keeping them accountable while the work is in progress. They will also oversee all the general workers, as well as being the liaison between the customer and the architect or engineer.

A general contractor who is skilled in certain construction areas (such as carpentry or drywalling) or is a jack-of-all-trades may handle these jobs and work alongside their people. Others take a more hands-off approach, choosing to outsource all the work and oversee its progress.

NECESSARY TRAINING

While formal education isn't required for someone to set themselves up as a general contractor, companies often want to see a certain level of experience and education in their GC—sometimes in the form of an associate or bachelor's degree. Specific certifications or accreditations will also be required.

USEFUL SKILLS, TALENTS, OR ABILITIES

Basic first aid, detail-oriented, dexterity, good with numbers, haggling, knowledge of explosives, leadership, mechanically inclined, multitasking, networking, predicting the weather, repurposing, sales, strength, woodworking

HELPFUL CHARACTER TRAITS

Adaptable, alert, ambitious, analytical, controlling, cooperative, courteous, decisive, diplomatic, disciplined, efficient, honest, honorable, humorless, industrious, intelligent, just, know-it-all, loyal, meticulous, observant, obsessive, organized, patient, perfectionist, persistent, persuasive, proactive, professional, pushy, resourceful, responsible, thrifty

SOURCES OF FRICTION

Losing a bid on a promising project
Prices that fluctuate and drive up costs
Falling behind the deadline
Receiving a shipment of incorrect or broken materials
Someone being injured on the job
Employees not showing up for work
Not being able to find suitable workers for a job
Unreasonable labor laws that make scheduling difficult
Demanding or indecisive customers
Sexual harassment on the job

Workers cutting corners that result in a low-quality or unsafe structure
Unforeseen circumstances that raise the cost of a job
Unethical or nitpicky inspectors
Working under a deadline and missing an important family event
Unpleasant weather making the job difficult
Finding that a job is beyond the character's ability to properly oversee
The job stalling due to lack of funds
Losing good workers to a competitor
Fears that make the job challenging (heights, enclosed spaces, being underground, etc.)
Business fluctuating seasonally, making planning difficult

PEOPLE THEY MIGHT INTERACT WITH
General construction workers, tradespeople (electricians, roofers, painters, etc.), architects and engineers, clients, office personnel, upper management (if the GC works for a company), inspectors, distributors, delivery people, suppliers, regulatory board officers, consultants

HOW THIS OCCUPATION MIGHT IMPACT THE CHARACTER'S NEEDS
Self-Actualization: A character who wants to excel and grow but finds himself unable to land the right jobs or move upward will grow frustrated and feel creatively limited.

Esteem and Recognition: A general contractor may chafe at the small-mindedness of those who look down on blue-collar workers.

Safety and Security: With so many tradespeople working at the same time, the risk is high. For example, an electrician could shut off power to work on wiring only to have a drywaller turn it on to run electric tools. A general contractor must ensure safeguards are in place so this doesn't happen, but human error does occur from time to time.

TWISTING THE FICTIONAL STEREOTYPE
To mix things up, consider a change of venue for your construction site. Maybe your GC is overseeing the restoration of an historical structure, building an amusement park, constructing a one-of-a-kind bridge, or is overseeing a project in a remote and rural location.

CHARACTERS MIGHT CHOOSE THIS PROFESSION BECAUSE THEY...
Grew up in an unhealthy building (with toxic mold, asbestos, etc.) and want to save others from those aftereffects
Were expected to participate in the family-run construction company
Want to move up from a laborer position
Enjoy the challenge of organizing and running large projects
Have a condition or cognitive challenge that makes silence unbearable

GEOLOGIST

OVERVIEW
Geologists study how the earth has formed over time, including how landscapes such as mountains, volcanoes, earthquakes, and oceans evolve. Businesses and other agencies hire geologists to better understand the environmental impacts of different initiatives, such as projects in the oil, gas, and mining sectors. They also consult on various issues, such as environmental protection, reclamation, and climate concerns, to name just a few.

Geologists research by studying rock structure and water flow, and by taking soil and rock samples. They may also map out areas using aerial photos, ground penetrating radar, surveys, and other equipment. In a lab, they will then analyze the data using microscopes, a geographic information system, and software so they can prepare their findings.

NECESSARY TRAINING
Geologists need a bachelor's degree in science. A master's degree is required for anyone wanting to specialize in fields such as paleontology, geophysics, oceanography, or volcanology. Field work can often be done as part of the schooling process, which is beneficial, since many companies are looking for geologists with both education and experience.

USEFUL SKILLS, TALENTS, OR ABILITIES
An aptitude for science, basic first aid, exceptional memory, knowledge of explosives, mechanically inclined, multilingualism, photographic memory, predicting the weather, research, stamina, strategic thinking, wilderness navigation, writing

HELPFUL CHARACTER TRAITS
Adaptable, ambitious, analytical, centered, compulsive, cooperative, curious, efficient, focused, fussy, independent, industrious, intelligent, nature-focused, objective, observant, organized, perceptive, perfectionist, persistent, proactive, professional, resourceful, responsible, socially aware, studious, workaholic

SOURCES OF FRICTION
Working with people who want to steer the study or put a spin on results
Poor weather conditions that make tests difficult or destabilize the landscape (an early thaw creating higher floodwaters, an unexpected snowfall, active volcanoes, mudslides, etc.)
Extreme weather that makes the work miserable (heat, cold, freezing rain, etc.)
Frequent travel, sometimes to remote locations or requiring stays in work camps
Having to carry a lot of equipment while out in the field
Frustration over the inability to get definitive answers from interpretive data
Managing conflicting personalities on a project
Running into a conflict-of-interest situation on a job
Having to keep up with technology advances (retraining and education)
Trying to do the job while adhering to pedantic safety rules
Struggling to balance economics, environment, and social impacts for a given project
Suspecting that data or materials are being manipulated to achieve a certain test result

Being stuck in the lab when the geologist really wants to be working in the field
(and vice versa)
Suffering a sprained ankle or knee injury that makes getting to a location difficult
Language barriers when working a job in a foreign country
Bureaucratic red tape that stalls a job or keeps it from getting started—e.g., needing a certain
permit or permission to work in an area
The worksite being picketed by an environmental group
Working with newer geologists who have a lot of questions
The geologist's results being questioned by other experts

PEOPLE THEY MIGHT INTERACT WITH
Other geologists, students, safety officers, laborers and engineers, company heads, project
managers, environmental groups, special interest groups, government officers, indigenous
peoples

HOW THIS OCCUPATION MIGHT IMPACT THE CHARACTER'S NEEDS
Self-Actualization: Geologists who uncover important data (say, shifts in ocean currents
or climate-related changes) may be limited by a non-disclosure agreement with employers in
the private sector. In this situation, they would be unable to share their findings with a wider
audience. If the geologist believes that withholding the data from the public is morally wrong,
their self-actualization may be threatened.

Safety and Security: Geologists traveling to unstable areas could encounter dangerous
conditions (flash flooding, earthquakes, an accident in a remote area, etc.).

TWISTING THE FICTIONAL STEREOTYPE
To be sure your geologist doesn't fall into the same old "scientist" stereotype, explore their
reasons for choosing this profession. Someone who loves working with the undeniable facts
of science is going to be different from a geologist who entered the field so they could affect important change, or one who simply loves the world and being in it. Personality and motivation
go hand in hand, so take that into consideration.

CHARACTERS MIGHT CHOOSE THIS PROFESSION BECAUSE THEY...
Are fascinated with the natural world
Have an aptitude for science combined with the desire to be outdoors
Want to solve an important problem, such as one involving pollution or waste management
Are seeking stability through working with dependable and solid materials
Want to make amends for a family business that was environmentally irresponsible
Feel a spiritual connection when they're working with the world's basic elements
Are highly analytical and enjoy working with data to draw conclusions

GHOSTWRITER

OVERVIEW

A ghostwriter is hired as a freelance writer to produce copy for a fee. They may work on staff, generating content (speeches, tweets, letters, blog posts, video scripts, website content, etc.) for a company or employer. Many also contract themselves out for a specific job like writing a novel or non-fiction book. Ghostwriters can also be part of a content marketing agency, pairing up with clients seeking help with specific projects.

In most cases, the ghostwriter will be given a flat fee for the job at hand (which may be paid in installments). In other cases, they may negotiate a smaller advance and be given a percentage of royalties. In most situations, the credit for the written work goes to the person or organization who hired the writer, but sometimes this is also negotiated, with the ghostwriter being listed as a co-author or contributor. Ghostwriters may also be asked to sign non-disclosure agreements.

NECESSARY TRAINING

Ghostwriters often have a solid backlog of writing credits to their name, which means anyone seeking employment in this field should have a lot of writing experience—and bylines—under their belt. Nonfiction ghostwriters might have training in that industry or area of expertise, providing them with not only the necessary background to knowledgeably write the content, but also credibility in the eyes of a potential employer.

USEFUL SKILLS, TALENTS, OR ABILITIES

Creativity, exceptional memory, good listening skills, networking, research, typing, vision, writing

HELPFUL CHARACTER TRAITS

Adaptable, cooperative, courteous, creative, curious, disciplined, discreet, enthusiastic, focused, honest, industrious, meticulous, organized, passionate, persistent, professional, responsible, studious, witty

SOURCES OF FRICTION

Frustrations over not getting credit for the work
A client who doesn't clearly communicate his needs or the scope of the project
The client not being happy with the final product
A perfectionistic or controlling client who micro-manages a project
Working on projects that aren't stimulating or fulfilling
Falling behind on a deadline
Family members who treat the character's job as a hobby
People who see ghostwriting as an unethical career choice
Tackling a job with content that proves difficult to grasp
Difficulty finding or landing new jobs
Former clients who don't help with referrals or networking
A lack of discipline that leads to a blown deadline

An illness or injury that makes the job hard, like carpal tunnel or chronic fatigue syndrome

Unexpected circumstances that interfere with writing, such as having to care for a sick child or take an elderly parent to an appointment

Environmental distractions that make focusing difficult (the air conditioner breaking, a noisy remodeling project, the neighbor's dog constantly barking, etc.)

Wanting to write full time but not making enough money to do so

Having to write content that makes the character uncomfortable (sex scenes, cruelty to animals, abuse, etc.)

A ghostwriter not having time to write their own books

Poor reviews for a project

A client who is over-involved, asking for rewrites that damage the story

A laptop crashing without being properly backed up, resulting in lost work

A celebrity client who tells everyone they wrote the book without assistance

PEOPLE THEY MIGHT INTERACT WITH

Clients, an employer, members of discussion and job-posting boards, other writers

HOW THIS OCCUPATION MIGHT IMPACT THE CHARACTER'S NEEDS

Self-Actualization: Many choose this field to make money while focusing on their own books. If they end up with little time for their own projects, they may become dissatisfied.

Esteem and Recognition: For writers whose esteem and self-respect depend on them being recognized by others, ghostwriting may lead to a void in this department.

TWISTING THE FICTIONAL STEREOTYPE

Writers are often portrayed as reclusive introverts, immured in their own worlds. To spice up your character, give your writer some unusual character traits or hobbies, or make them highly extroverted which helps them network well and gain new clients.

Because writers often work more than one job, also consider your character's primary (or secondary) career, and add some diversity there.

CHARACTERS MIGHT CHOOSE THIS PROFESSION BECAUSE THEY...

Are fascinated with words and enjoy transcribing other people's stories

Need to supplement their income (especially while working on their own writing projects)

Find it easier to write other people's stories than their own (due to of a past wound that resulted in underachieving or feelings of inadequacy)

Love writing but need to remain anonymous (perhaps they have an infamous family)

Want to simply write without having to do everything else required to be a successful novelist (marketing, networking, finding an agent, etc.)

GLASSBLOWER

OVERVIEW
A glassblower manipulates glass (either by blowing through a tube or relying on more advanced methods). They may shape it into various forms such as vases, dishware, jewelry, windowpanes, figurines, art, and other décor. Glassblowers can work in museums, universities, for a small business, or in a factory where they create custom glass pieces for suppliers, scientists, or manufacturers. Professionals in this career may also teach apprentices and conduct presentations for visitors. Some individuals work out of their own studio, selling their pieces to galleries and collectors.

NECESSARY TRAINING
Classes can be taken at trade schools and some colleges, but an apprenticeship with a master is the best way to become proficient in this field.

USEFUL SKILLS, TALENTS, OR ABILITIES
Creativity, detail-oriented, dexterity, networking, performing, promotion, sales, stamina, teaching, vision

HELPFUL CHARACTER TRAITS
Alert, calm, cooperative, creative, disciplined, enthusiastic, extravagant, focused, funny, fussy, imaginative, industrious, passionate, patient, perfectionist, persistent, resourceful, responsible, whimsical

SOURCES OF FRICTION
Friends and families who think the character should pursue a more lucrative career
Competitive or jealous rivals
Limited opportunities for training in the character's area
A physical disability that makes the job difficult
Internal doubts that make the character question their abilities
Limited finances
A competitive market
A change that results in the character having to work with inferior supplies (a depressed financial market, a monopoly on certain supplies, a change in manufacturer, etc.)
Being unable to break into a higher-end market
Having to teach to supplement income when it's not what the character wants to do
Falling short of a respected instructor's expectations
A demanding customer who is overly critical of the end result
The character not having time or energy to focus on their own art
Being pigeon-holed into making the same kinds of items over and over
Working with a distracted or unmotivated apprentice
Prices being undercut by other artisans in the area
Injuries on the job
Struggling to create the perfect color for a custom project

Working in an intensely hot environment
A fragile and labor-intensive item being broken through clumsy handling

PEOPLE THEY MIGHT INTERACT WITH
Other apprentices or students, a master glassblower or teacher, landlords, gallery owners and visitors, showroom personnel, delivery people, customers

HOW THIS OCCUPATION MIGHT IMPACT THE CHARACTER'S NEEDS
Self-Actualization: If the artist takes on a teaching or manufacturing job to cover the bills, he may find himself sacrificing his passion and stuck in a career that he doesn't enjoy.

Esteem and Recognition: This need can take a hit when criticism comes from professionals in the field, loved ones, or even the artist himself.

Safety and Security: On average, artisanal glassblowers in North America today make about $30,000 per year. Without a second job or an unusual level of success, it will be difficult for people in this field to be financially secure.

TWISTING THE FICTIONAL STEREOTYPE
The majority of glassblowers are men, so having a successful woman in this career would be a refreshing change.

Because of the dangerous materials and amount of training required to do well in this area, glassblowers are typically adults. So, creating the right circumstances for a teen or young adult to be involved in this trade could add an interesting twist.

Because of the beauty and artistry associated with glassblowers, their products tend to fall in the same vein: décor, jewelry, glassware, dishes, artwork, etc. To create an unusual scenario, consider what other, more unusual items your glassblower might produce.

CHARACTERS MIGHT CHOOSE THIS PROFESSION BECAUSE THEY...
Wanted to continue in the family business
Took advantage of an available apprenticeship that provided an opportunity for a different (better) life
Have an appreciation for art and want to make beautiful things
Have a well-developed imagination and the ability to visualize end results
Live in a town or province that is world-renowned for creating glassworks
Enjoy working with their hands and having a physically demanding job
Need a creative outlet and want to do something unusual or different

GRAPHIC DESIGNER

OVERVIEW

Graphic designers create physical or digital concepts to inform, inspire, and attract potential customers. They aim to make their clients memorable and prominent through the use of carefully selected layouts, fonts, colors, shapes, animation, logos, and other design elements. Their projects may include brochures, websites, packaging, social media material, advertisements, book covers, magazines, and more.

While some are employed by design agencies, others work in-house for a company or freelance on their own. A graphic designer going solo will also need to be versed in business practices and know how to market themselves to bring in sales.

NECESSARY TRAINING

A four-year degree in graphic design or a related field is typically necessary. Ongoing training in the field is expected for the designer to stay current with software, trends, and new marketing media.

USEFUL SKILLS, TALENTS, OR ABILITIES

A knack for making money, creativity, detail oriented, exceptional memory, good listening skills, haggling, multitasking, networking, out-of-the-box thinking, promotion, strategic thinking, writing

HELPFUL CHARACTER TRAITS

Analytical, creative, efficient, focused, honest, imaginative, independent, industrious, meticulous, organized, persuasive, professional, responsible, talented, thrifty, workaholic

SOURCES OF FRICTION

A client that is difficult to please
Having ideas that conflicts with a client or colleague's vision
Indecisive clients who request many revisions
Tight deadlines
Receiving harsh feedback
Changes in technology that keep the learning curve constant
A client providing vague direction, then criticizing the designer for the result
Pressure to generate original ideas
People naïvely believing the career is a simple one
Clients who balk at rates or conditions (such as a limited number of revisions being included in the price)
Being asked to design for free by a friend or family member
Creativity block
The designer's work being plagiarized
A software or hardware malfunction that results in lost work
Working in a market glutted with cheap amateurs who drive down design prices
Wanting to work on a project but knowing it doesn't fit their style

Competition among other graphic designers within a company
Receiving criticism for a product that wasn't sufficiently edited or tested
Inadvertently referencing or copying someone else's design element for a project
Taking on a project that is bigger than the designer can handle
Not scheduling enough time for a project, then encountering an emergency situation (i.e., a car accident and lengthy recovery) that pushes it past deadline

PEOPLE THEY MIGHT INTERACT WITH
Clients, art directors, project managers, graphic artists, production designers, web designers

HOW THIS OCCUPATION MIGHT IMPACT THE CHARACTER'S NEEDS
Self-Actualization: Graphic designers may have to compromise their own creative potential to accommodate a client or colleague's vision. Because they often work in the realm of marketing, they may question their ability to impact others in meaningful and intrinsic ways.

Esteem and Recognition: After many hours are invested in a project to get it right, the final product is associated with the client rather than the designer. This could be a problem for a character who desires recognition for their efforts.

Love and Belonging: Designers must use trial and error to perfect their projects, meaning a lot of time goes into each job. This work schedule coupled with hard deadlines could make it challenging for a designer to build and maintain personal relationships.

TWISTING THE FICTIONAL STEREOTYPE
Graphic designers are known to possess creative, analytical, and technological skills. What obstacles might spring up if your character has a serious deficiency in one of these areas?

Interpersonal skills are critical for graphic designers since they work closely with clients and colleagues. Why not create a character that struggles with listening, teamwork, motivation, empathy, or patience?

CHARACTERS MIGHT CHOOSE THIS PROFESSION BECAUSE THEY...
Have a natural eye for attractive design
Enjoy collaborating with clients and colleagues
Can do it while trying to get another career off the ground (designing video games, becoming a novelist, etc.)
Are technology savvy and want a career where they can set their own schedule
Are an artist at heart but lack the self-belief to pursue their own projects
Are introverted and prefer working with people online rather than in person

HOME HEALTH AIDE

OVERVIEW

A home health aide assists patients who are ill, injured, or unable to care for themselves. Some are live-in caregivers, working around the clock, while others assist the patient during specific hours. The schedule is often determined by what the patient is able to pay and which services their insurance company covers.

Working under the supervision of a medical professional (typically a nurse), an aide may provide any of the following services for the patient: helping with bathing, grooming, and other personal hygiene tasks; taking care of domestic duties, such as cleaning, doing laundry, shopping for groceries, or preparing healthy meals; transporting the patient to and from medical appointments; accompanying them on social outings; scheduling appointments; making sure the patient gets adequate exercise; helping with medical tasks, such as monitoring medication intake or changing bandages; keeping careful notes of their services; and working in cooperation with other professionals servicing the patient.

Aides may work independently or be part of an agency, with their hours being scheduled by an administrative employee.

NECESSARY TRAINING

Training varies, depending on the aide's location. Those working with an agency usually need a high school degree and must often acquire certain certifications. Training can be accomplished on the job or through vocational schools and community colleges. Background checks are usually required for people in this position.

USEFUL SKILLS, TALENTS, OR ABILITIES

Basic first aid, detail-oriented, empathy, exceptional memory, gaining the trust of others, good listening skills, hospitality, peacekeeping, reading people, stamina, strength

HELPFUL CHARACTER TRAITS

Adaptable, affectionate, alert, calm, cooperative, courteous, discreet, efficient, empathetic, friendly, gentle, honorable, hospitable, humble, kind, nurturing, organized, protective, responsible, sensible, supportive, unselfish

SOURCES OF FRICTION

Uncooperative patients
Patients who expect more help than the aide is supposed to provide
Patients who need more help but can't afford to pay for it
Conflict with insurance companies
Demanding or unreasonable family members
Patients who develop an unhealthy attachment or dependence on the aide
Absentee loved ones
Always being given the "difficult" patients or tasks
Being injured on the job and not being able to work
Working long or difficult hours

Sharing duties with other professionals and realizing the patient isn't receiving quality care
Seeing signs that a patient is being abused or neglected
Working in a home that is unsanitary or unsafe
Being accused of unethical behavior by the patient or their family members
Having to service a patient in an unsafe neighborhood
Roommates or live-in family members who make the aide feel unsafe

PEOPLE THEY MIGHT INTERACT WITH
Patients, the patient's family members or roommates, doctors, nurses, physical therapists, insurance personnel, other aides, administrative personnel (if the aide works out of an agency), police officers, social workers

HOW THIS OCCUPATION MIGHT IMPACT THE CHARACTER'S NEEDS
Self-Actualization: An aide who dreams of doing more with her career (like progressing to become a nurse) but is unable to do so may start to feel stifled and limited.

Esteem and Recognition: As support staff, aides may be treated as second-class citizens by some people. They can easily be overlooked, underestimated, or taken advantage of.

Love and Belonging: A home health care aide may choose this career as a way of connecting with many patients on a surface level. It could become a way to scratch the belonging itch without having to commit long-term or get really involved in someone's life.

Safety and Security: Aides may be injured while picking up patients or bodily moving them from one spot to another. They also can contract sicknesses if proper precautions aren't taken.

TWISTING THE FICTIONAL STEREOTYPE
While we often see aides servicing lower-income clientele, everyone needs help from time to time. What about a home health care agency that services the wealthy? Or an aide who specializes in working with large families or those with mental disabilities?

CHARACTERS MIGHT CHOOSE THIS PROFESSION BECAUSE THEY...
Needed a job and knew someone who was able to secure this one for them
Wanted a career where they could help others and be appreciated for their work
Spent a lot of time caring for an elderly parent or relative in the past
Have felt alone and unsupported and want to help people who feel the same
Have a lot of caregiving experience
Are highly compassionate and empathetic
Are estranged from their own family, and caring for others helps fill the void

HUMAN TEST SUBJECT

OVERVIEW

A human test subject is paid to participate in scientific experiments. If they're involved in a clinical trial, they might take specific drugs, vaccines, or supplements, or use a certain medical device to see what the effects are. Alternatively, they may offer biological contributions of blood, saliva, sperm, urine, skin cells, dandruff, etc., to be studied. They also could be part of a social science experiment to analyze behavior. In this situation, they would be asked specific questions, perform cognitive tasks, or be exposed to conditions that would alter their physical, mental, and emotional state. In any of these studies, the participant could be part of the test group or the control group, and usually do not know which. Other (safer) gigs would have the subject filling out surveys, participating in panel discussions for market research, testing products, or even participating in mock trials.

Depending on the criteria, test subjects may be chosen for specific reasons, say because they have a specific type of cancer, suffered frontal lobe damage after an accident, or they experience a phenomenon like synesthesia. They may be asked to adhere to a type of exercise, sleep, or dietary routines and abstain from taking any medication, supplements, or mood enhancers for the duration of the trial.

A character wishing to be a test subject would have to provide consent to be part of the study. They exchange money for their participation. Legitimate studies are regulated to prevent unethical experimentation.

NECESSARY TRAINING

No training is necessary, but the character must fit the parameters of the study. If the group is not randomly selected, the character might need to be within a specific height and weight range, be in good overall health, abstain from alcohol, and often be free of drugs and supplements (even over the counter ones) for a month before the trial begins.

USEFUL SKILLS, TALENTS, OR ABILITIES

Charm, exceptional memory, good listening skills, high pain tolerance, multitasking, stamina

HELPFUL CHARACTER TRAITS

Adaptable, adventurous, apathetic, calm, cooperative, curious, disciplined, easygoing, focused, honest, impulsive, obedient, observant, patient, simple, socially aware, uninhibited

SOURCES OF FRICTION

Being asked to do things within the trial that are uncomfortable, painful, or embarrassing
Becoming bored by repetitive duties or long hours performing tasks and answering questions
Being in a test group with annoying or uncooperative people
Experiencing symptoms that may or may not be normal (a sudden loss of libido, headaches, craving certain things, having to urinate frequently, etc.)
Feeling manipulated by researchers
Suffering a side effect that requires medical care

Suffering from minor side effects that must be endured for the length of the study (nausea, headaches, twitchy extremities, difficulty sleeping, etc.)

Missing work due to side effects and not being compensated for it

Experiencing side effects that last long after the study is finished

Regretting the decision to participate but having to see it through

Arguments with family members who disagree with the character's decision

Completing a trial and feeling like the compensation wasn't worth the risk

Breaking the rules of the trial—drinking alcohol, eating at a certain time of day, etc.—and being disqualified from continuing

Boredom arising from being sequestered for days at a time

Frequently having to have blood drawn

PEOPLE THEY MIGHT INTERACT WITH

Other test subjects, researchers, administrative staff, psychologists, doctors, dieticians, medical students

HOW THIS OCCUPATION MIGHT IMPACT THE CHARACTER'S NEEDS

Self-Actualization: If the testing produces a lasting side effect that disrupts a skill or ability, it may keep the subject from achieving a meaningful goal, leaving them feeling cheated.

Esteem and Recognition: A character who chooses this path may not have sufficient regard for their own health, indicating some self-esteem issues. Or, if the character is only thinking of the quick money and not the possible repercussions, they may realize later that they took foolhardy risks unnecessarily, leading to a self-esteem crisis.

Love and Belonging: Family members and close friends would likely not understand nor support the character's choice to be a test subject, creating friction in those relationships.

Safety and Security: Some tests (especially clinical trials) could have lasting negative effects that may not show up for years or even decades, and the character would have no recourse.

TWISTING THE FICTIONAL STEREOTYPE

People who take on jobs with an element of risk are often portrayed as desperate for money. Consider a different motivation for your human test subject choosing this career, such as a passion to eradicate a certain disease or the subconscious desire to punish him or herself.

CHARACTERS MIGHT CHOOSE THIS PROFESSION BECAUSE THEY...

Needed the money (for escalating debt, to pay for school, etc.)

Love science and wanted a job associated with the field

Have a self-destructive streak as a result of a past wound

Desperately need medical help

Are impulsive and live in the now, not thinking about the future

Possess a rare medical condition or advantage that is perfect for a certain study

HYPNOTHERAPIST

OVERVIEW
A hypnotherapist is a medical or mental health practitioner who is also certified in hypnosis. They guide a person into a highly relaxed state to focus their attention intensely on a specific idea or task. Once in this state, the hypnotherapist can assist a person in changing unwanted behaviors (such as smoking or overeating), address a phobia, or help them deal with a physical sensation like pain. Hypnotherapists may also attempt to unearth the psychological origins of a person's disorder or symptoms, explore past life regressions, and conduct inner child work.

NECESSARY TRAINING
Hypnotherapists must first earn the required degree(s) and/or licenses in their desired medical or mental health field, such as behavioral medicine, psychotherapy, dentistry, and so forth. They must enroll in a certified hypnotherapy school that is approved by their state or province and complete the required hours of coursework. After finishing an accredited program, they can apply for certification so they may practice.

USEFUL SKILLS, TALENTS, OR ABILITIES
Charm, empathy, exceptional memory, gaining the trust of others, good listening skills, leadership, making people laugh, mentalism, multilingualism, networking, out-of-the-box thinking, research

HELPFUL CHARACTER TRAITS
Calm, charming, confident, diplomatic, discreet, empathetic, intelligent, nurturing, observant, perceptive, professional, sensible, studious, wise

SOURCES OF FRICTION
Difficulty building a base of clientele
Skeptics delegitimizing the work hypnotherapists do
Being slandered by professionals in the health industry
Clients who are resistant to the process
Clients who don't really want to change their behaviors
Inadvertently creating false memories via leading questions or suggestions
Friends and family distancing themselves due to misconceptions or biases against the job
Clients with psychotic symptoms requiring different interventions
Struggling with a learning disability that makes certain administrative jobs difficult
Clients yielding information during hypnosis that may not be reliable
Finding it difficult to build rapport and trust with a client
Clients who have unrealistic expectations
Difficulty diagnosing or finding proper treatment for a client
Loving working with patients but hating the paperwork and administrative side of the job
People requesting "party tricks" in social situations, demonstrating a lack of respect for the career
Clients who cancel at the last minute or don't show up at all

Problems in a rented space that are outside of the hypnotherapist's control—a mold problem or pest infestation, a roof leak, etc.

Handling undesirable tasks to save money (cleaning the workspace, scheduling, etc.)

PEOPLE THEY MIGHT INTERACT WITH

Clients, guardians for underage clients, counselors, general practitioners, physical therapists, psychotherapists, acupuncturists, a receptionist

HOW THIS OCCUPATION MIGHT IMPACT THE CHARACTER'S NEEDS

Self-Actualization: While hypnotherapy's aim is to help others resolve issues, sometimes a therapist will have challenging clients or those who experience less success. This may lead the practitioner to question their ability to be a good care provider.

Esteem and Recognition: There is skepticism and distrust from the public when it comes to hypnotherapy. This may impact a practitioner's self-esteem, especially if colleagues in the health care industry also share this bias.

Love and Belonging: Public misconceptions about hypnotherapy can impact a practitioner's ability to build and maintain close relationships. Friends and family members may be fearful that a hypnotherapist could somehow use their skill set for nefarious purposes.

TWISTING THE FICTIONAL STEREOTYPE

Clients respond better to treatment if they have a good relationship with their hypnotherapist. Ratchet up tension by giving your character a bad bedside manner, a pessimistic outlook, or less-than-savory social skills.

Trained hypnotherapists are assumed to use their skills legitimately and to help others. Consider a character who is using hypnotherapy unethically (but be aware of the limitations by doing your research).

Hypnotherapy is about uncovering secrets and unravelling the cause for certain behaviors and disorders so clients can heal. What if your character, struggling with their own demons, chose this career to gain access to information held by specific people?

CHARACTERS MIGHT CHOOSE THIS PROFESSION BECAUSE THEY...

Were disillusioned with more traditionally accepted forms of health care

Experienced success with hypnotherapy and wanted to pay it forward to others

Have struggled with pain, addiction, or trauma in the past

Have a strong desire to help others

Believe in alternative health care

Lust for power and want to control other people

INTERPRETER

OVERVIEW
An interpreter is someone who orally or through sign language translates a person's words into a different language. This is different from a translator who does essentially the same thing but with words in a written format, such as in books or documents. Interpreters work most often in hospitals, schools, and courtrooms, but they also can be found at conferences, in political arenas, with the police when language barriers prevent communication, and in other situations. For long or challenging jobs, they may tag-team to combat mental fatigue. Interpreters can be part of an agency or freelance individually, and while they often work in person with others, they also can offer their services remotely, even from home.

NECESSARY TRAINING
Most interpreters need a bachelor's degree and all of them must be proficient in at least two languages. While further linguistic training isn't required, the more experience they have, the better; so having spent time immersed in the language and culture may give someone a leg up over the competition. Those working in certain fields, such as medical and legal environments, may need technical training in that area to bring them up to speed.

USEFUL SKILLS, TALENTS, OR ABILITIES
Charm, enhanced hearing, exceptional memory, good listening skills, lip-reading, multilingualism, multitasking, reading people

HELPFUL CHARACTER TRAITS
Adaptable, alert, charming, confident, cooperative, courteous, decisive, devious, diplomatic, focused, friendly, honest, honorable, just, nosy, objective, observant, professional, simple, studious

SOURCES OF FRICTION
Impatient clients who expect immediate and perfect translations
Being asked to work with a language the interpreter isn't proficient in
Not knowing the context of the conversation and being unable to interpret it accurately
A sickness that makes it difficult to focus
Noisy environmental distractions that make it hard to hear
Hearing something that raises a moral conflict (information that would be in the interpreter's best interest to convey a certain way, being asked by a client to interpret something incorrectly, etc.)
Mental fatigue from a long workday that compromises the interpreter's abilities
A competitor who is more knowledgeable in a preferred language than the character
Having to take on interpretation jobs that aren't stimulating or interesting
Working with a sub-standard fellow interpreter
Workplace politics that ensure the most desired jobs go to someone who isn't the best
Friction with family members due to the amount of time spent away from home
Uncooperative suspects or witnesses who use the language barrier to avoid incriminating

themselves or getting involving in someone else's business (e.g., witnesses—especially those worried about being deported or being punished for helping the police)

Growing heartsick from seeing and hearing the same kind of pain day in and day out (in foster care, the criminal system, a courtroom, etc.)

Preferring to work online but being asked to take on a face-to-face job

Overhearing something at work the interpreter wasn't meant to hear (incriminating information about a client; something that, should the interpreter share it, puts them at risk, etc.)

Trying to accurately interpret slang that is culture-specific or unfamiliar to the interpreter

PEOPLE THEY MIGHT INTERACT WITH

Other interpreters, administrators within the interpreter's firm, people specific to each job's environment (doctors, nurses, medical patients, lawyers, judges, social workers, administrators, students and parents, teachers, diplomats, leaders of foreign countries, CEOs and other business people, the police, etc.)

HOW THIS OCCUPATION MIGHT IMPACT THE CHARACTER'S NEEDS

Self-Actualization: As with any career, self-actualization becomes compromised if the job is no longer fulfilling. Ask yourself: why did the character pursue this job in the first place? What (if anything) has changed that makes them now unhappy in this career? Is there another occupation they'd rather have? What is it, and why?

Esteem and Recognition: This need could take a hit if the character's level of skill in a certain language is surpassed by a co-worker's—someone who seems to flourish without having to try while the character has to work like a dog to remain proficient.

Love and Belonging: Someone in this field would likely have a passion for their preferred language, and if a spouse or significant other showed no interest in learning that language or exploring the culture, it could cause friction. Problems may also arise if the interpreter's job requires frequent travel.

CHARACTERS MIGHT CHOOSE THIS PROFESSION BECAUSE THEY...

Overcame a language barrier (such as a speech impediment) that provided them with the strong communication skills needed for this job

Have a family member with a hearing disability who required advocacy and support

Have an affinity for different languages and an ear for tone and nuance

Have a secret need to be in the know or fear being kept out of the loop

Are naturally nurturing and enjoy making connections for others

Love to travel and interact with people from different cultures

Want to use their skills to help certain people groups (those in a refugee camp, immigrants seeking asylum, foster children, diplomats, etc.)

INVENTOR

OVERVIEW
An inventor creates a new device or process, often to address a problem or to improve upon an already-existing invention. To protect their creation, they will file for a patent that prevents others from making the exact same product or copying their process. The inventor can then sell their product or license it to interested parties.

   If an inventor works for a corporation, patents will be filed by the company on the inventor's behalf. According to the terms of the employee agreement, the company may own the rights to the patent in this situation.

NECESSARY TRAINING
There is no formal training to become an inventor, but strong background knowledge in science, math, engineering, technology, and consumer markets may be helpful. If an inventor works in a particular field, they will need education and experience related to that area to help them identify core needs or find opportunities for improvement.

USEFUL SKILLS, TALENTS, OR ABILITIES
A knack for making money, creativity, mechanically inclined, multitasking, networking, out-of-the-box thinking, photographic memory, promotion, repurposing, research, strategic thinking, vision, writing

HELPFUL CHARACTER TRAITS
Ambitious, analytical, creative, curious, focused, idealistic, imaginative, industrious, meticulous, observant, optimistic, organized, persistent, resourceful, talented, thrifty

SOURCES OF FRICTION
Struggling with repeated failure and rejection
Reluctance to outsource work to those with better sub-skills
Financial strain, especially if investors can't be secured early on
Competition with other inventors
Skeptical family and friends who think the character should get a "real job"
Creating an invention with unintended (negative) consequences
Struggling with self-doubt due to a poor track record
Having to present or pitch to investors (especially when the inventor isn't wired to do so)
Pressure to come up with new ideas
Lawsuits over patent infringements
Filing a patent too late (and a competitor reaping the benefits)
The inventor's ideas or materials being stolen
Selling the invention and realizing afterwards that they didn't get what it was worth
Being scammed by an unethical investor, business partner, or relative offering to "help out"
Not fully understanding the important parts of the process and losing time and money because of it (using the wrong material, choosing a co-packer or distributor based on the wrong criteria, etc.)

Getting ready to go to market with an invention and receiving poor feedback from market researchers that requires the inventor to start over

An angel investor that drops out (changing their minds, because the economy shifts, etc.)

PEOPLE THEY MIGHT INTERACT WITH

Other inventors, patent lawyers, patent office employees, market research firms, target audience members, employers, investors

HOW THIS OCCUPATION MIGHT IMPACT THE CHARACTER'S NEEDS

Self-Actualization: Inventors can directly improve the lives of others when they come up with creative and well-executed ideas. Failing to do so can create a lot of pressure and make them question their capabilities.

Esteem and Recognition: Inventing is riddled with failure and rejection, increasing the risk of lowered self-worth. It often requires the inventor to put themselves in vulnerable positions emotionally, mentally, and financially, with no guarantee of success. Having to outsource to those with greater skill in an area may also threaten the inventor's esteem.

Physiological Needs: In some instances, a discovery may be so valuable or important it attracts opportunists willing to do anything to secure it, including killing the inventor.

TWISTING THE FICTIONAL STEREOTYPE

Inventors are often viewed as risk-takers. But what if yours is a reluctant one? Perhaps they have a brilliant idea but struggle with bringing it to fruition? Maybe they are hesitant to give up the control necessary to outsource or are paralyzed by fear of failure.

We generally think of inventors as trying to improve life by creating solutions to problems. But what if your character is inventing things for darker, more sinister purposes?

An inventive mindset isn't limited by age or maturity. With increased STEM focus in our schools, kids are being given more opportunities than ever to come up with their own ideas. An important invention in your story that is created by a child or teenager could make for an interesting change.

CHARACTERS MIGHT CHOOSE THIS PROFESSION BECAUSE THEY...

Had former success with an invention

Enjoy problem-solving and can easily see deficiencies in existing products or processes

Feel driven to find "the next big thing"

Like experimenting and trial-and-error processes that lead to new discoveries

Are idealistic and want to make the world a better place

Are determined to change the fate of a loved one who is unable to fully enjoy life

Have a lot of ideas and naturally think outside of the box

JANITOR

OVERVIEW
A janitor maintains the physical appearance of schools, offices, hospitals, businesses, stadiums, and other facilities. They may clean and restock restrooms, remove garbage, maintain floors, and perform light maintenance. If higher-level repairs are needed, they will notify management. Their duties may also include groundskeeping tasks like shoveling snow, spreading salt or sand to clear ice, sweeping walkways, or mowing grass. Some members of the janitorial staff will be in charge of organizing, tracking, and ordering supplies for their department, following a set budget.

NECESSARY TRAINING
Janitors typically need a high school diploma or equivalent to demonstrate the basic skills required for administrative tasks. They may be more competitive as a candidate if they have previous experience in commercial cleaning or maintenance. Employers may provide training on equipment, standards, and practices, and some will provide an experienced mentor to train new janitors.

USEFUL SKILLS, TALENTS, OR ABILITIES
Basic first aid, detail-oriented, enhanced sense of smell, exceptional memory, mechanically inclined, multitasking, repurposing, stamina, strength, woodworking

HELPFUL CHARACTER TRAITS
Calm, centered, cooperative, disciplined, independent, industrious, obedient, observant, proactive, resourceful, responsible, tolerant, workaholic

SOURCES OF FRICTION
Low pay
An unusual work schedule that can include evening or weekend hours
Exposure to body fluids, germs, and generally gross stuff
A negative public perception (that janitors are uneducated, creepy, or unmotivated)
Inconsiderate behaviors by those utilizing the facility
Employees on power trips (purposely dumping their half-full coffee in the trash instead of emptying it in a nearby sink, etc.)
Personality conflicts with other janitors and building personnel
A lack of stimulation on the job
Being micromanaged by supervisors
A lack of respect from other employees in the building
Having to handle potentially toxic chemicals
High turnover among the staff, putting more stress on the other janitors
A big mess at the end of the day that requires the janitor to stay later than usual
Loved ones being embarrassed that their parent, spouse, etc. works as a janitor
Stumbling across confidential information (in a memo, in the garbage can, etc.) that the janitor

feels should be shared but would cost them their job to do so
Working with someone who is lazy but has higher seniority and so gets away with it

PEOPLE THEY MIGHT INTERACT WITH
People who share the janitor's workspace (students, patients, staff members, visitors, etc.), maintenance workers, members of management, inspectors

HOW THIS OCCUPATION MIGHT IMPACT THE CHARACTER'S NEEDS
Esteem and Recognition: Because janitors are not required to have higher education credentials and the work is manual, they may be looked down upon. Since they often work after hours, their efforts can go unrecognized by those they serve.

Love and Belonging: While janitors work in places like schools or hospitals, they are not typically viewed as part of the staff, making it a lonely position.

Safety and Security: Janitors often earn low wages, making it hard to attain financial security. They may also be exposed to chemicals or health risks found in hospitals, schools, and other public facilities.

TWISTING THE FICTIONAL STEREOTYPE
While it may be assumed that a janitor settled for their job due to a lack of education, perhaps your character purposefully chose this career. Maybe they wanted to avoid high-stress white-collar work, or it provides them access to specific things (like concerts or sporting events). Perhaps they wanted to be involved with a certain business or be near a loved one who is tied to the facility in some way. It's also possible that your character loves to clean and care for others, making this a highly rewarding job for them.

Many people can't imagine someone seeking out this profession, but it does offer the benefit of invisibility and provides access to areas that are off-limits to others. This combination is perfect for someone on a mission to advance their larger goals in a furtive way.

CHARACTERS MIGHT CHOOSE THIS PROFESSION BECAUSE THEY...
Needed a job with security and benefits
Prefer to work independently rather than with others
Are unable or unwilling to pursue higher education
Need to work close to home
Enjoy serving and caring for others
Want to be connected to a certain venue (a company doing important work, their kids' school, a city's sports complex, etc.)
Are able to make money on the side while pursuing other goals
Can do it during the school day or overnight, while their spouse takes care of the kids
Are mourning a recent loss and need a distraction that doesn't require a lot of brainpower
Have social anxiety and need to work in the off-hours when people generally aren't around

JEWELRY DESIGNER

OVERVIEW
There are many careers within this industry. For clarity, this entry will focus on people who design and manufacture jewelry. Some create artisan products from their own imaginations while others work for a larger company, manufacturing jewelry requested by those in charge.

NECESSARY TRAINING
No official training is required. Many people starting out in this field receive the necessary on-the-job training by apprenticing to a successful jeweler or working for one. Jewelry designers should be creative, but if they want to work independently, they'll also need to have some knowledge of business and marketing.

USEFUL SKILLS, TALENTS, OR ABILITIES
Creativity, dexterity, haggling, mechanically inclined, networking, promotion, repurposing, sales, vision

HELPFUL CHARACTER TRAITS
Ambitious, creative, curious, disciplined, imaginative, industrious, meticulous, passionate, patient, patriotic, quirky, resourceful, talented

SOURCES OF FRICTION
Being shortchanged by a customer
Struggling to make ends meet financially
Manufacturing a custom design that doesn't please the customer
Using a small or chaotic workspace that decreases efficiency
A customer's jewelry breaking due to a defect
Discovering that the jewels one has been using weren't sourced ethically
Changing suppliers and discovering too late that the quality of materials isn't up to par
The price of materials rising and affecting cost
Being robbed
Financial difficulties that make it impossible to buy new materials
The character's designs not being accepted by the public or critics
Knock-off competitors stealing the character's designs
Being blocked creatively and having difficulty coming up with new ideas
A hand or finger injury that makes the work difficult
Friends and loved ones who expect the designer to make jewelry for them for free or at discount
Being unable to succeed on their own and having to go into business for someone else
Impatient family members who want the character to give up the dream in favor of something more lucrative
Discovering that an employee is stealing from the designer
Being a talented designer but struggling with promotion or marketing
Spending precious resources to outsource unwanted duties and learning that the employee or

contractor is no good at their job

A post office mix-up that results in lost merchandise

Distractions common to working from home (the phone ringing, people stopping by, family members interrupting the designer's work, etc.)

Cash flow problems due to the high cost of materials

PEOPLE THEY MIGHT INTERACT WITH

Customers, suppliers, delivery people, landlords, retail personnel at stores where the jeweler shops for merchandise, trade show attendees and vendors, jewelry store personnel, personal shoppers

HOW THIS OCCUPATION MIGHT IMPACT THE CHARACTER'S NEEDS

Self-Actualization: It's notoriously hard to succeed financially in a creative field. A jewelry designer who has to work extra jobs or take on a related career that isn't satisfying can easily become personally unfulfilled.

Esteem and Recognition: Esteem can take a hit when customers, critics, or buyers aren't interested in or openly disparage the designer's creations.

Safety and Security: A designer who is unfamiliar or careless with the chemicals and metals they're working with may experience safety issues from misuse.

TWISTING THE FICTIONAL STEREOTYPE

People in this field typically work alone, but what about a partnership? While creative collaboration can be a wonderful thing, it also provides many opportunities for realistic tension and conflict.

Art doesn't always produce results that are traditionally beautiful. Instead of a jeweler who creates lovely things, how about one who specializes in disturbing or dark accessories?

CHARACTERS MIGHT CHOOSE THIS PROFESSION BECAUSE THEY...

Grew up in a wealthy or celebrity family where high-end fashion was admired

Grew up in a poor family and envied the beautiful and expensive baubles of the wealthy

Are inherently creative and deft with their hands

Have expensive tastes

Want to honor a dearly deceased loved one who had a passion for making or collecting jewelry

Can use the focus required to escape from painful memories

Enjoy expressing themselves by creating unusual or unnerving art

Want to step out of the shadow of a successful parent, sibling, or other important person

Want to be their own boss and open their own business

JUDGE

OVERVIEW
The roles of a judge vary widely depending on his or her jurisdiction. Regardless of the location and the type of work they do, their duties may include the following: listening to arguments and analyzing documents to determine whether cases deserve to go to trial, presiding over jury selection and providing jurors with instructions, overseeing court proceedings, ensuring proper legal procedures are followed, examining evidence and deciding if it is legal and proper, researching legal issues and applying the law to reach judgments, imposing penalties on those found guilty, negotiating and resolving administrative disputes, rendering decisions in legal disputes, granting search and arrest warrants, setting bail or release terms, performing marriage ceremonies, and issuing marriage licenses.

NECESSARY TRAINING
Because legal experience is usually required, most judges earn a law degree and practice for a number of years as a lawyer. While they are becoming familiar with the law and how the judicial system works, they will also be building a reputation and networking with influential people, since judges must be elected or appointed to their positions. Continuing education will be important throughout a judge's career, so they can stay abreast of changes in the law and courtroom proceedings.

USEFUL SKILLS, TALENTS, OR ABILITIES
Detail-oriented, empathy, enhanced hearing, equanimity, exceptional memory, good listening skills, leadership, networking, multilingualism, peacekeeping, public speaking, reading people, research

HELPFUL CHARACTER TRAITS
Analytical, calm, curious, decisive, diplomatic, disciplined, honest, honorable, intelligent, just, merciful, meticulous, objective, observant, pensive, perceptive, proactive, professional, proper, socially aware, tolerant, wise

SOURCES OF FRICTION
Having to always adhere to the letter of the law
Evidence that is difficult to hear or see
Political pressure being applied for the judge to issue a certain type of ruling
The weight of being responsible for someone's life or freedom
A loophole being exploited that the judge must abide by
Feeling empathy for the defendant
Releasing a defendant who goes on to commit an awful crime
Working with difficult court attorneys
Having to campaign for reelection
Being caught in a compromising situation
Laws that are constantly changing
Dealing with public scrutiny

Wrongly convicting someone
Personal experiences with crime influencing a judge's objectivity
Career burnout; struggling to process the psychological weight of difficult cases
Being threatened or targeted because of a past ruling or political stance

PEOPLE THEY MIGHT INTERACT WITH

Administrative and clerical staff, lawyers, defendants, witnesses, experts giving testimony, jury members, a courtroom deputy, court reporters, people attending a trial (the defendant's family members, reporters, law students, concerned community members, etc.)

HOW THIS OCCUPATION MIGHT IMPACT THE CHARACTER'S NEEDS

Self-Actualization: Judges are required to abide by the law and work with facts and evidence only. When they suspect someone is getting away with a crime due to a lack of evidence, this may cause them to question the legal system and their role within it.

Esteem and Recognition: A judge may catch a difficult case that results in a contentious ruling. This could place them in the negative crosshairs of public opinion, lowering their worth in the eyes of colleagues.

Love and Belonging: Because judges are the ultimate and sole authority in the courtroom, it can be a lonely job. Their work repeatedly exposes them to trauma they are expected to keep confidential, potentially isolating them in their personal relationships.

Safety and Security: A judge's safety can be threatened by criminal defendants, their associates, and disgruntled citizens.

TWISTING THE FICTIONAL STEREOTYPE

In most places, judges must have experience as lawyers in order to practice. But this isn't always the case. Consider a situation where a non-lawyer judge has been appointed. What surprising results might emerge?

We expect judges to be fair and law-abiding. How can you craft a character with passionate views who struggles to maintain objectivity in the courtroom?

CHARACTERS MIGHT CHOOSE THIS PROFESSION BECAUSE THEY...

Came from a family of lawyers and judges
Witnessed the ruin of a loved one's life by a shady, biased, or incompetent judge
Have respect for the law and want to serve their community
Seek to please others (especially family) by attaining prestige and power
Want to make a difference at a higher level
Want political power
Are seeking to become a federal judge with a lifetime appointment

LANDSCAPE DESIGNER

OVERVIEW

Landscape designers turn residential outdoor spaces into functional and attractive places for their customers. They meet with clients to ascertain their wants and needs, draw up plans, select plants, and propose their ideas. Those ideas may include plant beds, water features, decking and patios, walls, walkways, pools, and small structures. Once the design has been solidified, the designer will work with contractors to ensure it is implemented as intended and to the client's satisfaction.

NECESSARY TRAINING

No formal training is necessary, though courses can be taken and certifications and degrees obtained to enhance a designer's knowledge. Landscape architects, on the other hand, must be licensed and have a master's degree in order to practice.

USEFUL SKILLS, TALENTS, OR ABILITIES

Creativity, detail-oriented, gardening, good listening skills, leadership, repurposing, research, vision

HELPFUL CHARACTER TRAITS

Analytical, cooperative, courteous, creative, curious, focused, imaginative, industrious, meticulous, nature-focused, observant, patient, perfectionist, professional, responsible

SOURCES OF FRICTION

A fussy client who is never satisfied
Misunderstanding a client's desires
Introducing diseased shrubs that die quickly
Difficulty obtaining a permit
Nit-picky inspectors
Unreliable or dishonest employees
Weather difficulties (extreme hot or cold, a storm interrupting a project, etc.)
Disturbing an underground hornet's nest
Unforeseen issues (the ground being rockier than expected, problems with the soil, etc.) that push a project over-budget
Accidentally planting the wrong plants that won't thrive or don't get along
Contractors cutting corners and building structures that aren't reliable
A contractor becoming romantically involved with a client
Working with a dishonest partner or business administrator
Being great with plants but really bad with people (or managing finances, marketing, etc.)
Incomplete specs that cause construction delays
Clients with lots of ideas but small budgets
Working in a market that's saturated with designers, making it difficult to obtain clients
Unethical inspectors who require bribes to approve the designer's project
HOA restrictions that limit the designer's options

Neighbors disputing property lines, causing a project to stall
Poor reviews affecting the landscaper's ability to gain new clients
Sunburn, bug bites, poison ivy and other occupational hazards
Developing an ailment that impedes the character's ability to work (a sensitivity to sunlight, a fear of open spaces, etc.)

PEOPLE THEY MIGHT INTERACT WITH

Landscape employees, the company's owner, office personnel, clients, wholesalers and retailers (of plants, pavers, gardening equipment, etc.), plumbers, construction workers, inspectors, engineers and architects, neighbors

HOW THIS OCCUPATION MIGHT IMPACT THE CHARACTER'S NEEDS

Self-Actualization: Someone who entered this field so they could continue a parent's business or carry on someone else's legacy may find their self-actualization impacted if the job doesn't make them happy.

Esteem and Recognition: Someone seeking esteem may be unfulfilled if, despite doing a good job, they're unable to garner the kind of recognition and accolades they would like.

TWISTING THE FICTIONAL STEREOTYPE

Consider the friction possibilities if your landscape designer is part of a family business that is known for conflicting views, habits, and worldviews.

Another interesting twist would be to think about what unexpected items might be unearthed during a routine job: cursed objects long buried? Something considered a biohazard, a fortune in old coins or even a secured lockbox holding items suggesting a serial killer once lived there?

CHARACTERS MIGHT CHOOSE THIS PROFESSION BECAUSE THEY...

Spent many happy days in a neighbor's or friend's beautifully designed yard and are inspired by those memories
Grew up in urban poverty and view elegant outdoor spaces as a sign of wealth and success
Love being outdoors and want to create spaces that encourage others to enjoy it too
Are innately creative or artistic
Are a gardener at heart and want to earn a sustainable income while doing what they love
Have a strong appreciation for natural beauty
Have no children and are able to turn their nurturing nature toward plants
Enjoy turning boring or uninspired places into beautiful spaces
Are at peace working out-of-doors

LAWYER

OVERVIEW

Lawyers are licensed and can work individually or as part of a firm. Depending on the size or kind of firm they're with, they can be general practitioners or may specialize in one area, such as family, divorce, criminal, immigration, corporate, civil, or animal law.

A lawyer's duties include offering counsel, representing someone with respect to legal matters, preparing legal documents, defending or prosecuting in court, conducting research, and preparing evidence, among other things. Whatever their responsibilities, they're expected to fulfill those tasks while protecting their clients' rights. The roles and statutes for lawyers will differ depending on their jurisdiction, so further research may be necessary for writing a character with this occupation.

NECESSARY TRAINING

Lawyers must earn a four-year degree in any subject, after which point, they must pass an admissions test and be accepted into a law school. There, they typically complete hands-on, supervised training and eventually earn a Juris Doctor degree. They must then pass a bar examination in order to practice in a given jurisdiction.

USEFUL SKILLS, TALENTS, OR ABILITIES

Charm, exceptional memory, gaining the trust of others, good listening skills, haggling, multilingualism, performing, persuasion, promotion, research, strategic thinking, writing

HELPFUL CHARACTER TRAITS

Adaptable, alert, ambitious, analytical, decisive, disciplined, efficient, focused, honorable, industrious, intelligent, just, manipulative, meticulous, objective, observant, organized, persistent, persuasive, professional, resourceful, responsible, sensible, socially aware, wise

SOURCES OF FRICTION

Disagreeing with a client on a position
Having an untrustworthy or unlikable client
Going up against opposing counsel
Working with case agents and police
The burden of student debt
A poor work/life balance causing strained relationships with family and friends
A difficult schedule that includes working nights, weekends, and holidays
Competitive co-workers who try to steal the lawyer's cases or clients
Incompetent support staff
A case with gray-area ethical issues
A client not paying their legal fees
Working for a firm that requires a certain amount of billable hours
Substance abuse and other mental health concerns that are prevalent among lawyers
A case being threatened when the proper chain of evidence isn't followed
A client getting caught lying under oath

The pressure to win at all costs (even when the lawyer suspects their case is flawed)

A high-profile case with too many distractions (media involvement, constant scrutiny by the firm, etc.)

The temptation to cross ethical lines to obtain justice

Working for a small firm and having trouble paying the bills

Being accused of malpractice

PEOPLE THEY MIGHT INTERACT WITH

Judges, co-counsel, opposing counsel, clients, defendants, office staff, court staff, police or case agents, expert witnesses, court-appointed guardians or special advocates, bail-bondsmen, targets of investigations, interns, investigators

HOW THIS OCCUPATION MIGHT IMPACT THE CHARACTER'S NEEDS

Self-Actualization: Justice can be blind, and if loopholes are constantly exploited through which the lawyer sees witness tampering and politics-impacted cases, they may become disillusioned with this career.

Esteem and Recognition: It may be easy to feel overlooked and unappreciated when senior partners take credit for a lawyer's work. Losing an important case (or a series of cases) can also take its toll on the character's confidence.

Love and Belonging: Lawyers often struggle to leave work at work. Also, because they tend to see people at their worst, they may assume the worst about the people they know, which can prevent them from trusting others enough to develop loving relationships.

Safety and Security: Lawyers may receive threats to their safety from criminal defendants, disgruntled clients, ex-spouses of clients, or anyone else dissatisfied with a ruling.

TWISTING THE FICTIONAL STEREOTYPE

Lawyers are typically portrayed as unemotional and analytical. Twist this stereotype by crafting a character brimming with creativity, empathy, playfulness, or another un-lawyerly attribute.

We tend to see lawyers in literature who are fabulously wealthy. But what if your character doesn't make a ton of money because of their desire to do pro-bono work, a gambling or spending addiction, or some other reason?

CHARACTERS MIGHT CHOOSE THIS PROFESSION BECAUSE THEY...

Had parents who were lawyers

Experienced injustice at the hands of an inept or corrupt lawyer

Optimistically believe that they can change the world

Desire to champion human rights, the wrongfully convicted, the environment, etc.

Want to make a lot of money

Ultimately want to become a politician or judge

Love the art of debate

Desire power and prestige

Are justice-minded and want to be part of a system that helps mend what is broken

LIBRARIAN

OVERVIEW
Today's modern librarian is highly-educated, passionate about technology, and an expert at connecting people with relevant information. They are unafraid of technological advances, are adaptable, and have a seeming love of books that is actually a deep thirst for knowledge. They are great organizers, good with people, enjoy being facilitators of education, and can manage tight budgets, resources, and staff.

NECESSARY TRAINING
Most librarians must obtain a degree in library science, often a master's. If they work in a facility which is specialized, they may have a special focus or additional accreditation in that area. However, a librarian in a small town or school may not have the same education, say, as someone employed at a reference library tasked with curating specialized academic research. Schooling may be obtained in person (attending a campus), or mostly through online college programs (virtual learning).

USEFUL SKILLS, TALENTS, OR ABILITIES
Academics, charm, empathy, enhanced hearing, exceptional memory, good listening skills, hospitality, mechanically inclined, multilingualism, multitasking, photographic memory, reading people, research, strategic thinking, teaching, writing

HELPFUL CHARACTER TRAITS
Adaptable, alert, ambitious, analytical, centered, charming, confident, cooperative, courteous, creative, curious, decisive, diplomatic, disciplined, discreet, efficient, focused, friendly, hospitable, imaginative, independent, industrious, intelligent, nurturing, observant, organized, passionate, patient, pensive, perceptive, persuasive, protective, resourceful, responsible, socially aware, studious, thrifty, timid, uncommunicative, wise

SOURCES OF FRICTION
Patrons who are disruptive
People who are careless with books
Tight budgets
Having to let someone go because of a conflict or budget need
Working with uppity authors or experts who are holding events in the library
Book theft
People writing in books
Damage to property or resources (books, the copy machine, carving into tables, etc.)
Having patrons fight over popular books
Late fees that are difficult to collect
Patrons or local citizens protesting the inclusion of a certain book
Books being re-shelved incorrectly
Parents who let their kids run amok in the library
Patrons monopolizing the computers

Not having a book that a customer wants

Sharing property with other municipal buildings that don't contribute to a conducive library environment (alarms going off at the fire station, police cars shrieking out of the station, etc.)

PEOPLE THEY MIGHT INTERACT WITH

Other librarians, interns, volunteers, researchers, teachers, students, parents, patrons, book groups, authors, handymen, computer techs, booksellers, delivery people, professors and other subject matter experts

HOW THIS OCCUPATION MIGHT IMPACT THE CHARACTER'S NEEDS

Self-Actualization: Characters who greatly prize knowledge can be drawn to this position, so any threat to the librarian's ability to access information could cause them stress and grief. For example, living during a time when propaganda caused poisoned viewpoints and led to book burning or censorship would be difficult because it not only restricts access to unbiased information, it also disrespects books by presenting incorrect information as fact.

Esteem and Recognition: A librarian who loves books may view their workplace as an extension of him or herself. Budget cuts and decreased community involvement can run an establishment down, bringing the librarian's self-esteem with it.

TWISTING THE FICTIONAL STEREOTYPE

As someone who deals with the public and loves being a facilitator of knowledge, the stuffy, angry librarian who hates everyone under fifty doesn't make sense for this profession, so think past that cliché. Instead, bring to life a librarian who is young, enthusiastic, and possibly a knockout. While physical beauty isn't something to arbitrarily assign to our characters, if doing so knocks down a stereotype, it's something to keep in mind.

CHARACTERS MIGHT CHOOSE THIS PROFESSION BECAUSE THEY...

Found solace in books as a child and want to instill that passion in others

Love literature and reading

Want to help others obtain new knowledge and open their minds to what is possible

Are a passionate advocate of literacy

Value the past and want to make sure it's not forgotten

Are a lifelong learner and want access to unlimited knowledge as part of their career

View their library as the cultural and historical hub of the community and want to be part of that

LOBBYIST

OVERVIEW
A lobbyist attempts to influence legislators on behalf of an individual, group, or organization. They seek to persuade politicians to propose, pass, defeat, or amend legislation for the benefit of the interests they represent. Many do this by conducting research and providing the politician with information in the form of charts, polls, graphs, studies, and reports to plead their case. While they are prohibited from directly using money to achieve their ends, they will hold fundraisers as a means of garnering favor.

A lobbyist working on a politician's behalf will take part in community outreach to discover the constituents' issues so those can be folded into the campaign and addressed. They may create press releases, documents, and other informative materials to respond to voter concerns and sway public opinion.

NECESSARY TRAINING
There is no formal training for this career, but many lobbyists are former attorneys, government officials, or experts in policy. Most hold four-year or advanced degrees.

USEFUL SKILLS, TALENTS, OR ABILITIES
A knack for making money, charm, empathy, enhanced hearing, exceptional memory, gaining the trust of others, hospitality, performing, promotion, public speaking, research, writing

HELPFUL CHARACTER TRAITS
Ambitious, bold, charming, confident, confrontational, diplomatic, honorable, hospitable, idealistic, industrious, inflexible, just, loyal, manipulative, materialistic, obsessive, organized, patient, patriotic, persistent, persuasive, protective, pushy, resourceful, sophisticated, stubborn, unethical, workaholic

SOURCES OF FRICTION
Pressure to fundraise effectively for a politician
The responsibility of having to write legislative bills
Navigating the ethical and moral dilemma of the lobbying system
Unusual working hours due to entertaining politicians and hobnobbing with influencers
Limited cash flow
Being forced to work with other lobbyists whose personalities, ethics, or goals aren't a match
Unknowingly working with outdated information
Skepticism and distrust by the public
Family and friends who question the lobbyist's moral code
Loved ones questioning if the lobbyist is using their skills of persuasion or manipulation on them
Relationship conflict due to differences of opinion
An event that causes public backlash against a client (a mass shooting, a study that proves the client's product is unsafe, an executive being accused or convicted of a crime, etc.)
Making a discovery that threatens public safety and being asked by a client to repress it

PEOPLE THEY MIGHT INTERACT WITH
Politicians, fundraiser contributors, policy experts, other lobbyists, citizens, reporters

HOW THIS OCCUPATION MIGHT IMPACT THE CHARACTER'S NEEDS
Self-Actualization: A character in this career will knowingly exploit legal loopholes in order to achieve their ends and often approach politicians with job offers at their lobbying firms, effectively cornering a politician to stay in their good graces. Lobbyists also must secure funding for politicians via fundraising in order to achieve their clients' ends, earning them a questionable moral reputation. As time goes on, it may become difficult for them to reconcile with this identity. On the flip side, a lobbyist who adamantly believes they're fighting on the right side of an issue may become discouraged if their attempts to affect change are unsuccessful.

Esteem and Recognition: If they have a difficult client (such as a politician who is a PR nightmare or an automotive company known for its shady financial dealings), a lobbyist may find it hard to be a persuasive advocate. This can impact their self-esteem.

Love and Belonging: These characters may have difficulty connecting in personal relationships because of their unusual work schedule and calculating mindset. Romantic partners may question a lobbyist's ability to disengage from the person they are at work, especially as they tend to view people as chess pieces to move so goals can be achieved.

TWISTING THE FICTIONAL STEREOTYPE
Because lobbyists must mingle, entertain, and rub elbows with powerful people, consider a character with social anxiety. How might this difficulty add tension in your story?

Fictional lobbyists are often portrayed as unethical and power-hungry. Why not make your lobbyist ethical and moral, determined to be a catalyst for change that benefits those who need it most?

CHARACTERS MIGHT CHOOSE THIS PROFESSION BECAUSE THEY...
Experienced trauma that could have been avoided had laws been different
Are good at persuasion or manipulation
Are passionate about a cause, political party, politician, or their community
Enjoy the thrill of the lobbying process
Like to be entrenched in the political arena
Are a skilled tactician
Wish to bring about larger changes without being in the limelight (and dealing with everything that comes with it)

LOCKSMITH

OVERVIEW
A person in this field will be responsible for most any job involving locks: installing and changing them at residences, helping people get into locked cars and buildings, opening secured devices such as briefcases or boxes, installing and opening safes, and copying keys. A locksmith might work on his own or be employed by someone else.

NECESSARY TRAINING
A person can become a locksmith by completing an apprenticeship or by training at a vocational school. Because this field involves people's security, locksmiths are typically required to be licensed, bonded, and insured.

USEFUL SKILLS, TALENTS, OR ABILITIES
Exceptional memory, dexterity, mechanically inclined, putting people at ease, sales

HELPFUL CHARACTER TRAITS
Calm, centered, courteous, discreet, efficient, honorable, industrious, patient, persistent, professional, responsible

SOURCES OF FRICTION
A lock the character can't pick
Causing damage to a client's property while trying to complete a job
Having to work within a short timeline
A client's home or business being burgled just after the locks were installed
Accidentally letting a license or certification lapse
Misplacing the keys to a client's lock
Finding something disturbing in a customer's safe or home
Having low seniority at work and being assigned all the crappy jobs
Not being able to find a client's address
Having an accident that creates a mess of supplies in the back of the locksmith's van
Misplacing tools that must be paid for out-of-pocket
Not making enough money to make ends meet
Being asked to copy a key by someone who raises the character's suspicions
Failing to acquire a high-level certification (such as safe-cracking)
Being harassed by a client while on their property
A locksmith being robbed, and their tools or key cutting equipment being stolen
Being intimidated by a customer who wants to ensure their privacy is respected
Being asked to do something illegal
An injury that affects their dexterity

PEOPLE THEY MIGHT INTERACT WITH
Other locksmiths, customers, a dispatcher, a boss (a manager or the business owner), administrative personnel, vendors

HOW THIS OCCUPATION MIGHT IMPACT THE CHARACTER'S NEEDS

Self-Actualization: Picking locks can pay the bills, but someone who would rather be doing something else—maybe something creative or more mentally stimulating—might struggle in the long-term.

Esteem and Recognition: While it's an honest living, being a locksmith doesn't pay a lot. Someone who cares about what people think or frequently compares himself to others may find his esteem taking a hit.

Safety and Security: Any time a person is required to enter a stranger's home, there's the possibility of risk.

Physiological Needs: Because of this job's pay scale, locksmiths may find themselves unable to support a family on their salary. Add an expensive accident or illness, and the character's physiological needs may become threatened.

TWISTING THE FICTIONAL STEREOTYPE

This is another career field dominated largely by men. Make your locksmith a woman and you'll add a hint of freshness to the scenario.

Because of the security aspects of this career, it can also easily propel your character into conflict. Consider how the client (a mafia don or criminal) or the contents of the locked container (drugs, guns, or trafficking victims) might change the course of the protagonist's life.

CHARACTERS MIGHT CHOOSE THIS PROFESSION BECAUSE THEY...

Desperately needed employment and this work was available

Couldn't afford college tuition and so pursued a career that didn't require expensive training

Suffered a traumatic event involving being locked somewhere (in a closet, a chest, a shed, etc.), and they want to take their power back by mastering the locksmithing craft

Have a criminal past that created a proficiency in circumventing locks

Enjoy puzzles and solving problems

Are a voyeur, and the career allows them lawful access to personal spaces

Have a fascination with locks from growing up with secrets that were kept behind locked doors

Can use skills they hold dear without breaking the law as they once did

MAIL CARRIER

OVERVIEW
Mail carriers transport mail in the form of letters, circulars, packages, and bills from a distribution center to homes and businesses. While most of them use vehicles, urban mail carriers often walk their routes.

NECESSARY TRAINING
Mail carriers need a high school diploma or equivalent and must pass a written exam. They also must have a valid driver license, have a good driving record, and be able to pass a criminal background check.

USEFUL SKILLS, TALENTS, OR ABILITIES
A way with animals, being fit, exceptional memory, multilingualism, predicting the weather, stamina, swift-footedness

HELPFUL CHARACTER TRAITS
Alert, courteous, disciplined, discreet, efficient, focused, friendly, honest, independent, introverted, meticulous, organized, patient, professional, responsible

SOURCES OF FRICTION
Their van breaking down
Being threatened while delivering mail in a dangerous part of town
Customers not receiving their mail (because it was stolen or delivered to the wrong place)
Customers issuing complaints about the carrier's service
Working in miserable weather
Hand-delivering mail to someone who seems dangerous or unpredictable
Labor strikes
Feeling pressured to join a union when the character would rather not
Being injured on the job (slipping on ice and falling, being bitten by a dog, etc.)
Suffering an injury that makes it difficult to do the job
Working long hours (especially in the beginning of their career)
Mistakes at the distribution center that result in mail being delivered to the wrong address
Increased business over the holidays and not enough employees to handle it
Having to train a new carrier who is incompetent or annoying
Craving interactions with others but mostly working alone
Dealing with rude customers
Unfeeling or insensitive supervisors
Accidentally dropping a fragile package
A customer who refuses to accept delivery of a package
Delays at the distribution center that make the carrier late for their route
Handling a suspicious package
The physical effects of walking a long distance each day (if the carrier has a walking route)
Increased levels of fatigue as the character grows older

PEOPLE THEY MIGHT INTERACT WITH

Other mail carriers, a manager or supervisor, other postal service employees, union representatives, customers, drivers and pedestrians along the route, corporate security personnel

HOW THIS OCCUPATION MIGHT IMPACT THE CHARACTER'S NEEDS

Self-Actualization: There's only so much possibility for advancement in this position; someone who is looking for upward mobility within their career may soon feel like they're stuck and aren't able to realize their full potential.

Esteem and Recognition: Many people view college degrees and the careers that come with them as being more important, valuable, or desirable than ones where a degree isn't required. If a mail carrier interacts with these people, they may feel judged and question their own self-worth.

Love and Belonging: In the beginning, the hours are long; this can take a toll on personal relationships. And in many cases, a carrier is isolated, spending the majority of their day alone. This decreases the opportunities to meet and get to know people they might enter into relationship with.

Safety and Security: In certain situations, delivering the mail can be dangerous. This will depend on the neighborhood the carrier works in, the kinds and heaviness of traffic they encounter, and the dangers inherent when they exit their vehicle and step onto private property to deliver mail.

TWISTING THE FICTIONAL STEREOTYPE

Mail carriers tend to be background characters: quiet, introverted, and invisible. But characters in this occupation can be anything you want them to be. Just look at Newman, from *Seinfeld*. Give your mail carrier an unusual trait or two to bring them to life.

Also, consider carefully why your character has chosen this job. Is it because they don't have to work too closely with others? Because it requires hard work and long hours and allows them not to think about certain things? Because it keeps them out of the public eye? Knowing the reason behind this career choice can turn this option into something interesting with added depth.

CHARACTERS MIGHT CHOOSE THIS PROFESSION BECAUSE THEY...

Have a passion for the history of letter-writing as a form of communication

Want a job that encourages physical fitness without being too taxing

Enjoy solitary work and being able to limit their interaction with others

Are afraid to pursue a more challenging career, believing that doing so will result in failure

Want to feel part of a community but have social challenges that keep them from pursuing personal relationships

MAKEUP ARTIST

OVERVIEW

A makeup artist uses cosmetics to enhance or change a person's physical appearance. This type of artist may work as a clerk at a store, in a salon, as a personal makeup artist for a celebrity, at special events (such as a photo shoot, runway show, or wedding), or on staff for an entertainment production company. They may also work in a mortuary or funeral home, preparing corpses for viewing. At the extreme end of this career spectrum, makeup artists may use their techniques to create special effects in movies. People in this career field can either be freelance or employed in a permanent position.

NECESSARY TRAINING

Many makeup artists start their training by volunteering in the aforementioned roles and learning from professionals as they go. Certifications aren't required in all places, but sometimes they're necessary to work in the field, so many people choose to take cosmetology courses to become certified.

USEFUL SKILLS, TALENTS, OR ABILITIES

Creativity, detail-oriented, dexterity, good listening skills, multitasking, promotion, repurposing, vision

HELPFUL CHARACTER TRAITS

Adventurous, calm, cooperative, courteous, creative, enthusiastic, extravagant, gentle, imaginative, industrious, perfectionist, responsible, studious, talented, vain, verbose, whimsical

SOURCES OF FRICTION

A customer requesting something that's beyond the character's ability to accomplish
Perfectionistic customers who are impossible to please
A customer having an allergic reaction to a product
Financial limitations that force the character to work with inferior cosmetics and tools
Insecurities about their own appearance
Jealous or petty co-workers
Being unable to break into a desired area of the industry
Unhealthy practices at a salon or spa where the character works that lead to bad press and a decrease in customers
Having their techniques or ideas stolen
Clients with sensitive skin requiring expensive products (cutting into the artist's bottom line)
Family members disagreeing with this career choice (based on gender, religious beliefs, etc.)
Trying to stand out on social media when so many celebrity and Instagram influencers dominate the platform
Being on call and working odd hours with a production company or for a special event
Being hounded by paparazzi to give up dirt on celebrity clients

PEOPLE THEY MIGHT INTERACT WITH

Other makeup artists, customers and their entourages (mothers, friends, bridesmaids, etc.), managers (in a retail/commercial setting), hair stylists, fashion consultants, photographers, vendors, models, celebrities and their handlers

HOW THIS OCCUPATION MIGHT IMPACT THE CHARACTER'S NEEDS

Self-Actualization: An artist who wishes to do high-end makeup for a professional or creative work on a movie set but is unable to break into that field may be forced to work in a commercial environment as a fallback option. This could lead to dissatisfaction and a feeling of being unable to meet their full potential.

Esteem and Recognition: In this industry, the character may compare themselves to clients they consider to be more attractive or to peers who are more skilled or recognized, leading to self-esteem issues.

Love and Belonging: If someone in the character's life doesn't appreciate what they do or desires something more lucrative or esteemed for them, the relationship may suffer, and a void in this area may develop.

TWISTING THE FICTIONAL STEREOTYPE

Characters in the makeup and fashion industry are often viewed as vapid, superficial, or unintelligent. Avoid that misperception by fleshing out your character to include a variety of meaningful traits and interests. You can also mix things up by changing your character's place of work. Instead of placing them at a salon or movie set, what if they work as a professional YouTuber, at a Halloween-themed venue, or are part of a reality TV show?

Makeup artists are in a unique position of becoming the confidant of the people they serve. Consider the friction opportunities if rival celebrities or powerful people spill secrets and your character is caught in the middle.

Consider giving your character an interesting specialty, such as full body makeup or a specialization in 3-D artistic transformations.

CHARACTERS MIGHT CHOOSE THIS PROFESSION BECAUSE THEY...

Grew up with a beautiful sibling and felt "less than" as a result; makeup artistry lets the character manufacture beauty and compensate for the perceived lack

Love fashion and beauty

Want a career that will help other people look and feel their best

Are drawn to makeup application and rituals

Want to become renowned for their skill and work with models and celebrities

Have a physical flaw that they hide with makeup; embracing this career allows them to keep from dealing with the emotional wound (or avoid being defined by it)

MASSAGE THERAPIST

OVERVIEW

A massage therapist will evaluate a client for injuries and then manipulate muscle and soft tissue to relieve pain, help heal injuries, improve circulation, alleviate stress, and offer relaxation and overall wellness. They may specialize in a variety of modalities (such as Swedish, hot stone, aromatherapy, deep tissue, shiatsu, reflexology, sports massage, or pregnancy massage.) and work in spas, doctor's offices, sports clinics, hotels, chiropractic centers, fitness centers, and other environments. Some massage therapists work on location (going to someone's residence, office, or a hotel) bringing their own equipment, lotions, and oils. Others may run a salon from their own home or business space.

Massage therapists need healthy stamina, strength, and dexterity, because many sessions require 60-90 minutes of applying pressure and resistance techniques using the hands, fingers, knuckles, forearms, arms, and elbows. They must also be good at communication to ensure they can properly assess a client's condition and provide treatment options.

Once a session is finished, the therapist will recommend follow-up instructions (stretches, exercises, posture adjustments, avoiding certain activities) and make suggestions for managing symptoms or seeing a doctor for further diagnosis.

NECESSARY TRAINING

Most therapists enter a post-secondary program that is part classroom study, part hands-on massage. Programs often require 500 hours of practice and end with an exam. Additional time will be required to specialize in a modality. Depending on where they operate, certified therapists may require a license, have to pass a background check, and need to be certified in cardiopulmonary resuscitation (CPR).

USEFUL SKILLS, TALENTS, OR ABILITIES

Basic first aid, charm, clairvoyance, empathy, enhanced hearing, exceptional memory, gaining the trust of others, good listening skills, high pain tolerance, hospitality, multilingualism, reading people, regeneration, stamina, strategic thinking, strength, strong breath control

HELPFUL CHARACTER TRAITS

Adaptable, analytical, cautious, curious, controlling, disciplined, discreet, empathetic, focused, friendly, gossipy, industrious, meticulous, observant, organized, patient, perceptive, perfection-ist, persistent, professional, sensible, supportive, tolerant, workaholic

SOURCES OF FRICTION

A client being evasive about symptoms out of embarrassment
A client not disclosing a condition (like pregnancy) or injury
Treating a highly medicated client who isn't able to offer feedback about pain levels
Clients who don't like to be touched
Clients who "read into" the massage in a sexual way
A client gossiping or disclosing secrets about people the character knows
Demanding clients who try to tell the practitioner how to do their job

Clients who try to get out of payment after the service is complete
Credit cards that are declined
Working at an office with poor hygienic standards
Working at a clinic that requires the character to take on a too-high client load
Bad work contracts or poor benefit packages
Suffering an injury or strain on the job
Working on clients who are overly obese, which stretches the character's strength and stamina
A money-grabbing client falsely suing the therapist for causing injury
Clients who forget to tip

PEOPLE THEY MIGHT INTERACT WITH
Clients, doctors, chiropractors, administration, suppliers

HOW THIS OCCUPATION MIGHT IMPACT THE CHARACTER'S NEEDS
Esteem and Recognition: A character who has traditionally struggled with their own value may choose a career where they can directly influence the health and wellness of others. However, if they are criticized by an unhappy client, it may reawaken feelings of low self-worth.

Love and Belonging: If a character is in a rocky relationship with someone who requires a lot of massage therapy (say, after a car crash or workplace accident), they may question if the partner loves them or is just using them for what they can provide.

TWISTING THE FICTIONAL STEREOTYPE
Massage therapists are often portrayed as hot young guys or beautiful, small-framed women, but the reality is that the muscle manipulation requires a lot of core strength. Make sure your character's body type fits the profession and remember that the "hotness" level should have nothing to do with this career.

CHARACTERS MIGHT CHOOSE THIS PROFESSION BECAUSE THEY...
Found relief from chronic pain through massage and want to help others that way
Grew up in a family where massage was a cultural activity or the main source of livelihood
Lost a loved one as a result of mismanaged medication or surgery and wanted a career that would allow them to help others naturally
Strongly believe that natural methods are better for the body than drugs or surgery
Are rebelling against parents who pressured them to chase a more lucrative or highly esteemed profession

MASTER BREWER

OVERVIEW

A master brewer has extensive knowledge and experience when it comes to brewing beer. They oversee a brewery's production process to ensure batches turn out perfectly and efficiently. While master brewers may collaborate to develop recipes and brands, they have the final say and responsibility when it comes to product quality. Not only do they manage the people who work at the brewery, they often oversee the finances, as well.

NECESSARY TRAINING

There is no single path to becoming a master brewer. This designation is reserved for those with extensive knowledge and experience in beer production. Many people pursuing this title start in entry-level positions in a brew pub, brewery, or microbrewery and work their way up. Most have extensive experience as home or amateur brewers. To enhance their knowledge, they may pursue a four-year degree related to fermentation sciences, obtain various certifications, or attend one of the few programs dedicated specifically to master brewing (though no formal title is granted upon completion). The process to becoming a master brewer isn't clearly defined but is marked by many years of experience and a thirst for knowledge that is never quite quenched.

USEFUL SKILLS, TALENTS, OR ABILITIES

A knack for making money, a tolerance for alcohol, creativity, enhanced sense of smell, enhanced taste buds, exceptional memory, hospitality, mechanically inclined, promotion

HELPFUL CHARACTER TRAITS

Creative, curious, disciplined, enthusiastic, humble, imaginative, industrious, observant, organized, passionate, patient, persistent, quirky, studious, talented, workaholic

SOURCES OF FRICTION

Ruined brew batches
Financial strain in market downturns
Errors in data collection when monitoring a brew
Having an assistant brewer who resents their role (largely consisting of menial tasks)
Equipment malfunctions and expensive repairs
Difficulty developing new recipes
Being a female in a predominantly male work environment
The brewery changing ownership
Owners who micro-manage
Competition with other breweries
Having a poor business plan
Injury due to chemical or heat exposure
Discovering that a shipment contains subpar ingredients
Failing an inspection
A recipe being leaked to the competition
Being forced to relocate the brewery (e.g., due to a lease not being renewed)

Being limited by a lack of funds, making it impossible to buy high-quality ingredients or invest in the best equipment
Working with hobbyists rather than with passionate and knowledgeable brewers
Having to change suppliers and being unsure of the quality of their ingredients
Working for employers who don't know or care about beer
Launching a new beer to lackluster customer response

PEOPLE THEY MIGHT INTERACT WITH
Brewery owners, the head (lead) brewer, research and development brewers, shift brewers, assistant brewers, the cellar manager, inspectors, delivery drivers, administration staff, repair technicians, customers, suppliers

HOW THIS OCCUPATION MIGHT IMPACT THE CHARACTER'S NEEDS
Esteem and Recognition: The brewery itself may receive recognition while the hard work of its individuals is overlooked. This can be especially frustrating when the establishment's success is largely due to the master brewer's dedication to continuing education and developing new and popular recipes.

Safety and Security: Brewers are exposed to dangerous chemicals and hot temperatures. They work around heavy machinery and equipment. If care is not taken or someone fails to follow safety protocol, the master brewer could be hurt.

TWISTING THE FICTIONAL STEREOTYPE
Brewers were traditionally exclusively male, and this is how they're still often portrayed in literature. Bring your master brewer into the current century by turning him into a talented, beer-appreciating female lead.

Master brewers are highly educated and have years of experience in brewing. Consider crafting a character who comes from a much different background than readers might expect.

CHARACTERS MIGHT CHOOSE THIS PROFESSION BECAUSE THEY...
Love beer and the history of it
Are drawn to the challenges presented by chemistry and bioengineering
View chemistry as a vehicle for art
Love socializing and want to provide others with a memorable flavor experience
Want to turn their passion and hobby into a lucrative career

MECHANICAL ENGINEER

OVERVIEW
Mechanical engineering involves the study of motion, force, and energy. Engineers call upon their knowledge in this area by researching, designing, building, and maintaining mechanical tools, engines, machines, and large-scale plants and facilities. The products and systems created and developed by mechanical engineers are vast, from space shuttle vehicles to escalators to biomedical devices to power plants.

Their skills are needed in a variety of industries, including aerospace, automotive, pharmaceutical, robotics, construction, oil and gas, agriculture, and more, meaning there are many employment options for someone in this position.

NECESSARY TRAINING
To work in this field, a person must acquire a four-year mechanical engineering degree. Coursework leans heavily on knowledge of materials, statics, dynamics, thermodynamics, numerical methods, chemistry, and high-level mathematics. Innovation and well-developed problem-solving skills are a must in this field.

USEFUL SKILLS, TALENTS, OR ABILITIES
Detail-oriented, dexterity, good with numbers, mechanically inclined, repurposing, research

HELPFUL CHARACTER TRAITS
Analytical, cooperative, creative, curious, decisive, efficient, enthusiastic, focused, industrious, intelligent, meticulous, observant, organized, proactive, resourceful, responsible, sensible, studious

SOURCES OF FRICTION
Working on a team with uncooperative or unmotivated members
Racial or gender prejudice
Being unable to find the solution for a particular project
Being led by someone lacking sufficient knowledge or experience
Dealing with paperwork and red tape that keeps the engineer from doing their job
Working within unrealistic deadlines
Losing funding in the middle of a project
Unknowingly working with inferior parts, resulting in machines breaking down
A machine malfunctioning and causing an injury
The character being passed up for a project they really wanted to work on
Being pigeon-holed into only working on certain projects
Being great with machines but not so good with people
The engineer's ideas being stolen (by a boss, team member, or client)
A project being sabotaged by a jealous or competitive co-worker
A physical injury that interferes with the job, such as a traumatic brain injury or one affecting the hands or fingers
Being blamed for a failing project because higher-ups need a scapegoat

PEOPLE THEY MIGHT INTERACT WITH

Clients, a boss, office personnel, team members and co-workers, project managers, construction foremen and general contractors, engineers in other disciplines, corporate individuals (lawyers, finance people, human resources personnel, etc.)

HOW THIS OCCUPATION MIGHT IMPACT THE CHARACTER'S NEEDS

Self-Actualization: Because this career field is so vast, people may enter it with different goals. If a character was passionate about focusing on a specific area but gets stuck working on uninteresting products or in one space, they may become dissatisfied from not being able to do what they really want to do.

Esteem and Recognition: Someone who is always being out-performed by co-workers or is bypassed repeatedly for promotions may begin to doubt himself or lose esteem in the eyes of his peers.

Safety and Security: A mechanical engineer involved in the manufacture and testing of machinery could be injured if there is a malfunction or proper safety protocols aren't followed.

TWISTING THE FICTIONAL STEREOTYPE

Instead of sticking your mechanical engineer in the office, give them a project that requires them to visit interesting locations or places that are strategic to your plot.

Because of the analytical and structured nature of the job, engineers tend to be stereotyped as strait-laced, nerdy, and boring. To switch things up for your character, consider the different aspects of their personality and how you might bring in an unusual element. Hobbies, traits, secrets, phobias, and quirks can all be used to create a character who breaks the engineering mold. Consider, too, what negative traits and qualities might be overlooked by employers because your engineer is supremely talented and able to get results where others fail.

CHARACTERS MIGHT CHOOSE THIS PROFESSION BECAUSE THEY...

Were pressured by family members working in the field

Wanted to earn respect from a demanding parent who expected great things or withheld love

Are exceptionally intelligent

Want to create things that will have a far-reaching impact

Have a passion for science and innovation

Are fascinated with and have an innate understanding of how things work

Are passionate about an industry and want to create products and systems that enhance it

MIDWIFE

OVERVIEW
Midwives have been a pillar of women's health for thousands of years, and while techniques and perceptions have changed, the midwife's role remains largely the same: providing prenatal medical support, assistance during labor, and care for both the mother and infant in the postnatal period. They also provide advice on family planning and childcare, as well as on health, sexual, and reproductive matters. While midwives typically deliver babies on their own, part of their responsibility is to identify potential complications requiring treatment by other healthcare professionals.

NECESSARY TRAINING
In some places, a midwife must obtain a higher level of education, such as a graduate or bachelor's degree, before entering into the clinical phase of training. Other regions only require the person to complete certain courses and show competency in specified areas of knowledge and skill. Depending on their certification, midwives can work in the hospital, a birthing center, or a client's home.

USEFUL SKILLS, TALENTS, OR ABILITIES
Basic first aid, empathy, equanimity, gaining the trust of others, good listening skills, herbalism, hospitality, intuition, multitasking, peacekeeping, research, stamina, teaching

HELPFUL CHARACTER TRAITS
Adaptable, affectionate, alert, analytical, calm, confident, confrontational, courteous, decisive, diplomatic, disciplined, discreet, empathetic, fussy, gentle, kind, loyal, meticulous, nurturing, observant, organized, passionate, patient, perceptive, proactive, professional, protective, responsible, stubborn, supportive

SOURCES OF FRICTION
Prejudice from other healthcare officials or hospital administrations who harbor antiquated misperceptions about the midwifery career
Unforeseen circumstances during a delivery that cause complications
Failing a re-certification
Having to keep up with new certifications and course work
The death of a baby
Being unfairly blamed for something going wrong in the delivery
A patient who doesn't follow advice or care for herself properly
A patient refusing to deviate from her birth plan and putting herself or her baby in danger
Overbearing or hysterical relatives
Learning about a fellow midwife's unethical or inept actions (missing something obvious with the patient's prenatal care, becoming romantically involved with a patient's partner, etc.)
Administrators at the birthing center who are rude or difficult to work with
Multiple patients going into labor at the same time
Having to miss an important event because of an unexpected or longer-than-usual labor

Increasing numbers of patients suffering from postnatal depression and other mental health conditions

PEOPLE THEY MIGHT INTERACT WITH

Pregnant women, women seeking gynecological care, a patient's family members, other midwives, administrative personnel at a birthing center or hospital, OBGYNs and other doctors, nurses, doulas (birth attendants), other healthcare providers (psychiatrists, dieticians, etc.)

HOW THIS OCCUPATION MIGHT IMPACT THE CHARACTER'S NEEDS

Self-Actualization: A character who entered this field because of a love of motherhood may suffer a crisis if she discovers she is unable to bear children herself.

Esteem and Recognition: Outdated perceptions and stereotypes about midwifery still exist in some places. Someone who is accused of quackery or being "less than" other industry professionals will not receive the esteem and recognition that they deserve.

Love and Belonging: With the odd hours and level of responsibility required in this profession, some midwives could find it difficult to maintain the healthy work/life balance that keeps them in a loved one's good graces.

Safety and Security: For fictional purposes, certain scenarios could create risks for the midwife, such as a patient secretly carrying the child of a mafia don, unstable stalker, or powerful politician.

TWISTING THE FICTIONAL STEREOTYPE

Almost without exception, midwives are female—mostly because clients seeking them specifically want the care and support of a woman. To flip this stereotype and make your midwife male, you would need to change the culture in your story to account for this.

Female midwives tend to have certain innate traits, such as being nurturing, caring, and empathetic, so they're often portrayed in this way. But like other healthcare professionals, a midwife can be good at the clinical part of her job while having a terrible bedside manner. Consider giving your midwife unusual traits, such as flamboyancy, inflexibility, or even a heavy dose of superstition.

CHARACTERS MIGHT CHOOSE THIS PROFESSION BECAUSE THEY...

Assisted in a friend's home birth and found the experience empowering and satisfying
Worked as a doula and wanted to take their career to the next level
Had to deliver their baby alone and don't want others to go through the same experience
Believe that all life is sacred
Are unable to bear children and want to be as close to the process as they can
Have a nurturing nature and find satisfaction in coaching of any kind
Have a passion for supporting women

MILITARY OFFICER

OVERVIEW
A military officer is a member of a country's military forces who holds a position of authority. Their duties require them to oversee personnel units and may include planning missions, leading troops on those missions, managing subordinates, attending meetings, preparing training exercises, conducting safety drills, maintaining equipment, and filing significant paperwork. Military forces vary depending on the nation, but may include Air Force, Army/Land Forces, Coast Guard, Marine Corps, or Navy. Official positions include non-commissioned officers, commissioned officers, and warrant officers.

NECESSARY TRAINING
Non-commissioned officers (NCOs) attend basic training to prepare physically, mentally, and emotionally for military life. Afterward, they receive education in leadership and their military trade specialty.

Commissioned officers outrank all enlisted personnel and NCOs. They generally enter the military with a four-year college degree (though not all countries require one) and are commissioned in various ways. These include but are not limited to service academies or senior military colleges, Reserve Officer Training Corp (ROTC) programs through traditional colleges, Officer Candidate School, direct commissioning after college graduation, and programs that transition non-commissioned officers to commissioned ones.

Warrant officers are considered subject matter experts in specific technical areas. Their rank falls below the lowest commissioned officer but above the highest non-commissioned officer.

Additional training for the military officer is conducted over the entire span of their career though professional military education (PME). From Officer Basic to the War College, each grade of officer has a training course that must be attended to prepare them for leading at the next level.

USEFUL SKILLS, TALENTS, OR ABILITIES
Basic first aid, enhanced hearing, exceptional memory, high pain tolerance, knife throwing, knowledge of explosives, leadership, lip reading, lying, multilingualism, reading people, regeneration, self-defense, sharpshooting, stamina, strategic thinking, strength, strong breath control, survival skills, swift-footedness, wilderness navigation

HELPFUL CHARACTER TRAITS
Alert, ambitious, analytical, bold, calm, cautious, centered, confident, cooperative, disciplined, efficient, inflexible, loyal, obedient, patriotic, proactive, professional, subservient, workaholic

SOURCES OF FRICTION
Working with a leader who provides poor guidance
Personal beliefs that conflict with mission objectives
Acts of insubordination
Being frequently relocated to new posts
The loss of a fellow soldier
Suffering from work-related trauma

Undergoing challenging physical and mental training
Hours that mimic being constantly on-call
Having rigid rules for fraternization
Dangerous work environments
Being injured or growing ill on assignment, especially in a remote location
Relationship struggles as loved ones are impacted by the lifestyle
Being too strict or having unrealistic expectations as a parent
An affair overseas being discovered by the character's spouse
Coming home and discovering that a spouse has been unfaithful
Difficulty acclimating to civilian life
Getting a poor performance review (either deserved or underserved)
Having to navigate workplace politics
Failing a physical
The character's career stalling due to politics or nepotism

PEOPLE THEY MIGHT INTERACT WITH
Subordinate officers and non-commissioned officers, advisors for personnel actions, politicians, leaders within overseas communities

HOW THIS OCCUPATION MIGHT IMPACT THE CHARACTER'S NEEDS
Esteem and Recognition: Non-commissioned officers are known to be the "backbone" of the military, but the respect and pay they receive do not reflect their workload. Similarly, commissioned officers may be viewed as less esteemed when compared to lawyers, doctors, engineers, and other professionals.

Love and Belonging: Frequent moves may make it difficult to form long-lasting relationships and feel a sense of geographical community. Communication with loved ones may be limited, especially when the officer is deployed.

Safety and Security: Due to the living conditions in some countries, those who serve may be at higher risk of picking up illnesses, infections, and diseases.

Physiological Needs: Service members working in dangerous locations may be targeted (by missiles, through land mines, or in skirmishes) and killed.

TWISTING THE FICTIONAL STEREOTYPE
Military officers are generally thought of as male, aggressive, physically fit, and conservative in political views. Flip any one of these qualities to change things up. Also, consider giving your character a secret, condition, or challenge that must be hidden for them to be accepted in this career.

CHARACTERS MIGHT CHOOSE THIS PROFESSION BECAUSE THEY...
Came from a military family
Needed financial help with college tuition
Want to inspire and lead others
Have a deep need for structure and discipline
Are extremely patriotic
Wish to gain specialized training that would be difficult to come by elsewhere

MODEL

OVERVIEW

Most modeling falls into two categories: editorial (magazine spreads in chic magazines, fashion catwalks, high-end makeup ads) and commercial (catalogs, print ads for non-fashion products, commercials, and even showroom work). Models who are editorial often have something different or striking about their appearance, are quite tall, and adhere to specific weight and age ranges. They also will clearly display their personality to prospective agents and clients through their look but are expected to be flexible and opinionated. Commercial modeling is more about the products being showcased, making the appearance requirements for the models less stringent; they may be different ages, varying heights, and have more of a "girl or boy next door" appeal.

The career of an editorial model can start in their teens and go into the early twenties, while commercial modeling employs a wider range of ages. Models may also only use one of their features, such as their hands (for jewelry, skincare products, and accessories) or feet (to sell shoes, socks, or accessories) rather than the whole body.

Much of a model's time is spent off-camera, waiting for interviews, going to castings or auditions, being fitted, spending time in hair and makeup, exercising, and rushing between appointments.

NECESSARY TRAINING

Models may take classes to become acquainted with various aspects of the business, such as understanding the casting process, knowing how fittings work, dealing with criticism, the role of agents, the importance of building a name, creating a strong portfolio, working with photographers, and more. But this isn't a requirement. Models must, however, maintain strong hygiene, be in good health, and control their weight for them to succeed in this profession.

USEFUL SKILLS, TALENTS, OR ABILITIES

A knack for making money, a way with animals, charm, creativity, exceptional memory, gaining the trust of others, good listening skills, making people laugh, mimicking, multilingualism, multitasking, networking, performing, photographic memory, promotion, strength, strong breath control, swift-footedness

HELPFUL CHARACTER TRAITS

Adaptable, bold, charming, confident, cooperative, creative, discreet, easygoing, flamboyant, focused, friendly, funny, meticulous, obedient, passionate, patient, perfectionist, persuasive, professional, sensual, sophisticated, talented, thrifty, tolerant, uninhibited

SOURCES OF FRICTION

Untrustworthy agents
Being taken advantage of as a minor in the industry (exploitation)
People in positions of power using intimidation and threats to get what they want
Struggling to pay the bills
Sensitive skin that's prone to breakouts

The pressure to maintain an unhealthy weight causing eating disorders
Being worn down by criticism and suffering from anxiety and depression
Not having insurance to cover a health emergency
Over-processing leading to the model's hair being damaged
Being passed over for jobs in this fickle industry
Addictions to uppers, downers, or sleeping aids
Competitiveness between models
A "watch your back" industry that creates trust issues, causing loneliness
Tripping on the runway due to high platform shoes or avant-garde designs that restrict movement or reduce visibility
Working with an emotionally volatile or verbally abusive designer
The model's needs always coming last, resulting in poor self-care

PEOPLE THEY MIGHT INTERACT WITH

Agents, other models, model advocates or parents (for underage models), photographers, designers, high level executives (clients and VIPs) from different companies, celebrities, journalists, artists, delivery people, hair and makeup artists, clothing stylists

HOW THIS OCCUPATION MIGHT IMPACT THE CHARACTER'S NEEDS

Esteem and Recognition: So much emphasis on the physical appearance, criticism from professionals, and models being tempted to compare themselves to each other can all lead to esteem issues.

Love and Belonging: Very attractive individuals often worry that people are only interested in them because of their looks. This can lead to trust issues, difficulty opening up to others, or becoming jaded and viewing loving relationships as transactional rather than unconditional.

Safety and Security: Models who are highly visible are easily recognizable to the Average Joe and can become targets for stalkers and other unstable individuals.

Physiological Needs: When body image issues become serious enough to birth mental disorders like bulimia and anorexia, the person's very life may become endangered.

TWISTING THE FICTIONAL STEREOTYPE

Models have historically been presented as superficial and vapid, to the point of this stereotype becoming a trope. Make sure your model, like every other character, is well-rounded and multi-dimensional.

Fictional models often suffer from low self-esteem, so why not experiment with a character who understands their worth without being arrogant about it?

CHARACTERS MIGHT CHOOSE THIS PROFESSION BECAUSE THEY...

Were groomed by parents or caregivers to pursue a modeling career
Needed to pay for university, then discovered it was a lucrative career
See their looks as an advantage that they can monetize
Think it's the only way they can be exceptional
Have a passion for fashion, modeling, and the design industry

NANNY

OVERVIEW
Nannies are professional caretakers whose primary job is to tend to a family's children in their home. They provide a nurturing and safe environment, helping their charges grow and mature, and will educate and discipline as needed. They may prepare meals and do light housekeeping, take children to school and appointments, and accompany them on extracurricular activities. In some circumstances, they might be asked to join the family on vacations and continue their duties in those environments.

While nannies should be provided with a contract containing their full scope of duties, many are not, meaning their responsibilities evolve over time as parents pile on new roles without discussion. People in this position may work full- or part-time and live on their own or on site. It is common for them to become very attached to their charges and the family as a whole.

NECESSARY TRAINING
Nannies can have different levels of education; the more they have, the more they typically are paid. Different employers may also look for someone with specific qualities, such as speaking multiple languages, being physically fit, or experience working with children with learning disabilities, physical ailments, or other conditions.

USEFUL SKILLS, TALENTS, OR ABILITIES
Baking, basic first aid, blending in, charm, clairvoyance, empathy, enhanced hearing, enhanced sense of smell, exceptional memory, gaining the trust of others, gaming, hospitality, intuition, making friends, making people laugh, multilingualism, multitasking, peacekeeping, photographic memory, reading people, stamina, swift-footedness, teaching

HELPFUL CHARACTER TRAITS
Adaptable, affectionate, alert, calm, centered, charming, confident, cooperative, creative, diplomatic, disciplined, discreet, easygoing, efficient, empathetic, enthusiastic, friendly, frivolous, funny, generous, gentle, happy, honest, honorable, hospitable, imaginative, independent, industrious, kind, loyal, nurturing, obedient, observant, organized, passionate, patient, persuasive, playful, protective, responsible, sensible, tolerant

SOURCES OF FRICTION
Parents who micromanage or make unreasonable demands
Parents who expect the nanny to enforce certain behaviors but fail to follow through themselves
Parents who don't make time to discuss the children and what happened each day
Being paid an unfair wage for the work
Responsibilities being added without a corresponding increase in pay
New duties being added without consultation
Feeling isolated after long days with no interaction with other adults
Putting up with unhappy employment conditions because the character is attached to the kids

Disagreements over discipline or parenting
Watching parents neglect their children or place unreasonable demands on them
A lack of benefits and health care
Being expected to manage other people's children when the families get together
A lack of empathy or understanding if an emergency for the nanny disrupts a parent's schedule
Struggling with taxes (or establishing a credit rating, if the nanny is being paid under the table)
Feeling drained because so much energy is being expended at work
A parent becoming jealous of the nanny's strong relationship with their child
Parents who give the children pets and expect the nanny to care for those, too
The nanny learning something sensitive about a charge that they must share with others (abuse accusations, drug usage, a porn addiction, etc.)

PEOPLE THEY MIGHT INTERACT WITH
Parents, delivery people, teachers, librarians, coaches and other instructors, the kids' friends and their parents, medical personnel (the pediatrician, dentist, etc.)

HOW THIS OCCUPATION MIGHT IMPACT THE CHARACTER'S NEEDS
Self-Actualization: If the character is unable to have children of their own, this occupation can meet that missing need but also act as a constant reminder of what they cannot have.

Esteem and Recognition: If the character works for a family that doesn't respect the nanny's time, schedule, skills, or needs, this can sabotage their sense of self-worth.

Love and Belonging: A full-time live-in nanny may have difficulty finding a partner or maintaining the energy to devote to a romantic relationship. Additionally, a nanny with children of their own may not have energy for them at the end of the day, leading to relationship friction and resentment.

TWISTING THE FICTIONAL STEREOTYPE
Nannies are typically portrayed one of two ways: as foreign-born immigrants or sexy interlopers intent on seducing an employer. Resist these clichés by considering other motivations for this kind of work, such as gaining experience for a career in childcare, conducting research for a psychological thesis, or seeking to fill a void caused by the death of the nanny's only child.

CHARACTERS MIGHT CHOOSE THIS PROFESSION BECAUSE THEY...
Had a terrible home life with neglectful parents and want to protect other children
Wanted to immigrate to another country, and the job made that possible
Want to nurture children and help them discover who they are
Place a high value on time spent with children due to the loss of their own child
Need a steady income to pay for school or bills
Want to travel and see the world
Enjoy spending time with children but don't want to have any of their own

NOVELIST

OVERVIEW
A novelist is someone who writes fictional stories of novel-length.

NECESSARY TRAINING
Formal education is not required for this career. However, some novelists take courses or pursue degrees in creative writing, English, literature, and other related subjects. Writers may self-study the craft of writing by reading craft books, attending conferences, joining writer's groups, participating in workshops, and following industry-related blogs. To succeed, a novelist must spend a lot of time writing, as well as reading widely, especially in their chosen genre.

USEFUL SKILLS, TALENTS, OR ABILITIES
A knack for making money, creativity, exceptional memory, multitasking, outside-of-the-box thinking, promotion, public speaking, strategic thinking, typing, writing

HELPFUL CHARACTER TRAITS
Creative, curious, disciplined, extroverted, focused, imaginative, independent, industrious, passionate, patient, persistent, quirky, talented, thrifty, whimsical, wise, witty, workaholic

SOURCES OF FRICTION
Writer's block
Handling editorial or beta reader feedback
Being out on submission to editors
Scrambling to make deadlines
Being an introvert but having to market via social media and networking
Financial difficulties
Juggling writing and a full-time job or family
Low sales figures
Pressure to repeat a former publishing success
Having an agent who is poor at communication, selling, or advocating
Losing an agent
Unsupportive family members
Poor marketing support from a publisher
The novelist's book being orphaned when its assigned editor leaves the publishing house
A friend believing that they have inspired an unlikeable character
Having to decide which publishing path to choose
Struggling with criticism from readers and critique partners
Bullying reviewers
Technology difficulties
Balancing writing with marketing and promotion
Co-workers, friends, and relatives believing that writing a novel is easy and anyone can do it
The amount of time spent writing a novel and seeking publication
Making the decision to give up on a book

The temptation to write what will sell rather than writing about the novelist's passions
Having to invest (in education, materials, coaching sessions, etc.) before earnings come in
Jealousy toward other writers who write faster, sell more, or hit milestones quicker

PEOPLE THEY MIGHT INTERACT WITH
Readers, editors, literary agent, illustrator, librarians, bookstore employees, beta readers, critique group members, authenticity readers

HOW THIS OCCUPATION MIGHT IMPACT THE CHARACTER'S NEEDS
Self-Actualization: Novelists who have a hard time finding a home for their book or fail to draw in readers may question their abilities and wonder if a career in writing is a dream meant for other people.

Esteem and Recognition: Reaching publication is extremely difficult and competitive. Once published, reviews can be harsh and the pressure to write a more successful book can be daunting.

Love and Belonging: Writing can be a lonely endeavor. Friends and family members may not understand how difficult writing is, let alone how hard it is to get published. A lack of support can leave a writer feeling alone and misunderstood.

TWISTING THE FICTIONAL STEREOTYPE
People often think that novelists are all big names who write for a living, but most writers have other full- or part-time jobs. Consider twisting this misconception by giving your character a day job that may be dramatically different than writing.

Novelists are thought of as creative storytellers, but perhaps your character is something of a fraud, using a staunchly formulaic approach to their novels or even stealing ideas from others.

Successful novelists are usually portrayed as self-isolated introverts who rely on their agent and editor to handle the business and marketing side of their career. Dispel this myth and show your novelist embracing the whole job so they can grow their readership and run a successful business.

CHARACTERS MIGHT CHOOSE THIS PROFESSION BECAUSE THEY...
Find the process of story creation to be therapeutic and healing
Have a powerful imagination and love words
Have a deep appreciation for literature
Desire to use words to communicate ideas and beliefs to the world
Want to entertain readers or provide them with an escape
Believe the myth that most writers end up with fame and fortune

NURSE (RN)

OVERVIEW

Registered nurses are in charge of patient care, observing and recording symptoms and providing treatment instructions for loved ones and caregivers. Some RNs may have other roles, such as teaching or organizing a nursing crew. They may work in a hospital, clinic, long-term care facility, doctor's office, school, or even prison. If they're part of a home health care company, they'll travel to meet their patients in their homes or at other facilities. Depending on where they work, some nurses will focus primarily on a specialty area, such as pediatrics, geriatrics, plastic surgery, or dermatology.

NECESSARY TRAINING

Registered nurses need a four-year nursing degree and will have to pass a national licensing exam. Nurses with a graduate degree can seek certification in an advanced clinical profession to become a nurse practitioner, nurse midwife, or a specialist in another area.

USEFUL SKILLS, TALENTS, OR ABILITIES

Basic first aid, empathy, equanimity, gaining the trust of others, good listening skills, hospitality, leadership, multilingualism, multitasking, peacekeeping, reading people, research, stamina, teaching

HELPFUL CHARACTER TRAITS

Adaptable, affectionate, alert, calm, centered, cooperative, courteous, decisive, diplomatic, discreet, efficient, empathetic, friendly, fussy, hospitable, industrious, intelligent, kind, merciful, meticulous, nurturing, objective, observant, optimistic, organized, patient, perceptive, persuasive, professional, pushy, responsible, sensible, studious, supportive, unselfish

SOURCES OF FRICTION

Fractious or uncooperative patients
Patients who lie about their true condition or health habits
Missing important warning signs in a patient
Suspecting that an elderly or underage patient is being abused
Being unable to help a patient
Having to provide end-of-life care for a favorite patient
A patient being unable to afford treatment
Losing touch with a critically ill patient (because they moved unexpectedly, were transferred to a distant facility, etc.)
Becoming addicted to opioids or other medications
Being asked by a terminal loved one to help with their final transition
Undesirable work conditions
Working with patients who don't follow instructions and keep having the same problems
Overbearing or condescending doctors
Favoritism in the workplace
Budget cuts that result in understaffing and poorly maintained equipment

Seeing problems with a patient that the nurse can't treat (homelessness, toxic relationships, poor nutrition, etc.)
Treating a patient and discovering they have a dangerous and infectious disease
Suspecting a doctor of malpractice or incompetence
Harassment on the job

PEOPLE THEY MIGHT INTERACT WITH
Doctors, other nurses, other healthcare providers (physical therapists, psychologists, etc.), patients, hospital administrators, administrative staff, the patient's family members or caregivers, pharmaceutical reps

HOW THIS OCCUPATION MIGHT IMPACT THE CHARACTER'S NEEDS
Self-Actualization: Nursing is a rewarding career, but it also requires long hours and can be emotionally draining. Someone in a difficult work environment who is unable to move up or change specialty areas may begin to feel stifled and dissatisfied.

Esteem and Recognition: A nurse in the frequent company of a condescending doctor or disapproving relatives may come to doubt herself.

Love and Belonging: A nurse who becomes too emotionally attached to her patients may have a hard time attaching to others. Or she might connect with her patients in an attempt to keep from having to open up to the people in her life, either creating or reinforcing a void in this area.

Safety and Security: Safety could become an issue for a nurse who works in a dangerous part of town, treats volatile patients, or who doesn't practice sufficient self-care.

TWISTING THE FICTIONAL STEREOTYPE
While there are more men in the nursing field than ever before, most people still associate this career with women. Whatever the gender, make sure that your nurse has a combination of interesting and meaningful attributes and flaws. You can also switch things up by placing your nurse in an unusual location, such as a psychiatric ward or boarding school.

CHARACTERS MIGHT CHOOSE THIS PROFESSION BECAUSE THEY...
Were unable to save someone from dying in the past and are making up for it now
Wanted to be a doctor but were unable to do so (due to finances, time, academic limitations, etc.)
Are naturally nurturing and empathetic
Come from a family of nurses and doctors
Have a hard time connecting with the important people in their life and want to meet that need through their patients
Want to make a difference in people's lives and in the world
Are looking for access to drugs
Want to land a rich doctor as a spouse

OUTDOOR GUIDE

OVERVIEW

An outdoor guide is someone who leads excursions into natural areas. These trips may last anywhere from a few hours to weeks at a time and can occur year-round, depending on the location. An outdoor guide uses their skills and vast knowledge of the area to give guests an experience that only a seasoned outdoor enthusiast can provide. They take groups out to view scenery and animal activity using boats, quads, horses, skis, snowshoes, dog sled teams, or other means. This allows guests to safely explore hard-to-reach areas, or in the case of mountaineering, reach a summit. On longer trips, guides will also oversee camp preparations. This includes setting up camp, getting firewood, preparing meals, and filtering water, if needed.

NECESSARY TRAINING

Little formal training is required to start as a guide. They'll need previous field experience or be given on-the-job training about the terrain, various modes of transport, and area-related challenges. If for example, the travelling is primarily via horseback, guides will require additional education regarding the handling and care of horses, including any emergency situations that could crop up while they're away. They will have taken courses in first aid and possibly be a certified Wilderness First Responder (WFR) or a suitable equivalent. Because they're responsible for the safety and well-being of their guests, guides may or may not have firearms training and carry a gun.

USEFUL SKILLS, TALENTS, OR ABILITIES

A way with animals, archery, baking, basic first aid, charm, exceptional memory, fishing, foraging, gaining the trust of others, good listening skills, good sense of direction, high pain tolerance, hospitality, leadership, making people laugh, multilingualism, multitasking, predicting the weather, reading people, research, sharpshooting, stamina, strategic thinking, strength, survival skills, teaching, wilderness navigation

HELPFUL CHARACTER TRAITS

Adventurous, alert, calm, cautious, centered, charming, confident, courteous, curious, decisive, diplomatic, disciplined, easygoing, efficient, enthusiastic, extroverted, friendly, funny, hospitable, independent, mature, nature-focused, observant, optimistic, organized, persuasive, professional, protective, resourceful, responsible, sensible, simple, wholesome, wise, witty

SOURCES OF FRICTION

Difficult or whiny guests who underestimate "roughing it"
Bad weather making the trip miserable and limiting what can be experienced
Equipment malfunctions
Injuries for people and animals (if they're being used)
Dangerous animals wandering close to camp
Guests who try to get too close to wild animals
Personality conflicts between guests
Guests who are poor tippers

Guests who are not up to the fitness level needed for the excursion

A horse throwing a guest

Encountering a cougar, a bear with cubs, or another threat

A guest wandering away from the group and getting lost

An illness sweeping through the camp (food poisoning, a sickness from drinking water containing bacteria, etc.)

Exhausted guests who have trouble keeping up or finishing an excursion

Being tired and having to entertain or encourage guests

Losing crucial supplies in a freak accident (a bear getting into camp, a bag being carried away downstream, etc.)

PEOPLE THEY MIGHT INTERACT WITH

Outfitters, tourists and locals, ranch hands, fish and wildlife officers, photographers, outdoor enthusiasts, local landowners

HOW THIS OCCUPATION MIGHT IMPACT THE CHARACTER'S NEEDS

Self-Actualization: The day-to-day grind of dealing with entitled, rude, or overbearing clients on the trail may sour a guide's love of the wilds, leaving them unsatisfied and surprised by the mismatch of expectation and reality.

Esteem and Recognition: Because guiding can seem like self-isolation, people can make assumptions about someone in this career, believing them to be loners and somehow unfit for "the real world." Being judged in this way can impact the character's self-esteem.

Love and Belonging: Because a character is often away for days at a time and on constant rotation during tourist season, it can be difficult to create and nurture long-term relationships.

Safety and Security: Out in the wilds, the character may encounter dangerous animals or navigate difficult terrain. As guides are responsible for their party, they take on the biggest risk and could be hurt.

CHARACTERS MIGHT CHOOSE THIS PROFESSION BECAUSE THEY...

Were lost in the woods as a child and learned to be an expert navigator to keep the same thing from happening again

Love the outdoors and wish to share their passion with others

Prefer a solitary lifestyle

Are able to fund their outdoor hobbies and interests with the income

PALEONTOLOGIST

OVERVIEW

A paleontologist is someone who looks for fossils in the form of dinosaur bones, eggs, egg fragments, fossilized wood, excrement, leaves, footprints, and various other vertebrate and invertebrate skeletons. The work is slow and taxing, involving countless hours of sifting through layers of dirt and rock to uncover fossils and determine their age and habitat, among other things.

Many paleontologists travel to interesting locations, living simply while doing so, to analyze the animal remains found there. Their deductions can help the archeologists they sometimes work with to understand the diet of those ancient civilizations. Others may teach, write and publish papers, run educational programs, organize collections and maintain exhibits, work in museums, or conduct research for private companies. The hours can be long, and the pay is not always impressive, but the work is rewarding for those who love testing theories, uncovering the mysteries of the past, and possibly making a new discovery.

NECESSARY TRAINING

To gain employment, a degree in geology (with courses in paleontology), a master's degree, or a doctorate in paleontology is likely needed. Not many universities offer degree programs in this specialty area, so if education in the real world is a component of your story, some research will be required to find a school that will work for your character.

USEFUL SKILLS, TALENTS, OR ABILITIES

A knack for making money, basic first aid, detail-oriented, exceptional memory, fishing, foraging, gaining the trust of others, multilingualism, photographic memory, predicting the weather, promotion, research, sculpting, strategic thinking, teaching, wilderness navigation, woodworking, writing

HELPFUL CHARACTER TRAITS

Adaptable, adventurous, ambitious, analytical, cautious, cooperative, curious, diplomatic, disciplined, efficient, focused, fussy, independent, intelligent, meticulous, nature-focused, nosy, objective, observant, obsessive, optimistic, organized, passionate, patient, perfectionist, persistent, resourceful, responsible, simple, studious, workaholic

SOURCES OF FRICTION

Losing funding for a dig
The stress of not producing results (and possibly losing funding)
Inclement weather
Theft at a dig site
Loneliness
Personality conflicts while working with others in a remote place
Illnesses contracted (malaria, parasites, etc.) far from civilization
Suffering an injury and being far from adequate medical help
Accidentally damaging a find

Friction in personal relationships resulting from the character being away for long periods of time

Working with people who do not have the same work ethic or respect for rules and processes

Finds being damaged or lost in transport

Equipment or vehicle breakdowns

Difficulty integrating back into a busy world between assignments

Working a site for a long period of time and finding nothing

Philosophical arguments between colleagues

False alarms; being excited about finding something potentially important, then discovering that it's nothing

Missing the creature comforts of civilization

PEOPLE THEY MIGHT INTERACT WITH

Archeologists, students, interns, laborers, drivers, university staff, editors, researchers, locals (for obtaining resources, information, shelter, guiding, etc.)

HOW THIS OCCUPATION MIGHT IMPACT THE CHARACTER'S NEEDS

Self-Actualization: Paleontologists who dream of making a new discovery or proving a theory might become discouraged with the day-in, day-out routine of the job.

Esteem and Recognition: If colleagues or rivals are making interesting discoveries (and being acknowledged for them) while the character is not, he or she may begin to question their own abilities and aptitude.

Love and Belonging: This career could create challenges for characters who are always away on digs rather than spending time with their significant other (and children, if they exist).

Safety and Security: Funding can be problematic, which makes income less secure.

Physiological Needs: Exotic, remote locations can be dangerous. Opportunistic militant groups, aggressive animals, and viral threats could all threaten a character's life. Even a simple illness or accident could be fatal when they're far from help.

CHARACTERS MIGHT CHOOSE THIS PROFESSION BECAUSE THEY...

Had a nomadic childhood and draw comfort from remote locations

Are fascinated by the creatures of the past and the roots of mankind

Want to make a new discovery that could reshape what humanity knows about the past

Are an academic

Have a passion for science and history

Struggle with the modern world and wish to spend as much time in the past as possible

PARALEGAL

OVERVIEW
A paralegal is a qualified person retained by a lawyer to perform a variety of research and preparation tasks for legal cases. Duties might include working directly with the client to understand and catalogue the case's facts, booking and organizing meetings, researching and helping to interview witnesses and experts, preparing legal documents for the lawyer, organizing evidence, taking notes, preparing and filing documents in a timely manner, acting as a liaison with court officials and other parties, managing deadlines, and assisting the lawyer in whatever is needed. Paralegals are prohibited from any tasks that constitute "practicing law," such as accepting cases, offering legal advice, representing a client, or determining fees.

NECESSARY TRAINING
Paralegals can take a two-year certificate course or may also earn a degree. Because of the wide range of duties they perform, most paralegals will have strong computer, writing, organization, and communication skills, as well as some training in client interactions so they can present a professional face on the agency's behalf. They are incredibly detail-oriented and organized, as even the smallest mistake can be disastrous for a case.

USEFUL SKILLS, TALENTS, OR ABILITIES
Blending in, charm, detail-oriented, enhanced hearing, exceptional memory, gaining the trust of others, good listening skills, multilingualism, multitasking, photographic memory, reading people, research, strategic thinking, writing

HELPFUL CHARACTER TRAITS
Adaptable, alert, analytical, confident, cooperative, decisive, diplomatic, disciplined, discreet, efficient, empathetic, focused, honest, honorable, humble, independent, industrious, intelligent, loyal, meticulous, obedient, obsessive, organized, perfectionist, persistent, persuasive, proactive, professional, protective, resourceful, responsible, stubborn, workaholic

SOURCES OF FRICTION
Having too large of a workload because the firm refuses to hire more help
Being underappreciated for their work
Being mistreated by big personalities and fragile egos when things don't go well
Working with a disorganized lawyer who needs research, expert interviews, and documents immediately, creating stress for the paralegal
Long hours
Working weekends
Problems at home when family members resent the time the character gives to work
Having to navigate rules and red tape
Resentment toward others in the agency who do not adhere to the same work ethic
Discovering a lawyer's infidelity or overindulgences (drugs, gambling, etc.) and being asked to keep it quiet
Moral conflicts if they work for a lawyer who has flexible ethics

Misfiling and errors by the court that result in delays and lost time

Witnessing favoritism in the office where the closeness of a relationship is rewarded over hard work

Struggling to get in contact with a dodgy or reluctant witness

A paralegal watching their hard work go down the drain because of the missteps of an incompetent or lazy lawyer

Losing receipts and being unable to get much-needed reimbursement for work expenses

PEOPLE THEY MIGHT INTERACT WITH

Lawyers, other paralegals, legal assistants, clients and witnesses, bailiffs, judges, filing clerks, court reporters, criminals, expert witnesses (detectives, psychologists, accountants, etc.), anyone else with intimate knowledge of the case, delivery personnel, librarians at the law library, other staff members at the law firm, a client's family members

HOW THIS OCCUPATION MIGHT IMPACT THE CHARACTER'S NEEDS

Self-Actualization: A paralegal is limited in what they can do despite the growing knowledge, experience, and skills they gain on the job. Such narrowed prospects may squash the character's feeling of self-actualization despite their love of what they do.

Esteem and Recognition: It is not uncommon for the tremendous and important work or paralegals to go unrecognized, which can lead to declining self-worth.

Love and Belonging: Relationships may suffer because paralegals are very much at the beck and call of the lawyers they work for. Missing important life events (anniversaries, a weekend soccer game, etc.) or having little energy during downtime can cause strain with a spouse and other family members.

CHARACTERS MIGHT CHOOSE THIS PROFESSION BECAUSE THEY...

Were once denied justice

Wanted to be a lawyer but were unable to do so (due to lack of funds, flunking out of law school, circumstances that made time a commodity, etc.)

Watched a loved one lose something important because they did not have a legal advocate

Had a role model or family member in the justice system (as a lawyer, prosecutor, etc.)

Respect the justice system

Are incredibly organized, proactive, and investigative

Have a passion for the law but don't want to be in the spotlight

Are comfortable playing a supporting role

PAROLE OFFICER

OVERVIEW

When an offender is released from prison but is still on probation, a parole officer monitors them, ensuring they have registered with the local police, undergo drug testing, report to an officer at appointed times, and follow all conditions of their parole. Parole officers explain the rules of parole and will also make sure offenders are enrolled in rehabilitation and job training programs as determined by the court. It should be noted that a parole officer is slightly different than a probation officer, who monitors those who have been sentenced to serve probation rather than a jail sentence.

Parole officers handle a large caseload and keep detailed records on each offender (where they live, friends and family contacts, employment records, and the parolee's progress). They will make planned visits to the home of the parolee, talk to family members, neighbors, co-workers, and employers. In some cases, they'll use community associations and the offender's religious group to check on their behavior and ensure they are following all conditions of their parole. Ultimately, they decide if an offender is rehabilitated and integrating back into society appropriately or if the case needs to be reviewed by the parole board to determine if the parolee should be remanded back into custody.

A parole officer's work is challenging, as they are required to work a variety of hours—some in an office setting, some in the field, often in higher crime locations—and positively engage with individuals who are resistant to working with members of the justice system.

NECESSARY TRAINING

Generally, characters in this field have a bachelor's degree and have completed a program in criminal justice, social work, and/or psychology. They may be required to take a state-sponsored training program and a certification test. They often have to be certified to use a firearm, must pass background checks, and be trained to perform drug tests. This profession varies widely in duties and training from one location to another, so proper research is needed depending on where the story takes place.

USEFUL SKILLS, TALENTS, OR ABILITIES

Blending in, clairvoyance, empathy, enhanced hearing, enhanced sense of smell, exceptional memory, gaining the trust of others, intuition, making people laugh, mentalism, multilingualism, multitasking, peacekeeping, photographic memory, reading people, self-defense, sharpshooting, strategic thinking, writing

HELPFUL CHARACTER TRAITS

Adaptable, alert, cautious, controlling, courageous, diplomatic, disciplined, discreet, efficient, honest, honorable, inflexible, just, meticulous, observant, organized, persistent, persuasive, responsible, sensible, stubborn, supportive, suspicious, tolerant

SOURCES OF FRICTION

Working with volatile offenders (who probably should not have been released)
Safety concerns for parolees who informed on others to get a lessened sentence
Having to travel to high-crime areas
Burning out because of the job stress and high caseload
False accusations from vengeful offenders
A parolee using the character's personal information to intimidate or blackmail them
Being unable to adequately monitor all parolees due to an impossibly high caseload
Economic shifts and government cutbacks that reduce the programs and services that help
offenders succeed in the world
Problems at home due to long hours and job stress

PEOPLE THEY MIGHT INTERACT WITH

Criminals, members of community and religious groups, police officers, undercover detectives,
psychologists, people associated with the parolee (co-workers, employers, friends, and family),
people within the justice system

HOW THIS OCCUPATION MIGHT IMPACT THE CHARACTER'S NEEDS

Self-Actualization: A character who once was on a dark path but was helped early in life by
a mentor may be drawn to this profession out of a desire to do the same for others. But if their
offenders consistently return to crime, the character may question their career choice and suffer
a crisis of faith.

Esteem and Recognition: Parole officers will largely be looked down upon by a segment of
society—often, the very people they are working to help. Constant disdain and resentment can
cause these characters to feel badly about themselves.

Love and Belonging: The long, sometimes irregular hours and job stress could lead to
relationship problems or even a broken marriage.

Safety and Security: Home visits in high-crime locations, as well as the need to engage with
other criminals to fully monitor the offender, can place parole officers in harm's way.

Physiological Needs: Death threats or a violent altercation with criminals could place the
character in mortal jeopardy—especially in the case of an offender connected to people who
don't fear the law and are willing to do anything to get their hooks into them again.

CHARACTERS MIGHT CHOOSE THIS PROFESSION BECAUSE THEY...

Were given a second chance following a transgression and want other criminals to have the
same opportunity
Respect the justice system and want to be part of it
Want to keep society safe
Believe in a check-and-balance system for criminals and want to be part of the process

PERSONAL ASSISTANT TO A CELEBRITY

OVERVIEW
A personal assistant to a celebrity is required to always be on call and to perform many types of tasks. These include but aren't limited to scheduling appearances, organizing events, attending to social media, collecting work-related materials, planning travel, couriering sensitive personal documents or important items, juggling the celebrity's personal and professional calendar, and coordinating with other key personnel such as the nanny, personal trainers, hair stylists, makeup artists, fashion consultants, and the celebrity's agent. Some tasks are mere errands, running from the mundane (walking the dog, shuttling the celebrity's children, picking up their dry cleaning) to the unusual or outrageous, such as securing someone's phone number at the celebrity's request, obtaining a candy or coffee from another country, convincing a restaurant owner to open after closing for a private dinner, being a personal shopper, buying and delivering gifts for other people in the business, and even purchasing high-end items at the behest of the celebrity.

Having a personal life is difficult since the assistant's time is rarely their own. They run on the same professional schedule as their celebrity, attending the same events and traveling when they travel.

Assistants can often become confidants and secret keepers, so they witness not only the high moments, but the low ones, too. Some may have to cover up or minimize the fallout of their celebrity's actions, be asked to procure things that are illegal, cross personal moral lines, and perhaps even pay people off to fix the problems that crop up. For this reason, assistants usually are forced to sign non-disclosure agreements that forbid them from discussing their relationship with the celebrity.

NECESSARY TRAINING
While no official degree is required to become a personal assistant, connections in the industry can help the character procure a job. Having a strong network of facilitators ("I know a guy") is key, so the assistant must have established contacts or be willing to build these connections quickly.

USEFUL SKILLS, TALENTS, OR ABILITIES
Blending in, charm, clairvoyance, detail-oriented, empathy, enhanced hearing, exceptional memory, gaining the trust of others, good listening skills, haggling, hospitality, lip-reading, lying, making people laugh, mentalism, multilingualism, multitasking, networking, peace-keeping, photographic memory, predicting the weather, promotion, reading people, sewing, strategic thinking, swift-footedness, writing

HELPFUL CHARACTER TRAITS
Adaptable, alert, bold, calm, charming, cooperative, courteous, creative, decisive, diplomatic, disciplined, discreet, efficient, hospitable, loyal, mature, meticulous, obedient, observant, organized, proactive, professional, protective, resourceful, responsible, sophisticated, tolerant

SOURCES OF FRICTION
Dealing with an impossible request
Being asked to do something that makes the assistant uncomfortable

Being unfairly treated when the celebrity is upset

A celebrity that crosses the line and makes inappropriate advances

Having to take the blame for something the celebrity did to save their reputation

Being approached by another celebrity to work for them

An injury or illness that interferes with the assistant's ability to perform duties

Discovering something disturbing about the celebrity's friends and being asked to cover it up

Having to trade a personal life for the celebrity's narcissistic needs

Having to cancel an important personal event to deal with a work situation

Being asked to partake in illegal activities to prove loyalty

Becoming a target of paparazzi trying to gain information on the celebrity

The extravagant celebrity lifestyle bleeding into the assistant's personal life, resulting in over-spending and financial strain

PEOPLE THEY MIGHT INTERACT WITH

The celebrity's family and friends, agents, various handlers or advisors (a personal trainer, nutritionist, therapist, doctors, nannies, coaches, tutors, drivers, managers, etc.), travel specialists, hotel management and staff, venue staff, green room managers, industry executives, other celebrities and their assistants, business owners and managers, fans, club owners, fashion designers, photographers, paparazzi, artists, people of importance who run in the same circles

HOW THIS OCCUPATION MIGHT IMPACT THE CHARACTER'S NEEDS

Self-Actualization: A character who is caught up in this profession may never be able to take the time to pursue their own passions and dreams.

Love and Belonging: Family members who resent or don't understand the commitment needed for this career may soon become tired of playing second fiddle to the celebrity. Also, an assistant who has no time or energy for personal relationships may long for caring, loving connections that will allow them to be imperfect yet still cherished and valued.

Safety and Security: Being closely tied to a celebrity could be dangerous as many have fans who are rabidly devoted. These fans, and those who are certified stalkers, may go to any length to obtain access to or information about the celebrity.

TWISTING THE FICTIONAL STEREOTYPE

Personal assistants are often relatives or friends of the celebrity. Instead, why not bring in someone from the celebrity's past who was a rival but happens to be the best in the business?

What about someone who was a celebrity but fell from grace and is seeking a way to get back into the business? What if their motivation is to discover who caused her downfall and exact revenge?

CHARACTERS MIGHT CHOOSE THIS PROFESSION BECAUSE THEY...

Grew up with an exceptionally talented sibling and became used to the supportive role

Were plagued by self-doubt that kept them from pursuing a career in entertainment

Love the Hollywood lifestyle but lack the talent to pursue an entertainment career

Have a condition or challenge that makes a career in the limelight impossible

Are a fierce advocate of a famous relative and worry about them being exploited

PERSONAL SHOPPER

OVERVIEW
Personal shoppers assist clients in making retail purchases by shopping alongside them and offering their expert advice or buying items on their behalf. Some clients also hire them to buy gifts for others. These shoppers tailor their services to suit an individual client's tastes and needs while utilizing their own expertise of trends and their knowledge of what the client will like. They may be employed by a store or work in a freelance capacity in-person or online.

NECESSARY TRAINING
Formal education is not required to become a personal shopper, but a retail or industry-related degree, like fashion merchandising, may prove useful. Experience is key, particularly in demonstrating proven sales records and client satisfaction in similar industries.

USEFUL SKILLS, TALENTS, OR ABILITIES
Charm, exceptional memory, gaining the trust of others, good listening skills, haggling, multitasking, reading people, sales

HELPFUL CHARACTER TRAITS
Charming, confident, cooperative, creative, diplomatic, discreet, easygoing, efficient, extravagant, friendly, honest, know-it-all, loyal, nurturing, objective, organized, persuasive, resourceful, sophisticated, spunky, talented, thrifty

SOURCES OF FRICTION
Demanding clients with unrealistic expectations
Clients who are resistant to suggestions or change
Balancing honesty with diplomacy when it comes to offering feedback
Pressure to keep up with trends
Clients who have gained weight yet refuse to try on suggested sizing that reflects this
Being expected to meet sales quotas
Dealing with a client's entourage
Competition with other personal shoppers
Working unusual hours to accommodate a client's needs
Handling clients with insecurities
Inconsistent income, particularly if the shopper works on commission
Sacrificing income to maintain a trendy wardrobe that clients expect to see
Balancing rapport with clients and the need to sell
Setting aside personal tastes to satisfy a client
Being limited by a client's narrow budget
Hearing unwelcome gossip from a client
Struggling to deal with clients who are overly superficial or materialistic
Experiencing product envy when purchasing for clients
Moral conflict over pushing certain items to receive a kickback and suggesting what's best for the client

Being tempted to add a personal purchase to a wealthy client's tab because they would never notice

Having to spend the day with a chatty, extroverted client when the shopper would rather work alone

Mixing up the preferences of multiple clients while shopping online and sending the wrong products to the wrong person

PEOPLE THEY MIGHT INTERACT WITH

Clients, salespeople, fashion designers, store managers, other personal shoppers

HOW THIS OCCUPATION MIGHT IMPACT THE CHARACTER'S NEEDS

Esteem and Recognition: Personal shoppers can be looked down upon or seen as a frivolous expense, since people tend to think that all they do is shop. The industry knowledge and entrepreneurial skills needed to draw in new clientele and maintain existing clients is often undervalued or overlooked.

Love and Belonging: Long hours and on-call work can make it hard for a shopper to nurture their personal relationships.

TWISTING THE FICTIONAL STEREOTYPE

If personal shoppers are expected to tailor everything to a client's needs, why not imbue your character with selfish behaviors, such as an I-know-better-than-you attitude?

A personal shopper's livelihood depends on their knowledge of trends and clients being willing to spend money. What if your character has strong opinions and secretly denounces material things and money?

We often associate women with shopping. Flip the stereotype by creating a male personal shopper, or even male clients.

CHARACTERS MIGHT CHOOSE THIS PROFESSION BECAUSE THEY...

Have an appreciation for retail and fashion trends

Possess strong interpersonal skills

Enjoy matching items to a client's tastes

Thrive on the thrill of making a sale and reaching goals

Crave the reward of making others look and feel good about themselves

Love the fashion industry but lack the talent to become a designer

Wish to gain access to people with wealth or power

PERSONAL TRAINER

OVERVIEW
A personal trainer works one-on-one and with small groups of clients to help them achieve their physical fitness goals. This usually involves leading them in an exercise regimen meant to help them reach a healthy weight and advising them in regard to nutrition. Trainers may specialize in certain areas, such as yoga, aerobics, or strength training. While they typically work in public venues, many large-scale organizations now have their own fitness centers and personal trainers for their employees to utilize. Some clients may opt to pay for a trainer to come to their home.

NECESSARY TRAINING
While many companies prefer trainers who hold a health- or fitness-related degree, some only require certain certifications. It also helps to be certified in specialization areas, such as performance enhancement, post-rehab training, and senior fitness conditioning. And some additional training, such as in basic CPR and first aid, is required.

USEFUL SKILLS, TALENTS, OR ABILITIES
Basic first aid, high pain tolerance, parkour, sales, stamina, strength, strong breath control, teaching

HELPFUL CHARACTER TRAITS
Bold, confident, cooperative, courteous, disciplined, empathetic, enthusiastic, inspirational, observant, optimistic, persistent, persuasive, supportive

SOURCES OF FRICTION
A client being hurt during a session
Being unable to afford the necessary equipment or materials
Wanting to open an independent practice but being stuck working for someone else
Sustaining an injury or acquiring an illness that makes it hard for the trainer to stay fit
Being unable to help a client achieve their goals
Dishonest clients who make it difficult for them to achieve their fitness goals
Becoming romantically attracted to a client
Unhealthy competition with other trainers at the workplace
Sexual harassment
Being accused of maintaining an impressive physique through questionable means (doping, abusing diuretics, getting surgical implants, etc.)
A fitness trainer who has no time to pursue their true passion, such as becoming a professional bodybuilder or weightlifter
Fitting in work around family, personal workouts, and other commitments
Being employed by a gym and having to work around other trainers' schedules
Becoming passionate about a new tool or training method that the gym owners aren't interested in implementing

Endorsing a nutrition product, then discovering it's not what it seems (the producers billed it as a healthy product but it's full of chemicals, adequate testing wasn't done before going to market, etc.)

Getting too involved in a client's personal life

Having to work evenings and weekends, when clients have more availability

The financial burden of having to maintain expensive certifications

PEOPLE THEY MIGHT INTERACT WITH

Clients, gym rats, other personal trainers, workout partners, gym managers and owners, administrative personnel, people they would run into during their own personal fitness training (spin class attendees, a yoga instructor, runners at the local track, etc.)

HOW THIS OCCUPATION MIGHT IMPACT THE CHARACTER'S NEEDS

Self-Actualization: If a trainer took this job to finance their own desire to become a competitive athlete but the work becomes too time-consuming, their inability to pursue their passion might cause them to regret their decision.

Esteem and Recognition: It's natural for trainers to notice people's bodies; if in comparing themselves to others they find themselves lacking, this can lead to a self-esteem problem.

Love and Belonging: A person in this field might find it difficult to make true connections with others if they feel that potential romantic partners are only interested in them for their looks, or that the partner's interest will only remain as long as they maintain a certain physique.

Physiological Needs: As with any healthy desire, wanting to be physically fit can be taken to an unhealthy extreme-even to the point of a character's health or very life being threatened.

TWISTING THE FICTIONAL STEREOTYPE

The hard-nosed, borderline-abusive personal trainer yelling and spitting into the client's face has been done to death. Likewise, the sex kitten bombshell female trainer. Consider a different angle.

CHARACTERS MIGHT CHOOSE THIS PROFESSION BECAUSE THEY...

Wanted to continue their health journey after weight loss and a lifestyle change

Overcame an eating disorder and wanted to stay focused on health and a positive body image

Were unable to make it in a sporting career but still wanted to be involved with athletes

Needed an exit career after being a competitive bodybuilder

Have a passion for physical fitness, health, and nutrition

Want to help people with certain health issues (obesity, heart disease, those recovering from physical trauma, people suffering from a disorder like multiple sclerosis, etc.)

PEST CONTROL TECHNICIAN

OVERVIEW
A pest control technician removes unwanted pests from residential and commercial areas. The types of pests will be dependent on the location, but commonly these include ants, roaches, bedbugs, termites, ticks, spiders, wasps, rats, and mice that infest structures (or crops, in a farm or orchard). In some areas, technicians may also be called in to take care of snakes, scorpions, crocodiles, birds, or alligators. Technicians run site inspections and assessments and carry out fumigations and removals using spraying equipment, power fog machines, bait guns, and traps. Because technicians may be required to kneel, crawl, enter small spaces, and possibly work in sewers or other undesirable locations, a reasonable level of fitness and strong mental constitution is required.

NECESSARY TRAINING
Characters looking to get into this profession usually need a high school diploma or equivalent and often must have a certification to practice. On-the-job training is provided that educates new technicians about the chemicals and pesticides they'll use and how to apply them safely. All work must be done in accordance with any local environmental laws and regulations. Having skills in math is also important to accurately plan the quantities of pesticides needed as well as the time it will take to complete the task—especially when fumigating or using chemicals in residential areas. Technicians must have a valid driver license for transporting equipment and driving to locations to assess problems.

USEFUL SKILLS, TALENTS, OR ABILITIES
A way with animals, basic first aid, blending in, enhanced hearing, exceptional memory, foraging, high pain tolerance, mechanically inclined, parkour, predicting the weather, self-defense, strategic thinking, strength, strong breath control, swift-footedness, wilderness navigation, woodworking, wrestling

HELPFUL CHARACTER TRAITS
Adaptable, adventurous, alert, analytical, cautious, centered, courageous, cruel, cynical, disciplined, efficient, independent, industrious, observant, organized, patient, perfectionist, proactive, professional, resourceful, responsible, stubborn

SOURCES OF FRICTION
Irresponsible homeowners who are part of the infestation problem (by not getting rid of trash, not adequately caring for the property, etc.)
Pests that are resistant to the technician's methods
Homeowners who take out their anger on the technician
Dealing with poisonous pests in a tight or dangerous area
Questioning the company's methods or policies
Working with a partner who is unnecessarily cruel
Being accused of theft after fumigating a home
Discovering the pest is a protected species and being forced to deliver bad news to the homeowners

PEOPLE THEY MIGHT INTERACT WITH

Homeowners and building managers, wildlife officers (in the case of larger pests), other technicians, supply reps, health and safety inspectors, business owners

HOW THIS OCCUPATION MIGHT IMPACT THE CHARACTER'S NEEDS

Esteem and Recognition: The public perception of this work can be undesirable, which may affect the character's self-esteem and feelings of self-worth.

Love and Belonging: Possible partners might make unfair assumptions about the character because of their job and may not be able to look past their disgust of the work, creating hurdles in the romance department.

Safety and Security: Because a character often must go where homeowners and property managers dare not, safety is a concern, especially if the pests are poisonous or dangerous.

Physiological Needs: The nature of a pest control technician's work is risky, and if they mishandle their equipment and poisons, the result could be deadly.

TWISTING THE FICTIONAL STEREOTYPE

Characters in this occupation are often portrayed as uneducated or social misfits. Break your technician free of these stereotypes. The work requires very specific handling of toxic pesticides and sometimes dangerous pests, so the character would have to be intelligent enough to work safely in this field.

Another way to differentiate the circumstances for your technician is to have them encounter something beyond the norm on a call, such as a colony of squirrels living in the attic of an historical building, a skunk under someone's porch, or alligators in a residential retention pond.

CHARACTERS MIGHT CHOOSE THIS PROFESSION BECAUSE THEY...

Had a criminal record and employment options were limited

Needed a job and this one was available

Wanted a career that provides no joy or satisfaction (as a punishment for past actions)

Grew up in an environment where pests were treated inhumanely and are seeking to make up for past transgressions or address that problem

Want to face a fear or phobia of insects or other pests

Derive joy from killing things without repercussion

Are continuing in the family business

Strongly believe that all pestilence should be eradicated

PHARMACIST

OVERVIEW
A pharmacist's primary duties have to do with distributing drugs and medicines. They fill prescriptions from doctors (sometimes speaking with the physician to obtain information about the patient), documenting drug orders, and offer advice to customers. Some may also provide vaccinations and manage interns, assistants, or technicians.

While we often picture the pharmacist in a drugstore environment, they can work in other settings, such as hospitals, grocery stores, private practices, and even research facilities. Because of the importance of their duties and the level of trust granted by their customers, the pharmacist profession is typically a highly regarded one.

NECESSARY TRAINING
In the United States, most pharmacists obtain a Doctor of Pharmacy, a program which usually takes anywhere from six to eight years, including undergraduate courses. In some countries, only a bachelor's or master's degree is required to become a pharmacist. To practice, a pharmacist has to become licensed and typically must complete some standard examinations.

USEFUL SKILLS, TALENTS, OR ABILITIES
Basic first aid, detail-oriented, dexterity, equanimity, multilingualism, photographic memory, reading people, research, strategic thinking, teaching

HELPFUL CHARACTER TRAITS
Analytical, cautious, centered, courteous, discreet, focused, friendly, honest, intelligent, observant, organized, persuasive, proactive, professional

SOURCES OF FRICTION
Dealing with temperamental customers (who are in pain, anxious, or frustrated by insurance limitations)
Accidentally filling the wrong prescription or dosage
Not being able to pay off student loans
Having to deny a request (because of the customer's inability to pay, a problem with a prescription, etc.)
Customers who appear to have dependency issues
Interacting with a patient who has communication difficulties or disorders
Dealing with a patient who doesn't adhere to instructions
Training an intern who makes too many mistakes
Struggling with a mental health crisis that makes it difficult to focus
A doctor who prescribes too many drugs at once, or drugs that shouldn't be taken together
Getting blamed for a mistake that wasn't the pharmacist's fault
Trying to resolve problems with an insurance company
Frazzled parents seeking help for their child
Being targeted and robbed for medications and cash
Discovering a patient's unrecorded allergy to a specific medicine

Elderly patients with memory issues
Needing to do too many things at once
Customers complaining about wait times
Miscommunication with pharmaceutical benefit managers or drug manufacturers
A potentially harmful drug being recalled after it was in distribution
Many orders coming in at once, causing long delays

PEOPLE THEY MIGHT INTERACT WITH

Technicians, assistants, doctors, dentists, psychiatrists, nurses, interns, customers and patients, parents, other pharmacists, supervisors, delivery drivers, drug company representatives

HOW THIS OCCUPATION MIGHT IMPACT THE CHARACTER'S NEEDS

Self-Actualization: Because of the routine nature of their work, many pharmacists don't know if they're really making a difference. They rarely get to see the fruits of their labor.

Esteem and Recognition: In a pharmacy, one slip could lead to serious consequences. Even a small mistake could cost a character their job and their reputation.

Safety and Security: If a pharmacist makes a mistake (real or perceived), they could find themselves named in a lawsuit. This could affect their financial security if their insurance coverage isn't sufficient or too many claims result in the pharmacist becoming uninsurable. Additionally, they spend a lot of time around sick people, so there is some risk of becoming ill.

TWISTING THE FICTIONAL STEREOTYPE

Nearly all pharmacists are portrayed in white coats and surrounded by high-tech medical equipment. Try switching up the setting in which your pharmacist works. Maybe they are in a poorer urban area where new technology is not readily available, or in an area of high crime where additional security measures are needed.

CHARACTERS MIGHT CHOOSE THIS PROFESSION BECAUSE THEY...

Experienced the loss of a family member due to a medication mix-up
Had a parent who believed in natural medicine and refused to vaccinate their children
Are extroverted and want to work with and help a variety of people
Have an interest in healthcare and the medical field
Have a desire to help a specific group of people, such as the elderly, diabetes patients, etc.
Are driven to help people who can't afford necessary medication

PHYSICAL THERAPIST

OVERVIEW
A physical therapist (PT) specializes in the recovery of patients who have had injuries, illnesses, or surgeries that impact their mobility and comfort. This kind of therapy can also be used to safely rebuild muscle tissue and flexibility if it has been lost (due to age or malnutrition) or to prevent further degradation.

Physical therapists are trained to listen to the symptoms of a patient, diagnose what the problem may be, and then create a plan to treat the injured site. Once a therapy plan is made, the PT will administer therapy using a variety of methods: massage, muscle manipulation and mobilization, ultrasound, isokinetic bands and devices for tension stretching, ice and heat therapy, electrical muscle stimulation (EMS), exercise balls, exercise bikes, and other equipment to allow for low, medium, or high impact workouts.

The PT will also document and modify the therapy as needed, consulting with doctors or other healthcare professionals if it becomes necessary. They provide a listening ear, encouragement, and empathetic support so the patent makes the best recovery possible and is incentivized to continue with at-home habits that will prevent re-injury.

NECESSARY TRAINING
A PT will need a university degree in a science-related field. To practice, they must obtain a doctoral degree in physical therapy (DPT), which includes up to a year in clinical application, plus a residency or internship. After this time, specializations can be obtain in areas such as sports, wound management, oncology, or pediatrics.

USEFUL SKILLS, TALENTS, OR ABILITIES
Basic first aid, charm, empathy, enhanced hearing, enhanced sense of smell, exceptional memory, gaining the trust of others, good listening skills, high pain tolerance, hospitality, intuition, making people laugh, multilingualism, multitasking, reading people, regeneration, strategic thinking, strength, strong breath control, teaching

HELPFUL CHARACTER TRAITS
Adaptable, cautious, charming, confident, curious, disciplined, discreet, easygoing, efficient, empathetic, friendly, industrious, know-it-all, observant, obsessive, optimistic, organized, patient, perfectionist, persistent, persuasive, proactive, professional, workaholic

SOURCES OF FRICTION
Patients who are uncommunicative and so make the diagnosis more difficult
Patients who lie about how they were injured (out of embarrassment)
Having too many patients
Difficulty navigating the different coverage thresholds for insurance providers
Poorly maintained equipment
Patients who don't want to put in effort for their recovery
Trying to work as a PT while running the business
Drama with co-workers

Overhearing a patient complain about a previous experience with the PT
Patients who divulge too much personal information
People who expect to be seen without an appointment or referral
Becoming injured during a session with a client
Trying to manage a client load and keep up with new developments in treatment and therapy
Conflict with related practitioners, such as chiropractors, acupuncturists, or general physicians
Other PTs calling in sick and the character having to handle their patients as well as their own
Working for a practice that doesn't have the necessary equipment or resources

PEOPLE THEY MIGHT INTERACT WITH

Other physical therapists, clinic employees, doctors and physician's assistants, nurse practitioners, patients, insurance agents, coaches, athletic and personal trainers, massage therapists, acupuncturists, naturopathic doctors, product representatives

HOW THIS OCCUPATION MIGHT IMPACT THE CHARACTER'S NEEDS

Self-Actualization: A character who dreams of consulting with high-profile athletes may not gain the same sort of fulfillment from working in a general clinic.

Esteem and Recognition: If the character is unable to help a patient to the desired degree or they become embroiled in a malpractice lawsuit, it may cause them to question their own abilities, leading to lower self-worth.

Love and Belonging: The long hours and physicality of this work may leave the character with little energy for loved ones once the day is finished, which could lead to frustration and resentment from their partner or children.

Safety and Security: A PT working with a client who requires a high level of flexibility and strength could become injured and temporarily unable to practice, causing financial hardship.

CHARACTERS MIGHT CHOOSE THIS PROFESSION BECAUSE THEY...

Recovered from an accident with physiotherapy and want to help others do the same
Were pushed into surgery when therapy was an option and they want to save others from the same experience
Were a caregiver to a loved one whose physiotherapist helped provide a better quality of life
Want to help people recover from injuries without relying heavily on medication (perhaps because their parent was addicted to pain meds)
Have a strong interest in sports and want to help athletes stay in top shape

PILOT

OVERVIEW
There are a few kinds of jobs available for people wanting to make a living as a pilot. Namely, they would need to be employed by an airline, serve in the military, or do commercial work.

As the name suggests, airline pilots fly airliners. Commercial pilots may work for a private company or own their own business transporting passengers and cargo, running rescue missions, dusting crops, or doing aerial photography. Military pilots obviously fly in the military; they may be career pilots or could be fulfilling a tour of duty as a means of gaining flight training and experience. They often have no trouble transitioning to a civilian pilot's career once their time is up.

Airline pilots don't tend to have the typical nine-to-five work schedule; instead they work a series of days followed by a number of days off. A commercial pilot's workweek may be more regulated, depending on what they're doing. The former must be twenty-three years old while the latter can begin working earlier, at eighteen.

NECESSARY TRAINING
Pilots will need a certification that consists of a combination of ground school (any training done on the ground) and flight training. Training can take place at a flight school, through a collegiate program, or with a private instructor. A medical certificate (first class for aviation pilots, second class for commercial pilots) is also required.

Beyond certification, most commercial jobs require that a pilot have a certain number of flight hours under their belt. Many times, their flight training doesn't provide the required hours; in this case, pilots will need to gain experience before applying with their desired company. Military training is obviously a different animal, with varying requirements depending on the country and branch of service.

USEFUL SKILLS, TALENTS, OR ABILITIES
Detail-oriented, equanimity, exceptional memory, good sense of direction, good with numbers, leadership, mechanically inclined, multitasking, predicting the weather

HELPFUL CHARACTER TRAITS
Adaptable, adventurous, alert, confident, cooperative, decisive, disciplined, focused, meticulous, perfectionist, responsible, studious

SOURCES OF FRICTION
Working with a difficult or lazy co-pilot
Flying a plane with mechanical difficulties
Flying in difficult weather
Having to conduct an emergency landing
Romantic entanglements with members of the flight crew
Failing a drug test
Being faced with a terrorist or hijacking situation
Delayed flights that cause the pilot to miss an important event, such as a child's birthday party

or a vital counseling session

Having to take less-desired flights due to other pilots having seniority

Being stationed in a place where they don't want to live

Medical issues that threaten their career

Difficulties at home that make it difficult to be gone for long stretches (a serious medical diagnosis, a spouse's promotion that requires them to travel, too, etc.)

PEOPLE THEY MIGHT INTERACT WITH

Co-pilots, air traffic controllers, flight attendants, airport personnel, union officials, passengers, ground crew, shuttle operators, hotel personnel

HOW THIS OCCUPATION MIGHT IMPACT THE CHARACTER'S NEEDS

Self-Actualization: A pilot who is unable to obtain his desired certification may be stuck doing jobs that are unsatisfying. This could also happen if personal circumstances required him to take a job with more flexibility and traditional hours.

Love and Belonging: If the pilot's work hours and time away from home create problems, it could lead to a break up, strained relationships with children, or both.

Safety and Security: Even with all the training and experience, flying is still a dangerous endeavor. If a pilot encounters a life-threatening situation, it may haunt them, hindering their flying attempts in the future.

TWISTING THE FICTIONAL STEREOTYPE

Gender-wise, pilots are largely male, so making yours female can provide a seldom-seen twist.

Pilots are typically portrayed as either highly adventurous adrenaline junkies or strait-laced, by-the-book types. When you're building your pilot's personality, consider uncommon traits that aren't usually associated with this career, such as sentimental, philosophical, sleazy, verbose, or morbid.

CHARACTERS MIGHT CHOOSE THIS PROFESSION BECAUSE THEY...

Wanted to be an astronaut but weren't suited for that career

Had a parent involved in aviation (as a mechanic, pilot, member of the air force, etc.)

Love planes and flying

Want to go places and see things that others cannot

Want to defeat a fear of flying and heights

Enjoy responsibility and being in charge

Love travel and experiencing new places

PODCASTER

OVERVIEW
Podcasters provide information or entertainment to the public through audio recordings that focus on a specific content area. Episodes are available to the public on various apps and websites that allow users to download them and listen at their leisure.

Successful podcasters need to create quality recordings, which requires a certain level of technical savvy. These duties may be handled by the podcaster or a team of workers. They also should publish material in a timely manner, frequently providing their followers with new content. To reach and grow their audience, they must be able to market and promote themselves and find ways to bring in revenue, which might include advertising, selling merchandise, obtaining sponsorships, or putting on live events. Some podcasts are not free to download or may require a subscription; this can be an additional way to make profit.

NECESSARY TRAINING
Naturally, a podcaster must be educated on their chosen topic. They will also need to have strong interview skills, be personable, and understand their audience's interests and needs. Podcasters should also possess basic knowledge of audio recording and editing, possess quality recording equipment, and have an ideal location for taping where background noise can be minimized or eradicated.

One of the most important pieces of equipment in the podcaster's arsenal is their voice. Whether they use a professional vocal trainer or go the do-it-yourself route, a podcaster will need to hone their skills so they can speak with clarity, eliminate vocal tics (such as frequent throat clearing, word repetitions, or too many *umms*), and address any other issue that might be irritating to listeners.

USEFUL SKILLS, TALENTS, OR ABILITIES
A knack for making money, charm, enhanced hearing, gaining the trust of others, good listening skills, making people laugh, networking, research

HELPFUL CHARACTER TRAITS
Adaptable, curious, enthusiastic, friendly, inspirational, organized, passionate, socially aware, talented, thrifty, witty

SOURCES OF FRICTION
A microphone or other recording equipment malfunctioning
Their cohost having different views or wanting to go in a different direction with the show
Having another job or responsibility that makes it difficult to find time to record
Dealing with burnout or a creativity block
An antagonistic or disrespectful guest who tries to use the podcast as a personal soapbox
Having a cold that affects sound quality
A computer crashing and losing all its data
Haters trying to sabotage the channel's ratings
Expensive equipment being stolen

Being accused of infringing on someone's music, artwork, or other media copyright

A scheduled interviewee canceling at the last minute

A rivalry with another podcaster who covers the same subject matter

Disappointed fans (if the podcaster changes focus, ends a popular series, doesn't publish frequently enough, etc.)

The mind going blank during an interview

Being turned down when asking people to be interviewed

A glitch on the podcast host site

The audience shrinking, causing a crisis of faith for the podcaster

PEOPLE THEY MIGHT INTERACT WITH

Cohosts, other podcasters, fans, sponsors, co-workers (editors, content writers, marketing professionals, etc.), guest speakers, experts or celebrities in their chosen niche

HOW THIS OCCUPATION MIGHT IMPACT THE CHARACTER'S NEEDS

Self-Actualization: This job can become draining and tiresome if the podcaster feels that not enough people are listening. This could cause them to question whether or not they're cut out for this career.

Esteem and Recognition: Like many art and entertainment industries, it can be a long slog to become an established podcaster. Slow progress combined with the temptation to compare themselves to successful people in the field can lead to a lack of self-confidence.

Safety and Security: This job doesn't necessarily provide a secure income, especially when the podcaster is just starting out. It may be necessary for them to hold a second job or source of income to make ends meet.

TWISTING THE FICTIONAL STEREOTYPE

Since this is a fairly modern industry, many podcasters are young and trendy. Why not have an elderly couple who run a podcast channel, or turn it into a family business where multiple generations record episodes together?

Also, consider the topic of your character's show. Think past the common subjects in existence and see what fresh and interesting ideas your podcaster might choose to explore.

CHARACTERS MIGHT CHOOSE THIS PROFESSION BECAUSE THEY...

Had limited access to learning and knowledge as a child

Want to reach out to people who are interested in their passion

Love digital technology and podcasting

Want to steer conversations that encourage ideas or innovation in a particular field

Are introverted or reclusive but want a controlled way to connect with people

Want to be an online phenom or celebrity

POLICE OFFICER

OVERVIEW
Police officers serve and protect, keeping the peace, often putting themselves at great risk to do so. In the scope of their duties they enforce laws, interview suspects and witnesses, respond to emergencies, and investigate suspicious circumstances or crimes that have taken place. Through their work, officers are in a position to help victims navigate difficult situations by showing compassion and empathy and using their knowledge and resources. They also deal with people on the wrong path (drug addicts, thieves, gang members) and have the opportunity to encourage them to make life changes before it is too late.

Police officers are usually assigned an area to patrol and work with a partner. Their beat will determine the people and situations they tend to encounter.

NECESSARY TRAINING
While the specifics of education and training will vary depending on where your story takes place, a police officer must be a high school graduate, pass a thorough background check, be in good physical condition, and graduate from a police academy. There they will learn state and constitutional laws, local ordinances, civil rights, and accident investigation. Recruits also learn about traffic control, first-aid, emergency response, firearms, and self-defense. Officers will need to pass written, physical, and psychological tests, as well as a polygraph.

USEFUL SKILLS, TALENTS, OR ABILITIES
Basic first aid, blending in, enhanced hearing, equanimity, exceptional memory, gaining the trust of others, good listening skills, high pain tolerance, lip-reading, lying, making people laugh, multilingualism, peacekeeping, photographic memory, reading people, self-defense, sharpshooting, stamina, strategic thinking, strength, strong breath control, survival skills, swift-footedness, wilderness navigation

HELPFUL CHARACTER TRAITS
Adaptable, alert, analytical, calm, cautious, charming, confident, courageous, decisive, diplomatic, disciplined, easygoing, efficient, empathetic, focused, friendly, honest, honorable, independent, just, loyal, objective, observant, organized, patient, perceptive, persistent, persuasive, proactive, professional, proper, protective, resourceful, responsible, socially aware, tolerant, wise, workaholic

SOURCES OF FRICTION
Losing a fellow officer in the line of duty
Having to kill someone in the line of duty
Every decision being scrutinized
Dealing with the politics of the job
Dirty cops that give all cops a bad name
Having to notify families of someone's passing
Being repeatedly exposed to traumatic situations and struggling to process it all
Walking into dangerous situations, such as those dealing with active shooters, terrorism, drug

operations, and chemical threats

Trying to separate work and home life

Difficulty relaxing in places and situations that are typically dangerous on the job (exploring narrow streets while shopping on a holiday, being in tight crowds, etc.)

Having to walk the line between persuasion and manipulation outside of work

Easily recognizing when a loved one or friend is lying, but not wanting to create drama

Seeing or suspecting racism, sexism, or criminal activity from a fellow officer and struggling to do the right thing

A family member breaking the law, casting a shadow on the officer's reputation

The character's children rebelling against strict parenting and getting caught breaking the law

Making a mistake (arresting a bystander, shooting a child, misreading a situation, etc.)

Having personal biases that influence decisions and actions at work

PEOPLE THEY MIGHT INTERACT WITH

Suspects, criminals, members of the press, firefighters, coroners, detectives, FBI or other government agents, the public, victims and their families, paramedics, witnesses, other police officers, city officials, judges, lawyers

HOW THIS OCCUPATION MIGHT IMPACT THE CHARACTER'S NEEDS

Self-Actualization: If an officer joins the force to affect change but finds himself making little difference, it may lead to disillusionment at choosing this path.

Esteem and Recognition: A character who is deemed guilty by association due to a very public mistake by another officer could take an esteem hit.

Love and Belonging: The long hours, emotional struggles, and necessity of not disclosing work details at home may leave a partner feeling like they aren't a priority.

Safety and Security: A police officer's job is inherently dangerous, meaning safety and security will always be tenuous at times. This risk could spill over to family members if the officer is targeted for intimidation or revenge.

Physiological Needs: Because police officers run toward danger when others flee and often work in high-crime areas, there are many situations that could end their lives.

TWISTING THE FICTIONAL STEREOTYPE

Some police officers move into this career from a parallel one, such as a paramedic. Consider the interesting plot ramifications if your character has multiple skillsets of a first responder, and why they might have chosen to move from one role to another.

CHARACTERS MIGHT CHOOSE THIS PROFESSION BECAUSE THEY...

Grew up in a law-enforcement family

Were victimized in the past and chose this career to reclaim their power

Have a strong moral compass and sense of duty

Want to protect people and keep them safe

Are part of a criminal group that needed to have a mole in the system

POLITICIAN

OVERVIEW
Politicians are elected by the constituents in their jurisdictions. Once elected, they form the government, from national roles to those associated with local municipalities. Because they're elected, garnering support from others is vital to their success. For this reason, politicians are typically charismatic by nature and will have experience as leaders in the community, either in business or on a volunteer basis. These elected officials do a lot of campaigning to sell themselves—via town hall meetings, debates with other politicians, interviews, publicity-based events (fundraisers, nonprofit benefits, goodwill activities) and other media that will allow them to share their ideas and beliefs with their constituents.

The day-to-day duties will vary for politicians depending on the position they hold. But because the basis of their work is supporting their platform or ideals, much of their day is spent in activities that further that goal. They attend many meetings, advocate for their goals with influential people, form alliances with others (often using a quid pro quo format), read and write legislation, address and solve problems, discuss strategy, inform public opinion, and shape policies.

It should be noted that some politicians are appointed rather than elected. These roles are usually tied to the person that appointed them or for a certain length of time. Because they do not need votes, how they deal with their constituents and responsibilities will be very different.

NECESSARY TRAINING
Each political position has its own requirements, and these will vary by region. Many potential candidates will obtain a political science degree, though this isn't always necessary. Regardless, most will gain experience serving at the local level (as an elected official or volunteer) and working their way up to more prestigious positions. Marketing and promotion are hugely important in this field, so knowledge and experience in this area are a must.

USEFUL SKILLS, TALENTS, OR ABILITIES
Charm, empathy, equanimity, gaining the trust of others, good listening skills, hospitality, leadership, making people laugh, multitasking, networking, organization, promotion, public speaking, reading people, strategic thinking, vision

HELPFUL CHARACTER TRAITS
Adaptable, alert, ambitious, analytical, calm, charming, confident, confrontational, controlling, cooperative, courteous, decisive, diplomatic, discreet, enthusiastic, extroverted, focused, idealistic, inspirational, passionate, patriotic, persistent, persuasive, professional, resourceful, responsible, socially aware, tolerant, uninhibited, verbose, wise, workaholic

SOURCES OF FRICTION
Freezing during a public debate
The character's words being taken out of context and used against him or her
Going up against a formidable competitor
Skeletons from the past being brought to light

A public relations nightmare
A smear campaign by the opposing party
A crisis of faith that causes a shift in the character's ideals
Being tempted to do something unethical (accepting a bribe, turning a blind eye to injustice)
Getting caught in a lie
Being accused of sexual misconduct
Physical exhaustion from working long hours
Emotional strain from constantly being in the spotlight
Being embarrassed by a rebellious child or opinionated relative
Being stalked
An assassination attempt
The character trying to appeal to everyone and ending up alienating their constituents
Falling ill during an important campaign
An important staff member switching teams to work with a competitor
Making promises but being unable to keep them due to situational developments
The weight of constant criticism from the opposition
Having little to no privacy

PEOPLE THEY MIGHT INTERACT WITH
Other politicians, volunteers, interns, administrative personnel, voters and constituents, reporters, campaign managers, lobbyists, analysts

HOW THIS OCCUPATION MIGHT IMPACT THE CHARACTER'S NEEDS
Self-Actualization: Politicians who want to affect change but are consumed with the need to please certain people or groups may lose sight of their own values and identity.

Esteem and Recognition: Politics is largely a popularity contest, and people in this field are often driven by the opinions of others. When someone falls out of favor and the public's interest wanes, this need can be impacted.

Love and Belonging: Politicians put in long hours and are often slaves to their schedules, meaning family and friends will take a back seat to work.

Physiological Needs: Physical attacks from disgruntled or unhinged citizens are part of the landscape, making this a potentially dangerous career choice.

TWISTING THE FICTIONAL STEREOTYPE
Forget the selfless public servants and fickle baby-kissers. Avoid clichés by knowing your character deeply, including their motivation for choosing this job, their personality, and the kinds of conflict they're dealing with. Consideration of these factors will ensure that you end up with a well-rounded politician instead of one we've seen a million times.

CHARACTERS MIGHT CHOOSE THIS PROFESSION BECAUSE THEY...
Grew up in a political family
Want to affect change in their community or country
Crave being in the spotlight
Believe strongly in servant leadership
Are passionate about a platform, idea, or social issue

PRIVATE DETECTIVE

OVERVIEW

Private detectives are hired by an individual or organization to gather specific information. Working freelance or as part of an agency, they may be tasked with tracking someone's whereabouts (such as a spouse suspected of infidelity), checking a potential employee's background, finding a missing person, or proving that a prominent community figure is involved in criminal activity.

In pursuit of goals like these, private detectives (also called investigators) spend a lot of time doing research, interviewing people, and conducting surveillance. They also may be called upon to testify in court.

NECESSARY TRAINING

The training regimen for private detectives varies widely depending on where they want to practice. They may need a high school diploma or a criminal justice-related degree, and a minimum amount of experience might be necessary. Regulations commonly include limitations surrounding age, national citizenship, and the person's criminal record.

Once any requirements have been met, private detectives must become licensed to practice. If the individual wants to carry a firearm while working (and the state or locality allows them to do so), additional training and ongoing instruction will be required for that. Anyone working in this field will also need to be familiar with local laws so they can work within them (or break them, should your story require them to do so).

USEFUL SKILLS, TALENTS, OR ABILITIES

Blending in, charm, computer hacking, detail-oriented, enhanced hearing, equanimity, gaining the trust of others, good listening skills, haggling, lip-reading, multilingualism, networking, organization, out-of-the-box thinking, peacekeeping, performing, photographic memory, reading people, self-defense, stamina

HELPFUL CHARACTER TRAITS

Adventurous, alert, analytical, bold, calm, cautious, charming, confrontational, cooperative, courteous, curious, decisive, diplomatic, disciplined, discreet, evasive, focused, friendly, industrious, intelligent, manipulative, meticulous, nosy, objective, observant, organized, patient, perceptive, persistent, persuasive, pushy, resourceful, responsible, suspicious, workaholic

SOURCES OF FRICTION

Being threatened or attacked by a volatile suspect
Working an impossible case; not being able to find the desired information
Interviewing someone who lies or withholds information
The character's car breaking down or becoming unreliable
Boring stakeouts
Dealing with nefarious individuals
Being limited by the law
Breaking the law and getting caught
The character's cover being blown

Not doing thorough research and passing along bad information to the client

Clients with unrealistic expectations, timelines, and budgets

Difficulty finding new clients

The detective or his family being targeted by the person he or she is investigating

Wasting time on a dead-end lead

Losing a valuable source of information

Working irregular hours that interfere with family time

Physical problems from sitting for long periods of time at a desk or in a car (back pain, weight gain, etc.)

Tracking someone with the same secrets as the character

Discovering an employer's shady dealings during a routine investigation

Being asked to break the law or cross a moral line by a client

Losing a valuable snitch (because the informant is sent to jail, killed, or is no longer willing to offer information, for example)

PEOPLE THEY MIGHT INTERACT WITH

Clients, information sources (the suspect's friends, family, neighbors, co-workers, etc.), administrative or managerial personnel (if the character works out of an agency), subject experts

HOW THIS OCCUPATION MIGHT IMPACT THE CHARACTER'S NEEDS

Self-Actualization: If the character chose this career because they were unable to do what they really wanted (such as police or military work), they may become dissatisfied.

Esteem and Recognition: This career is largely a background one, with private detectives working in the shadows and providing information to higher-ups as it comes along. Someone desiring recognition and accolades may begin to chafe at playing the support role.

Love and Belonging: If a private detective's loved ones aren't understanding about irregular work hours and extensive travel, those relationships may sour.

Safety and Security: In most cases, the subject of an investigation doesn't want to be investigated. When they find out someone's been prying into their personal business, they may react with threats, altercations, or even physical violence.

TWISTING THE FICTIONAL STEREOTYPE

While many private detectives have a police or military background, this isn't always the case. Give your character an interesting and unique past that provides the experiences and skills to make them good at this job.

CHARACTERS MIGHT CHOOSE THIS PROFESSION BECAUSE THEY...

Are gifted at research and problem solving

Are incurably nosy and have a knack for figuring out people's secrets

Have a background in law enforcement

Want to see justice prevail but chafe at the constraints of traditional police work

PROFESSIONAL ATHLETE

OVERVIEW
Professional athletes participate in a sport for a living. They may make money off of ticket sales, medals and top placements received in sporting events, endorsements, corporate sponsorships, grants, and merchandising. Some may work a part-time job (often in a related field) to help cover the bills. While most athletes don't reach the millionaire level of fame and fortune that star players do, many can make a living as long as they stay healthy and on top of their game.

While much of an athlete's time is dedicated to practicing their sport, their workday might also be spent reviewing footage of past performances, analyzing an opponent's practices, working out, adhering to a fastidious diet regime, participating in promotional activities, and attending meetings with agents, coaches, and team members. Players of certain sports can live where they want and travel to and from events while others can be traded at the whim of management and have to relocate. This can happen multiple times throughout their career.

NECESSARY TRAINING
Professional athletes only reach their level of skill through extreme discipline and years of diligent practice. Many work with private coaches to speed up the learning curve. Most athletes start playing their sport as a child and continue honing their abilities through high school and college. While some athletes begin their professional careers directly after high school, most are drafted out of college, so they must have the academic foundation to get into a university and succeed there as they wait for the right opportunity to arrive.

USEFUL SKILLS, TALENTS, OR ABILITIES
Basic first aid, dexterity, equanimity, high pain tolerance, leadership, performing, promotion, stamina, strategic thinking, strength, swift-footedness

HELPFUL CHARACTER TRAITS
Ambitious, analytical, confident, confrontational, cooperative, decisive, disciplined, enthusiastic, focused, inspirational, obsessive, passionate, perfectionist, persistent, responsible, studious, talented, uninhibited, workaholic

SOURCES OF FRICTION
A nagging or career-ending injury
Negative social media interactions being resurrected and tainting their reputation
Trusting the wrong people (a greedy agent, friends interested in the athlete's fame or money, etc.)
Failing a drug test
Being replaced by a younger and more talented athlete
Internal and external pressure to perform and succeed
A crisis of confidence
Being traded and having to move to a new location
Falling into temptation while on the road (one-night stands, drugs, etc.)
An unfavorable change in management or coaching staff

A coach that plays favorites

An athlete mismanaging their finances and burning through vast amounts of money

Being accused of sexual harassment or fathering someone's child

Being sexually harassed on tour

Losing a key sponsor or endorsement opportunity

Injuring another player during a game or event

Having parents who love conditionally, based on the athlete's performance or success

Being caught in a compromising situation (buying drugs, getting into a bar fight, trespassing, hanging out with known criminals, etc.)

The athlete's child struggling to adapt after a move to a new town

Struggling to maintain a certain kind of public image

Declining performance (due to age, injury, mental well-being, etc.)

PEOPLE THEY MIGHT INTERACT WITH

Teammates, competitors, coaches, agents and managers, personal trainers, nutritionists, doctors, physical therapists, fans

HOW THIS OCCUPATION MIGHT IMPACT THE CHARACTER'S NEEDS

Esteem and Recognition: An athlete who is unable to deal well with the constant criticism inherent with this career may quickly find their self-esteem bottoming out.

Love and Belonging: Athletes who have to travel a lot or move away temporarily from family members may find it hard to maintain loving and loyal romantic relationships.

Safety and Security: Career-ending and dangerous injuries, such as concussions and the like, can present a safety threat for many professional athletes.

TWISTING THE FICTIONAL STEREOTYPE

Stories about athletes typically involve the underdog hero going up against the well-funded, well-connected, legacy-type antagonist. Keep this in mind and switch up your characters' roles to bring something fresh to the page.

Also consider the activity your protagonist will pursue. Popular sports are, well, popular for story fodder. But what about the less-romanticized choices? Skeet shooting, equestrian dressage, fencing, wrestling, rowing, and Paralympic events can provide the same competitive and stressful environments while allowing you to cover new ground for readers.

CHARACTERS MIGHT CHOOSE THIS PROFESSION BECAUSE THEY...

Have an aptitude for the sport and are naturally competitive and driven

Want to live up to family or social pressures to succeed in a high-profile area

Want to escape undesirable living conditions

Are seeking fame and fortune

PROFESSIONAL MOURNER

OVERVIEW

When a family member or loved one dies, professional mourners, also called moirologists, are sometimes paid to attend the funeral and pretend to grieve. This could be the case if the deceased had very few relations or the family wants it look like they were more popular than they actually were.

The professional mourner will play a role at the funeral—usually that of a distant relative, long-lost friend, previous co-worker, or acquaintance. They must stay in character without revealing their true identity, even while interacting with other guests.

Religion and culture help to define funeral traditions, meaning the particulars will vary from job to job. The mourner will need to be familiar with the cultural norms and religious customs that are in play for each funeral in order to blend in and not blow their cover.

NECESSARY TRAINING

No formal education or training is required in this field, but acting or improvisation classes might benefit the professional mourner. Job listings aren't even posted publicly, so prospective mourners usually will have to do some extra digging to find work.

USEFUL SKILLS, TALENTS, OR ABILITIES

Blending in, creativity, detail-oriented, exceptional memory, lying, multilingualism, peacekeeping, performing, reading people, talking with the dead

HELPFUL CHARACTER TRAITS

Adaptable, centered, courteous, creative, discreet, empathetic, loyal, mature, morbid, obedient, patient, persuasive, proper, supportive, unethical

SOURCES OF FRICTION

Someone getting suspicious and asking too many questions
Accidentally slipping out of character
The deceased's family setting extremely high expectations for the mourner
Unfamiliar religious rituals at the funeral
Uncovering evidence that suggests foul play or even murder
Getting pulled into a family feud
Running into someone the mourner knows at the funeral
Struggling with the constant exposure to other people's grief
The mourner overhearing something private
Harassment from a family member or other attendee
Their car breaking down on the way to a funeral
Another mourner at the same funeral trying to one-up the character's performance
Finding out they have a distant connection to the deceased
A family member becoming upset when they learn that a professional mourner was hired
A guest asking for advice on a private family matter that causes the mourner to feel like a fraud
An event during a funeral that causes the mourner to feel shame or guilt for their actions,

making it hard to stay in character

A guest getting too chatty or asking awkward questions

A reporter at a high-profile funeral getting suspicious and investigating, leading to a public outing that damages the mourner's career opportunities

The family stiffing the mourner because they know he or she won't risk going public with a lawsuit.

PEOPLE THEY MIGHT INTERACT WITH

Parents or siblings of the deceased, other family members or friends, pastors or priests, professional mourners attending the same funeral, funeral planners, florists, caterers

HOW THIS OCCUPATION MIGHT IMPACT THE CHARACTER'S NEEDS

Esteem and Recognition: Some people feel that faking emotions and lying to people, especially at a vulnerable time, is unethical. They may direct harsh criticism toward professional mourners because of that.

Love and Belonging: If public opinion about this career isn't popular, the mourner may have trouble making meaningful connections due to judgment and a lack of understanding.

Safety and Security: Funerals are volatile places where emotions run high. If the mourner is discovered, an altercation could ensue that results in physical harm.

TWISTING THE FICTIONAL STEREOTYPE

Traditionally, professional mourners are women, because in many cultures it was and may still be more socially acceptable for them to openly display emotions than men. How might your story benefit from a male professional mourner?

As with most "unsavory" careers, the person involved is usually a reluctant one who can't wait to get out. What if, instead, the character loves and relishes their job?

CHARACTERS MIGHT CHOOSE THIS PROFESSION BECAUSE THEY...

Experienced disrespect and disappointment when relatives failed to attend a family member's service

Love acting

Have a fascination with death, funeral rites, and the grieving process

Want to feel like they're part of a family, if only for a short time

Are excited by the thrill of living out a false persona

Struggle being their true self, and this career lets them continue this behavior without facing reality

PROFESSIONAL POKER PLAYER

OVERVIEW
A professional poker player is someone who plays poker for a living, drawing wages from their winnings rather than by clocking hours. People in this field may gamble in person at a casino or professional card room or play online against opponents located anywhere in the world. Some professionals enter tournaments that may require a sizable buy-in and last hours or even days. Players who like to travel will attend international tournaments and go on tours while others prefer working close to home.

NECESSARY TRAINING
Just like any other skill, poker requires practice, with some players logging an average of eight hours per day. This may include playing casually with friends or simply showing up to lower-stakes games. Professional players also need to study everything there is to know about their game; antes and blinds may go up depending on which variant of poker is being played, and the rules for each are different. In addition, players need to develop mathematical accuracy and analytical skills, since these are vital for gambling wisely and managing their bankroll.

USEFUL SKILLS, TALENTS, OR ABILITIES
A knack for making money, clairvoyance, dexterity, equanimity, good with numbers, intuition, lying, photographic memory, reading people, sleight of hand, strategic thinking

HELPFUL CHARACTER TRAITS
Alert, ambitious, analytical, bold, calm, disciplined, focused, manipulative, observant, obsessive, patient, superstitious, talented, thrifty, uncommunicative, withdrawn

SOURCES OF FRICTION
Playing with someone who's cheating
Family members who insist it's time to get "a real job"
Pushing the body past healthy limits (not sleeping enough, overusing stimulants, not exercising, etc.)
Making a miscalculation with their bankroll
Developing an addiction (to gambling, alcohol, caffeine, etc.)
Being accused of cheating
Being banned from a casino
Conflicts or rivalries with other professional players
Amateur opponents who lose and make threats or want payback
A computer freezing in the middle of an online game
Becoming stressed during an intense game
A personal or family crisis that impact's the character's playing
Misreading an opponent
Family members who believe gambling is wrong
An opponent calling the player's bluff
Playing while impaired

Being mugged after a big win

Having to move to a state where professional gambling is illegal

Not being able to get a seat at big tournaments

Becoming obsessed with rituals or superstitions that supposedly bring luck

PEOPLE THEY MIGHT INTERACT WITH

Other players (virtual or in-person), dealers, spectators, announcers, waiters and waitresses, bouncers, security guards, casino management, concierges, reporters

HOW THIS OCCUPATION MIGHT IMPACT THE CHARACTER'S NEEDS

Esteem and Recognition: Few professional poker players become famous, and those who do will lose attention the moment someone else starts winning more than them. This can create a rollercoaster of fluctuating self-worth.

Love and Belonging: In order to reach the professional level, poker players must practice extensively and may become so engrossed in their craft that they neglect relationships with a spouse, children, family, or friends.

Safety and Security: Playing poker as a profession does not guarantee a fixed income. All professional players go on losing streaks from time to time, which could result in serious debt.

Physiological Needs: Poker involves sitting at a table or in front of a computer for hours at a time. Exercise, sleep, and nutrition are necessary, but some players may become so involved in the game that self-care becomes an issue.

TWISTING THE FICTIONAL STEREOTYPE

For legal reasons, most professional poker players are adults, but in some countries, teenagers or even children can gamble. To add an interesting twist, try making your poker phenom unconventionally young.

Professionals in this field have a consistent look, wearing similar jewelry, clothing styles, or colors. Why not write a poker player who dresses purposely to shake things up and unsettle opponents?

CHARACTERS MIGHT CHOOSE THIS PROFESSION BECAUSE THEY...

Grew up around this industry (parents owned a casino, were professional gamblers, etc.)

Lost their former job and were desperate for a source of income

Struggled academically but wanted to excel at something intellectual

Love the game, risk, and adrenaline rush of winning big

Don't want to be tied down to a desk job or work for someone else

Have a gambling problem

PROFESSOR

OVERVIEW

A professor is an instructor in a college or university. Some co-teach with other instructors, teach in a classroom, or offer online education. The demand for online teaching offers many professors a more flexible schedule and the convenience of working from home.

Regardless of where classes take place, a professor's responsibilities include planning out their courses, giving lectures and presentations, grading tests and papers, interacting with students, and adhering to the codes of conduct and responsibilities set out by the institution to which they belong. If they're pursuing tenure, they may also conduct research in their area of study, seek publication, sponsor student groups or university programs, and sit on committees. Renowned professors might be invited to speak at events on campus as well as travel around the world to lead conferences or workshops on behalf of their school.

NECESSARY TRAINING

A professor usually must hold a doctoral degree, but a master's degree may be sufficient for some universities and community colleges. Certain areas of education will have more competitors vying for an appointment, so having additional education, experience, accolades, or political clout can help a character win the position.

USEFUL SKILLS, TALENTS, OR ABILITIES

Leadership, multitasking, public speaking, research, teaching, throwing one's voice, writing

HELPFUL CHARACTER TRAITS

Confident, creative, curious, focused, friendly, honorable, inspirational, intelligent, just, objective, organized, patient, persuasive, philosophical, professional, proper, wise, witty, workaholic

SOURCES OF FRICTION

Watching a student go through a dark time and not being able to help
Being criticized by fellow professors
Students who are rude or disruptive
Being in a highly competitive research field
An inability to know students personally because of large class sizes
A student with a learning disability or condition that comes with added challenges
Students who don't want to be in class
The character's personal views or their research causing colleagues to look down on them
A lockdown occurring because of a significant threat on campus
Being accused of plagiarism or impropriety
Experiencing racial, religious, or gender discrimination
Competing with another professor for a tenure-track position
The college or university discontinuing a degree program that directly affects the classes the character teaches
Getting laid off because of a financial crisis

Not getting along with a teaching assistant

Necessary equipment breaking before an important lecture

Being traditionally minded and having a hard time keeping up with work-related technological advances (grades being posted online, students reaching out via email, etc.)

The temptation to pursue an inappropriate relationship with a student or teacher's aide

PEOPLE THEY MIGHT INTERACT WITH

Students, other professors, the department chair, alumni, custodians, IT technicians, university personnel, prospective students and their parents

HOW THIS OCCUPATION MIGHT IMPACT THE CHARACTER'S NEEDS

Self-Actualization: College students are usually required to take certain general education courses whether they want to or not. This can be challenging for the professor because students may not value the material or lectures as much as they should.

Esteem and Recognition: The inability to publish or attain certain accolades may cause the character to feel they have come up short.

Love and Belonging: Professors have a high workload. Some can become married to the job, so consumed that they have no time to invest in a family of their own.

Safety and Security: Smaller colleges do not pay nearly as much as larger universities. In fact, a second source of income will sometimes be necessary.

TWISTING THE FICTIONAL STEREOTYPE

Professors are oftentimes portrayed as being serious or humorless. Try giving your character a more laid-back personality—maybe they're always cracking jokes about their favorite movies or prefer to sit on their desk while they give lectures.

Professors don't have to devote their entire life to the subjects they teach. What if your professor was passionate about a hobby, such as being an avid fantasy writer or skydiving on the weekends?

CHARACTERS MIGHT CHOOSE THIS PROFESSION BECAUSE THEY...

Wanted to teach elementary school but knew their highbrow family wouldn't approve

Come from a family of educators

Are passionate about their chosen academic field

Love to teach

Place a high value on education

Wish to help shape and mentor emerging adults

Have fond memories of their college years and want to stay connected to the institution

RADIO DJ

OVERVIEW

Radio disc jockeys (DJs) work for community or college radio stations. They're mostly associated with music, but DJs can be hired for any type of show, including those that focus on sports, news, politics, pop culture, or another specific area of interest. Either way, the DJ does the talking between songs or clips. If the station does provide music to its listeners, the DJ may have some say in what's being played, or those decisions could be made by the higher-ups. While most DJs work for a station, some are self-employed, recording their shows on their own and pitching them to stations who will put them on the air.

As budgets shrink and the industry becomes more automated, DJs are required to do more than play music and talk on air. They also may have to take on the social media promotion, do live events in the community, create content, or help with sales for the station.

NECESSARY TRAINING

Some DJ positions require only a high school diploma, but most stations are looking for DJs with a bachelor's degree in communications, broadcast journalism, or a similar field. Experience can always be gained by volunteering at a college or even a high school station. Because of the amount of technology involved, it also helps to have training or expertise in this area.

USEFUL SKILLS, TALENTS, OR ABILITIES

A soothing voice, charm, good listening skills, making people laugh, mechanically inclined, multitasking, networking, performing, promotion, reading people, writing

HELPFUL CHARACTER TRAITS

Adaptable, charming, confident, confrontational, cooperative, creative, curious, diplomatic, efficient, enthusiastic, friendly, funny, gossipy, melodramatic, mischievous, nosy, observant, optimistic, organized, passionate, persuasive, playful, pushy, socially aware, spontaneous, spunky, studious, uninhibited, wise, witty, workaholic

SOURCES OF FRICTION

Out-of-touch members of management pushing the show in the wrong direction
Budget cuts
Outdated equipment
Integration of new technology the DJ is unfamiliar with
Saying something on-air that gets them in trouble with the bosses
The DJ saying something troublesome when they thought they were not on-air
Having to do things that make them uncomfortable (sales, promotion, in-person events, etc.)
An interviewee who turns argumentative or combative
An interview or segment falling flat
Pitching an idea that the executives aren't interested in
Difficult work hours (particularly at the start of a career) which make it hard to build relationships
Their personal beliefs being shared on-air and bringing bad PR to the station

Physical ailments that threaten their career (a chronic illness that changes their voice, vocal nodules, throat or mouth cancer, etc.)

Stalkers and over-zealous fans

Not being prepared for an interview and saying something stupid or offensive

PEOPLE THEY MIGHT INTERACT WITH

Station managers and executives, other DJs, a producer, guests (being interviewed in person or over the phone), janitorial and administrative staff, celebrities or politicians

HOW THIS OCCUPATION MIGHT IMPACT THE CHARACTER'S NEEDS

Self-Actualization: As this industry changes, jobs may become scarcer, making it difficult for radio DJs to get the jobs they want. Someone stuck on a show they're not passionate about may no longer feel fulfilled.

Esteem and Recognition: This could become an issue for someone who wants more recognition than they're likely to get for their work.

Safety and Security: Any person working a job that makes them well-known, even in small circles, will have fans. If one of those fans is psychotic or imbalanced, they could become a danger for the DJ.

TWISTING THE FICTIONAL STEREOTYPE

People are often surprised when they meet someone whose voice they've heard on air, because their appearance doesn't match the image in listeners' minds. Play on this by considering what unusual physical characteristics a radio personality might have that wouldn't be known unless they were seen in person.

You can also make your DJ memorable by figuring out what personality traits might set him or her apart from the crowd. Howard Stern's shock jock persona and Frasier Crane's snooty and ambitious character traits make them memorable standouts.

CHARACTERS MIGHT CHOOSE THIS PROFESSION BECAUSE THEY...

Were constantly told growing up that they had a voice for radio

Have a passion for a certain genre of music or a desire to interact with music and musicians

Are a talker, and the job provides a platform to share their thoughts

Find it safer to connect with people via the radio than in person (due to social difficulties, bad past relationships, being stalked, etc.)

RANCHER

OVERVIEW
Ranchers handle the day-to-day operations of running a ranch. Their duties may include choosing which livestock to raise, breeding the animals, feeding and watering them, seeing to their physical health, hiring and overseeing the necessary personnel, selling livestock, and maintaining the ranch's physical structures. They may also choose to raise crops that can be used on the ranch as feed for the animals.

NECESSARY TRAINING
Many ranches are family-owned, and the necessary skills are taught from one generation to the next. An outsider entering this career field might sign on with an existing ranch to gain experience, or they could take over a ranch and hire skilled workers to do the manual labor.

USEFUL SKILLS, TALENTS, OR ABILITIES
A knack for making money, a way with animals, basic first aid, exceptional memory, farming, haggling, mechanically inclined, multitasking, predicting the weather, repurposing, sales, sharpshooting, stamina, strength, survival skills, whittling, wilderness navigation, woodworking

HELPFUL CHARACTER TRAITS
Adaptable, adventurous, alert, ambitious, calm, cooperative, courageous, disciplined, focused, gentle, independent, know-it-all, macho, mature, nature-focused, nurturing, observant, organized, patient, persistent, resourceful, sensible, stubborn, workaholic

SOURCES OF FRICTION
A local illness that attacks livestock, such as an avian or porcine disease
A predator preying on the animals
Poachers
The rancher's land being taken away (by the government, in a lawsuit, etc.)
An accident befalling a careless worker
The animals being mistreated by workers
Financial difficulties
A drought or famine
Strife between family members about how the ranch should be run
Bad PR—e.g., people protesting the treatment of the rancher's animals
Family members who want out of the business
Wanting to travel but being unable to because the ranch requires constant management
An illness or condition that requires frequent trips to the city to see a doctor, cutting into work time
Kids getting onto the property and engaging in unhealthy or dangerous activities
Difficult animal births that require a vet's intervention, causing unexpected expenses
Social or cultural changes that make a specific type of livestock or their byproducts undesirable (the vegan lifestyle making beef an unwanted commodity, studies showing that the rancher's product is unhealthy, etc.)

PEOPLE THEY MIGHT INTERACT WITH
Ranch workers, family members who live on the ranch, veterinarians, farriers, inspectors, delivery people, breeders, customers seeking to buy the livestock or their byproducts

HOW THIS OCCUPATION MIGHT IMPACT THE CHARACTER'S NEEDS
Self-Actualization: If a character is working the farm out of a sense of duty, rather than because they really want to, this could cause them to resent their work and feel unfulfilled.

Esteem and Recognition: A rancher's esteem could take a hit if they're awful at certain aspects of the job and are being shown up by their workers. Someone with a growth mindset would likely learn from their employees, but a rancher who is more fixed may internalize failures and begin to doubt their abilities.

Safety and Security: Ranching doesn't always carry a wide profit margin. A disease that spreads easily between livestock, a downturn in the economy, restricted trade, climate change, and a number of other scenarios could threaten your character's financial stability.

TWISTING THE FICTIONAL STEREOTYPE
Ranchers are typically portrayed as men. A woman in this role might be just the ticket for providing a twist on this stereotype.

Also, because ranches are usually family-owned businesses, the people running them are typically familiar with the setting. What about someone from the outside taking over, or a group of ranches being run by a co-op?

CHARACTERS MIGHT CHOOSE THIS PROFESSION BECAUSE THEY...
Grew up on a farm or ranch

Idolized cowboys and cowgirls as a child

Wanted sustainable country living rather than life in the city

Have fond childhood memories of visiting a grandparent or other relative on their ranch

Identify with the cowboy culture and the freedom of having a large tract of land

Struggle with a challenge (PTSD, a disfigurement, a speech impediment, etc.), and being surrounded by animals and nature makes it easier to bear

Want autonomy (they're distrustful of the government, are preparing for a possible apocalyptic event, etc.)

See what urban living is doing to their children and want a different life for them

See issues with our food supply production and distribution and want to solve those problems

REAL ESTATE AGENT

OVERVIEW

A real estate agent oversees the buying and selling of homes and properties. They may represent the seller or the buyer and will take on many different duties depending on the situation. These responsibilities include investigating comparative properties, setting up listings for a seller, setting up open houses, accompanying a buyer to a showing, finding answers to their questions about a certain listing, submitting offers, and negotiating between parties.

NECESSARY TRAINING

Agents take a pre-licensing course (the length of which depends on the country and state) where they learn realty practices, lending rules, banking processes and assessments, how to assess a home's value, and how to be an effective advocate and negotiator. Once training is complete, they must pass their licensing exam and pay for a license to practice.

When starting out, a character in this field will most likely join a brokerage so they can utilize the networking of a larger firm. Later, they may choose to set out on their own. In a more populated area, agents may choose a specialty, be it homes in a specific part of the city, working with either residential or commercial properties, focusing on ranches and farms, or only taking on listings in a certain price range. An agent in a smaller town will likely have a variety of clients and listings, ensuring they'll make enough commission to live on.

USEFUL SKILLS, TALENTS, OR ABILITIES

A knack for making money, charm, exceptional memory, gaining the trust of others, good listening skills, haggling, hospitality, lip-reading, lying, making people laugh, multilingualism, multitasking, networking, photographic memory, predicting the weather, promotion, reading people, research, sales, writing

HELPFUL CHARACTER TRAITS

Adaptable, ambitious, analytical, bold, calm, charming, confident, decisive, diplomatic, disciplined, efficient, extroverted, meticulous, organized, perceptive, persuasive, professional

SOURCES OF FRICTION

Clients who aren't ready to buy and just want to see what's out there, wasting everyone's time
Competitive agents vying for the same sale (few listings and many real estate agents)
Clients who are late or especially demanding
Clients who are hoarders or leave their home a mess before a showing
A theft that happens during an open house
Clients who delay financial pre-approval and get angry when they lose out on an offer
Clients with an unrealistic view of what their home is worth
Showing homes to clients who have big expectations but a small budget
Having to put up with inappropriate commentary while showing a house to a client
An angry past client who tries to unfairly smear the agent's good name
Deals falling through
Making a mistake on the paperwork that exposes a client in some way

Trying to sell a problematic home (it's a bank foreclosure, is located next to something undesirable like a landfill or factory, was the site of a suicide, etc.)

Other real estate agents within the firm poaching clients

A downturn in the economy that means lower-priced houses and less commission

A break-in at a home resulting from a lock box not being secured

Property being damaged during an open house

Feeling unsafe when alone with a client

Having to ditch family events to meet with a client who is ready to purchase

PEOPLE THEY MIGHT INTERACT WITH

Administration staff, bank employees and mortgage brokers, freelance photographers and copy writers, other real estate agents, home inspectors, homeowners, home buyers, family members of the clients, contractors hired to spruce up the building (painters, landscapers, pressure washers, etc.)

HOW THIS OCCUPATION MIGHT IMPACT THE CHARACTER'S NEEDS

Self-Actualization: Because of the huge time commitment and irregularity of hours in this profession, a character may find him or herself unable to pursue meaningful goals or grow their knowledge and skills in other areas.

Esteem and Recognition: Within the industry, quarterly and yearly sales are constantly being used as a metric to judge the agent's abilities, and competition is fierce. A poor month or two can lead to a bad year, and the character's standing may drop among peers in the industry, causing self-doubt and low self-esteem.

Love and Belonging: The unsteady hours and need to always be hustling for work means often family and relationships come second, leading to resentment at home.

Safety and Security: Because an agent doesn't always know who's going to show up for an appointment or attend an open house, they could be in danger if caught in a home alone with the wrong person.

TWISTING THE FICTIONAL STEREOTYPE

In fiction, real estate agents always come across as a bit pushy and overly friendly, and usually only point out the highlights of the property. Why not have your character's ethics and values cause them to be overly honest, even if it means costing them a sale?

Characters cast in this role are usually well-groomed and articulate. Instead, consider a character who doesn't care about appearances but is exceptionally good at what they do, so much so that rumpled clothing or rougher language is overlooked.

CHARACTERS MIGHT CHOOSE THIS PROFESSION BECAUSE THEY...

Derive joy from helping people find a home

Have a love affair with houses and homes

Never felt like they had a home; helping people find one meets that need for them

Have strong matchmaking skills and have adapted this instinct to match people with homes

Know everyone in their town and believe they can do well

Falsely believe they can make a lot of money in real estate without much effort

RECEPTIONIST

OVERVIEW

A receptionist works at the front desk of an office or business and, therefore, usually makes the first impression on clients. They're responsible for welcoming guests, distributing and filing paperwork, and answering the phone. They can have additional duties, such as making appointments, ordering office supplies, billing, bookkeeping, checking the mail, training new administrative employees, and escorting clients around the facility. Some receptionists might also be responsible for scheduling or arranging professional services, such as building repairs or website design.

NECESSARY TRAINING

A high school diploma is usually required to work as a receptionist. However, in some facilities, high school students may be employed as office help and take on some of the duties. Most training, such as learning office protocol and how to use the company's software system, occurs on the job. Receptionists are often required to have baseline words-per-minute typing skills and proficiencies with common computer programs.

USEFUL SKILLS, TALENTS, OR ABILITIES

Charm, computer hacking, detail-oriented, exceptional memory, good with numbers, hospitality, making people laugh, multitasking, peacekeeping, reading people, research, typing, writing

HELPFUL CHARACTER TRAITS

Charming, cooperative, courteous, diplomatic, efficient, honest, loyal, obedient, observant, proactive, professional, protective, resourceful, responsible, supportive

SOURCES OF FRICTION

Haughty co-workers with more seniority or education than the receptionist
Misplacing important paperwork
Being asked to do things that are demeaning or not in the job description (janitorial tasks, running personal errands for people in the office, lying to the boss's spouse, etc.)
Having to deal with angry clients or customers
Feuds among co-workers
A power outage that brings work to a halt
Dealing with an insurance company that refuses to pay
Interacting with a talkative or flirty customer
Catching a sickness from a patient or co-worker
Sexual harassment or discrimination
Poor pay and benefits
Having to take on more responsibility when co-workers are laid off
A boss who condescends, micromanages, or is unreasonably demanding
Customers who never seem to be satisfied
Patients who always miss their appointments
Having to deal with a complicated situation they've never encountered before

Frequent turnover that requires the receptionist to train new office personnel, impacting efficiency

Training new assistants who don't listen or adhere to processes

A family emergency occurring during the workday

Accidentally breaking client confidentiality

Noticing suspicious activity within the company and not knowing what to do about it

Not having time to take a break

A personal fear that is related to the work environment—e.g., working in a doctor's office but being afraid of blood or needles

PEOPLE THEY MIGHT INTERACT WITH

Patients, clients or customers, other receptionists or office managers, onsite professionals (accountants, doctors, nurses, counselors, lawyers, teachers, dentists, etc.), students on work experience programs, applicants for job openings, delivery personnel

HOW THIS OCCUPATION MIGHT IMPACT THE CHARACTER'S NEEDS

Self-Actualization: The duties of a receptionist can sometimes become repetitive and boring, which could lead to thoughts of *Is this really all there is?*

Esteem and Recognition: It's not uncommon for a receptionist to get blamed for something that wasn't their fault. On the flip slide, when they do fix a big problem, they're not often recognized for the accomplishment.

Love and Belonging: Relationships with bosses and co-workers can be problematic, especially for a receptionist who is dedicated to solving problems in the office. This could lead to unhealthy rivalries or feelings of isolation.

TWISTING THE FICTIONAL STEREOTYPE

When it comes to receptionists, it has all been done before: attractive and flirty, comedically sloppy, painfully organized, bored and disillusioned. Work to ensure that your character rises above these clichéd personas. Maybe they have a big and lively personality, are sullen and lackluster, or are so passionate about being the vital hub within the company that they live and breathe their motto and do things around the office to brighten everyone's day.

CHARACTERS MIGHT CHOOSE THIS PROFESSION BECAUSE THEY...

Had no reliable transportation and needed a job close to home

Love interacting with all types of people

Want a good summer job

Have strong organizational skills

Want a steady, predictable career

Love the organization they work for (a non-profit, their kid's school, a company owned by a beloved friend, etc.)

Want to experience an industry from the ground up

Have limited education

RECRUITER

OVERVIEW

A recruiter is a human resource specialist who vets and interviews interested job candidates on a business's behalf, screening them and recommending them for certain positions. Some work as internal recruiters within their own company, while external recruiters are hired by a firm as a third party to do this job.

People in this position may also be tasked with locating possible candidates—even those who are employed elsewhere and aren't actively seeking a change—for a job opening. These individuals, called headhunters, will be well-connected and tech-savvy, using social media and special databases to search for passive candidates and reach out to them.

Recruiters may be engaged by a business, work solely on a big project (like a new condo or office building being built), conduct executive searches for high-level positions, pursue athletes for a sports agency or university, or seek enlistees for the military, to name a few possibilities. Depending on their resources, they may invest time and money "wooing" a client to secure a contract with that company.

People looking for work may also seek out a recruiter in hopes of finding employment quicker. That professional is contracted by certain businesses and will be compensated by them should he or she make a suitable match, so the job-seeker doesn't have to pay them for their time.

NECESSARY TRAINING

In most cases, a recruiter will need to earn a bachelor's degree in human resources or business administration and complete a certification program. They'll also need to be an expert in the field for which they're recruiting so they can recognize which people would make good employees.

By paying attention to the little things and being adept in the interview room, a recruiter can use their skills to secure their candidate a job. For example, should they know a prospective employer enjoys painting as a hobby, and they know that their candidate has the same interest, they may suggest the candidate bring this up during the interview. However, this must be done authentically and in the right situation, not as a way to encourage an employer to overlook the faults and shortcomings of a mediocre match.

USEFUL SKILLS, TALENTS, OR ABILITIES

A knack for making money, charm, clairvoyance, detail-oriented, empathy, enhanced hearing, exceptional memory, gaining the trust of others, good listening skills, haggling, hospitality, making people laugh, multilingualism, multitasking, networking, persuasion, promotion, reading people, sales

HELPFUL CHARACTER TRAITS

Adaptable, ambitious, analytical, charming, confident, cooperative, courteous, diplomatic, discreet, easygoing, efficient, extroverted, friendly, honest, honorable, hospitable, industrious, intelligent, loyal, observant, obsessive, organized, patient, perceptive, perfectionist, persuasive, proactive, professional, resourceful, workaholic

SOURCES OF FRICTION

Clients who aren't specific enough regarding hiring specifications, leading to wasted hours of searching

Learning that a new hire lied about their qualifications

A job candidate who has an impressive resume but does subpar work

Being asked to loosen standards or fast-track sourcing in order to receive payment

Placing a candidate, then learning that they switched companies due to unethical meddling

Having a friend apply for a position but, based on certain weakness or a lack of specific experience, not being able to recommend them for it

Being accused of favoritism

Losing a big client to a rival within the recruiter's firm

Finding the perfect applicant but being unable to reach them due to a typo in their contact information

Being hired to fill a position, then being secretly "leaned on" by management to give the job to a certain person

Being swayed by a candidate who is a master manipulator or a pathological liar

A recruiter being tempted to fill a position just to get it off their plate (because they're over-worked, haven't been able to find the perfect candidate, are physically exhausted, etc.)

PEOPLE THEY MIGHT INTERACT WITH

Business executives (CEOs, CIOs, COOs, etc.), prospective candidates, social media managers, technology specialists, other recruiters, executive assistants

HOW THIS OCCUPATION MIGHT IMPACT THE CHARACTER'S NEEDS

Esteem and Recognition: Constantly placing others in dream job positions might cause dissatisfaction and self-doubt for a recruiter as they question if they settled in their own career.

Safety and Security: If a character becomes embroiled in an ethics review due to poor hiring practices in their recruitment firm, they could lose their job or find it hard to find employment elsewhere (whether they were involved or not).

TWISTING THE FICTIONAL STEREOTYPE

Recruiters can be portrayed as being unethical or willing to do anything to secure a commis-sion. But in an industry where reputation is everything, disappointing clients by providing candidates who aren't the best fit for a position will only hurt the recruiter's practice. A recruiter who is good at what they do will take the time to really get to know a client's needs and strive to bring them exactly what they want, time after time.

CHARACTERS MIGHT CHOOSE THIS PROFESSION BECAUSE THEY...

Enjoy connecting people with the jobs that will bring them satisfaction and self-worth

Are adept at reading people and unearthing their talents and areas of expertise

Gain satisfaction from determining and deciding what someone really needs

Value the fine art of persuasion and negotiation due to a past influencer who loved to barter

REFEREE

OVERVIEW
Referees oversee sporting events to ensure rules are being followed, good sportsmanship is upheld, and the players are kept safe. Officials are needed at various levels, from professional sports to college to high school and intramurals. Those refereeing intramural sports and community games for kids may be relatively untrained—high school or college students with knowledge of the particular sport—making this a viable job option not only for adults but for young people as well.

NECESSARY TRAINING
A high-school diploma or equivalent is required to ref in most official capacities. Specific training is also necessary and might be offered through a college or sports organization. Certain registrations and certifications often have to be met as well. Candidates tend to start out at the lower level, overseeing high school or minor league sporting events, for instance, before moving upward.

USEFUL SKILLS, TALENTS, OR ABILITIES
Enhanced hearing, equanimity, exceptional memory, multitasking, peacekeeping, predicting the weather, stamina, swift-footedness

HELPFUL CHARACTER TRAITS
Alert, calm, confrontational, cooperative, courteous, decisive, diplomatic, disciplined, honest, honorable, humorless, just, objective, observant, passionate, perfectionist, professional, responsible

SOURCES OF FRICTION
Being injured on the job
Making a mistake that determines the outcome of a game
Being threatened or stalked by an angry fan
Working the field with an incompetent referee
Disagreeing with a fellow ref over an important call
Running into a key player and causing an injury
Difficulty remembering certain rules or consequences
Not staying up-to-date on new rules and regulations
Personal bias that leads to prejudicial decisions
Losing their cool with a perturbed player
Frequent travel taking the referee away from family
Getting used to calling the shots at work and struggling to turn that off at home
A diagnosis of chronic illness or pain that makes it difficult to work
Loving the job but struggling financially
Being unable to move upward and reach their preferred level
Lacking discipline and losing the physical fitness necessary to do the job well
Working a long game with extended overtimes

Working in extreme weather conditions
Being offered a bribe to call a game a certain way

PEOPLE THEY MIGHT INTERACT WITH

Players, coaches, other referees, facilities personnel (groundskeepers, maintenance people, stadium managers, janitorial staff), parents (at the lower levels)

HOW THIS OCCUPATION MIGHT IMPACT THE CHARACTER'S NEEDS

Self-Actualization: This need might take a hit for a character who is unable to referee their preferred sport or reach the desired level (i.e., NCAA Division 1, NBA, or NFL).

Esteem and Recognition: Refs are typically pursuing a passion, which makes the job worthwhile despite the lower compensation. But if financial status is important, they may wrestle with esteem issues when comparing their wages to those of friends in other careers.

Safety and Security: Referees get hit in contact sports all the time, making it a career where injuries are more likely to happen. If an incident makes it impossible for the referee to work and provide for family, this could create financial strain.

TWISTING THE FICTIONAL STEREOTYPE

This career is male-centric; while women are making their way slowly into the field, they're rare. A female ref could provide the twist you're looking for.

Refs also tend to be strait-laced and by-the-book. One with unusual characteristics—say, flamboyant, mischievous, or overly nervous—would stand out.

Instead of falling back on the traditionally popular sports for your ref, consider one with less visibility, such as rugby, lacrosse, roller derby, or wrestling. You might also think about placing him in an unusual venue, such as the Olympics or overseeing games for people with special needs.

Many fictional refs choose this as a fallback career because they were unable to play professionally. What about a character who never desired to be in the limelight and just has a passion for the sport and the players?

CHARACTERS MIGHT CHOOSE THIS PROFESSION BECAUSE THEY...

Wanted to make someone happy (such as a teen seeking to please his parents by refereeing his younger sibling's games)
Love sports and being close to the camaraderie of teams
Have grown too old to continue playing the game
Want to participate in an activity that brought enjoyment (and possibly empowerment) as a child
Have the necessary qualities, such as an innate sense of fairness, a respect for structure, and being a rule-follower

REIKI MASTER

OVERVIEW
Reiki is a Japanese healing practice that uses energy to provide physical, mental, and spiritual wellness. Though it is not a religion, it is often associated with spirituality.

A typical Reiki session is performed by a practitioner or master who has been through an attunement process that allows them to channel the healing energy to their clients. Individual sessions may target a specific illness or injury, or it might focus on an underlying cause (such as stress) that is inhibiting good health.

Because many practitioners in this field will seek out the coveted rank of Reiki Master, those who have already attained this level will often offer training as well as healing services. They may work out of a private practice or in other facilities, such as a hospital, assisted living facility, or spa.

NECESSARY TRAINING
Reiki Masters must first become practitioners. This is achieved by receiving attunements from a Master that will give them access to Reiki energy so they can channel it to others. Practitioners must then proceed through a series of levels, becoming attuned to various symbols that will increase their power. Once they've attained the third level, they will become a Master and will be able to teach. Some practitioners may also undergo an apprenticeship as part of the process.

USEFUL SKILLS, TALENTS, OR ABILITIES
Astral projection, basic first aid, charm, clairvoyance, dexterity, empathy, gaining the trust of others, herbalism, intuition, out-of-the-box thinking, reading people, regeneration, stamina

HELPFUL CHARACTER TRAITS
Calm, centered, confident, courteous, disciplined, empathetic, focused, gentle, honorable, kind, nature-focused, nurturing, passionate, perceptive, proper, protective, spiritual, talented, tolerant, wise

SOURCES OF FRICTION
A client who is anxious about being touched
A religious family member who is uncomfortable with the idea of energy healing
A young client who finds it hard to stay still
Feeling drained or tired after a session (or multiple sessions)
Rudeness and judgment from skeptics who know nothing about Reiki
A client who complains about strange side effects
A family member who refuses healing and then starts deteriorating
Being unfamiliar with the financial management side of running a business
An enthusiastic student who is unable to pay for training
A client who is uncomfortable with the spiritual aspects of Reiki
Liability issues
A client who refuses to pay for their session
Working with a fellow practitioner who disagrees with the character's business model or ethics

A client who feels they are not experiencing the effects of Reiki as strongly as they did at first
Struggling to achieve the level of "master" despite much hard work and dedication
The workplace being broken into
A client becoming overly attached due to the nature of the healing sessions
An injury (such as a concussion) that prevents the character from practicing
Struggling to build a book of business and grow a practice

PEOPLE THEY MIGHT INTERACT WITH
Clients, other Reiki masters or practitioners, doctors, nurses, hospital staff, Reiki students, the client's family members or advocates

HOW THIS OCCUPATION MIGHT IMPACT THE CHARACTER'S NEEDS
Self-Actualization: Since Reiki is associated with many spiritual ideas, it is easy for a master to constantly seek a higher connection with God or a higher consciousness. This can become difficult when they aren't feeling particularly enlightened or are struggling to help clients as much as they would like.

Esteem and Recognition: Some people have strong opinions against Reiki. Despite numerous testimonies about its effectiveness, very little scientific research exists to support it. Thus, some Reiki masters may feel challenged or even disrespected.

Love and Belonging: Potential love interests may be put off by the practice of energy healing, making it challenging for someone in this field to find a romantic partner.

TWISTING THE FICTIONAL STEREOTYPE
Not all Reiki masters are hardcore spiritual and mystical, though that is certainly the case some of the time. Perhaps your character likes to work in conjunction with doctors or counselors. Or maybe they associate healing and relaxation with an unusual music genre.

Most Reiki masters use Reiki on people. What if your character specializes in using Reiki to treat pets or wildlife?

CHARACTERS MIGHT CHOOSE THIS PROFESSION BECAUSE THEY...
Experienced personal healing from Reiki
Believe that spirituality and healthcare can go hand in hand
Have an interest in spirituality, natural medicine, and healing
Possess psychic abilities or clairvoyance and wish to use their insight to help others
Are nurturing and feel very connected to people and nature
Are seeking opportunities for spiritual growth

REPORTER

OVERVIEW

Reporters may work for different industries, such as news channels and websites, magazines and newspapers, or radio stations. Many write within a niche, focusing primarily on sports, politics, local happenings, health, crime, the world of entertainment, etc., so research is integral to their work. Once their information has been gathered, it may be shared through written articles, interviews, recorded videos, or live news reports.

Sometimes, the terms *reporter* and *journalist* are used interchangeably, but there is a slight distinction between the two. A journalist is anyone who gathers and shares information on public affairs; this might be a reporter, editor, news anchor, columnist, etc. A reporter is a specific kind of journalist whose role is to glean and communicate information in a direct fashion, such as through interviews or press conferences.

NECESSARY TRAINING

Many reporters will pursue a bachelor's degree in a field like communications or journalism, but this isn't always necessary. More important is experience, which budding reporters can gain through an internship with a media outlet. As with most careers, reporters often will start at the bottom of the ladder, as an editor or blogger, and work their way up to their desired position.

USEFUL SKILLS, TALENTS, OR ABILITIES

Blending in, charm, detail-oriented, equanimity, gaining the trust of others, good listening skills, multilingualism, multitasking, networking, organization, photographic memory, public speaking, reading people, research, strategic thinking

HELPFUL CHARACTER TRAITS

Alert, ambitious, analytical, bold, charming, confident, confrontational, cooperative, courteous, curious, diplomatic, extroverted, gossipy, industrious, manipulative, meticulous, nosy, objective, observant, organized, passionate, patient, persistent, persuasive, professional, pushy, resourceful, socially aware, spunky, studious, unethical, uninhibited

SOURCES OF FRICTION

Intense competition with other reporters
Being criticized for their views or reporting style
Competition with another news channel, magazine, etc.
Having to make time to edit their own articles
Becoming emotional while reporting a story
Interviewees who dodge questions
Reporting or observing in a dangerous place (a house fire, a riot, a natural disaster, etc.)
Being accused of plagiarism, sloppy fact-checking, or politicking
Working within a hard deadline
Being biased or opinionated and only being allowed to report facts (or vice-versa)
Having to look confident and put together, even when they're not
Having their hours dictated by the people and events they are covering

Friction at home with their spouse or children when work takes over

Being threatened by people who have a vested interest in keeping certain facts quiet

Having a story killed because it doesn't align with the company's political beliefs

Difficulty finding childcare when the boss calls with a last-minute job that requires travel

Focusing primarily on difficult or traumatic situations and struggling with compassion fatigue as a result

PEOPLE THEY MIGHT INTERACT WITH

News anchors, journalists, photographers or camera operators, other reporters, witnesses, interviewees, spectators, police officers and first responders, sports figures and professional coaches, politicians, editors, criminals, victims of crime

HOW THIS OCCUPATION MIGHT IMPACT THE CHARACTER'S NEEDS

Self-Actualization: Newbie reporters will be given assignments that may not match their interests, while experienced reporters are given the high-profile work. If the former feel constantly held back, it could cause them to question their career path.

Esteem and Recognition: A reporter may feel looked-down-upon if the publication they're working for is small or lacks credibility.

Safety and Security: A reporter traveling to the site of a natural disaster, war zone, or other crisis may find themselves in danger.

Physiological Needs: Reporters have unfortunately been killed in the line of duty, so, depending on the character's assignment, this is a realistic possibility.

TWISTING THE FICTIONAL STEREOTYPE

Since reporters who face the camera appear professional and put-together, that's how they're mostly portrayed. What if you had a casual, carefree reporter who writes articles for print or the web and observes from the shadows?

Most reporters are relatively young. To switch things up, consider an elderly reporter who is wildly successful because he or she knows how to get people to trust and open up.

CHARACTERS MIGHT CHOOSE THIS PROFESSION BECAUSE THEY...

Are driven to bring truth to the public

Are intensely interested in what goes on behind the scenes of political elections, natural disasters, contentious public debates or meetings, etc.

Want to personally uncover facts rather than hear them from others

Are suspicious of the government and media and want information firsthand

ROBOTICS ENGINEER

OVERVIEW
Robotics engineers work in an array of industries, such as manufacturing, film and entertainment, mining, and space exploration. This job involves a large amount of research and design to establish the concept for the robot, followed by its construction, and, finally, thorough testing to be sure it works as intended. If the robot already exists, the engineer is tasked with developing new applications or software for it. Regardless, for most projects, the engineer will work collaboratively with others rather than independently.

NECESSARY TRAINING
Some universities offer degree programs specifically in robotics, but typically, engineers just need to have a bachelor's degree in a related field (like mechanical engineering). Licensing is required for those who wish to work independently or pursue higher-level jobs, and certain career paths, such as teaching in the field, will require a master's or doctorate degree. Because new research is being published at a steady rate, continuing education is a priority for anyone in this position.

USEFUL SKILLS, TALENTS, OR ABILITIES
Creativity, detail-oriented, dexterity, good with numbers, mechanically inclined, organization, out-of-the-box thinking, repurposing, research, teaching, vision

HELPFUL CHARACTER TRAITS
Adaptable, analytical, cooperative, creative, curious, focused, industrious, intelligent, meticulous, mischievous, organized, perfectionist, persistent, proactive, resourceful, responsible, studious

SOURCES OF FRICTION
Working with military secrets and having to keep projects completely confidential
Being unable to figure out why a robot isn't working properly
A computer failure that results in lost data
Having a great idea and not being able to make it work
A family member who is paranoid about robots or technology
Having a spouse in a field where their work is being outsourced to robots
An accident while building the robot that leaves the character injured
Fighting a mental or physical malady that makes it difficult to concentrate (migraines, depression, etc.)
Being unable to implement designs because of protocol or budget cuts
Struggling to find work and pay off student debt
A co-worker becoming competitive with a project
Struggling to keep up with new research
Having to design robots that will be used in a way that causes a moral conflict
Projects being shelved, leading to frustration at the wasted time and effort
Conspiracy theories surrounding artificial intelligence gaining traction in the culture

A robot malfunctioning shortly after it was bought by a customer
Going significantly over budget or past deadline on a project
Having a vision for a new robot but being unable to garner the support to build it
Being approached by a competitor and asked to cross ethical lines for compensation

PEOPLE THEY MIGHT INTERACT WITH

Interns, other robotics engineers, supervisors and managers, scientists, film directors, car manufacturers, military personnel, medical personnel

HOW THIS OCCUPATION MIGHT IMPACT THE CHARACTER'S NEEDS

Self-Actualization: Some mental conditions, such as OCD or ADHD, make it harder to concentrate or get work done. This kind of limitation could make it difficult for the character to achieve their true potential in their career.

Esteem and Recognition: Conspiracy theories about robots and technology being dangerous or threatening aren't unusual. This can sometimes cause engineers in this field to feel criticized, disrespected, or even villainized for the work they do.

Physiological Needs: Due to the nature of their job, most robotics engineers work long hours, which can lead to physical and mental exhaustion and declining health.

TWISTING THE FICTIONAL STEREOTYPE

Robotics engineers in fiction and film usually are background characters who only appear when needed. Try making your engineer the protagonist or giving him an affinity for the spotlight.

Most of these characters are portrayed creating items for the manufacturing and automotive industries. Why not have your engineer build creations that are a little more unusual, such as new animatronics equipment for an amusement park or production studio?

Characters in this field are often written as geeky, bookish, and better able to relate to machines than humans. Play with your engineer's personality traits, physical looks, and interests to break them from the mold.

CHARACTERS MIGHT CHOOSE THIS PROFESSION BECAUSE THEY...

Were introduced to it through a robotics club at school
Were told that technology was bad, and they want to prove otherwise
Love building things in a new or innovative way
Want humankind to be able to explore new places that are currently inaccessible
Want to make meaningful advances in the field of artificial intelligence
Are mechanically inclined and science-minded
Are interested in cutting-edge technology and advancements

SECRET SERVICE AGENT

OVERVIEW
Secret Service agents protect high-profile government officials such as presidents, vice-presidents, and visiting heads of state. They also lead investigations into money laundering, cyber-attacks, fraud, and other crimes that threaten national systems of banking, technology, etc. Depending on the assignment, frequent and lengthy travel can be required.

NECESSARY TRAINING
Applicants for this position must be US citizens between twenty-one and thirty-seven years of age (thirty-nine, for applicants with a veteran's status) and in superb physical condition, including having 20/20 corrected vision. They must pass a written exam, a physical abilities and psychological evaluation, and in-depth background checks. In addition, they can have no visible body or facial tattoos.

Once hired, an agent will go through two extensive training programs lasting a total of twenty-seven weeks. Both programs must be passed on the first try. After completion of training, an agent's first field assignment is to a U.S.-based office and lasts six to eight years. This is followed by a three- to five-year protective assignment. After that, an agent can pursue placements in various locations, including international offices.

USEFUL SKILLS, TALENTS, OR ABILITIES
Basic first aid, blending in, computer hacking, enhanced hearing, equanimity, gaining the trust of others, good listening skills, intuition, knife-throwing, knowledge of explosives, leadership, mentalism, multilingualism, peacekeeping, photographic memory, reading people, research, self-defense, sharpshooting, stamina, strategic thinking

HELPFUL CHARACTER TRAITS
Adventurous, alert, analytical, bold, confident, confrontational, decisive, patient, patriotic, perceptive, perfectionist, persistent, resourceful, responsible, spunky, suspicious, unselfish

SOURCES OF FRICTION
Being assigned to an undesirable field office
Applying for a certain assignment and being denied
Having to escort someone in an activity the agent doesn't enjoy (riding horses, deep-sea fishing, etc.)
Having to protect someone the agent doesn't like or agree with on a moral level
Chaotic events that are difficult to secure, such as the president shaking hands in a crowd outside a hotel
Dismissing someone as a threat who then makes an assassination attempt
An injury that makes it difficult to do the job (a sprained ankle, a torn ligament, etc.)
Getting sick and having difficulty focusing
Dealing with violent or mentally imbalanced suspects
Fatigue from having to be on call and on high alert all the time
Becoming so used to suspecting everyone that it's hard to trust anyone

The agent being easily bored off the job

Dealing with uncooperative staff at a location where an event is being held (a hotel, restaurant, convention center, etc.)

Friction with family members when work overrides home life

The pressure of working a case that, if unresolved, has potentially catastrophic results

Suspecting that there's a mole in the department

Protecting someone who takes foolhardy risks

PEOPLE THEY MIGHT INTERACT WITH

The government official they're protecting (a former vice-president and their spouse, a candidate for president, a visiting dignitary, etc.), other agents, people suspected of posing a threat (a suspicious bystander, a mentally unwell person seeking an audience with the president, a suspect in a fraud case, etc.), witnesses in a case, staff at an event where someone is being protected

HOW THIS OCCUPATION MIGHT IMPACT THE CHARACTER'S NEEDS

Self-Actualization: A character who is in this position for moral reasons may become frustrated if they're asked to protect someone or fight for something they don't believe in.

Esteem and Recognition: Secret Service agents are the cream of the crop, meaning competition for positions is brutal. An agent who doesn't measure up is going to lose standing in his own eyes and in the eyes of those around them.

Love and Belonging: In an elite agency where few are chosen, those who make it could easily begin to think too highly of themselves, leading to a haughty, cocky, and condescending character that others will not connect with.

Safety and Security: A character in this career faces danger constantly. This danger could extend to family members if an enemy wanted to compromise the agent.

Physiological Needs: Agents in protective assignments literally put their lives on the line on a day-to-day basis, making this a potentially dangerous occupation.

TWISTING THE FICTIONAL STEREOTYPE

These characters are usually portrayed as loyal patriots who would gladly take a bullet for the president. But what about a conflicted agent who, for whatever reason, is less than enthusiastic about their assignment?

CHARACTERS MIGHT CHOOSE THIS PROFESSION BECAUSE THEY...

Were part of a military family

Want to be the best of the best, admired and respected

Are a loyal patriot who wants to serve their country

SECURITY GUARD

OVERVIEW
Security guards monitor and patrol an area to ensure the safety of those nearby and the security of the property. They may work freelance and be hired directly by a company (such as a bank, casino, night club, apartment complex, hotel, retail store, or school) or work through an agency. Some jobs are stationary (monitoring cameras or guarding an entrance) while others require the guard to patrol an area (on foot, by car or bicycle, etc.).

Guards are on the lookout for anyone breaking the law, disturbances that could escalate into violence, and any suspicious activity. While their presence is largely meant to deter crimes, misconduct does occur. In these cases, the guard will have additional duties, such as documenting infractions, detaining suspects until the proper authorities arrive, and testifying in court. Guards may also be in charge of ensuring that all safety and security mechanisms (such as smoke alarms, digital locks, and video cameras) are in working order. And because they are seen as safe and trustworthy, they may find themselves answering questions, giving directions, and providing other customer service-related information.

NECESSARY TRAINING
Most security guards must have a high school diploma to enter the workforce. They'll also have to be fingerprinted and pass a criminal background check. Armed guards must become certified and maintain their certification in various training and safety courses associated with carrying a gun.

USEFUL SKILLS, TALENTS, OR ABILITIES
Basic first aid, enhanced hearing, enhanced sense of smell, equanimity, gaining the trust of others, intuition, lip-reading, mentalism, multilingualism, peacekeeping, reading people, self-defense, sharpshooting, stamina, strength, swift-footedness, wrestling

HELPFUL CHARACTER TRAITS
Adaptable, alert, bold, calm, confident, confrontational, controlling, decisive, diplomatic, disciplined, focused, humorless, just, mature, nosy, objective, observant, obsessive, persuasive, protective, resourceful, sensible, suspicious, uninhibited

SOURCES OF FRICTION
Uncooperative suspects
Lack of sleep slowing reflexes and reaction times
Boredom or distraction causing the guard to miss something important
Being baited by bored teenagers
Law enforcement or emergency personnel taking longer than usual to arrive
Suspecting someone of wrongdoing but having no proof
Being hurt by a suspect
Being accused of unnecessary roughness or abuse
A physical decline that makes it difficult to do the job (failing eyesight, an old knee injury worsening and making it hard to walk around all day, etc.)

Favoritism or prejudice making it difficult for the guard to be objective

Dissatisfaction over what they're able to do or accomplish as a security guard

Having to deal with a situation beyond their abilities (finding a bomb, facing multiple violent suspects, having to offer life-saving measures in the wake of an armed robbery, etc.)

Not being taken seriously by law enforcement personnel or members of the community

PEOPLE THEY MIGHT INTERACT WITH

People commonly found in the area the guard monitors (customers, business owners, business employees, pedestrians, etc.), their employer (a business owner or the manager of a security firm), other guards, law enforcement personnel, suspects

HOW THIS OCCUPATION MIGHT IMPACT THE CHARACTER'S NEEDS

Self-Actualization: Someone who entered the business to make a difference may become stymied if they find themselves merely slapping a bandage on the community's problems or dealing with the same issues over and over.

Esteem and Recognition: Many security guards are perceived as "rent-a-cops" or wannabe police officers. This lack of esteem by others can have an impact on the way the character views him or herself.

Safety and Security: Physical risk is a part of this job, both for the guard and those they are seeking to protect.

Physiological Needs: Any security detail can go badly, resulting in a guard being killed.

TWISTING THE FICTIONAL STEREOTYPE

If your security guard is ex-law enforcement, consider why they chose to leave the force yet seek a job that still centers on the safety of citizens and property.

In fiction, security guards are sometimes little more than paper obstacles that serve the plot. Defeat boring clichés by making sure your character is fully developed. Give them unexpected skills that make them effective at their job and weaknesses that provide a true challenge to overcome.

CHARACTERS MIGHT CHOOSE THIS PROFESSION BECAUSE THEY...

Wanted to be a police officer but were unable to do so (due to a physical shortcoming, fear, insecurity, psychological ailment, etc.)

Were attacked, robbed, etc. in the past and want to stop it from happening to others

Are hoping to make up for a past wrong (not stopping a fight before it became deadly, etc.)

Need a job that provides the flexibility for them to pursue other interests or obligations

Value justice, protectiveness, and being community-minded

SERVER

OVERVIEW

A server is someone who interacts directly with the patrons of a restaurant, bar, café, diner, pub, or other location where food and drink are served. They oversee the customer experience, greeting and seating guests, relaying any specials, answering questions about the menu items, taking orders, passing special requests or dietary conditions to the cooking staff, bringing food and drinks as they are prepared, and delivering the bill when the customer is finished. Servers may also be responsible for collecting payment, carrying away dishes, packing up leftovers, dealing with customer complaints, and light food preparation (such as plating salads and premade desserts).

NECESSARY TRAINING

In most situations, no post-secondary education is required to be a server, but a high school diploma is often the benchmark for many employers. Depending on the restaurant's pedigree, extra courses and training may be required or encouraged. A server may also need to take training to obtain a permit to serve alcohol.

Servers will receive onsite mentoring and instruction on specific business protocols, be trained on any technology systems used by the restaurant, educated on food preparation and safety, and taught how to handle and execute customer requests.

USEFUL SKILLS, TALENTS, OR ABILITIES

Charm, empathy, enhanced hearing, enhanced sense of smell, enhanced taste buds, exceptional memory, good listening skills, hospitality, making people laugh, multilingualism, multitasking, peacekeeping, promotion, reading people, sales, stamina

HELPFUL CHARACTER TRAITS

Adaptable, calm, charming, confident, cooperative, courteous, diplomatic, easygoing, efficient, enthusiastic, extroverted, friendly, funny, gossipy, hospitable, independent, industrious, obedient, observant, organized, perfectionist, persuasive, professional, proper, quirky, resourceful, responsible, sensible, sophisticated, tolerant, witty, workaholic

SOURCES OF FRICTION

Customers who are rude or impossible to please
Dine-and-dashers
Patrons with extreme food allergies who expect menus to be altered to suit them
Being blamed for mistakes made by the cooking staff
Other servers stealing tips
Being given too many tables during a shift and struggling to provide quality service
Giving exceptional service but being tipped poorly
Management who insist on micromanaging
A request for time off being denied
Not having enough staff working to serve the patrons adequately
Having to make excuses to a customer when the cooking staff messes up an order

Customers who flirt or make unwanted advances
Being forced to share tips with those who put in subpar effort
Working with people the server doesn't like or respect
Struggling to make a living wage
Creepy regulars who ask prying or personal questions or refuse to be served by anyone else

PEOPLE THEY MIGHT INTERACT WITH

Customers, management, cooking and prep staff, dishwashers, restaurant greeters, delivery people, food and beverage reps, food and safety inspectors, district managers or other people from the head office (if the restaurant is a chain)

HOW THIS OCCUPATION MIGHT IMPACT THE CHARACTER'S NEEDS

Self-Actualization: There is only so much advancement opportunity in the food service industry. A character who is unable to move up the chain can easily become dissatisfied with their work, especially when they feel they are not being fairly compensated for the effort.

Esteem and Recognition: A server surrounded by people with higher paying or better respected jobs could begin to feel badly about their career choice, lowing their sense of self-worth.

TWISTING THE FICTIONAL STEREOTYPE

Servers are often portrayed as washed out, jaded workers, or even as being bubbly and "not too bright." In reality, good servers do what's necessary to give customers an enjoyable experience so they'll want to return. Know the skills required to be an effective server and keep those in mind when creating your character to steer clear of those one-note clichés. Remember that, in most places, a good portion of the server's income will come from tipping, so they're invested in making sure the customer receives strong, friendly service.

CHARACTERS MIGHT CHOOSE THIS PROFESSION BECAUSE THEY...

Lacked the post-secondary education required in many other jobs
Need to supplement their income to meet immediate financial needs
Have a hospitable nature and want to help people enjoy a specific part of their day
Have friends who work at the same restaurant
Are gaining experience for a future career, such as becoming a provider for the food industry
Want to contaminate large quantities of food or make individual customers ill
Want to spy on a person of power who frequents the establishment—e.g., gathering details about the person's work while serving him or her
Know that important influencers (talent scouts, modeling agents, etc.) hang out there

SKYDIVING INSTRUCTOR

OVERVIEW
Skydiving instructors teach willing participants the basics of safe skydiving. Then they take them miles into the sky to help them to jump out of a plane with a parachute, either solo or in tandem dives. Instructors will teach, pack parachutes, answer clients' questions, help them gear up, and ensure all safety regulations are followed.

Instructors must be highly alert, dedicated, calm, decisive, and strong communicators. They'll need to work well with others in a high-pressure environment, exude confidence and enthusiasm that encourages trust, and have a strong work ethic. A healthy sense of adventure and the ability to analyze and mitigate risk are also helpful qualities to have in this job.

NECESSARY TRAINING
Career options will be determined by the instructor's number of dives, their certifications, and their own personal areas of interest. With the proper credentials, they might become coaches, skydiving photographers, AFF instructors, or tandem instructors. In addition to the jumps and classroom time, they must be able to pass challenging written and oral exams. There are also additional courses an instructor can take to qualify them to teach in specialized areas.

USEFUL SKILLS, TALENTS, OR ABILITIES
A knack for making money, charm, equanimity, gaining the trust of others, good listening skills, hospitality, lip-reading, making people laugh, mechanically inclined, multilingualism, photographic memory, predicting the weather, promotion, reading people, strategic thinking, strength, strong breath control, teaching, throwing one's voice, wilderness navigation

HELPFUL CHARACTER TRAITS
Adaptable, adventurous, alert, ambitious, analytical, calm, courageous, decisive, diplomatic, disciplined, easygoing, efficient, enthusiastic, extroverted, focused, friendly, independent, meticulous, nature-focused, observant, obsessive, organized, passionate, perfectionist, persuasive, professional, protective, responsible, spontaneous, thrifty, uninhibited

SOURCES OF FRICTION
Working for a company that runs a tight budget (walking the safety line)
Struggling to make ends meet as an instructor
Friction between instructors and staff over preferential treatment or work ethic imbalances
Clients who change their minds mid-flight
Clients who don't follow instructions or who take risks
An inattentive skydiver whose actions lead to a near-miss or even a collision
A malfunction with a skydiver's automatic activation device (AAD)
A jumper blacking out
A near-collision with a plane or drone
Camera malfunctions
Bad weather
Plane issues that scrap the day's dives, resulting in no one getting paid

A difficult landing that leads to injuries
Being sued by a client
Having a death occur within the skydiving community (especially if it happens onsite)
Economic changes that drive up costs and prices, resulting in fewer customers
Discovering suspicious cargo on the plane

PEOPLE THEY MIGHT INTERACT WITH
Other skydivers, clients, facility staff, pilots, students, family members of participants

HOW THIS OCCUPATION MIGHT IMPACT THE CHARACTER'S NEEDS
Self-Actualization: A character who becomes addicted to the rush of skydiving may struggle with feeling satisfied on the ground.

Esteem and Recognition: A character who dreams of competing and being the best in this field may have trouble meeting that goal if most of their time is spent teaching others.

Safety and Security: A career as a skydiving instructor does not pay well, and as the sport is expensive, a portion of the earnings will go right back into skydiving. This can create a financial hardship if the character is not frugal or has a family to support.

Physiological Needs: While parachute malfunctions and other accidents are rare, skydiving means ever-present risk to an instructor's life.

TWISTING THE FICTIONAL STEREOTYPE
Characters in this field are usually described as fearless, but many of them originally took up skydiving as a way to master a fear of heights. And though they love the experience and have parlayed it into a career as an instructor, it doesn't mean the fear has gone away. Think carefully about scenarios like this and what you can add to your character's personality, past, or mindset that might save them from the stereotypical portrayal.

While skydivers in fiction are often drawn as reckless, instructors are anything but. They take their responsibility to clients seriously, understanding risk and working to mitigate it. It's our job as authors to make our characters one-of-a-kind, but sometimes, the storybook portrayal is the one that needs to be avoided. This can often be done by looking to reality for inspiration.

CHARACTERS MIGHT CHOOSE THIS PROFESSION BECAUSE THEY...
Wanted to overcome a phobia of heights, falling, suffocating, or dying
Wanted to face past experiences where there were bound, held, or restricted in some way
Are an adrenaline junkie
Have overcome a fear that limited their life and wanted to help others do the same
Are embracing freedom and joy after being wrongfully imprisoned for a long period of time
Are a skydiving enthusiast and need a way to pay for their hobby

SMALL BUSINESS OWNER

OVERVIEW

A small business owner may choose from a number of structures for their company—such as a sole proprietorship, C corporation, S corporation, or limited liability company—and concentrate in any number of areas. Businesses tend to be product- or service-focused and may target individual consumers (via a clothing store, mechanic's shop, or pottery studio), corporations (via a safety training company servicing oil companies or an art supplier for creatives), or both.

Small business owners wear many hats; they'll need to excel at managing all aspects of the business or outsource those duties to employees or other companies. Aside from providing the highest quality product or service, the owner must concentrate on business development and customer retention, navigate market changes, gain financing, and handle legal affairs (such as securing sensitive information appropriately, obtaining insurance, keeping licenses and permits up-to-date, training employees, and paying taxes). They also need to pay bills, issue payroll, manage cash flow, understand their assets, and make reinvestment decisions—things like buying new equipment, hiring more employees, doing a website overhaul, etc. Owners should concentrate on building good relationships with suppliers and other local businesses and will need to be proficient at marketing and creating a business plan. Over the long-term, they'll have to scale up to grow, and if they are struggling, scale down to stay afloat.

Small business owners, although time- and cash-stretched, often give back to the community through personal involvement, sponsorship of events, charitable donations, or a mixture of these, which raises their profile in the community.

NECESSARY TRAINING

Training will vary depending on the type of business that's being run, expertise needed, and the certifications required for the company to operate. Generally speaking, having a background in business management, marketing, and/or accounting will greatly help a small business owner be successful and navigate the many challenges that can affect their operations.

It's also beneficial to have experience with the service or product being provided. Working for someone else (perhaps as an apprentice) and understanding the business from the inside will help an owner start and grow a company effectively. Managerial experience with a different sort of business can also give them an advantage when it comes to handling the administrative side of things.

USEFUL SKILLS, TALENTS, OR ABILITIES

A knack for making money, exceptional memory, gaining the trust of others, haggling, hospitality, leadership, making people laugh, mechanically inclined, multitasking, networking, out-of-the-box thinking, promotion, reading people, sales, strategic thinking, writing

HELPFUL CHARACTER TRAITS

Ambitious, bold, calm, controlling, courteous, disciplined, efficient, focused, honest, industrious, intelligent, meticulous, organized, passionate, patient, perfectionist, persistent, proactive, professional, resourceful, responsible, stubborn, talented, thrifty, workaholic

SOURCES OF FRICTION
Being an expert in the field but having no aptitude for the business end of things
Changes in the market that make it more expensive to do business
High maintenance employees
Money going missing or being skimmed by an employee, a business partner, etc.
An expensive insurance claim (after a fire, vandalism, theft, sewers backing up, etc.)
Being "shaken down" by local thugs demanding protection payments
New competition entering the marketplace
Enemies using their influence or power to kill a business deal, ruin the owner's reputation, etc.
Struggling to pay bills and employees
A divorce that requires the owner to sell the company
Harassment complaints from employees against someone in the company
Never being able to take time off of work
Problems obtaining product (due to factory strikes, a distributor going out of business, etc.)

PEOPLE THEY MIGHT INTERACT WITH
Customers, accountants, delivery drivers, reporters, other business owners, inspectors, product reps, employees, couriers, non-profit representatives or community organizers looking for a corporate sponsorship, candidates dropping off resumés or coming in for interviews, tradespeople (electricians, plumbers, construction workers, etc.)

HOW THIS OCCUPATION MIGHT IMPACT THE CHARACTER'S NEEDS
Esteem and Recognition: A character who fails to see the growth they imagined may start to believe they don't have what it takes.

Love and Belonging: Long hours spent at a job that often is the owner's highest priority can cause him or her to neglect the important people at home, leading to rocky relationships.

Safety and Security: Having a business in a high crime area of a city can increase the chance of robberies and break-ins, endangering the character and the people who work there.

CHARACTERS MIGHT CHOOSE THIS PROFESSION BECAUSE THEY...
Have an entrepreneurial spirit and want to be their own boss
Needed to take over the family business from aging parents
Have skills or knowledge that can meet a need and make life easier for others
Would rather take on an existing enterprise (such as a family business) than risk striking out on their own and possibly failing
Want to prove their capability and success to a disapproving sibling or peer

SOCIAL MEDIA MANAGER

OVERVIEW

Nearly every industry, from filmmaking to nutrition to education, employs social media managers. These people are responsible for creating and maintaining the company or industry's online presence while appealing to customers and promoting the establishment's brand. Duties might include running a blog, responding to emails, monitoring and updating a website, and managing social media platforms.

People in this field can work at the office or from home. If they freelance, they may juggle several clients or work on a part-time basis.

NECESSARY TRAINING

While some professional companies are looking for social media managers with four-year degrees in a field like journalism or marketing, this isn't always the case. Many times, applicants can prove their competency and skillset to potential employers via their own social media accounts, so those will need to be nurtured and well-maintained. Starting out as a freelancer to gain experience and learn necessary skills is also common. Both avenues give social media managers the opportunity to learn the various platforms inside and out so they can use them to interact with customers and promote the company's brand.

USEFUL SKILLS, TALENTS, OR ABILITIES

Detail-oriented, gaining the trust of others, haggling, multitasking, networking, organization, promotion, research, sales

HELPFUL CHARACTER TRAITS

Cooperative, courteous, diplomatic, enthusiastic, friendly, funny, hospitable, industrious, organized, persuasive, professional, resourceful, responsible, socially aware, studious

SOURCES OF FRICTION

Being hacked
Angry comments or reviews that damage the company's reputation
Unwanted messages or spam
Being expected to fulfill duties the character is not trained for or qualified to perform
Not being valued as a freelancer
Unreliable internet or Wi-Fi service
The company getting a bad rap from a trusted source
Online trolls who have a beef with the company
Struggling with distractibility online
Being accused of copyright infringement (from a photo used on a blog post, an unauthorized quote, etc.)
A social media platform bug that prohibits potential customers from seeing posts
Being stalked online
A family matter interfering with work (especially if the character works from home)
Having to take up the slack when other managers neglect their responsibilities

Work-related health problems (headaches or migraines from staring at a screen, failing vision, back problems due to sitting for long periods of time, etc.)

Struggling with accountability and time management

Having to keep up with social site algorithms that affect a company's discoverability

Being blamed for a poor marketing performance when the character didn't create the marketing plan

Frustration at a site's promotional rules that hamstring online marketing efforts

Fallout from a client's public misstep (a flagship product is recalled because it poses a danger to consumers, the CFO is accused of fraud, etc.)

PEOPLE THEY MIGHT INTERACT WITH

Company management, interns, online associates (customers, fans, advocates, rivals, etc.), support techs, people within the marketing department, graphic designers, copywriters

HOW THIS OCCUPATION MIGHT IMPACT THE CHARACTER'S NEEDS

Self-Actualization: Even though the social media manager is representing a brand, it can be difficult not to take customer feedback personally. And because the character is at least partly responsible for the company's public persona, limitations outside of their control can keep them from being able to do the job to the best of their ability.

Esteem and Recognition: Some people don't take social media managers seriously, seeing the job as a "soft" one where the person gets to spend all day online. A lack of recognition for the value they add might get under the character's skin.

TWISTING THE FICTIONAL STEREOTYPE

Social media managers are often portrayed as young, enthusiastic individuals who are wired into today's culture. Why not choose this career for a character who is older and enjoys technology? Online interactions could also be a draw for someone who feels isolated, possibly due to a physical limitation, an estrangement from family members, or being widowed.

CHARACTERS MIGHT CHOOSE THIS PROFESSION BECAUSE THEY...

Can do it part-time while getting a degree, providing caregiver support to a parent, etc.

Love the company or organization and want to support it—e.g., it's a non-profit cause they believe in or a company owned by a dear friend

Have a knack for running successful online platforms

Like to solve problems and build relationships

Are highly introverted and find it easier to interact with people online than in person

Want to work primarily online (due to a speech impediment, a mental disorder that makes leaving the house difficult, etc.)

SOCIAL WORKER

OVERVIEW

A social worker strives to connect people and can work in a variety of circumstances, depending on their specialty. They may pair children with foster or adoptive parents, support the elderly, connect the homeless with potential employers, provide aid to those with disabilities, or work with addicts. Clinical social workers have more foundational duties, including diagnosing and treating clients' disorders.

This work requires flexibility, since a social worker's daily schedule will vary. Besides meeting with clients, they may also be responsible for referring them to community resources or health specialists, meeting with lawyers, filing paperwork, performing home or supervised visits, and communicating with insurance companies on the client's behalf.

NECESSARY TRAINING

Most social workers will need to have a bachelor's degree in social work or a related field, such as child psychology. Clinical social workers must hold a master's degree and gain a certain amount of experience (often via an internship) before being able to practice independently. After obtaining a degree, most social workers will need to become licensed. This process varies depending on which kind of work the applicant is pursuing, what degree they hold, and the requirements of the state or province where they'll be employed.

USEFUL SKILLS, TALENTS, OR ABILITIES

Detail-oriented, empathy, equanimity, gaining the trust of others, good listening skills, hospitality, multitasking, peacekeeping, reading people

HELPFUL CHARACTER TRAITS

Adaptable, affectionate, bold, calm, confrontational, cooperative, courteous, decisive, discreet, efficient, empathetic, focused, friendly, gentle, honorable, just, kind, nosy, nurturing, objective, observant, perceptive, persistent, persuasive, professional, protective, pushy, resourceful, socially aware, supportive, unselfish, workaholic

SOURCES OF FRICTION

Being overwhelmed with paperwork and red tape
Having too many cases at once
Becoming emotionally weighed down from the pain they've witnessed
Lengthy court proceedings that slow the process for a child's adoption
Having to call a family and give bad news (more waiting time for a refugee resettlement, an adoption falling through at the last minute, etc.)
Having to move and leave the cases and clients they've come to care for
Being part of a team that makes hard decisions, such as removing a child from their home
Situations where there seems to be no obvious solution
Being unable to leave work at work
A complication in an already tough case—e.g., an academically struggling child whose parents decide to get a divorce

Clients who don't answer calls, respond to emails, or show up for appointments on time
Finding something disturbing or unsettling during a home visit
A client who has trouble communicating in their non-native language
Clients who withhold the truth or otherwise won't cooperate
Suspecting something bad is happening but not having the evidence to intervene
Struggling with prejudice or bias

PEOPLE THEY MIGHT INTERACT WITH

Foster parents and children, other social workers, a child's birth parents or guardian, refugees, teachers, lawyers, police officers, probation officers, mental health patients, counselors and psychologists, doctors, nurses, nursing home residents and staff

HOW THIS OCCUPATION MIGHT IMPACT THE CHARACTER'S NEEDS

Self-Actualization: A character who entered the field with the desire to help others may find themselves discouraged by their inability to affect change when bureaucracy and politics get in the way.

Esteem and Belonging: Social workers may take on unwarranted blame for cases that go bad or clients they're unable to help, which can undermine their confidence.

Love and Belonging: This work is demanding and can take a heavy toll, draining the character of their optimism and emotional energy. Over time, they may not be able to offer a partner the proper support, encouragement, and positivity, which could lead to the relationship collapsing.

Safety and Security: Entering certain environments may pose safety risks. The character's mental health can also be impacted if a case triggers an unresolved wound.

TWISTING THE FICTIONAL STEREOTYPE

Many social workers are portrayed as being tired and jaded or blindly optimistic and out of touch with their charges. Instead of leaning too far in a clichéd direction, consider a combination: a social worker who is tired and discouraged but incredibly discerning, able to instinctively see what's going on with her clients. Or maybe your character is wildly glass-half-full but connects deeply with her clients, drawing them out through the force of her love and belief in them.

CHARACTERS MIGHT CHOOSE THIS PROFESSION BECAUSE THEY...

Grew up in close proximity to refugee camps or a large homeless population
Were adopted as a child or grew up with adopted siblings
Needed an advocate as a child and want to be that advocate for others
Feel connected to a specific group of people (foster children, refugees, the elderly, etc.)
See social work as the solution to many of society's ills
Are highly empathetic and want to help others

SOFTWARE DEVELOPER

OVERVIEW
Software developers create many of the computer programs people use on a daily basis, from entire systems to smaller, add-on applications. They can develop a wide variety of programs, such as video games, apps, or security software. The product may be created for the company they work for, a client who hires them as a freelancer, or on their own initiative. In addition to designing and coding a product, developers do some testing, fix bugs, and provide upgrades down the road.

Software developers may be independent freelancers or part of a team, working from home, an office, or both. If they work for a client or as part of a group, they will meet regularly, either virtually or in person, to discuss designs and solutions to tough problems, assess progress on a current job, or brainstorm and plan new projects.

NECESSARY TRAINING
Some companies prefer software developers to hold a bachelor's degree, such as one in computer science, while others require nothing more than completion of certain certifications. If the company offers junior positions or internships, developers may utilize these opportunities to gain experience and on-the-job training. Continuing education is highly important in this field since the language of computers, as well as the computers themselves, are constantly changing.

USEFUL SKILLS, TALENTS, OR ABILITIES
Computer hacking, creativity, detail-oriented, gaming, leadership, out-of-the-box thinking, research, typing, vision

HELPFUL CHARACTER TRAITS
Ambitious, analytical, cooperative, creative, curious, disciplined, efficient, focused, imaginative, industrious, intelligent, meticulous, obsessive, organized, passionate, perfectionist, persistent, proactive, responsible, studious

SOURCES OF FRICTION
Spending more time debugging an existing program than creating new material
Beta testers not providing the kind of feedback the developer needs
An employer's unreasonable demands (tight deadlines, adding to the scope of work, etc.)
Having to choose between writing good, functional code and getting it done quickly
Being overwhelmed by a big project
Competition amongst fellow developers
Getting distracted while surfing the internet for solutions to work problems
Having trouble finding a good solution to a persisting problem
Testing a new feature and finding more problems than was expected
Discovering that a co-worker has been taking shortcuts
Difficulty accepting constructive criticism
Struggling to juggle other job-related responsibilities (managing finances, negotiating contracts, etc.)

Being assigned a project the character lacks the training or knowledge to complete
A micro-managing and overly fussy project leader
Having to work for someone who thinks they're tech savvy but aren't
A project taking much longer than expected
Preferring to work alone but having to work with a team on a certain job
Making a mistake on a collaborative project
Doing or saying something that reveals a lack of knowledge about an important piece
of software

PEOPLE THEY MIGHT INTERACT WITH

Other developers or engineers, beta testers, customers, managers or supervisors, third party
service providers

HOW THIS OCCUPATION MIGHT IMPACT THE CHARACTER'S NEEDS

Self-Actualization: If the character is stuck developing software that isn't challenging or
what they want to work on, a lack of fulfillment may drain their passion for the work.

Esteem and Recognition: A persistent or seemingly unsolvable problem can lower a
character's confidence, especially if they believe they are missing an obvious solution.

Love and Belonging: Freelance work can be very solitary. A character may become so
isolated (especially if overworked) they fail to invest in or maintain real-world relationships.

TWISTING THE FICTIONAL STEREOTYPE

Software developers are sometimes portrayed as introverts who sit alone at their computer
all day, yet this is not often the case. Many developers work in an office as part of a team,
talking through problems and working on creative solutions together.

People tend to assume that older people are not competent with technology. To mix things
up, why not have a retiree who has taken up software development in their free time?

CHARACTERS MIGHT CHOOSE THIS PROFESSION BECAUSE THEY...

Enjoyed software development as a hobby and have decided to pursue it as a career
Love the intellectual challenge of figuring out solutions to tough problems
Want to set their own schedule and work from home
Want to work their way up to a prestigious software company, such as Apple or Google
Enjoy meticulous and detail-oriented work
Love technology and are passionate about its development
Have a lot of ideas and need an outlet for their creativity

SOMMELIER

OVERVIEW

A sommelier is a wine master who typically works in a fine dining restaurant, helping guests choose a wine to go with their meal. Their knowledge goes way beyond simply suggesting the right pairing, however, since they have to know and be able to recognize many different types of wine. They may bring out several options and refill glasses when requested, as well as take inventory of the restaurant's wine and restock it as needed. Some sommeliers parlay their expertise into a teaching career, sharing their knowledge through seminars, published articles, or private tasting events.

NECESSARY TRAINING

Sommeliers can take a variety of courses to gain their designation and must take four examinations that include written and practical portions, including a blind tasting to identify various kinds and qualities of wine. The fourth examination is to obtain the rank of master, and according to the Court of Master Sommeliers, fewer than 300 people have earned this prestigious title since its inception, making it a very difficult rank to obtain.

USEFUL SKILLS, TALENTS, OR ABILITIES

Charm, enhanced sense of smell, enhanced taste buds, hospitality, promotion, reading people, research, sales, teaching

HELPFUL CHARACTER TRAITS

Appreciative, confident, courteous, decisive, enthusiastic, generous, hospitable, passionate, patient, perfectionist, persuasive, proactive, professional, sensible, sophisticated, studious

SOURCES OF FRICTION

Unreasonable, demanding, or rude customers
The restaurant or winery being broken into
Underage patrons lying about their ages
Becoming pregnant and having to abstain from drinking wine
Clearly intoxicated patrons
Serving a very tense and combative couple
A shipment of wine not arriving on time
Being pushed by management to pitch a subpar wine
Being challenged by a chef or a waiter who thinks they know better than the sommelier
A stain on the sommelier's uniform making him or her self-conscious
A patron who makes unreasonable demands and refuses to listen to suggestions
Getting blamed for a patron's bad experience
Becoming self-conscious due to weight gain from rich wine and food
Being looked down upon by those who don't know the extent of the sommelier's knowledge
Making a mistake when taking inventory
Too many late nights or early mornings
Developing a cold that impacts their sense of smell and taste

Studying to become a master sommelier and working at the same time
Customers who consider themselves wine experts
Suffering a trauma and becoming dependent on alcohol in the aftermath
Having to take medication that can't be combined with alcohol
A fear of flying that makes it difficult to travel and obtain additional training
Failing the examination to become a master sommelier
Seeing others in the profession become masters and move up in the world

PEOPLE THEY MIGHT INTERACT WITH
Guests and patrons, chefs and cooks, waiters and waitresses, other sommeliers, winery owners, wine tasters, wine sellers

HOW THIS OCCUPATION MIGHT IMPACT THE CHARACTER'S NEEDS
Self-Actualization: The Master Sommelier Diploma Examination is one of the most difficult tests in the world to pass. The passing rate is extremely low, and after spending countless hours learning and studying, it can be hard for a sommelier seeking master status not to get discouraged if they fail.

Esteem and Recognition: Sommeliers go through difficult training, yet they hardly ever receive appreciation or even recognition for their hard work. Most people are not even aware of how much energy has gone into their achievements.

TWISTING THE FICTIONAL STEREOTYPE
Because of the prestigious titles and formal training, sommeliers are typically employed in expensive restaurants. Try adding another layer to the sommelier in your story. Maybe he runs a small business on the side, leads wine-tasting tours to exotic locations, runs a successful blog, or periodically hosts informal wine tastings for his family and friends.

This career is often associated with the rich and well-to-do, so it stands to reason that people in this field would be sophisticated and mannerly—even a bit pretentious. What about a sommelier with a great palate who lacks the refinement associated with this profession?

CHARACTERS MIGHT CHOOSE THIS PROFESSION BECAUSE THEY...
Expected to inherit the family winery
Wanted a career that gave them easy access to people with wealth and power
Grew up on a grape vineyard and took a natural interest in wine
Grew up poor and wanted a distinguished career associated with wealth and status
Love the thrill of pursuing a very rare and prestigious job title
Have a refined and sensitive palate and a passion for wine

STREET PERFORMER

OVERVIEW
Also known as buskers, street performers put their talents or skills on display in a public space. This might be a street corner, shopping mall, or subway station, to name just a few possibilities. Many street performers are musicians, but they may exhibit other talents, such as dancing, painting, sleight-of-hand, circus acts, poetry reading, or storytelling.

Depending on the location and circumstances (if they're hawking merchandise, for instance), some performers will have to obtain a permit to use the space, so take that into consideration if your character chooses to follow this career.

NECESSARY TRAINING
No formal training or education is required to be a street performer. However, if they want to be successful, they should be trained accordingly in their area of expertise. A musician should have a strong repertoire, gymnasts should be able to perform impressive routines, and artists should be skilled in order to draw the attention of potential customers.

USEFUL SKILLS, TALENTS, OR ABILITIES
Charm, creativity, dancing, dexterity, equanimity, making people laugh, musicality, parkour, performing, promotion, public speaking, reading people, sales, sleight-of-hand, stamina

HELPFUL CHARACTER TRAITS
Adaptable, alert, bold, confident, confrontational, creative, diplomatic, disciplined, enthusiastic, extroverted, friendly, funny, impulsive, independent, industrious, melodramatic, mischievous, observant, persistent, persuasive, playful, quirky, resourceful, responsible, spontaneous, spunky, talented, uninhibited

SOURCES OF FRICTION
Performance anxiety
Unexpected weather that drives away potential customers
Rude or insulting comments from audiences
Being paid with counterfeit money
Being overshadowed by another street performer
The character's original songs, dances, etc., being plagiarized
Not being allowed to perform in an ideal place
Impossible requests from audience members
Getting sick and not being able to perform
The performer's earnings being stolen by a passerby
Getting injured on the job
Videos or recordings of performances being posted on social media without permission
Getting mugged as the character walks to or from favorite performance spots
Being stalked by a fan
Having to perform in awful weather
Family members nagging them about getting a "real" job

Struggling financially during the tourist slow season or an economic downturn
Another busker claiming the performer's usual spot

PEOPLE THEY MIGHT INTERACT WITH

Other members of their band or troupe (if they do not perform alone), passersby and audience members (shoppers, travelers, bar-goers, tourists, etc.), security personnel and police officers, local shopkeepers, other performers, street vendors

HOW THIS OCCUPATION MIGHT IMPACT THE CHARACTER'S NEEDS

Self-Actualization: Some performers see busking as a way to gain experience and perfect a talent so they can one day make it professionally. A character stuck for too long as a street performer may become dissatisfied, wishing they could do something more.

Esteem and Recognition: Dealing with criticism is inevitable for street performers. There will always be people who complain about their abilities, and some are rude and insulting. Some days it may seem as if no one is stopping to watch at all. All of this can be detrimental to a street performer's self-esteem.

Safety and Security: Performers don't always work in the safest of places. Many set up in whatever spots they can find or have to cross through a bad part of town to get to an ideal location, putting themselves at risk.

TWISTING THE FICTIONAL STEREOTYPE

Street performers are typically portrayed as one guy with an acoustic guitar. While this is sometimes the case, groups of performers are not uncommon, nor are individuals playing other instruments, performing illusions, dancing, or showcasing other unique talents. Because musical performers are so common, try having your performer specialize in something else. Maybe they put on magic shows for children, dress up as statues and do tricks, or run through comedy routines.

CHARACTERS MIGHT CHOOSE THIS PROFESSION BECAUSE THEY...

Have a deep passion for a certain skill or talent
Are using it as a stepping-stone for a more professional career
Like to treat others to unexpected performances, a flash mob, or an unusual routine
Want to make a little extra money to pay the bills or donate to charity
Are talented but feel unable to make it professionally due to insecurity, a phobia, a wounding event that holds them back, or a lack of mastery
Like to travel and earn a living as they go rather than be tied to one place
Are a natural performer who loves working a crowd

TALENT AGENT

OVERVIEW

Talent agents work with many different types of people, including artists, musicians and bands, writers, actors, models, and athletes. Most agents work with people in more than one area of specialty (depending on their own interest and expertise). Their duties revolve around marketing their clients and "selling" them to potential employers. This includes meeting with interested parties, attending social and cultural events as a means of networking, scheduling auditions or important events for the client, handling travel details, and negotiating contract terms.

Newcomers to this business will usually first seek employment with an agency but end up starting their own operation. They can be located anywhere, but agents representing certain types of talent may have more success working in areas associated with their clientele (Nashville for country singers, Hollywood for actors, etc.).

NECESSARY TRAINING

Most people interested in this career will begin as interns at an agency, where they'll likely assist agents or work in another capacity, such as that of a receptionist. Many agencies are looking for agents with at least a bachelor's degree, so obtaining one in a field like communications, marketing, or business is a good first step. Interns can seek employment as a full-fledged agent once their internship is complete.

USEFUL SKILLS, TALENTS, OR ABILITIES

A knack for making money, charm, detail-oriented, gaining the trust of others, good listening skills, haggling, leadership, multitasking, networking, organization, out-of-the-box thinking, promotion, reading people, sales, vision

HELPFUL CHARACTER TRAITS

Ambitious, analytical, bold, callous, confident, confrontational, controlling, cooperative, diplomatic, disciplined, discreet, efficient, enthusiastic, honorable, loyal, manipulative, meticulous, observant, optimistic, organized, persistent, persuasive, professional, protective, pushy, resourceful, responsible

SOURCES OF FRICTION

Competition with another agent or agency
A client missing an audition opportunity because of schedule conflicts
Harassment from clients or co-workers
Nagging clients who are constantly asking for updates
Dealing with the demanding or disrespectful parents of child star clients
Last-minute flight or hotel complications
A client with a habit of not communicating in a timely fashion
Burning out from the constant work schedule
A client with unreasonable aspirations or expectations
Having to tell a client they didn't get the audition or role that they wanted

A client suffering an injury that renders them unable to perform, play, tour, etc.
A client becoming discouraged from the lack of opportunities
Irresponsible or entitled clients that need a lot of micro-managing
Losing a long-standing client or promising new client to a rival
Turning down a potential client who ends up hitting it big
A difficult client burning bridges and making it harder for the agent to do their job
A client's misbehavior that results in a PR nightmare
Having to let a client go
Knowing that a client is struggling with an addiction but not being able to help them

PEOPLE THEY MIGHT INTERACT WITH
Athletes, models, musicians, singers, writers, artists, parents of clients (if the client is a youth), other agents, receptionists, accountants, film directors, coaches, personal trainers

HOW THIS OCCUPATION MIGHT IMPACT THE CHARACTER'S NEEDS
Self-Actualization: An agent who fails to catch the "big fish" and consistently works with mid-listers may find themselves chafing at being limited in their career field.

Esteem and Recognition: The entertainment and talent industries are notoriously competitive. A character who compares him or herself to highly successful agents may quickly come to doubt their own abilities. It could go the other way, also, with high-powered agents scorning those they deem as being farther down the professional ladder.

Love and Belonging: If a client needs hand-holding, that job will often fall to the agent, who must rearrange their own schedule to make sure things go smoothly. This can cause problems at home when loved ones start to feel they're playing second fiddle to the talent.

TWISTING THE FICTIONAL STEREOTYPE
When people think of talent agents, they often think of agents managing rich actors in Hollywood or Los Angeles. Why not have an agent who works with lesser-known actors, or even someone who specializes in a completely different field? Perhaps they have a passion for puppeteers, artists, clowns, magicians, or a brand-new genre of music.

CHARACTERS MIGHT CHOOSE THIS PROFESSION BECAUSE THEY...
Grew up believing they weren't talented enough at something to make it big
Were poised to be a successful actor, athlete, musician, etc. when an injury, illness, or other obstacle ended their career
Have a passion for a specific field or industry (acting, filmmaking, athletics, fashion, etc.)
Want to help others further their talents and succeed
Want to be part of the glamour of Hollywood, Broadway, the high-end art scene, etc.

TATTOO ARTIST

OVERVIEW
Tattoo artists are responsible for using needles and ink to paint a person's skin. They may copy a customer's design or render an original one based on what the client wants. These artists may work for a studio or be independent freelancers.

NECESSARY TRAINING
While no formal education or training are required, most people begin their career working as an apprentice and expand their craft under the eye of a master tattooist.

USEFUL SKILLS, TALENTS, OR ABILITIES
Creativity, detail-oriented, dexterity, good listening skills, high pain tolerance, promotion, stamina

HELPFUL CHARACTER TRAITS
Calm, confident, cooperative, creative, imaginative, kind, meticulous, patient, persuasive, quirky, responsible, sentimental, supportive, talented, tolerant

SOURCES OF FRICTION
An indecisive customer who can't decide what they want
Overzealous health inspectors
A client asking for a design that's offensive or taboo
Customers with low pain tolerances
Tattooing a customer who has self-medicated in an effort to proactively manage the pain
Working for a parlor that takes shortcuts, resulting in a customer getting sick
A customer requesting a design that's too complicated for the artist
Tattooing a customer with an undisclosed health risk (hemophilia, specific allergies, etc.)
Contracting an illness from a client
Difficulties arising from working at a parlor in a dangerous part of town
Conflict with family members who are morally opposed to the character's occupation
An underage client lying about their age
Developing an allergy to tattoo dyes that makes it difficult to do the job
A competitor who is copying the character's style or aesthetic
The parlor's lease being taken over by someone who is opposed to tattoos
Being sued by a customer who contracts an illness or experiences an allergic reaction after receiving their tattoo
Experiencing a traumatic event that makes the character faint at the sight of blood
A disgruntled customer leaving bad reviews and trying to ruin the character's reputation
Having to provide a facial tattoo, and knowing that the majority of customers who ask for one will come to regret it
Satisfied customers who won't leave reviews, slowing the business's growth
Being very good at copying an image but lacking the imagination to create them
Developing a condition that limits the tattoo artist's abilities (going color blind, developing

muscle tremors, an illness that causes numbness in the extremities, etc.)
Working with tattoo artists who despise each other
A hesitant client changing their mind partway through
Making an error with a tattoo (misspelling a word, leaving out an important detail, etc.)

PEOPLE THEY MIGHT INTERACT WITH
Other tattoo artists, a landlord, administrative personnel, vendors, customers

HOW THIS OCCUPATION MIGHT IMPACT THE CHARACTER'S NEEDS
Self-Actualization: Many tattoo artists choose this profession because it enables them to satisfy their creative needs. But this need could go unmet if their work situation requires them to do more commercial, standard work that doesn't allow them to flex their imaginative muscles.

Esteem and Recognition: While the old stigma regarding tattoos has largely gone away, there are still certain people and cultures who look down on the profession. This could be a problem if the naysayers are important or influential people in the character's life.

Safety and Security: There is always a health risk when you're working with needles and other people's blood. An artist who cuts corners, is distracted, or is working with inferior equipment could end up contracting an illness from a customer.

TWISTING THE FICTIONAL STEREOTYPE
Tattoo artists are usually fairly well inked themselves. But what about a character who couldn't get tattoos due to a health problem but pursued the job so he could be creative?

You could also play with the kinds of tattoos an artist creates. Maybe their work is philanthropically based, such as turning scars into art, disguising old gang tats, or covering prison, slave, or concentration camp markings.

CHARACTERS MIGHT CHOOSE THIS PROFESSION BECAUSE THEY...
Were exposed to tattoos during their upbringing
Were able to move past their own hate and bigotry and want to help others do the same by specializing in racist tattoo removals or alterations
Love unusual artforms—especially personally meaningful art pieces
Have a creative mind and an artist's skill
Have role models with tattoos who shared the meanings behind them
Want to make people feel better about themselves by transforming their scars into art
Believe strongly in the importance of empowering others through self-expression

TAXIDERMIST

OVERVIEW

Taxidermists are trained in the art of animal preservation, restoring a variety of animals to a lifelike state while drawing out their original beauty and strength. They often have specialties, including pets, fish, reptiles, birds, small animals, or large game. They may have a shop where they handle pets and local wildlife or focus more on animal trophies (located in an area frequented by hunters or as part of a commercial operation dealing in exotics). A few highly skilled taxidermists also work with natural history museums, creating displays used for educational purposes and repairing items already in the collection.

Taxidermists view their profession as artistic and are passionate about recreating the breath of life through their work, which they usually take great pride in. Some practitioners in this field will take any job they feel skilled to handle since work can be sporadic or revolve around hunting seasons. Others have ethical boundaries and will avoid certain jobs, such as preserving endangered animals or those shot for sport.

Clients may be hunters looking to obtain trophies, pet lovers struggling to release a beloved companion, and people who find dead animals and want to preserve the beauty of their forms.

NECESSARY TRAINING

Several certifications and diploma programs exist for this field, but a degree is not necessary. As part of these courses, students learn how to treat and tan skins and feathers, construct habitats, work with forms, and become proficient in air brushing and other finishing procedures. Often people get their start by apprenticing under a licensed taxidermist, learning on the job and taking classes as needed or to specialize in a particular area.

A person is required to have a license to practice, they may need special permits to work with migratory birds or endangered species, and they must abide by regulations set by fish and wildlife services.

A great deal of research is needed to understand an animal's structure and movement to create a lifelike end product. Taxidermists usually have an impressive collection of reference books, pictures, and videos to help them with the shaping of subjects that they work on.

USEFUL SKILLS, TALENTS, OR ABILITIES

A way with animals, creativity, dexterity, empathy, multitasking, photographic memory, repurposing, sculpting, sewing, strategic thinking, woodworking

HELPFUL CHARACTER TRAITS

Calm, cautious, centered, creative, focused, imaginative, independent, morbid, nature-focused, observant, resourceful, talented, thrifty, withdrawn

SOURCES OF FRICTION

Clients who don't pay or who have impossible demands
Being asked to prepare an animal that was an illegal kill
People who discriminate against the taxidermist for their work
Difficulties keeping a seasonal business afloat

Being asked to take on a project that raises ethical concerns for the taxidermist
Making a mistake that causes the animal to be misshapen or ruined in some way
A break-in
An economic downturn that cuts into the taxidermist's business
Shifting social perspectives that cast taxidermy in a bad light
A grieving customer being disappointed with (rather than comforted by) the finished product
Changing suppliers and ending with lesser-quality chemicals
Improper use of chemicals that leads to sickness

PEOPLE THEY MIGHT INTERACT WITH
Neighbors, hunters, wildlife officers, commercial agencies, delivery people, locals

HOW THIS OCCUPATION MIGHT IMPACT THE CHARACTER'S NEEDS
Self-Actualization: A character who views taxidermy as a way to honor the dead by restoring their beauty might be devastated if exposure to chemicals led to health complications, forcing them to retire.

Esteem and Recognition: Characters in this job will likely be misunderstood as most people view taxidermy as a morbid practice. A character in this field who looks outward for acceptance may struggle at finding a lack of it.

TWISTING THE FICTIONAL STEREOTYPE
A taxidermist known for incorporating humor into their work might create sought after collector pieces. This might soften the public's attitude toward this profession so they see it in a more creative and artistic light. Alternatively, a taxidermist known for taboo projects (displaying animals in a way that depicts cruelty rather than compassion, or even using human subjects) might be an interesting alternative.

CHARACTERS MIGHT CHOOSE THIS PROFESSION BECAUSE THEY...
Grew up with a close relative in the business
Lost a beloved pet as a child and were gifted with a preserved version of it; they want to offer the same comfort to others
Revere animals and want to preserve their beauty even after death
Have a healthy (or unhealthy) fascination with death
Have a passion for hunting and using all the parts of the kill
Wish to work with an unusual medium for their art

TEACHER

OVERVIEW

A wide range of jobs are available to those interested in education. Teachers work at various levels, from prekindergarten through college. Public schools are fairly standard, with the teacher's requirements being dictated at the county, state, and national levels. Private schools are more varied; they may follow the traditional public-school model, espouse a certain educational method (Montessori, etc.), or be affiliated with a religious organization.

Teachers' duties and education requirements vary depending on their area of focus. Through the elementary level, most teachers are responsible for a small group of students for the entire year, instructing them in the core education areas (math, language arts, science, and social studies). Special-area teachers focus on a specific area of instruction, such as physical education, art, music, band, or computer skills. This model continues into middle and high school, where teachers are certified in a subject area and teach that subject throughout the day to a wide range of students. Professors do the same at the college level.

Teachers' duties include preparing lesson plans based on established curriculum standards, teaching lessons to accommodate the needs and ability levels of many different students, assessing students, attending faculty meetings, conferencing with parents, and participating in workshops and other ongoing education opportunities. Some teachers may have additional duties as well, such as monitoring students at lunchtime or recess, coaching a sports team, leading a student club or organization, and other before- and after-school responsibilities.

NECESSARY TRAINING

Teaching certifications depend upon a number of criteria. In the US, many pre-K programs require no formal education for their teachers. Elementary and secondary teachers need a four-year degree, though they can go on to get their master's or doctorate degrees for better pay and the opportunity to move into an administrative capacity. Unaccredited private schools may have more lenient requirements. Professors are usually required to have a master's or doctorate degree.

USEFUL SKILLS, TALENTS, OR ABILITIES

Empathy, enhanced hearing, gaining the trust of others, good listening skills, hospitality, leadership, multitasking, out-of-the-box thinking, peacekeeping, research, teaching

HELPFUL CHARACTER TRAITS

Adaptable, affectionate, alert, calm, cooperative, decisive, diplomatic, disciplined, discreet, enthusiastic, gentle, honorable, industrious, inspirational, intelligent, nurturing, objective, observant, optimistic, organized, passionate, patient, protective, resourceful, responsible, studious, tolerant, wise, workaholic

SOURCES OF FRICTION

Unreasonable administrative expectations
Frequently changing curriculum and teaching methods
Increasing pressure for students to score well on standardized testing

Co-teaching with someone whose methods or philosophies are different from the character's
Limited funding that requires the teacher to supplement supplies
Conflict with parents (who don't support the teacher, want preferential treatment, etc.)
Seeing a student fail despite the character's best efforts to help him or her
Conflict among students
Being accused of inappropriateness by a student
Suspecting that a student might be a victim of abuse
Being unable to connect with a student and gain their trust
Suspecting that a student is being bullied but being unable to catch the offender
Struggling to find time to adequately teach the core subjects (due to frequent behavior problems, school assemblies or programs focusing on other topics, not having the necessary supplies, etc.)
Being unable to connect with a struggling student
Having students at different ability levels and trying to meet them each where they are

PEOPLE THEY MIGHT INTERACT WITH
Administrators, students, parents, other teachers, classroom aides, mentors

HOW THIS OCCUPATION MIGHT IMPACT THE CHARACTER'S NEEDS
Self-Actualization: As with so many occupations, the dream doesn't always match the reality. Teachers spend a large portion of their time doing things other than teaching. They can easily find themselves doing very little of what they love, making them dissatisfied with their chosen profession.

Esteem and Recognition: While teachers are slowly gaining the respect they deserve, there are still people who would rather their loved ones choose occupations that pay higher wages or garner more prestige. A teacher whose parent, spouse, or other influential person puts pressure on them to find "better" employment may feel that their work isn't as important as they thought it was.

Physiological Needs: The rise of school violence has made this scenario a sadly believable one that could threaten a teacher's survival.

CHARACTERS MIGHT CHOOSE THIS PROFESSION BECAUSE THEY...
Wanted to please their parents by pursuing a career they deemed respectable
Wanted access to children in order to protect them (knowing what to look for because of their own history of being abused or mistreated)
Wanted access to children for a darker reason (as a pedophile, a child trafficker, etc.)
Have positive past experiences with teachers, resulting in a desire to help others the same way
Recognize, from personal experience, the necessary escape school represents for some children and the role teachers play in their lives
Love learning and want to share their knowledge with others

THERAPIST (MENTAL HEALTH)

OVERVIEW
A mental health therapist provides help to those who are struggling with mental or emotional problems. A therapist may open their doors to any clientele or focus on an area of specialization (such as marriages and families, substance abuse, grief, or life coaching). Some will own their own business, while others choose to be part of a practice. They may work in a specific location, such as a hospital, prison or detention facility, detox center or halfway house, church, or school system. Online counseling is also a popular option for those seeking support.

Many mental health occupations are mentioned synonymously, but there are distinct differences. It should be noted that while psychologists may provide therapy, many of them choose to work in academic or research settings. Likewise, a psychiatrist holds a higher degree and has the distinction of being able to prescribe medication.

NECESSARY TRAINING
A four-year degree is required in the U.S., with certain kinds of therapy also requiring a master's degree. Many clinical hours are necessary to achieve the needed on-the-ground training before a therapist can hang their shingle.

USEFUL SKILLS, TALENTS, OR ABILITIES
Clairvoyance, empathy, exceptional memory, gaining the trust of others, good listening skills, hospitality, out-of-the-box thinking, peacekeeping, reading people, research, teaching

HELPFUL CHARACTER TRAITS
Analytical, calm, cooperative, curious, diplomatic, discreet, efficient, empathetic, friendly, gentle, honest, kind, nurturing, observant, optimistic, organized, patient, perceptive, persistent, persuasive, proactive, professional, responsible, studious, supportive, tolerant, wise

SOURCES OF FRICTION
Being unable to find the solution that works for a client
A client who is unable or unwilling to open up and be honest about their situation
A client's dysfunction escalating while in the therapist's care, resulting in them attempting suicide, abusing a child, killing someone, etc.)
Misreading or misdiagnosing a client
Becoming romantically involved with a client
Harboring prejudice against a client
Having to break confidentiality for safety reasons but knowing it will impact the client's trust
Tempers flaring in a group therapy session
A client with uncooperative family members or caregivers who undermine progress
Alienating loved ones through constant psychoanalysis
Bringing work home with them (being unable to keep from obsessing over a client or the difficult life circumstances they hear about daily)
Seeing clearly how to help others but having blind spots in their own personal life
A client in crisis interfering with the therapist's personal life

Being stalked or attacked by an unstable client or someone close to that person
Maintaining a professional relationship when the therapist knows the client personally
Taking on too many pro bono clients
Suffering from burnout and compassion fatigue
Having to testify in court about a case relating to a client

PEOPLE THEY MIGHT INTERACT WITH

Clients (children, teens, couples, inmates, veterans, the elderly, etc.), the client's family members or caregivers, other mental health practitioners (social workers, psychiatrists, etc.), medical doctors, school officials, administrative personnel

HOW THIS OCCUPATION MIGHT IMPACT THE CHARACTER'S NEEDS

Esteem and Recognition: Not every therapist can help every client, but a professional who has more than their share of failures may begin to doubt their capabilities—even if the fault isn't theirs. The therapist may also suffer a lack of esteem if their choice of clientele (e.g., pedophiles or serial killers) brings them low in the eyes of others.

Love and Belonging: It's said that some therapists follow this career path out of a desire to fix themselves, but this is easier said than done. If a therapist is deeply wounded, they may have difficulty getting along with others or connecting in healthy ways on a personal level. Their need to "fix" people can also cause problems when they consistently try to do this with loved ones.

Safety and Security: If a therapist's practice takes them into an unsafe place, such as a dangerous neighborhood or high-security prison, their safety may be threatened on a regular basis.

TWISTING THE FICTIONAL STEREOTYPE

In stories, therapists tend to play the mentor role. But what about a therapist villain who is out to emotionally destroy others, or a therapist love interest who creates unusual sources of conflict for the protagonist?

CHARACTERS MIGHT CHOOSE THIS PROFESSION BECAUSE THEY...

Subconsciously wanted to identify and slay their own demons
Changed their own life with the help of a therapist and want to provide that chance for others
Can avoid dealing with their own issues when they're focused on other people's problems
Want to help a certain segment of society (abused children, refugees, women, addicts, etc.)
Are discerning and have a knack for encouraging people to open up about their problems
Are trying to make up for a past failure when they weren't there for someone who needed them

TOUR GUIDE

OVERVIEW

Similar to an outdoor guide, a tour guide acts as a knowledgeable companion for a group of people wishing to experience local sights in a safe and educational way. Excursions might be a few hours to several weeks, depending on the type of tour. Guides travel with their group, showing them landmarks, historical sites, and other areas of interest, encouraging tourists to immerse themselves in the culture, activities, cuisine, and adventure of the place they have traveled to.

If the tour is a longer one, the guide also acts as a go-between, communicating with hotel and restaurant staff, transportation companies, and excursion personnel on the group's behalf. They will also interpret for clients if there is a language barrier. During a tour, the guide will advise travelers on how to purchase items and make recommendations for things to see and do during free time. They will also inform travelers about local laws and customs and will warn them of dangers (if there are any). Tour guides may operate within a city, take their group to multiple locations in a specified area, travel with them to different parts of the country, or even accompany the group on an international trip.

NECESSARY TRAINING

Degrees aren't required to work in this field, but many tour guides may choose to get a four-year degree to flesh out their resumé. Once hired, supplemental training and education pertaining to their area of focus will be necessary. For example, a guide who focuses on a specific location such as a museum or historical site will be deeply familiar with it and possibly have a related degree (in art history, for instance). If a guide covers a specific town or city, they will have significant knowledge of the history, landmarks, culture, arts, and language of that location. Their expertise will enable them to field a wide variety of questions from their group.

Guides who work longer excursions will have a broader skill set since they will have to know about each area they visit. If the tour is international, they will navigate clients through border crossings and customs, which may be very different from the processes they are used to in their home country. Guides are responsible for the safety of their guests and will receive training from the company they are affiliated with.

USEFUL SKILLS, TALENTS, OR ABILITIES

Basic first aid, charm, exceptional memory, good sense of direction, haggling, hospitality, making people laugh, multilingualism, multitasking, peacekeeping, predicting the weather, promotion, public speaking, reading people, research, stamina, throwing one's voice, wilderness navigation

HELPFUL CHARACTER TRAITS

Adaptable, adventurous, calm, charming, confident, courteous, diplomatic, disciplined, discreet, easygoing, efficient, enthusiastic, extroverted, friendly, funny, gossipy, hospitable, intelligent, introverted, nosy, observant, optimistic, organized, passionate, patient, socially aware, spunky, thrifty, tolerant, wholesome, wise, witty

SOURCES OF FRICTION

A group member entering an off-limits area at a historical site or causing damage to property
Clients who wander away during the tour
Accommodation mix-ups (not enough rooms at a hotel, rooms being less than ideal, etc.)
Personality conflicts between group members
A transport breakdown or travel delays
A client being pickpocketed
A client breaking a law because it's not a big deal where they are from
A group member being injured or growing ill and needing a hospital
A mix-up in transfers (a van doesn't arrive when it should, or the tuk tuks are a no-show)
Group members being late, causing everyone to wait
Language barriers
Entitled clients who don't follow through on group responsibilities (being on time, being organized, helping to clean up group areas, etc.)
Demanding clients who expect their personal tastes and desires to be catered to
Freeloading tourists who try to slip into the group to benefit from the guide's knowledge

PEOPLE THEY MIGHT INTERACT WITH

Travelers, bus and cab drivers, other tour group leaders, customs officials, museum curators and employees, security personal, hotel staff, airport staff, restaurant staff, shopkeepers

HOW THIS OCCUPATION MIGHT IMPACT THE CHARACTER'S NEEDS

Love and Belonging: A guide will be away from home often and put in long (or odd) hours. Their energy levels may be sapped from having to look after others, jet lag, or both. This could make it hard to maintain certain types of relationships.

Safety and Security: If members of the group don't realize the danger of certain areas, they can put everyone in danger.

CHARACTERS MIGHT CHOOSE THIS PROFESSION BECAUSE THEY...

Moved many times as a kid and have become comfortable with living on the go
Love to travel and want to see the world
Want to help others broaden their knowledge and care more about other cultures
Like the mobility it offers (enabling them to escape their past or evade pursuers)
Are able to meet new people while avoiding deep relationships
Are passionate about a specific geographic location or piece of history
Have a personal tie to a location, legend, etc. and want to stay close to it

TREASURE HUNTER

OVERVIEW
A treasure hunter is someone with an inquisitive nature who uses their investigative talents to find lost, stolen, or forgotten treasure. It may be buried, sunken, hidden, part of a recovery mission, a historical find, or a prize as part of an elaborate hunt created by a person with means.

NECESSARY TRAINING
Depending on the type of treasure being recovered, different types of education will be necessary or aid in the hunter's success. For example, someone who salvages shipwrecks would need their diver certification and be able to pilot a boat. Hunters will need training and skills specific to the job, such as knowledge of history, map reading and navigational skills, familiarity with certain cultures, proficiency in obscure languages and written forms, an understanding of local customs and superstitions, and intimate knowledge of the person who originally hid the treasure. Hunters will also need equipment—ranging from a metal detector to deep sea salvage gear to explosives, and more—and be proficient in their use.

USEFUL SKILLS, TALENTS, OR ABILITIES
A knack for making money, basic first aid, enhanced hearing, exceptional memory, foraging, gaining the trust of others, good listening skills, haggling, lip-reading, lying, mechanically inclined, multilingualism, out-of-the-box thinking, predicting the weather, promotion, reading people, repurposing, research, self-defense, sharpshooting, sleight of hand, stamina, strategic thinking, strong breath control, survival skills, wilderness navigation

HELPFUL CHARACTER TRAITS
Adaptable, addictive, adventurous, alert, ambitious, analytical, bold, calm, cocky, courageous, curious, decisive, devious, disciplined, discreet, dishonest, evasive, focused, imaginative, independent, industrious, know-it-all, macho, manipulative, materialistic, meticulous, observant, obsessive, optimistic, organized, patient, persistent, persuasive, resourceful, stubborn, superstitious, suspicious, thrifty, unethical, wise

SOURCES OF FRICTION
Rival treasure hunters unraveling clues before or at the same pace the character does
Tight-lipped locals who don't trust outsiders
Maps that have degraded with age
Old equipment that barely functions or breaks just when it is needed most
False leads that waste time and provide the competition with an advantage
Trying to bribe an official or police officer, and it backfiring
Finding a treasure only to have someone else try to claim it
A hunter's equipment or vehicle being sabotaged by a rival
Personality conflicts within the crew or group
Discovering that a curse tied to a treasure's lore is true
Buying a treasure at auction or in a yard sale and finding it to be a fake

Trying to circumvent the law and being arrested

Being attacked or injured during a job

Reaching a treasure's location only to discover that someone got there first

A client running out of money before the treasure is found

The clues taking a hunter into territory they can't enter, such as protected land or a city that's under quarantine

Going to great lengths to find a treasure, then discovering that it's worthless (due to exposure, it being broken, it not being what the client expected, etc.)

Unethical partners causing legal problems for the treasure hunter

An emergency at home that interrupts a project, bringing it to a halt

PEOPLE THEY MIGHT INTERACT WITH

Museum curators, archeologists, historians, police, government officials, local guides, drivers, laborers, fellow treasure hunters, captains, experts, financial backers

HOW THIS OCCUPATION MIGHT IMPACT THE CHARACTER'S NEEDS

Self-Actualization: If a treasure hunter's desire to find a big score is their sole focus and this never materializes, it may threaten their sense of self and make them wonder if they have wasted their life.

Esteem and Recognition: A character in this field who is always one-upped by other hunters may develop self-esteem issues.

Safety and Security: In the scope of their work, treasure seekers may travel to locations that are hazardous. Whenever a large finder's fee is in the offering, humans can present a danger, too.

TWISTING THE FICTIONAL STEREOTYPE

A lot of treasure hunters are portrayed as men, but women can have the adventurer's spirit too. Why not consider this career for your next female protagonist?

CHARACTERS MIGHT CHOOSE THIS PROFESSION BECAUSE THEY...

Found something valuable as a child—an item that was hidden, buried, or lost

Had a parent with a passion for gambling who scored big

Grew up in a family that antiqued or collected and refurbished high-end items

Have a parent who was an archeologist or museum curator and worked with valuable artifacts

Have a passion for the history of a certain area

Have a knack for finding lost things through natural or psychic means

VETERINARIAN

OVERVIEW
Veterinarians care for the furry, scaled, feathered, and otherwise non-human members of our families. They can work in a general practice or specialize in certain kinds of animals, such as exotics (birds, reptiles, and rodents), equines, or other farm animals (cows, pigs, and sheep). Vets can also work in the inspection field, visiting livestock and other food animals to test and treat them and make sure government standards are being met. Research veterinarians spend more time in a lab than in a practice, doing clinical research on various health issues.

NECESSARY TRAINING
In the United States, a vet must complete four years of undergraduate school and four years of veterinary school. Obtaining board certification in a specialty area, such as surgery, oncology, or reproduction, will require additional education. Slots in a vet program are highly sought after and extremely competitive, meaning many qualified students may not be accepted.

USEFUL SKILLS, TALENTS, OR ABILITIES
A way with animals, empathy, gaining the trust of others, peacekeeping, research

HELPFUL CHARACTER TRAITS
Affectionate, bold, calm, cooperative, efficient, fussy, gentle, intelligent, merciful, nurturing, observant, organized, passionate, patient, perceptive, playful, professional, studious, suspicious

SOURCES OF FRICTION
Volatile or nervous pets
Difficult owners
Conflicts between staff members
Having to put a pet down
Seeing neglect cases and not being able to do anything about them
Having to confront an abusive owner
A rude or insensitive staff member driving away customers
A contagious disease spreading through the animals being boarded
Dogs or cats fighting in the waiting room
A bigger and more successful practice opening up nearby
Endorsing a pet product that ends up being recalled
Being unable to gain a pet's trust
An animal escaping the boarding facility and running away
Self-doubt arising from a misdiagnosis that ended in death
Financial difficulties that result in having to let staff go or not being able to pay the bills
Suffering from symptoms of compassion fatigue (apathy, depression, substance abuse, etc.)
Being asked by friends or neighbors to diagnose and treat their pets for free
Dealing with people who want to know why the character didn't become a "real" doctor
Pet owners who won't take advice—perhaps because it conflicts with something they read online or heard from the employee at the local pet store

PEOPLE THEY MIGHT INTERACT WITH
Pet owners, other vets in the practice, administrative staff members, vet techs, vendors (selling medical equipment, medicines, pet supplies, etc.), people with pet rescue groups

HOW THIS OCCUPATION MIGHT IMPACT THE CHARACTER'S NEEDS
Esteem and Recognition: Vets tend to be take-charge people who are deeply invested in a pet's welfare. So when something isn't going well, they may take the blame on themselves and become mired in self-doubt, especially if they believe they made a mistake.

Safety and Security: Safety should always be a concern around volatile animals. Not only will some bite, kick, charge, or trample out of the desire to protect themselves from perceived harm, many of them can cause serious injury unintentionally. And whenever blood is drawn, the risk of infection is real.

Physiological Needs: Care has to be taken around sick or injured animals—particularly the large or unpredictable ones—which can inflict injuries resulting in death.

TWISTING THE FICTIONAL STEREOTYPE
Vets are almost always represented in a friendly office setting. But what about a different situation, such as a vet who works in slaughterhouses maintaining the health of the animals, or one whose passion lies with test tubes and microscopes rather than the animals themselves?

Another way to twist the stereotype is with your veterinarian's specialization or the kinds of pets they treat. Maybe, in their free time, they volunteer at an animal preserve or bird rescue. Or your vet might specialize in dentistry, ophthalmology, or another field.

CHARACTERS MIGHT CHOOSE THIS PROFESSION BECAUSE THEY...
Grew up where animals were commonly abused and they want to fight such treatment
Grew up taking care of animals (on a farm, by taking in rescues or injured animals, etc.)
Experienced a trauma that makes them feel safer with animals than people
Grew up with a support animal and want to honor him or her with their career
Deeply love animals
Have a desire to safeguard animals from harm
Have a family member who mistreated animals (arranging cock fights, running a puppy mill, etc.) and they feel morally compelled to choose a different path

WEDDING PLANNER

OVERVIEW

A wedding planner's job is to take the stress off the engaged couple on their happy day. They do this by figuring out what kind of wedding is wanted, knowing their budget, and then bringing together options for venues, entertainment, decor, and other vendors for the couple to consider. The hundreds of small decisions and pressure to make the day memorable can create a lot of stress. A planner will narrow the options for the couple in a way that aligns with their vision, making the decision-making process more manageable.

A planner can use their contacts to find vendors (such as entertainers and musicians, caterers, cake decorators, florists, photographers, and videographers) to make the event not only special but affordable. They can help with the delivery and tracking of invitations, offer counsel on navigating difficult family dynamics (divorced parents, feuds in the family, or controlling in-laws), reserve a venue, manage seating, arrange for tasting or menu viewing with caterers and bakeries, create timelines for the days leading up to the wedding, and even assist in planning the travel for the honeymoon.

On the day of the wedding, the planner will be onsite to ensure that everything proceeds smoothly, managing all the moving pieces. It is their job to handle any problems that crop up and protect the couple from any forces (relatives or otherwise) who seek to interfere or take away from the specialness of the big day.

NECESSARY TRAINING

While no training is necessary, people pursuing this career may take a course or diploma program that covers the different aspects of wedding planning and client relations. In many cases, these courses can be taken online over several months.

USEFUL SKILLS, TALENTS, OR ABILITIES

Blending in, charm, empathy, enhanced hearing, enhanced sense of smell, enhanced taste buds, exceptional memory, gaining the trust of others, good listening skills, haggling, hospitality, making people laugh, multitasking, photographic memory, predicting the weather, promotion, reading people, repurposing, sewing, strategic thinking, swift-footedness, throwing one's voice, writing

HELPFUL CHARACTER TRAITS

Adaptable, analytical, calm, centered, charming, confident, cooperative, courteous, creative, decisive, detail-oriented, diplomatic, disciplined, discreet, easygoing, efficient, focused, friendly, honest, hospitable, imaginative, loyal, networking, observant, organized, patient, persuasive, proactive, professional, proper, protective, resourceful, responsible, supportive, thrifty, tolerant, workaholic, vision

SOURCES OF FRICTION

Interfering family members who don't respect the wishes of the wedding couple
In-fighting among the bridal party
A problem at a venue (a fire, a foreclosure, etc.) that makes a booking suddenly unavailable
A vendor going out of business close to the big day
A mishap with the bridal wear (lost during shipping, an error with the alterations, etc.)
A cake that falls apart as it's being delivered to the reception
Feuding family members who disrupt the service or reception
An unwanted guest showing up (an ex, a deadbeat parent, a trouble-making cousin, etc.)
A couple with huge expectations and a tiny budget, making the job nearly impossible
Not being paid in a timely manner
A relationship with a vendor being damaged by a disrespectful bride or groom
Last-minute requests for changes that are difficult to manage
A guest who didn't disclose an allergy
Alcohol reigniting old family feuds
Servers who are unprofessional, unhygienic, or who behave inappropriately
A vendor making a big mistake, such as a photographer "losing" the pictures or a caterer giving everyone food poisoning at the reception
The bride ordering products or services without telling the wedding planner

PEOPLE THEY MIGHT INTERACT WITH

The couple, family members, vendors, caterers, photographers, ushers, venue management and staff, guests, musicians, staff at the church (if the ceremony is being held there), vendor employees, delivery people, limo drivers for the bridal party (if applicable), travel agents and hotel staff (if honeymoon planning is part of the role)

HOW THIS OCCUPATION MIGHT IMPACT THE CHARACTER'S NEEDS

Esteem and Recognition: A character in this role may be passionate about weddings but struggle in other ways, due to being disorganized, indecisive, or cracking under pressure. Frequent mistakes may keep them from succeeding in this field and create self-doubt.

Love and Belonging: A character who has not yet found a life partner (and is starting to believe that they never will) may find it hard to repeatedly help others gain their happily-ever-afters.

CHARACTERS MIGHT CHOOSE THIS PROFESSION BECAUSE THEY...

Have a fascination with weddings, romance, and happy endings
Want to have a fairy tale wedding once they find the right partner
Hold to superstitious beliefs that for a marriage to succeed, it must start off perfectly
Had a wedding that was a train wreck due to poor organization, and they want to save other brides from the same disaster

YOGA INSTRUCTOR

OVERVIEW
A yoga instructor specializes in helping others create a harmonious union between the body and mind through breathing exercises (pranayama) and postures (asanas). They assist clients in becoming more flexible while strengthening their bodies, as well as developing a more balanced, peace-seeking mindset through visualization and meditation. While teaching classes (at a studio, health center, spa, in a natural setting, on a retreat, or in a private home), a good instructor will pay close attention to the needs of their clients and design a program that is tailored to them. For example, a class for pregnant women, children, or senior citizens will require specialized stretches, just as customized programming will be necessary for individuals recovering from a surgery, injury, or other vulnerability. A yoga instructor must pay careful attention to each client to avoid injuries.

Yoga instructors also will put considerable effort into the business end of their practice, which means spending time on things like accounting, time management, promotion, and client outreach. This also includes choosing what specialties to teach (Ashtanga, Bikram, Hatha, Iyengar, Kripalu, to name a few), creating playlists and routines for the group, building relationships with clients, evaluating progress to best decide when clients are ready to move on to more complex postures, and being available to answer questions and guide clients toward meditative solutions that may help them through personal challenges.

NECESSARY TRAINING
There are many schools and programs that teach the philosophies and history of yoga and certification in a variety of practices. After becoming certified, many instructors will develop specialties. These will all require further education. For devout practitioners, continuing education will remain a steady focus throughout their career.

USEFUL SKILLS, TALENTS, OR ABILITIES
A knack for making money, basic first aid, charm, empathy, enhanced hearing, exceptional memory, gaining the trust of others, intuition, making people laugh, promotion, reading people, regeneration, stamina, strong breath control, teaching, throwing one's voice

HELPFUL CHARACTER TRAITS
Calm, centered, creative, empathetic, enthusiastic, friendly, generous, gentle, happy, inspirational, kind, loyal, mature, nature-focused, nurturing, optimistic, organized, passionate, patient, perceptive, quirky, socially aware, spiritual, supportive, wholesome

SOURCES OF FRICTION
Balancing studio sessions and private clients (and finding a work-life balance)
Having to travel to multiple locations each day (a studio, clients' homes, a gym, etc.)
A car breakdown
An injury or illness that puts the instructor out of commission for a time
Private clients who cancel or ask to reschedule with little notice
Clients who assume one yoga instructor is the same as the next

Misunderstanding a vulnerable person's challenges and them being hurt during a yoga session
Clients not being upfront about conditions and injuries
Attendees who join for the wrong reasons (hoping to meet a romantic partner, etc.)
Building a practice that creates a steady income and livable wage
Being a poor business person and neglecting that aspect of the practice, resulting in financial or even legal troubles
Less-qualified instructors undercutting the character's pricing and market share
Problems with the studio (booking issues, malfunctioning equipment, an unclean space, etc.)
Clients who ask for help but fail to follow through on advice

PEOPLE THEY MIGHT INTERACT WITH
Clients, studio owners, gym management, community hall employees, other instructors

HOW THIS OCCUPATION MIGHT IMPACT THE CHARACTER'S NEEDS
Self-Actualization: If the character is unable to find clients with similar ideologies and a true desire to grow, they may end up teaching yoga to people who think it's fashionable or trendy, and disillusionment may set in.

Esteem and Recognition: A character who struggles to maintain a steady practice because of too much competition, being undercut on pricing, or other economic factors, may start questioning their ability to succeed.

TWISTING THE FICTIONAL STEREOTYPE
Characters in this career don't have to always fit into the "young and beautiful" category. Consider how an older instructor will not only reinforce the idea of following a passion, they will also have valuable insight into life and may offer a more balanced outlook, which can add something special to the story.

Fad yoga practices (like goat yoga) may date your manuscript. If you want to make a character's practice unique, consider an instructor that takes clients on retreats to foreign locations or on mountain hikes that end with a yoga session at the summit.

CHARACTERS MIGHT CHOOSE THIS PROFESSION BECAUSE THEY...
Grew up in a family that was grounded in meditation and natural healing
Are spiritually wired and health-conscious
Derive enjoyment from group activities that focus on health and mental well-being
Want to share the enlightenment of meditation with others
Struggle with a condition that requires daily meditation and focus, and this career will keep them accountable to that routine

OCCUPATION: _____

Can't find the job you're looking for? Peruse a list of job entries contributed by our readers (https://writershelpingwriters.net/contributed-occupations/), visit https://onestopforwriters.com to search an expanded version of the Occupation Thesaurus, or flex your research muscles and create your own entry using this template.

OVERVIEW

NECESSARY TRAINING

USEFUL SKILLS, TALENTS, OR ABILITIES
(TIP: Our large list of Talents and Skills at https://onestopforwriters.com can help you brainstorm.)

HELPFUL CHARACTER TRAITS
(TIP: Our lists of Positive and Negative Traits at https://onestopforwriters.com can help you brainstorm.)

SOURCES OF FRICTION

PEOPLE THEY MIGHT INTERACT WITH

HOW THIS OCCUPATION MIGHT IMPACT THE CHARACTER'S NEEDS
Self-Actualization:

Esteem and Recognition:

Love and Belonging:

Safety and Security:

Physiological Needs:

TWISTING THE FICTIONAL STEREOTYPE

CHARACTERS MIGHT CHOOSE THIS PROFESSION BECAUSE THEY...

OCCUPATION: _____

OVERVIEW

NECESSARY TRAINING

USEFUL SKILLS, TALENTS, OR ABILITIES
(TIP: Our large list of Talents and Skills at https://onestopforwriters.com can help you brainstorm.)

HELPFUL CHARACTER TRAITS
(TIP: Our lists of Positive and Negative Traits at https://onestopforwriters.com can help you brainstorm.)

SOURCES OF FRICTION

PEOPLE THEY MIGHT INTERACT WITH

HOW THIS OCCUPATION MIGHT IMPACT THE CHARACTER'S NEEDS
Self-Actualization:

Esteem and Recognition:

Love and Belonging:

Safety and Security:

Physiological Needs:

TWISTING THE FICTIONAL STEREOTYPE

CHARACTERS MIGHT CHOOSE THIS PROFESSION BECAUSE THEY...

OCCUPATION: _____

OVERVIEW

NECESSARY TRAINING

USEFUL SKILLS, TALENTS, OR ABILITIES
(TIP: Our large list of Talents and Skills at https://onestopforwriters.com can help you brainstorm.)

HELPFUL CHARACTER TRAITS
(TIP: Our lists of Positive and Negative Traits at https://nestopforwriters.com can help you brainstorm.)

SOURCES OF FRICTION

PEOPLE THEY MIGHT INTERACT WITH

HOW THIS OCCUPATION MIGHT IMPACT THE CHARACTER'S NEEDS
Self-Actualization:

Esteem and Recognition:

Love and Belonging:

Safety and Security:

Physiological Needs:

TWISTING THE FICTIONAL STEREOTYPE

CHARACTERS MIGHT CHOOSE THIS PROFESSION BECAUSE THEY...

APPENDIX A: OCCUPATION SPEED DATING

With so many jobs to choose from, finding the right fit can be a challenge. Start by identifying a standout trait for your character, then try some speed dating and see if you find an occupation match.

INDEPENDENT
(Likes working on their own)

Animal Rescue Worker
Janitor
Farmer
Novelist
Carpenter
Deep Sea Diver
Animal Trainer
Locksmith
Robotics Engineer
Geologist
Coroner
INDEPENDENT
Book Conservator
Ghostwriter
Ethical Hacker
Graphic Designer
Software Developer
Baker
Dog Groomer
Rancher
Auto Mechanic
Private Detective
Antiques Dealer
Pest Control Technician

OUTGOING
(Likes interacting with others)

Actor
Yoga Instructor
Bouncer
Professional Mourner
Receptionist
Babysitter
Barista
Politician
Recruiter
Cashier
Children's Entertainer
Radio DJ
Tour Guide
OUTGOING
Bartender
Reporter
Social Media Manager
Concierge
Docent
Driver (Car)
Wedding Planner
Lobbyist
Mail Carrier
Talent Agent
Fundraiser
Personal Assistant
Server

CREATIVE
(Driven by creativity and self-expression)

Actor
Dancer
Chocolatier
Jewelry Designer
Software Designer
Baker
Chef
Model
Ghostwriter
Podcaster
Tattoo Artist
Graphic Designer
Makeup Artist
Fashion Designer
CREATIVE
Architect
Master Brewer
Conductor
Novelist
Inventor
Robotics Engineer
Street Performer
Taxidermist
Children's Entertainer
Glassblower
Landscape Designer
Food Stylist
Dog Groomer
Carpenter

PASSIONATE
(Dedicated to a form of meaningful work)

Actor
Chef
Docent
Book Conservator
Food Critic
Conductor
Lobbyist
Model
Inventor
Paleontologist
Politician
Treasure Hunter
Professional Poker Player
Skydiving Instructor
PASSIONATE
Small Business Owner
Sommelier
Wedding Planner
Yoga Instructor
Professional Athlete
Reporter
Personal Trainer
Novelist
Fashion Designer
Master Brewer
Dancer
Jewelry Designer
Baker
Business Tycoon
Chocolatier

ALTRUISTIC
(Seeks actualization through helping others)

Animal Rescue Worker Nanny
Massage Therapist Physical Therapist
Social Worker
Emergency Medical Responder Funeral Director
Therapist
Professor Hypnotherapist

ALTRUISTIC

Midwife Clergy Member
Teacher Emergency Room Physician Librarian
Veterinarian
Home Health Aide
Reiki Master
Police Officer Nurse

AUTHORATIVE
(Drawn to positions of authority and leadership)

Air Traffic Controller Diplomat General Contractor
Firefighter Referee
Parole Officer Babysitter
Bounty Hunter Lawyer Secret Service Agent
Conductor Politician

AUTHORATIVE

Corrections Officer Emergency Room Physician
Private Detective
Military Officer Security Guard
Animal Trainer
Business Tycoon Flight Attendant
Judge Bouncer Police Officer

PROFESSIONAL
(Highly responsible, proper, and respectable)

Architect Judge Emergency Room Physician
Book Conservator Mechanical Engineer
Real Estate Agent Dentist
Nurse
Fundraiser Therapist Pilot
Pharmacist Emergency Dispatcher

PROFESSIONAL

Business Tycoon Diplomat Paralegal
Coroner Lawyer Flight Attendant
Politician Emergency Medical Responder Midwife
Paleontologist
Small Business Owner Receptionist
Interpreter Professor

ACADEMIC
(Knowledge-seeking; well-educated)

Lawyer Inventor Nurse
Hypnotherapist
Therapist Software Developer
Paralegal Ethical Hacker
Business Tycoon
Professor
Mechanical Engineer Dentist Emergency Medical Responder

ACADEMIC

Master Brewer Military Officer
Robotics Engineer
Pharmacist Interpreter
Judge Geologist Paleontologist
Teacher Veterinarian Emergency Room Physician
Antiques Dealer Coroner Dietitian

UNCONVENTIONAL
(Atypical; drawn to uncommon interests and activities)

Talent Agent Skydiving Instructor Tattoo Artist
Reiki Master Makeup Artist Children's Entertainer
Personal Shopper Jewelry Designer
Private Detective Glassblower Deep Sea Diver
Fashion Designer Professional Mourner
Food Critic Bounty Hunter Animal Trainer

UNCONVENTIONAL

Dream Interpreter Ethical Hacker Street Performer
Inventor Food Stylist Pest Control Technician
Funeral Director Model Taxidermist Coroner
Professional Poker Player Master Brewer Sommelier
Radio DJ Treasure Hunter Crime Scene Cleaner
Book Conservator Bouncer Human Test Subject

ADVENTUROUS
(Intrepid; disposed to trying new things and taking risks)

Pilot Military Officer Reporter
Human Test Subject Bounty Hunter
Professional Poker Player Business Tycoon
Secret Service Agent Firefighter

ADVENTUROUS

Police Officer Deep Sea Diver
Inventor Emergency Medical Responder
Private Detective
Diplomat Skydiving Instructor
Outdoor Guide Treasure Hunter

RUGGED
(Hardworking, tough, likes to be hands-on)

Military Officer Animal Rescue Worker
Outdoor Guide Glassblower
Deep Sea Diver Carpenter
Farmer Janitor Tour Guide

RUGGED

Firefighter Locksmith
General Contractor Mail Carrier
Crime Scene Cleaner Auto Mechanic
Personal Trainer
Treasure Hunter Rancher

TRAIT: _____
Definition: _____

APPENDIX B: CAREER ASSESSMENT

When matching a career to a character, it can be helpful to think about influential elements. Work your way through the boxes below, filling in any important factors on the left and adding possible jobs for each on the right. Once you've finished, look for commonalities. Is there a job that matches several important factors? For more help, view the sample assessment and references on the pages that follow.

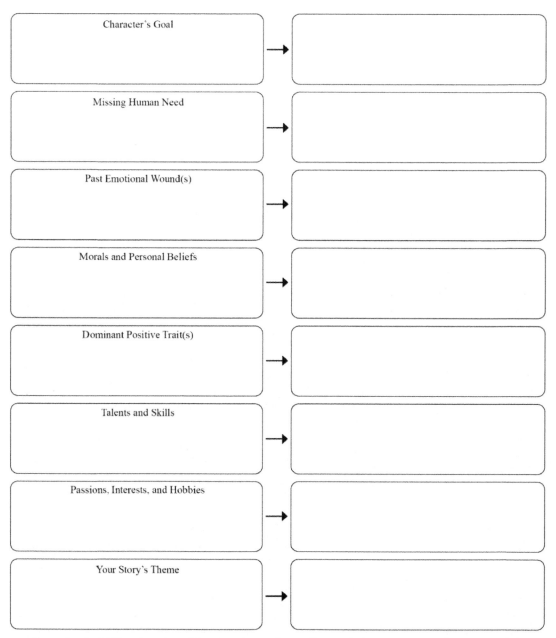

Character's Goal	→
Missing Human Need	→
Past Emotional Wound(s)	→
Morals and Personal Beliefs	→
Dominant Positive Trait(s)	→
Talents and Skills	→
Passions, Interests, and Hobbies	→
Your Story's Theme	→

Download additional copies of this template at https://writershelpingwriters.net/writing-tools/.

CAREER ASSESSMENT
(EXAMPLE)

Character's Goal To find her birth parents	Social worker, private detective
Missing Human Need Safety and Security: She has critical health issues that dramatically impact her way of life.	Coroner, dietitian, personal trainer, nurse, ER doctor, pharmacist
Past Emotional Wound(s) Living with chronic pain or illness (something genetic)	A job with flexibility that can be done alone or at home
Morals and Personal Beliefs Origins are important.	n/a
Dominant Positive Trait(s) Optimistic and creative	Small business owner, novelist
Talents and Skills Multilingual, gaming, detail-oriented	Interpreter, software designer, hacker
Passions, Interests, and Hobbies Making jewelry, reading, painting	Jewelry designer
Your Story's Theme Finding and living one's truth	Book conservator ★

CAREER ASSESSMENT CHEAT SHEET

To get the most out of this Career Assessment, writers should have a good grasp of **influential story factors**. Below is a condensed explanation of each, sourced from this book and the extensive tutorials and resources at One Stop for Writers (https://onestopforwriters.com). This site has a free trial, which will allow you to explore any of the **thesauruses** mentioned here.

Character's Goal: The overall goal (outer motivation) is the obvious thing your character is trying to achieve by the story's end. As examples, Frodo's goal in *The Lord of the Rings* is to destroy the one ring, while Katniss Everdeen wants to survive the Hunger Games. We recommend revisiting the Professions that Help or Hinder Goal Achievement section for more information (p. 25). **The Character Motivation Thesaurus** also explores possible goals and how to plot a character's route toward them.

Missing Human Need: All people have five basic needs that, when fulfilled, make them feel complete: physiological, safety and security, love and belonging, esteem and recognition, and self-actualization. If one of these needs is threatened or taken away, your character will become motivated to regain it. For more information, review the Basic Needs section (p. 3).

Past Emotional Wound(s): An emotional wound is a negative experience that causes pain on a deep psychological level. This event happened before the story began and changed the way the character views the world and him or herself. It may lead to biases, fears, and insecurities and can cause your character to limit themselves or avoid certain types of people or situations that they fear might hurt them again. We recommend revisiting the Unresolved Wounds section for more information (p. 7). And for a detailed breakdown of the fallout associated with different types of trauma, visit **The Emotional Wound Thesaurus.**

Morals and Personal Beliefs: These concepts are rooted in the character's foundational ideas about right and wrong and are tied to identity, helping to define who the character is. They are part of a personal code that steers decision making and establishes boundaries on what a character will or will not do. The Moral Conflict section (p. 14) explores this in detail.

Dominant Positive Trait(s): Positive attributes are traits that produce personal growth or aid a character in achieving goals through healthy means. They also help the character display their identity, live their moral beliefs, and communicate with others, fostering strong relationships. To dig into this more deeply, return to the Personality Traits section (p. 9). You can also explore the **Positive Trait Thesaurus** to brainstorm a character's dominant trait.

Talents and Skills: Your character possesses certain aptitudes and abilities, both learned and innate. These provide authors with opportunities to individualize a run-of-the-mill character while also arming him or her with the capabilities needed to win in the story. For more information, see the section on Talents and Skills (p. 9), and check out the **Talent and Skill Thesaurus**.

Passions, Interests, and Hobbies: Everyone has activities they enjoy, and characters should be no exception. Beyond simply rounding out a character, these areas of interest can serve a deeper purpose in the story itself, providing a skill, experience, or knowledge that is vital to their success. We recommend revisiting the section on Hobbies and Passions (p. 10), and if you wish to brainstorm ideas, try the One Stop for Writers' **Idea Generator.**

<u>Your Story's Theme:</u> A theme is a central idea or message that is subtly conveyed throughout the story. Common themes include redemption, coming of age, sacrifice, and power. A thematic statement represents the author's take on that idea and often becomes the overall message in a literary work. We recommend reviewing the section on Vocations as Thematic Devices (p. 26), and you may also find the **Symbolism and Motif Thesaurus** helpful in finding symbols to represent common story themes.

REFERENCES

Much research was required to gather and confirm the details for so many occupations, and we found the following websites to be very helpful. As you continue to explore jobs for your characters, they might also be of use to you.

Academic Invest (https://www.academicinvest.com)
A lot (https://www.alot.com)
CareerAddict (https://www.careeraddict.com)
CareerExplorer (https://www.careerexplorer.com)
CareerMatch (https://www.careermatch.com)
Career Trend (https://careertrend.com)
Chron (https://work.chron.com)
CollegeGrad (https://collegegrad.com/about)
CriminalJusticeDegreesSchool.com (https://www.criminaljusticedegreeschools.com)
ExploreHealthCareers.org (https://explorehealthcareers.org)
Forbes (https://www.forbes.com)
HowStuffWorks (https://www.howstuffworks.com)
HowToBecome.com (https://www.howtobecome.com)
Innovators Guide (http://www.innovatorsguide.org/index.htm)
Insider.com (https://www.insider.com)
Job Lense (http://www.joblense.com)
LearningPath.org (https://learningpath.org)
Los Angeles Times (https://www.latimes.com)
Medium (https://medium.com)
MyPlan.com (https://www.myplan.com/index.php)
My Perfect Resume (https://www.myperfectresume.com)
New York Times (https://www.nytimes.com)
OwlGuru.com (https://www.owlguru.com)
Psychology Today (https://www.psychologytoday.com/us)
Small Business Trends (https://smallbiztrends.com)
Study.com (https://study.com)
The Balance Careers (https://www.thebalancecareers.com)
U. S. Bureau of Labor Statistics (https://www.bls.gov)
wikiHow (https://www.wikihow.com/Main-Page)
Workable (https://www.workable.com)
YourFreeCareerTest (https://www.yourfreecareertest.com)

ADDITIONAL EXPERT SOURCES

To verify the information contained in these entries, we enlisted experts in as many occupational fields as possible. We are deeply grateful to those who offered their insight and advice.

Aime Jakubowicz Sund
Allyson Lindt
Andrew Cleveland
Anthony J. Harrison
Billy Mac
Blythe Cappello Asher
Bobbi Davidson
Boni Wagner-Stafford
Brenda Kaye
Brent Nicols
Calvin D. Jim
Carol Gavin
Cassie Robertson
Chris Ackerman
Chris Marrs
Donna Maloy
Dr. Laura Elliott, PT, DPT, PPSC
Ed Khossossy
Elisha DeZwart
Erika Lange
Florence Seiler
Gaby Triana
Gloria Singendonk
Harrison Lake
Holly Rabon
Ian Hugh McAllister
J. M. Bird

Jan Safran
Jason Cyr
Jennifer Cheung
Jennifer Rimoldi Hale
Judith Brown
Korri MacMillan
Kristin Bartley Lenz
Laurie Hodges
Lori Ackerman
Lorraine Paton
Major Robert D. Carter, Armor, U.S. Army
Megan Jane Colville
Michelle Miles
Monica-Marie Vincent
Nicolle M. Browne
Rachel Lauderdale
Rachel Lauderdale
Sacha Black
Samantha Davidson
Sandi Melnychuk
Sarah Elizabeth Isaksen
Stacey Kondla
Tammy Archambeau
Tracey Rosen
Tyson Mowat
Vicki Tharp
Wade Tharp

RECOMMENDED READING

Every powerful novel begins with a realistic, well-layered protagonist and memorable supporting cast. These writing guides will help you create characters strong enough to carry the weight of their stories.

Creating Character Arcs: The Masterful Author's Guide to Uniting Story Structure helps you look deeper into the story beats that create realistic and compelling character arcs. (K.M. Weiland)

Writing Screenplays That Sell, New Twentieth Anniversary Edition teaches all writers to think deeply about their characters' motivations, story structure, and the art of selling. (Michael Hauge)

10 Steps to Hero: How to Craft a Kickass Protagonist is a step-by-step guide that takes you from character-twinkle-in-your-eye through conflict, motives, character arc and all the way to finished novel. (Sacha Black)

Several of our Writers Helping Writers® guides cover critical areas of characterization. To build standout characters, we suggest the following volumes:

The Emotion Thesaurus: A Writer's Guide to Character Expression, expanded to a whopping 130 emotions, is packed with lists of body language, thoughts, dialogue cues, and visceral sensations to describe whatever feeling your character experiences.

The Emotional Wound Thesaurus: A Writer's Guide to Psychological Trauma digs into the heart of your character's backstory to find a painful past event that shook them to their core, leaving fear, dysfunction, and unmet needs in its wake. This guide's comprehensive lists of behavioral and cognitive fallout will help you write the actions and choices of your damaged characters with authenticity.

The Positive Trait Thesaurus: A Writer's Guide to Character Attributes is one half of the character-building puzzle that helps you create a memorable story cast. With an arsenal of positive traits and their defining characteristics, you will be able to create convincing, rich characters that fascinate readers.

The Negative Trait Thesaurus: A Writer's Guide to Character Flaws looks at your character's dark side and the realistic flaws that hold him or her back while complicating your plot. Believable characters have both positive and negative qualities, and understanding their disagreeable aspects is a pathway to understanding their insecurities and fears, both of which must be overcome to achieve their goal.

If you're up for a characterization adventure, might we also suggest the Character Builder at One Stop for Writers (https://onestopforwriters.com)? It's powered by the largest description database for characters that's available anywhere. Take advantage of the site's two-week free trial to give it a test drive.

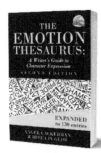  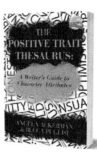 

  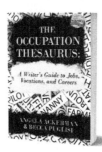 

PRAISE FOR...

THE EMOTION THESAURUS

"One of the challenges a fiction writer faces, especially when prolific, is coming up with fresh ways to describe emotions. This handy compendium fills that need. It is both a reference and a brainstorming tool, and one of the resources I'll be turning to most often as I write my own books."
~ **James Scott Bell, best-selling author of *Deceived* and *Plot & Structure***

THE POSITIVE AND NEGATIVE TRAIT THESAURUSES

"In these brilliantly conceived, superbly organized and astonishingly thorough volumes, Angela Ackerman and Becca Puglisi have created an invaluable resource for writers and storytellers. Whether you are searching for new and unique ways to add and define characters, or brainstorming methods for revealing those characters without resorting to clichés, it is hard to imagine two more powerful tools for adding depth and dimension to your screenplays, novels or plays."
~ **Michael Hauge, Hollywood script consultant and author of *Writing Screenplays That Sell***

THE URBAN AND RURAL SETTING THESAURUSES

"The one thing I always appreciate about Ackerman and Puglisi's Thesauri series is how comprehensive they are. They never stop at just the obvious, and they always over-deliver. Their Setting Thesauri are no different, offering not just the obvious notes of the various settings they've covered but going into easy-to-miss details like smells and tastes. They even offer to jumpstart the brainstorming with categories on potential sources of conflict."
~ **K.M. Weiland, best-selling author of** *Creating Character Arcs* **and** *Structuring Your Novel*

THE EMOTIONAL WOUND THESAURUS

"This is far more than a brilliant, thorough, insightful, and unique thesaurus. This is the best primer on story—and what REALLY hooks and holds readers—that I have ever read."
~ **Lisa Cron, TEDx Speaker and best-selling author of** *Wired For Story* **and** *Story Genius*

ADD WRITERS HELPING WRITERS® TO YOUR TOOLKIT!

Over a decade of articles are waiting to help you grow your writing skills, navigate publishing and marketing, and assist you on your career path. And if you'd like to stay informed about forthcoming books, discover unique writing resources, and access even more practical writing tips, sign up for our newsletter onsite.

ONE STOP
F O R
WRITERS

Writers, are you ready for a game-changer?

In a flooded market, exceptional novels rise above the rest, and to get noticed, authors must bring their A-game. One Stop for Writers gives creatives an edge with powerful, one-of-a-kind story and character resources, helping them deliver fresh, compelling fiction that readers crave.

Brought to you by the minds behind *The Occupation Thesaurus,* One Stop is home to the largest show-don't-tell description database available anywhere and contains an innovative toolkit that makes storytelling almost criminally easy. A fan favorite is the hyper-intelligent Character Builder, which helps you explore a character's deepest layers to uncover their desires, fears, motivations, and needs that drive the story. It will even create an accurate Character Arc Blueprint for you, making it easier to marry the plot to your character's internal journey. And the site's story structure maps, timelines, worldbuilding surveys, generators, and tutorials give you what you need when you need it. So forget about staring at the screen wondering what to write. Those days are over, friend.

If you think it's time someone made writing easier, join us at https://www.onestopforwriters.com and give our **two-week free trial** a spin. If you choose to subscribe, use the code **ONESTOPFORWRITERS** for a one-time discount of 25% off any plan*. We're Writers Helping Writers, remember?

See you at One Stop!

Becca Puglisi & Angela Ackerman

*For full details and conditions, see our Coupon Redemption guidelines at https://onestopforwriters.com/coupon.

Printed in Great Britain
by Amazon